YEATS, ELIOT, POUND
AND THE POLITICS OF POETRY

YEATS, ELIOT, POUND and the POLITICS OF POETRY

RICHEST TO THE RICHEST

Cairns Craig

CROOM HELM
London & Canberra

© 1982 Cairns Craig
Croom Helm Ltd, 2-10 St John's Road, London SW11

British Library Cataloguing in Publication Data

Craig, Cairns
    Yeats, Eliot, Pound and the politics of
    poetry.
    1. English poetry — 20th century — History
    and criticism
    I. Title
    821'.91209   PR601
    ISBN 0-85664-997-X

Printed and bound in Great Britain
 by Billing and Sons Limited
Guildford, London, Oxford, Worcester

CONTENTS

Acknowledgements

Preface 1

1. Introduction: Poetry and Politics 2

2. The Associationist Tradition 26

3. Openings 65

4. Yeats: the Art of Memory 72

5. Eliot, Pound and the Memory of Art 112

6. Closures 146

7. Yeats: the Loss and Recovery of Memory 155

8. Eliot, Pound: Memory's Broken Bridge 204

9. The Politics of Poetry 251

Abbreviations and Editions of Texts Cited 290

Notes 292

Select Bibliography 313

Index 319

In gratitude for their struggle to give us what they had never had themselves this book is dedicated to my parents, Bill and Jean.

ACKNOWLEDGEMENTS

The publishers and author would like to thank the following for permission to quote copyright material: The Ezra Pound Literary Trust and Faber and Faber Ltd for the use of uncollected prose work, © The Ezra Pound Literary Property Trust 1981; Mrs Valerie Eliot and Faber and Faber Ltd for the use of uncollected prose work, © Set Copyrights Ltd 1981; Faber and Faber Ltd for *Collected Shorter Poems, Literary Essays, ABC of Reading, Jefferson and/or Mussolini* and *Selected Prose* by Ezra Pound; Faber and Faber Ltd for *Collected Poems 1909-1962, Selected Essays and Notes Towards the Definition of Culture* by T.S. Eliot; Farrar, Straus and Giroux, Inc., and Faber and Faber Ltd for *Knowledge and Experience in the Philosophy of F.H. Bradley* and *On Poetry and Poets* by T.S. Eliot; Harvard University Press and Faber and Faber Ltd for *The Use of Poetry and the Use of Criticism* by T.S. Eliot; Methuen and Co. for *The Sacred Wood* by T.S. Eliot; Macmillan and Co. for *Autobiographies, The Collected Poems of W.B. Yeats, Essays* (1924), *Essays and Introductions, Explorations, Mythologies, Memoirs: Autobiography – first draft – and Journal, Uncollected Prose* volumes 1 and 2, *The Variorum Edition of the Poems of W.B. Yeats* and *A Vision* by W.B. Yeats. Excerpts from the poetry of T.S. Eliot are also reprinted by permission of Harcourt Brace Jovanovich, Inc., from his volume *Collected Poems 1909-1962*, copyright 1936 by Harcourt Brace Jovanovich, Inc.; copyright © 1943, 1963, 1964 by T.S. Eliot; copyright 1971 by Esme Valerie Eliot.

PREFACE

A first book, as this is, must carry with it the debts of one's whole intellectual life, and as will be evident I owe a great deal to those critics who have formulated the issues with which this study is concerned, especially to Frank Kermode, who was — unknowingly — an essential participant in my debate, and to Denis Donoghue, Conor Cruise O'Brien, Robert Langbaum, Hugh Kenner, and to all who have concerned themselves with associationist theories of literature. Equally, however, this work reflects — in whatever virtues it might have, its faults being entirely the author's — the influence of my former teachers, some of whom are now my colleagues, at Edinburgh University. I am particularly grateful to J.R. Mulryne, now Professor at Warwick, and Helen Williams, with whom I first worked on modern poetry as a postgraduate student.

To my former colleagues at the University of Aberdeen I am grateful for several very happy and stimulating years during which most of the work for this book was done. George Watson, David Fuller and John Roach will all find here echoes of past conversations and I hope they will forgive me if I have been unable to distinguish and footnote their individual contributions: their ideas, their criticisms and their encouragement were invaluable.

Working on several different fields of enquiry was made considerably easier by the help of the librarians at Aberdeen and Edinburgh University Libraries and at the National Library of Scotland, and the final preparation of the manuscript benefited enormously from Chris Johnstone's typing skills. Edinburgh University also helped with research and typing grants. I would also like to thank the editors of *Stand*, *The Dalhousie Review*, and *Helix* in which some of the thoughts, though not the chapters as they now exist, have previously appeared.

Finally, my thanks to Douglas Martin, without whom none of this would have happened — I hope it is worthy of his inspiration — and, most of all, to Phyl, who knows where it began and who made its completion possible.

1

1   *INTRODUCTION: POETRY AND POLITICS*

1933: in Ireland, in Italy, in the United States, three men who had, in the years around the First World War, produced a revolution in poetry, who had shaped an art we still describe as 'modern' because it succeeded in bringing the modern world into poetry and poetry into the modern world, struggle to make sense of the crisis-torn decade and by their writings try to give shape to a new civilisation. In Ireland, W.B. Yeats, 58 years old, Nobel prize winner, Protestant senator for six years in a Catholic Ireland the existence of which was due in part to the national revival in the arts that he had led before 1914, has General O'Duffy, new leader of the Irish Fascists, the Blue Shirts, brought to him so that O'Duffy can hear him 'talk his anti-democratic philosophy'.[1] On 13 July, in high excitement, Yeats writes to his old friend Olivia Shakespear:

> Politics are growing heroic. De Valera has forced political thought to face the most fundamental issues. A Fascist opposition is forming behind the scenes to be ready should some tragic situation develop. I find myself constantly urging the despotic rule of the educated classes as the only end to our troubles ... Our chosen colour is blue, and blue shirts are marching all over the country, and their organiser tells me it was my suggestion.[2]

In Italy, Ezra Pound, rebellious American who had helped modernise the style of Yeats's poetry when he acted as his secretary in the winters of 1913 to 1915, a man whose ceaseless propaganda had helped bring the new movement in the arts to public attention and to whom almost every major literary figure of the period was indebted, succeeds in obtaining an interview with his hero, Mussolini, and presents him with a copy of his poetry:

> 'MA QVESTO,'
>   said the Boss 'è divertente'
> catching the point before the aesthetes had got there.[3]

Throughout the year Pound is at work on a book entitled *Jefferson and/or Mussolini* that is to reveal the true heritage of the American

Revolution to be the Italian Fascist State in which Pound is living: 'The heritage of Jefferson, Quincey Adams, old John Adams, Jackson, Van Buren is HERE, NOW in the Italian Peninsula at the beginning of the fascist second decennion, not in Massachusetts or Delaware.'[4] In the United States, T.S. Eliot, self-proclaimed Anglo-Catholic and royalist, having returned to his homeland as the central figure of British literary life, having written the most influential of post-war poems, *The Waste Land*, and having provided contemporary criticism with its fundamental tenets in *The Sacred Wood*, delivers a series of lectures at the University of Virginia attacking a society which he describes as 'worm-eaten with liberalism'.[5] The term 'tradition', which he had made a central concept for contemporary criticism, is given more than literary significance as he defines the nature of a worthwhile society:

> The population should be homogeneous; where two or more cultures exist in the same place they are likely either to be fiercely self-conscious or both to become adulterate. What is still more important is unity of religious background; and reasons of race and culture combine to make any large number of free-thinking Jews undesirable. There must be a proper balance between urban and rural, industrial and agricultural development. And a spirit of excessive tolerance is to be deprecated.[6]

1933: no longer in close communication with each other as they had been in London in those years of the poetic revolution, the three major poets of the English-speaking world agree that democracy must be replaced by a society that is hierarchical, authoritarian and, ultimately, founded on purity of blood.

Are such views but the coincidence of their personalities? Or the pressure of historical events on sensitive human beings who respond to extreme situations with extreme solutions? Or is there a deep-seated relationship between the modernity of their art and the reactionary nature of their politics? The responses of 1933 may be extreme — Yeats may rapidly come to see the Blue Shirts as potentially comic rather than tragic, Eliot may refuse to have *After Strange Gods* reprinted — but they remain an expression of their common and fundamental belief that the values of art and the values of democracy are inimical.

Yeats made his early reputation as the poet and folklorist of the Celtic Twilight, but his interest in the folk, despite the intensity of his nationalism and his connections with William Morris's circle and their socialist views, did not prevent him, in a review of 1896, when he was 31, taking note of the theory that

> 'civilised' or 'progressive communities' began when a race of superior intellectual power compelled or persuaded a race of lesser intellectual power to feed it and house it, in return for the religion and science which it had thus found the leisure to make, and to pass on from generation to generation in ever growing complexity. This contest, the contest of subtlety against force, the subtlety often of a very few against the force of a multitude, gradually changed from a contest between men of different races to a compact between men of different classes, and so created the modern world.[7]

It is a theory that Yeats hopes will turn out to be true, 'being no democrat in intellectual things, and altogether persuaded that elaborate beauty has never come but from the mind of a deliberate artist writing at leisure and in peace'.[8] Forty years later Yeats was to celebrate precisely that theory of history in 'Blood and the Moon',

> Blessed be this place,
> More blessed still this tower;
> A bloody, arrogant power
> Rose out of the race
> Uttering, mastering it,
> Rose like these walls from these
> Storm beaten cottages —[9]

but with the added component that only force could create the opportunity for subtlety. The 'race of superior intellectual power' Yeats had found in his own Anglo-Irish ancestry, the image of that leisure in which elaborate beauty could be created in the house of his patron and friend Lady Gregory, fulfilling his expectation that the artist and the aristocrat share the same values, and the same enemies. By 1909 he could write:

> Every day I notice a new analogy between [the] long-established life of the well-born and the artist's life. We come from permanent things and create them, and instead of old blood we have old emotions and we carry in our head that form of society which aristocracies create now and again for some brief moment at Urbino or

Versailles. We too despise the mob and suffer at its hands.[10]

For Yeats, therefore, the overthrow of aristocracy was the overthrow of art, of its essential condition at any rate, and in Ireland the 'the new class, which had begun to rise into power under the shadow of Parnell',[11] the Catholic urban middle class, became an image for him of the degeneration that modern civilisation was undergoing. In the final years of his life, in desperation at the loss of that leisured life, he was to advocate eugenic solutions so that the civilised could be bred and the uncivilised prevented from breeding:

> Since about 1900 the better stocks have not been replacing their numbers, while the stupider and less healthy have been more than replacing theirs. Unless there is a change in the public mind every rank above the lowest must degenerate, and, as inferior men push up into its gaps, degenerate more and more quickly. The results are already visible in the degeneration of literature, newspapers, amusements . . .[12]

The historical conception of the imposition of one group upon another as the source of culture provides Yeats with his model for how civilisation is to be saved: 'the danger is that there will be no war, that the skilled will attempt nothing, that European civilisation, like those older civilisations that saw the triumph of their gangrel stocks, will accept decay.'[13] Poets are often the opponents of their times, perhaps necessarily so, but how are we to read a poetry that tells us that we ourselves are the destroyers of culture, part of the philistine modern world, 'Base-born products of base beds'?[14]

The problem is even more intense in the case of Pound, for his politics do not have the advantage of seeming so divorced from the actualities of the modern world as to constitute a myth of history rather than an involvement with it. Pound took the wrong side in one of the central historical conflicts of our century — and for the reasons that make it the wrong side. Had he been content to express his desire for hierarchy in the context of the ancient China whose poetry was to influence his own technique, it could have been passed over as a merely aesthetic concern: but for Pound an eternal truth was eternal because it could be applied in the present:

> Is there 'a race' left in England? Has it any will to survive? You can carry slaughter to Ireland, but will that save you? Nothing can save

you save a purge. Nothing can save you but an affirmation that you
are English.

Hore-Belisha is not. Isaacs is not. No Sassoon is an Englishman
racially. No Rothschild is English, no Streiker is English, no Roose-
velt is English, no Barush ... Schiff, Sieff, or Solomon was ever
yet born Anglo-Saxon. And it is for this filth you fight.[15]

It is rhetoric, of course, insane rhetoric perhaps, but the rhetoric is
there in the poetry as well: is it transformed into something else by
its aesthetic context?

> Remarked Ben: better keep out the jews
>   or yr/ grand children will curse you
> jews, real jews, chazims, and *neschek*[16]

Pound's anti-Semitism was the result of his incessant battle with what
he saw as the destruction of life's proper values by usury,[17] by the
charging of interest to produce a profit that had not been earned by
any kind of production. Usury is, for Pound, against nature and therefore the cause of social corruption, but nature he sees as ruled over
by an eternal order the equivalent of which, in the social realm, is
poetry:

> The statements of 'analytics' [equations of geometry] are 'lords'
> over fact. They are the thrones and dominations that rule over
> form and recurrence. And in like manner are great works of art
> lords over fact, over race-long recurrent moods, and over to-
> morrow.[18]

The analogy — thrones, lords — is in itself significant, but what Pound
sought, in Major Douglas's social credit economics and in Fascism, was
a system that would recognise the rule of art, a rule that could only
be achieved through the 'domination' of events by the elite who had
grasped the 'analytics' of reality, by a ruler who knew the value of
poets.

Pound's disordered writings of the 1920s and 1930s, his obsessive
concern with the rightness of 'a few simple and known facts'[19] that
constitute the fundamental truths of poetry and of economics, are
usually regarded now as the products of an unbalanced mind;[20] Eliot,
on the other hand, is generally presented by his critics as a responsible
thinker, a man whose conservatism remained, barring the occasion of

After Strange Gods, within the terms of a reasonable debate about the needs of contemporary society.[21] Eliot himself wrote to the *Times Literary Supplement* in 1957[22] to deny that he had ever been a supporter of Fascism, and to deny specifically that any approval of Fascism could be drawn from a review he wrote in the *Criterion* in 1928, containing the following:

> I am all the more suspicious of fascism as a panacea because I fail to find in it any important element, beyond the comfortable feeling that we will all be benevolently ordered about, which was not already in existence. Most of the concepts which might have attracted me in fascism I seem already to have found, in a more digestible form, in the work of Charles Maurras. I say more digestible form, because I think they have a closer applicability to England than those of fascism.[23]

The question, of course, is the extent to which the 'concepts that might have attracted' him in Fascism did not do so because in Charles Maurras' *Action Française* he had already found a Fascist ideology. Nolte, in his study *Three Faces of Fascism*, includes the *Action Française*, though like most writers treats it as a crypto- or proto-Fascism, one that provided an appropriate atmosphere for the development of fully-fledged Fascist movements, and that also encouraged, in France, the collaboration with the Nazis as a result of which Maurras, for his part in the Vichy government, was sentenced to death in 1946. The *Action Française* was reactionary, both in the sense that it began as a response to a revulsion from the success of what its members saw as liberalism in the Dreyfus affair, and in the sense that they desired a return to a previous condition of society, basically to the pre-Revolutionary *ancien régime*. It was this aspect of a return to a specific past that attracted Eliot — or that formed Eliot's political notions: 'The *Action Française* insists upon the importance of continuity by Kingship and hereditary class, upon something which has some analogy with what the government of England was, formerly, at least, supposed to be . . .'[24] The definition of the present by the past also occurs in Eliot's attitude to democracy. Eliot never accepted totalitarian ideas of social organisation, but his definition of democracy is, to say the least, eccentric to contemporary political debate:

> A real democracy is always a restricted democracy, and can only flourish with some limitation by hereditary rights and respons-

ibilities. The United States of America, for instance, were more or
less democratic up to 1829, when Andrew Jackson became Presi-
dent . . .[25]

The credit for having avoided Pound's commitment to Fascism is
achieved on a not very substantial distinction, perhaps only on the
basis that, living in England, his adoption of the *status quo* of Church,
State and King turned out to be safer than Pound's support of the
Italian state:

> Both fascism and communism seem to me to be well-meaning
> revolts against 'capitalism', but revolts which do not appear to get
> to the bottom of the matter; so that they are likely to be merely
> transformations of the present system which will completely satisfy
> the materialistic interpretation of history . . .
>   . . . I confess to a preference for fascism in practice, which I
> dare say most of my readers share; and I will not admit this prefer-
> ence is itself wholly irrational. I believe that the fascist form of un-
> reason is less remote from my own than is that of the communists,
> but that my own is a more reasonable form of unreason.[26]

Eliot's support of the monarchy was based on his desire to re-establish
a hierarchical society which would maintain order and tradition: Pound
saw in Italy a situation in which only a man of strength and will could
impose such hierarchy.

What keeps Eliot within the terms of 'reasonable' political discussion — though his reason is based on unreason — is his commitment
to the Church of England as an established Church of the state. But
even after the War, after the trial, condemnation and reprieve from
the death sentence of Maurras, Eliot's political theory retains the same
fundamental characteristics. The terminology is derived from sociology
now rather than politics, but the implications of the theory are un-
changed:

> I incline to believe that no true democracy can maintain itself
> unless it contains different levels of culture. The levels of culture
> may also be seen as levels of power, to the extent that a smaller
> group at a higher level will have equal power with a larger group
> at a lower level; for it may be argued that complete equality means
> universal irresponsibility; and in such a society as I envisage, each
> individual would inherit greater or lesser responsibility towards

the commonwealth, according to the position in society which he inherited. . .[27]

A hierarchical society of inherited wealth (or the lack of it) and power (or the lack of it) remains Eliot's ideal, and it must be a single culture — it must be ethnically integral. The loss of an organic aristocracy based on land and a culture without ethnic differentiation is, for Eliot, the fundamental break in American history:

> The real revolution in that country was not what is called the Revolution in the history books, but is a consequence of the Civil War; after which arose a plutocratic elite; after which the expansion and material development of the country was accelerated; after which was swollen that stream of mixed immigration, bringing (or rather multiplying) the danger of development into a caste system, which has not yet been quite dispelled.[28]

The danger to the unity of the culture is not a function of the attitudes of the already existing hierarchy, but is brought by that mixed immigration which the language, in its inversions and parentheses, can hardly bear to voice. How are we to respond to Eliot's poetry when it seems, in its own nature, to seek to enforce what Eliot believed of culture in general, that 'it is an essential condition of the preservation of the quality of the culture of the minority, that it should continue to be a minority culture'?[29] How do we read such poetry when it is designed to refuse itself to all but those who have somehow attained the status of belonging to that minority?

Reading Yeats, Eliot or Pound we are thrust back — reluctantly, apologetically, polemically, or just bemusedly, but inevitably — upon the question of its relation to the social and political views which I have sketched here. These views have been analysed in depth by various critics, by Conor Cruise O'Brien,[30] by Roger Kojecky, by William M. Chace, but what we do with such historical information, how we treat the poetry in the light of it or vice versa, remains problematic. The fullest effort to comprehend the interconnections between the two is contained in John Harrison's *The Reactionaries*, which argues that the social views are so unacceptable to the vast majority of readers, and so integral to the poetic works themselves, that they cannot help but lessen our evaluation of the art:

The writer's views may, as in the case of Yeats, help to work some wonderful transformation in technique, but the reader's enjoyment is almost certainly reduced by his antipathy to the content of what he is reading. It might also be argued that the writer's achievement is lessened.[31]

It is one of the canons of modern criticism that there can be no divorce between form and content — though it is a canon rarely adhered to with any rigour — and one of the values of Harrison's book is that he does at least try to see how form and content match one another: in Yeats's later poetry, he insists, 'the attitude, feeling, style, rhythm, metaphors all merge . . . to produce some of the most intellectual, authoritarian, passionate and, as far as texture goes, the hardest poetry ever written.'[32] In what sense, however, a metaphor can be authoritarian, what consistutes 'hardness' of texture, why intellectual and authoritarian should be linked, remains unclear. Harrison wants to read the poems as in some sense necessitating a reactionary politics by the very nature of their formal concerns, but he reduces himself continually to discussing the stated contents of the works as assertions of a political point of view which is therefore equally true of the poetic technique. That a poem asserts a certain point of view is entirely different from its technique implying or necessitating such a view, except by virtue of the critical dogma that if the poem is successful there must be a union of form and content. It may be true that there is 'a definite correspondence in Yeats's later poetry between his "tendency" (that is the direction which his thinking followed on political and sociological matters, and the attitude he adopted) and his literary style',[33] but Harrison's study does more to document the writers' views than it does to justify or explain such a correspondence.

When Harrison's study was published it was received less than enthusiastically by the critics. It would appear that there is still a general hope that time will do away with the problem, that in the perspective of history the men will become irrelevant and we will be left only with the poetry we admire. Or, if not, that at least we will be able to interpret their poltitical stances in ways that make them more acceptable to ourselves and perhaps more honourable in the writers. Stephen Spender, for instance, writing in the shadow cast by Harrison's book, offers the following defence:

The political attitudes of Yeats, Eliot, Pound, Lewis, Lawrence, consist largely of gestures towards some movement, idea, leadership, which *seems* to correspond to the writer's deeply held traditionalism. Such gestures are largely rhetorical. For the politics of these writers are secondary effects of their thoughts about the tragedy of culture in modern industrial societies. They are some-times conscientious, sometimes irresponsible attempts to trans-late the traditionalist standpoint into programs of action.[34]

The problem with this is twofold. In the first place it is itself largely a *rhetorical* translation of terms from the apparently dangerous sphere of politics — 'reactionary', 'authoritarian' or 'Fascistic' are the ones usually invoked — to the commendatory sphere of purely cultural analysis — 'tradition', 'gesture', 'tragedy'. What is reactionary in the cultural sphere is not therefore insulated from politics, and ges-tures are not necessarily mere theatre: many political acts consist precisely of gestures. Secondly, it fails to explain the connection between modernist art and 'traditonalism', which is even more paradoxical, on the face of it, than the connection with reactionary politics; for modernism was seen, and indeed saw itself, as a revolu-tion in the arts. How is its revolutionary nature related to its 'deeply held traditionalism'? And why is traditionalism not a political stance in itself, rather than something that generates politics as a 'secondary effect'? The implicit answer is that the poets were men who should not have raised their heads from the 'cultural' sphere: as artists they might see deeply into the nature of the contemporary world, but only where that world impinges directly on their own specialist field: we have to allow them their significance as artists by insisting that in politics they were myopic, that they were silly— and, therefore, excusable — citizens. This is no doubt a comforting doctrine for those of us who are responsible citizens, for it allows us to entertain the art as a part of our cultural experience without allowing that it can challenge any of our own attitudes and values. The art is neutralised by preserving its aesthetic value within the insulated world of 'culture', for we make ourselves impervious to its doing us any good as well as any harm. The value of the art becomes the value of culture itself in a world where culture is threatened, and any specific values which the art enforces are subsumed within this higher value: it is more important to preserve culture than to question anything specific cul-tural works might wish to press upon us.

Spender's analysis, destructive though its implications are for art, points us to one of the major strands both in modern art and in con-temporary criticism. We live in a world in which Wilde's dictum that art does not imitate life, life imitates art, has become true almost as a matter of their quantitative priority within our experience. We live in a world of art; we are wrapped round by it; it flows into our homes, travels with us in our transport, meets us in the landscapes we consume as tourists. The 'tragedy of culture' is that there is no world in which culture has its place, because our cultural artifacts have made themselves omnipresent; there is no way in which aesthetic objects can force us to attend to the world, since they are the constant objects of our attention. No matter how violent, disturbing, moving, shocking, thought-provoking, liberating, a work of art may be, we joyfully consume its every challenge; 'high seriousness' for modern art — and this is implicit in Spender's formulation of the problem — is attention to itself, the restriction of itself to purely cultural ends, to purely technical considerations. Art becomes a play, however serious, with its medium in the effort to evade the trivialisation of meanings created by the increase in media. The defence of the artist against the world is formalism.

It is precisely such a conception that has motivated both the old New Critics who wanted us to attend to the words of the poem and to ignore such matters as biography and authorial intentions, and the new New Criticism that sees the author as the invention of his text rather than the text as his creation. The removal of the author allows us to see the work, independently of its historical situation, as being progressive in terms of its cultural contribution, and whether, therefore, we wish to separate works from the consequences of their authors' views, or whether we ourselves want to escape from historical determination, we accord to cultural artifacts the honorific values of a 'progress' of which we despair in our historical crisis. For the old New Criticism progress was implicit in the development of tradition: a work's value lay in its furthering the developments which were integral to the cultural tradition of which it was to form a part. So that though the stances of the New Critics were largely conservative in social matters, the realm of culture became the preserve of a true sense of progress. In the new New Criticism, progress has been largely removed from the work and given to the critic: it is in the critic's treatment of literature that progress is truly observable, since he confers upon the text that freedom from determination which it was once the aim of radical politics to achieve for human beings, but which has now become chimerical except in the realm of language itself. Thus, for instance, Roland Barthes has argued that we must see literature in terms of 'texts' and not of 'works', and the nature of the Text is that it is 'plural':

This does not mean just that it has several meanings, but rather that it achieves plurality of meaning, an irreducible plurality. The Text is not coexistence of meanings but passage, traversal; thus it answers not to an interpretation, liberal though it may be, but to an explosion, a dissemination . . .

. . . the Text is that which goes to the limit of the rules of enunciation (rationality, readability, and so on). The Text tries to situate itself exactly behind the limit of *doxa* (is not public opinion — constitutive of our democratic societies and powerfully aided by mass communication — defined by its limits, its energy of exclusion, its censorship?) One could literally say that the Text is always paradoxical.[35]

The text which defies *doxa* (orthodoxy) takes on all the characteristics that used to be applied to revolutions: it is a passage, a traversal, linearity that is not single dimensional but offers, like continuous revolution, the eruption into a qualitatively different state. The revolutions which have failed to move that suffocating censorship of 'liberal' society are transferred from the streets to the libraries, from politics to culture. In the realm of culture the progress which we deny or which has been denied to us is rewritten: and the true paradox is that the necessity for change, for consumption and replacement, is inscribed in the structure of culture, in its praise of experiment and renewal, at the very moment that it claims to oppose or to transcend the values of a society dedicated to consumption.

One of the earliest defences of Yeats, which attempted this separation of author from work that the work might remain in its progressive purity, was W.H. Auden's spoof trial of Yeats's ghost — a touch that Yeats, great ghost seeker, would have appreciated — shortly after Yeats's death in 1939:

But there is one field in which the poet is a man of action, the field of language, and it is precisely in this that the greatness of the deceased is most obviously shown. However false or undemocratic his ideas, his diction shows a continuous evolution toward what one might call the true democratic style. The social virtues of real democracy are brotherhood and intelligence, and the parallel linguistic virtues are strength and clarity, virtues which appear even more clearly through successive volumes by the deceased.[36]

In the famous elegy, written at the same time, Auden claimed that poetry 'made nothing happen', but the poetry is to be saved not by its inconsequentiality, but because its 'successive' improvement of its language is towards a style that is identical with an acceptable politics. The author is recreated on the model of the virtues attributed to his style: 'The diction of *The Winding Stair* is the diction of a just man, and it is for this reason that just men will always recognise the author as a master.'[37] The technique allows one to damn authors as well as justify them, but the recreation of the author as a function of his style and the interpretation of the style as part of a cultural politics are the essential moves, whether one is denying Milton or Balzac, praising Donne or Mallarmé. Auden, of course, was writing – as indeed was Spender – with one eye on his own political involvement in the 'low dishonest decade' of the 1930s; to save others from the consequences of their politics might be to save themselves, to unburden their works of the past. But the critics who practise the same kind of intellectual quarantine are also trying to unload the weight of the past: as Eric Homberger commented on the criticisms of Pound's *Pisan Cantos* in 1967,

> These cantos have been scrutinised with as much care as anything Pound ever wrote. Curiously enough, they have been read no differently in kind than if Pound had never left Church Walk, Kensington, as if, we are forced to say, nothing had ever happened to him.[38]

Such evasions of the past are not merely refusals to deal with history or with a wider perspective than the cultural: they are pointers to an underlying fear from which formalist criticism is a recoil, fear that art itself is a regression from the norms of the civilised mind. The metaphor of progress is so insidiously present in formalist criticism, because it implies that art keeps pace with the rest of our historical development, that it is not at base a reversion – however necessary to the economy of our minds – to modes of cognition, patterns of experience which, in the rapidity of our drive towards technological domination of the world, we have not yet managed to redeem from nature. It is a fear that, instead of being a fundamental expression of our civility, art may be our divesting of civilisation in the name of culture.

The most influential regressive theory of art is, of course, Freud's conception of art as wish-fulfilment, carrying into waking life the business of sleep and into adult life the fantasies of childhood.[39] The most destructive theory, however, as Eliot noted in 1916 when he commented on its 'interesting pessimism with respect to the future of art',[40] was probably Nietzsche's. In *Human, All Too Human*, Nietzsche suggested that the lengthening of our historical perspectives into evolutionary time-scales had surprised us with,

> how lately the more acute logical thinking, the strict determination of cause and effect, has been developed, when our reasoning and understanding still hark back to those primitive forms of deduction, and when we pass about half our life in [dreaming]. The poet, too, and the artist assign causes for their moods and conditions which are by no means the true ones: in this they recall an older humanity and can assist us to the understanding of it.[41]

Where formalism treats art as a progressive institution and, fundamentally, as an index of civilisation, Nietzsche sees art, by its form, as essentially archaic, an interesting living fossil that will eventually be allowed to wither away entirely. Concentration on the purely formal aspects of the work of art, given the power with which the regressive view has been stated in the past century, seems to be an evasion of the essential issue. Eliot could not help asking in a review in 1924, 'Is it possible or justifiable for art, the creation of beautiful objects and of literature, to persist indefinitely without its primitive purposes: is it possible for the aesthetic object to be a direct object of attention?'[42] And for art to remain viable it had, for Eliot, to remain in touch with those 'primitive purposes': 'the stage — not only in its remotest origins, but always — is a ritual, and the failure of the contemporary stage to satisfy the craving for ritual is one of the reasons why it is not a living art.'[43] This is not to raise the issue of 'belief' as a part of a poet's statement about the world, but the issue of 'belief in poetry': Yeats, Eliot and Pound demanded that we take seriously the question of whether we believe in poetry as a means to certain kinds of knowledge and insight. It is a question which, by concentrating on poems as purely formal constructions, or by translating all they wrote into 'gestures' about the 'tragedy of culture', we evade, allowing ourselves to maintain in the realm of culture values which they or we would not choose to apply to society in general.

The most important discussion of these issues by a contemporary critic is Frank Kermode's in *The Sense of an Ending*. Kermode argues that literature is essentially 'fiction' in the specialised sense which Vaihinger gives to the term in his philosophy of 'as if': fictional 'as if' is to be distinguished from a 'hypothesis' because we drop it as soon as we have used it to find something out; a 'fiction' is not, like a hypothesis, put to the test of experiment for it is not subject to proof or disconfirmation, but only to loss of 'operational effectiveness', to neglect.[44] At the same time, and most importantly, the fictional 'as if' has to be distinguished from 'myth', for myths present themselves as beliefs, as fundamental and total accounts of what really is the case, accounts which cannot be replaced and must not be neglected:

> Fictions can degenerate into myths whenever they are not consciously held to be fictive. In this sense anti-Semitism is a degenerate fiction, a myth; and Lear is a fiction. Myth operates within the diagrams of ritual, which presupposes total and adequate explanations for things as they are and were; it is a sequence of radically unchangeable gestures. Fictions are made for finding things out, and they change as the needs of sense-making change. Myths are the agents of stability, fictions the agents of change.[45]

Fictions, in other words, are 'progressive', not only in being a historical development from the stage of civilisation that believed in myth, but in their encouragement of a world of change, in their parallel with the most profound theories of the physical sciences – Kermode refers us to the Complementarity Theory – in our time. Spender's word 'gesture' returns, but this time to characterise the realm of myth which is impervious to change. But what is the opposite of gesture for Kermode? Is it action, choice, commitment? No, it is 'sense-making', involving 'conditional assent' to purely intellectual formulations. For Kermode, we can never act according to the conditional assents we give to the 'truths' of fiction: this is precisely, for him, the explanation of the relation between modernist art and reactionary politics, for as 'fictions' their works are perfectly acceptable; unhappily those fictions are connected to fictions that other people have used as myths, that the poets themselves may have taken as myths sometimes:

> The fictions of modernist literature were revolutionary, new, though affirming a relation of complementarity with the past. These fictions were, I think it is clear, related to others, which helped to shape the disastrous history of our time. Fictions, notably the fiction of apocalypse, turn easily into myths; people will live by that which was designed only to know by.[46]

But if a fiction is to have any explanatory power at all it cannot merely receive our conditional assent as an intellectual construct: the assent may be conditional but until it is retracted our behaviour will be modified by our knowledge. Conditional assent it still assent; what Kermode wants to do is to emphasise its conditional nature to the point at which we would never trust the fiction far enough to allow it into our lives, but in the process of making decisions about our day-to-day concerns we cannot enforce such total separations. Kermode's fictions are purely 'cultural' in the sense of 'cultural' that opposes it to ordinary life, that makes of culture a realm of the pure spirit opposed to the fallen world of the flesh:

> We are never in danger of thinking that the death of King Lear, which explains so much, is true . . . we make an experimental assent. If we make it well, the gain is that we shall never quite resume the posture towards life and death that we formerly held. Of course, it may be said that in changing ourselves we have, in the best possible indirect way, changed the world.[47]

Apart from playing fast and loose with the word 'true', confusing the sense in which a work of drama is experientially real while we suspend our disbelief and the sense in which it offers propositional knowledge, Kermode makes our knowledge a purely perceptual matter. We do not here commit ourselves even to a 'gesture', we hold ourselves in a 'posture': the world is changed by the way we look at it. For Kermode there can be no truths of action, for all action is a turning of fiction into myth. To function constantly in the full consciousness of the fictionality of all our knowledge, however, could only lead to a self-induced intellectual *aboulia*, a complete atrophy of the will. And that, indeed, is the condition of Kermode's 'clerkly scepticism', for he ends by imaging the situation of the reader in terms of a prisoner of war imaginatively giving meaning to his world in solitary confinement. Such a model is essential precisely because Kermode cannot allow the slightest step beyond a merely intellectual conception of the world without descending from fiction into myth. But the fictional assents of science apply only in its purely theoretical domain; at some point we also have to trust our fictions enough to walk across the bridges they have constructed, we have to walk through the world which our 'making sense' perceives.

Kermode distrusts fiction so intensely, as do post-modernist artists and critics in general, because he fears its consequences, its closeness to regressive modes of knowing the world. The unleashing of a new experimentalism that we have seen in the literature of the 1960s and

1970s is largely founded on the treatment of art as game: since there is no reality with which it has to correspond, it is free to exploit whatever is possible within its own medium. We can give, in Kermode's terminology, conditional assent to anything. The experimentalism of the old modernism, at least in Yeats, Eliot and Pound, was founded on precisely the opposite premise: that whatever art assented to was true, that reality was what we knew in art and not something we suspended in order to experience art, that the real was what the 'clerkly sceptic' would regard as regressive: 'all the machineries of poetry are parts of the convictions of antiquity, and readily become again convictions in minds that brood over them with visionary intensity.'[48] So wrote Yeats in 'The Philosophy of Shelley's Poetry', to be echoed by Pound in the *Guide to Kulchur*,

> Romantic poetry . . . almost requires the concept of reincarnation as part of its mechanism. No apter metaphor having been found for certain emotional colours. I assert that the Gods exist . . . I assert that a great treasure of verity exists for mankind in Ovid and in the subject matter of Ovid's long poem, and that only in this form could it be registered.[49]

For Yeats and Pound, metaphors are not illusions to be held in the mind in a frame of fictional assent, they are closer to the real than any of our rational knowledge and if we concentrate upon them sufficiently not only will we see the world differently, but the world will be so different that it will demand that we act differently:

> Plotinus said that we should not 'baulk at this limitlessness of the intellectual; it is an infinitude having nothing to do with number or part' (*Ennead* V. 7. I); yet it seems that it can at will re-enter number and part and thereby make itself apparent to our minds. If we accept this idea many strange and beautiful things become credible. The Indian pilgrim has not deceived us; he did hear the bed where the sage of his devotion slept a thousand years ago creak as though someone had turned over in it . . . the gamekeeper did hear those footsteps the other night that sounded like the footsteps of a stag where stag has not passed these hundred years. All about us there seems to start up a precise inexplicable teeming life, and the earth becomes once more, not in rhetorical metaphor, but in reality, sacred.[50]

Yeats's conclusion to his introduction to *The Words upon the Window-pane* are representative of the regression the modernists accept as part of their art, accept because they believe in art. It is significant that Kermode wishes to see the novel as the central form of the contemporary imagination because it cannot enter so easily into the world of myth, and significant that so many critics want to dilute the emphasis on the *reality* that Yeats and Pound ascribe to such perception and return them to the realm of 'metaphor', the realm where, as Dekker insists in his study,[51] myth is 'a record of delightful psychic experience'. But for Pound as for Yeats the psychic is not the psychological: it is the reality which our materialism cannot accept, it is an 'eternal state of mind'[52] beyond our own mind. In *The Spirit of Romance* Pound points us to his Greek source for such a conception in the idea of the 'phantastikon':

> We have about us the universe of fluid force, and below us the germinal universe of wood alive, stone alive . . . the consciousness of some (men) seems to rest, or have its centre more properly, in what Greek psychologists called the *phantastikon*. Their minds are, that is, circuminvolved about them like soap bubbles reflecting sundry patches of the macrocosmos.[53]

Neither Yeats nor Pound would be confident of such views all the time, but they are an indication of how seriously they took the truth of poetry as a regression to forgotten connections between the mind of the individual and the world around him.

The paradox of our desire to release modernist poetry from its regressive stance is that the formalist or culture oriented criticism, in its effort to concentrate attention on the art alone, mirrors the position from which the poets themselves started, a position which they felt they had to reject. What many critics of Pound wish to do, for instance, is to remove − from our attention if not from the poem − the elements that Yeats found unacceptable in his predecessors: 'I saw that . . . Swinburne in one way, Browning in another, and Tennyson in a third, had filled their work with what I called "impurities", curiosities about politics, about science, about history, about religion; and that we must create once more the pure work.'[54] The curiosities with which Yeats filled his own poetry have proved just as problematic and Eliot's allusiveness is hardly less appreciated by modern readers. The 'pure' poem was the starting point for all three poets and though they did not regard purity in a technical but in an emotive sense there is an obvious line of development from a statement like the following, by Eliot, in 1917, to the linguistic formalisms which have dominated our critical procedures:

> M. de Bosschere is an intellectual by his obstinate refusal to adulterate his poetic emotions with human emotions. Instead of refining ordinary human emotions (and I do not mean tepid human emotion, but — however intense — in the crude living state) he aims direct at the emotions of art. He thereby limits the number of his readers and leaves the majority groping for a clue that does not exist.[55]

Eliot completely separates the 'emotions of art' from the ordinary emotions of life and regards it as no longer necessary, or interesting, that the poet should lead his readers to art emotions by giving them directions via ordinary life emotions. The evident pleasure in the discomfiture of the ordinary reader and the smug sense of belonging to an elect point forward to Eliot's elitist conceptions of society, but one would not have expected the political involvement of the 1920s and 1930s from a writer so committed to the distinctness of art from life. Nor would one have anticipated the harsh political stances of that period from the Celtic or Provençal dreamers that were Yeats and Pound in 1900 and 1909.

The pattern in all three careers is, however, the same: the initial effort to maintain a 'pure' poetry led them to analyse the problems of poetry as lying in the social world, and solving poetic problems became, therefore, a matter of solving social problems. The purity of poetry could only be maintained in a world that allowed for the existence of a pure art and the effort to discover the failures in the society that prevented the poet's full achievement led to an incorporation of 'impure' elements into the poetry itself. Eliot, for instance, in 1926, offered readers of the *Criterion* this dejected rewriting of Shelley, in which the unacknowledged poets of the age become the legislators of the future:

> The artist in the modern world . . . is heavily hampered in ways that the public does not understand. He finds himself, if he is a man of intellect, unable to realise his art to his own satisfaction, and he may be driven to examining the elements in the situation — political, social, philosophical or religious — which frustrate his labour. In this unfortunate position he is accused of 'neglecting his art'. But

it is likely that some of the strongest influences on the thought of the next generation may be those of dispossessed artists.[56]

The date may suggest that the General Strike was not altogether unconnected with Eliot's sense of a social crisis, but the determination of the possibilities of art by the society that the artist has to live in had already become evident to Yeats before the War. Discussing the paintings of Augustus John, he argued that they were all imperfect because of the physical defects of his subjects:

> A gymnast set to train the body would find in all of these some defect to overcome, and when he had overcome them he would have brought them in every case nearer to that ancient canon which comes down to us from the gymnasium of Greece, and which, when it is present marks, like any other literary element, a compact between the artist and society, a purpose held in common with his time to create emotions or forms which Nature also desires.[57]

The 'compact between artist and society' represents Yeats's recognition that a pure poetry is not by its purity released from the history of its time; indeed, the purer it seeks to be the more it needs the collaboration of its society. That collaboration had to work both ways, however, and a diary entry of 1910 recognises poetry's obligations to its society:

> I now see that the literary element in painting, the moral element in poetry are the means whereby the two arts are accepted into the social order and become a part of life, and not things of the study and exhibition. Supreme art is a traditional statement of certain heroic and religious truths passed on from age to age . . .[58]

For Yeats engagement in society has become an essential part of the aesthetic value of poetry: supreme art is not the 'pure' art that he had sought in the art-for-art's sake atmosphere of the 1890s. What Yeats discovered in his work with the Abbey Theatre — for the drama, with its direct relation with a public, deeply affected Yeats's view of poetry — Eliot and Pound were to discover in the political and social crisis that followed from the First World War. Pound bade an ironic farewell to his aestheticist attitudes in 'Hugh Selwyn Mauberley' (1920):

> For three years, out of key with his time,
> He strove to resuscitate the dead art

Of poetry; to maintain 'the sublime'
In the old sense. Wrong from the start.[59]

Had Pound remained within that stance, 'Unaffected by "the march
of events" ', then he would, in his opinion, have 'passed from men's
memory in *l'an trentuniesme / De son eage'*, but what he learned was
'usury age-old and age-thick/and liars in public places'. By 1942 the
relation between art and economics is not merely that art depends
upon economics: one can learn one's economics from the arts and
their history:

> The emphasis given to economics by Shakespeare, Bacon, Hume
> and Berkeley does not seem to have been enough to have kept it
> prominent in the Anglo-Saxon public conscience. After the arch-
> heretic Calvin, it seems, discussion of usury has gone out of fashion.
> A pity! As long as the Mother Church concerned itself with this
> matter one continued to build cathedrals.[60]

And Eliot might well have been explaining Pound to readers of the
Criterion when he wrote in November 1927:

> The man of letters today is interested in a great many subjects —
> not because he has many interests, but because he finds that the
> study of his own subject leads him irresistibly to the study of
> others; and he must study the others if only to disentangle his
> own, to find out what he is really doing himself . . . Politics has
> become too serious a matter to be left to politicians. We are com-
> pelled, to the extent of our abilities, to be amateur economists,
> in an age when politics and economics can no longer be kept wholly
> apart. Everything is in question . . .[61]

This was not merely a response to the pressure of events: the pattern
of a passage from the pure engagement with an art to the recognition
of that art's involvement with and dependence on matters of politics
and economics is so insistent in all three as to seem to flow directly
from their conception of — or from the very nature of — poetry itself. There is no obvious correlation between modernist novelists —
Joyce, Woolf, Faulkner — and the kinds of politics we find in Yeats,
Eliot and Pound and it would seem, therefore, that it was not merely
the pressure of external events that drove them to see the demands
of their poetry as coterminous with the ends of reactionary politics:

the relation is intrinsic, not extrinsic.

To refuse to take account of that necessity in our criticism is not only to refuse the poets' insights into their own art, the poet's own conception of their purposes, but to ignore the fact that we too may, however unconsciously, be subscribing to values that have an insistent political dimension. If poetry cannot be a 'direct object of attention' then the effort to compartmentalise poetry from our other concerns may be encouraging precisely those translations of cultural into political gestures which it tries to avoid, encouraging them because it cannot acknowledge the consequences of its aesthetic values. The problems we face with modernist poetry are not new: William Hazlitt posed precisely the question of poetry's natural political inclination when he tried to make sense of what he saw as the betrayal of democracy by those Romantic poets who had been the heroes, and friends, of his youth. In his despair over the politics of poets Hazlitt was driven to question even his favourite Shakespeare:

> Shakespeare himself seems to have a leaning to the arbitrary side of the question, perhaps from some feeling of contempt for his own origin . . . The cause of the people is indeed but little calculated as a subject for poetry; it admits of rhetoric, which goes into argument and explanation, but it presents no immediate or distinct images to the mind . . . The language of poetry naturally falls in with the language of power. The imagination is an exaggerating and exclusive faculty; it takes from one thing to add to another; it accumulates circumstances together to give the greatest possible effect to a favourable object. The understanding is a dividing and measuring faculty: it judges of things not according to their immediate impression on the mind, but according to their relations with one another. The one is a monopolising faculty which seeks the greatest quantity of present excitement by inequality and disproportion; the other is a distributive faculty, which seeks the greatest quantity of ultimate good, by justice and proportion. The one is aristocratical, the other a republican faculty. The principle of poetry is a very anti-levelling principle . . . Kings, priests, nobles, are its train bearers, tyrants and slaves its executioners — 'Carnage is its daughter' — Poetry is right royal. It puts the individual before the species, the one above the infinite many, might before right . . . [62]

If Hazlitt is right, then the problem is not merely that we might mistake fictions for myths, but that all poetry is, by the categorical imperative of its originating faculty, necessarily sympathetic to reactionary, totalitarian politics. It is not a matter of poets' stated opinions, but of the very mental structures which are called into play in the creation of poems. Poetry is not merely regressive — which might, on a Freudian model, be cathartic — it is a way of perceiving the world the consequence of which is necessarily a refusal of the claims of a mass of humanity to our attention and concern. If poetry is indeed 'right royal' then Eliot's monarchism, Yeats's love of aristocrats, Pound's admiration for dictators are the appropriate reactions of poets to the problems of a mass society, but what is the appropriate response to poetry of those who do not share such political leanings?[63]

Hazlitt's challenge is one we have not met. As Kermode comments in *The Sense of an Ending*, the 'correlation between early modernist literature and authoritarian politics . . . is more often noticed than explained',[64] and until we have managed to explain it we cannot know if it is a function of a specific conception of poetry, of an unrepeatable historical crisis, or of the very nature of poetry itself. Explaining it requires, I think, three things: we have to understand the dynamics of the process that led Yeats, Eliot and Pound from a 'pure' poetry to a poetry of social involvement; we have to understand why that involvement should be based on values of historical regression; and we have to understand how the formal characteristics of their poetry enact those social and historical values, and to what extent those values are inherent in the very workings of the poetry. The chapters that follow represent an effort to answer these questions. They begin by re-examining the aesthetic context in which we see the workings of the poetry, an aesthetic context which has been dominated, I want to suggest, by the romantic conception of the power of the imagination. In the following chapter I offer a different tradition and a different context as the appropriate one for understanding the poetry; one that stems from associationist psychology and that is directed not at explaining (as theories of the imagination usually are) the poet's creative processes, but the reader's experience of the work, an experience which, it turns out, is entirely dependent on the power of memory. The impetus behind the development of the poetry and its related politics lies, I will argue, in the defence of memory. Chapters 4 and 5 examine the role of memory in the poetic theory and some of the poetry in order to establish the centrality it has to the work of all three, and in Chapters 7 and 8 I attempt to show how the dynamic of the development of an aesthetic based on the workings of memory carries with it distinct political implications. Yeats receives fullest treatment and

Pound scantiest: this is in part an indication of my valuation of the poets and in part a constraint of space, but it is also an assertion of what seems to me a real historical priority. We have not yet, I think, understood the extent of the shared poetic values of all three nor the decisive influence of Yeats in shaping what we now know as modernist poetry. I hope what I have to say about the poems I discuss will have its application to the bulk of their work upon which I have not touched.

My own political views are necessarily involved in some of my judgements: that many may be more sympathetic to the views of Yeats, Eliot and Pound than I at one time suspected has been made clear by recent events, by the revival of right-wing radicalism across Europe in the late 1970s, but I write about what I see as the problem of their politics only because I am an admirer of the poetry, and I trust that I have not only been faithful to my love of their poetry, but that the effort to understand their art has given me a view of their political commitments which is not simply hostile or a matter of immediate revulsion. I disagree profoundly with their politics and with those who might find support in the views of these poets, but I do not, for that reason, think their poetry false or a mere smokescreen for ideology. Nor is a poem a fiction, an 'as if', to be taken up or dropped depending on what it can teach us. It is a part of the culture which has made us more than we have made it, a part of the repertoire of gestures, postures, stances, even actions, which we have inherited: we can no more drop it from our existence than we can drop a past experience of our own lives. It is, to paraphrase Yeats, a part of our being, not of our knowledge, though for that reason only knowledge of it will allow us to understand its — and our own — limitations.

2 THE ASSOCIATIONIST TRADITION

What has characterised successive interpretations of modernist poetry is their gradual assimilation back into the mainstream of English literary history of modes of poetry that once seemed to represent a radical break in the continuity of our literary culture. The moderns who had propagated a myth of the disruption of the tradition in order to justify their own break with their predecessors have been gradually but surely drawn back into the very tradition they were so resolute in denying. Early critics tended to take Eliot's self-confessed poetic beginnings as the starting point for modernist writings, and related the radical break either to the influence of the French symbolists — as Edmund Wilson did in his influential *Axel's Castle* — or back to the Jacobean dramatists and the metaphysicals — as Cleanth Brooks did in *Modern Poetry and the Tradition*.[1] The emphasis was either on the poetry as an excess of connotation over denotation, on its suggestiveness and its non-logical structure, or on its play of wit, its ability to be 'constantly amalgamating disparate experience', 'forming new wholes'.[2] With two books of the 1950s, however, Robert Langbaum's *The Poetry of Experience* and Frank Kermode's *Romantic Image*,[3] the perspective shifted back to the immediate predecessors of modernism, to the Victorian dramatic monologue and to the romantic conception of a moment of perception in which an object is freed from time and space and becomes a gateway to 'radiant truth'.[4] In both cases modernist writers are seen to be working directly within their inheritance from romanticism, an inheritance that makes the influence of French symbolism or of the metaphysicals a matter of rhetorical style, a disguise within which the true tradition can be concealed behind gestures of novelty.

The assimilation of modern to romantic has proceeded apace since that time, despite one or two dissenting voices[5] In the work of Frye, Bloom and Bornstein,[6] Yeats, Eliot and Pound are finally forced to remove the mask of modernity and to stand forth as authors of poems the structure of which is that of the 'internalised quest' or which are versions of the 'Greater Romantic Lyric'. And it is from such an assimilation of the moderns to their romantic predecessors that Denis Donoghue has derived one of the most suggestive accounts yet offered of the political implications of their poetry. Its connection with Hazlitt's understanding of the force of the imagination as conceived by the romantics will be clear:

> Think of modern aesthetics, with politics half in mind. The single
> article of faith which goes undisputed in the Babel of modern
> criticism is the primacy of the creative imagination. It bloweth
> where it listeth, indisputable and imperious, it gives no quarter.
> In extreme versions it concedes no rights to nature, history, other
> people, the world of natural forms is grist to its mill. It is strange
> that we have accepted such an authoritarian notion in aesthetics
> while professing to be scandalised by its equivalent in politics.
> The poet is free to deal with nature as he wishes, whatever form
> the imposition takes . . . The freedom conceded to the poet's
> imagination is fundamental to European Romanticism, represented
> accurately enough by Coleridge. The modern understanding of
> imagination assumes that order is imposed upon experience by those
> exceptional men, the few, capable of doing so, as an act which
> issues from a prior capacity. It would be possible . . . to devise an
> aesthetic which would consort with a democratic politics, but no
> such aesthetic has flourished in modern literature. If you start with
> the imagination, you propose an elite of exceptional men; their
> special quality is power of vision. This relation between the elite
> and the masses is bound to be a critical one, and is likely to proceed
> by authority.[7]

The imagination is 'imperious' because the creative work of the artist
informs those imaginative structures through which we see the world
and without which the world would have no sense for us at all. The
mind of each of us creates the world it perceives, but the artist creates
the forms through which our lower order imaginations will work. If
imagination were only this, it would, however, lock us into an anthro-
pomorphic world from which there was no escape. For Coleridge the
imagination not only structured our world, but also revealed the truth
about it, because the imagination was an 'echo' of the divine act of
creation which had infused the world with spiritual meaning from
its inception. Imagination is our salvation, assuring us that we are not
surrounded by a world of dead matter because it penetrates to the
spiritual organisation of reality. Without a divinity to substantiate
its claims to knowledge the Coleridgean imagination can impose itself on the world only as a solipsistic gesture towards a meaningfulness which the world will never confirm or disconfirm. The declension
described by Harold Bloom, in *The Ringers in the Tower*, from the

romantic to the modern is not really a declension in 'faith in the creative power of imagination', but in the imagination as a means to faith by its revelation of a spiritual source which supports imaginative perception:

> Where Wordsworth and Keats, followed by Mill and Arnold, fought imaginatively against excessive self-consciousness, Pater welcomes it . . . What Pater, and modernist masters after him, lack is not energy of apprehension but rather the active force of a synthesising imagination . . . Yet this loss — in Yeats, Joyce, Stevens — is only an honest recognition of necessity . . . the faith in the saving creative power of imagination subsides in our time. Here too Pater is the hinge, for the epiphanies of Marius only help him to live what life he has — they do not save him, nor in the context of his world, or Pater's or ours can anyone be saved.[8]

The crucial element in this decline is faith in the imagination as linked to some transcendent source: without that the Coleridgean imagination become self-regarding. But if Bloom is right Donoghue's appropriation of Yeats to Coleridge's conception of the imagination must undergo some qualification — the imagination that helps the poet 'live what life he has' is not the same as the imperious imagination that imposes itself on all around it. What is important in Donoghue's conception, however, is his insistence — itself a romantic inheritance — that the poem is not merely a formal structure of language, a design on paper, but the enactment of particular processes of the mind: the formal qualities of the poem will be the result of the conception of the mind which the poet assumes to be operating in the process of creation. The romantics believed this to be true because they saw all art — successful art — as stemming from and as a revelation of the imagination; but in retrospect we can see that that was only one possible way in which a conception of the mind shapes the formal structures that the poet adopts. To understand the structuring both of the poem and of the world as the poet perceives it, we need to grasp the central element which defines, at a particular moment in history, the epistemology that links creative process, poem and world. That element, for modernism, is not the imagination.

In the perspective of literary history Coleridge's conception seems such a striking leap to a qualitatively different order of awareness that we read all subsequent literature as developing within the terms set by the new order of understanding. The pattern of nineteenth-century literature is viewed with the romantic aesthetic as the point of focus. We consider the primacy of the imagination and the organicist metaphor of art as the significant ideas to which any important artist of the period will be responding. Progressive models for the arts, however, are the imposition, by analogy, of our expectations of progress in other fields of human activity, and there is a moment in one of Eliot's essays from 1933 that ought to alert us to the dubiety of such models, a moment when Eliot is tempted to an anachronism that he cannot allow himself because it would be a disavowal of historical progression:

> There is the probability that this imagery had some personal satura-
> tion value, so to speak, for Seneca; another for Chapman, and
> another for myself, who have borrowed it twice from Chapman. I
> suggest what gives it such intensity as it has in each case is its satura-
> tion — I will not say with 'associations', for I do not want to revert
> to Hartley — but with feelings too obscure for the authors even
> to know quite what they were.[9]

Why can't Eliot revert to the terminology of Hartley? Why can't he use the word associations? It is because he knows that Hartley had been 'disproved' by Coleridge; that Coleridge had replaced an inferior mechanistic theory of mind — based on the principle of the association of ideas — with a more complex, more 'modern', more 'organic' theory. Earlier in *The Use of Poetry and the Use of Criticism*, the book from which this passage is drawn, Eliot had argued that 'in estimating for ourselves the greatness of a poet we have to take into account also the history of his greatness. Wordsworth is an essential part of history; Landor only a magnificent by-product.'[10] Replace Wordsworth with Coleridge, Landor with Hartley, and Eliot's reluctance to revert to Hartley is clear: there is no history of the significance of his ideas to justify their continued claim on our attention. Eliot in effect subscribes to a history of literature which perhaps has been given its most forceful statement by Frank Kermode in *Romantic Image*, although it is one that is standard to most literary criticism of the period:[11]

> Whether the objects of one's hatred are Bacon, Locke and Newton,
> or Darwin, Huxley and Lepage, or other monsters chosen by nine-
> teenth century Frenchmen, one is going, whenever one uses language
> about art, to be involved in some organicist challenge to the basic
> eighteenth century mechanist treatment of the subject. The most
> famous statement of this challenge in English is in *Biographia*

Literaria where Coleridge refutes Hartley's mechanistic psychology ... Before this there had been a prolonged effort by eighteenth century aestheticians and psychologists in the tradition of Hartley ... to develop within the Locke-Hartley tradition a certain freedom from pure determinism, without abandoning that uniformity of impulse which made the imagination as much as the memory dependent upon the nervous reorganization of sense impressions. But however ingenious such attempts might be, they could never have led to an organicist theory of art, because they could only conceive of extremely complicated mechanical processes performed upon material supplied by the 'vegetative' world.

The eighteenth-century mechanist idea of the mind is the reduction of all mental processes to the 'association of ideas' and that mechanist theory, identified with the works of Hartley, is overthrown by Coleridge.

But the terminology of association had not died with Hartley. Eliot, indeed, was not loath to use it without qualification in some of his influential essays of the 1920s. Discussing some stanzas of Herbert's, for instance, he identifies their power as residing 'in the richness of association which is at the same time borrowed from and given to' a specific word;[12] and in Donne's imagery he finds that what is characteristic is 'a development by rapid association of thought which requires considerable agility on the part of the reader.'[13] Yeats, too, was willing to adopt this anachronistic terminology, and indeed, in *Per Amica Silentia Lunae*, took the process of association to be the very foundation of the reading experience:

One must allow the images to form with all their associations before one criticises. If you suspend the critical faculty, I have discovered, either as a result of training, or, if you have the gift, by passing into a slight trance, images pass rapidly before you. If you suspend also desire, and let them form of their own will, your absorption becomes complete and they are more clear in colour, more precise in articulation. But the images pass before you linked by certain associations, and indeed in the first instance you have called them up by their association with traditional forms and sounds.[14]

A method of reading that operated by such a suspension of the critical faculty might lead to an increase in academic unemployment, but for Yeats and Eliot the principle of association was not just an outmoded literary theory, but an active element in their conception of what constituted the poetic 'modern'.

'Association' is a word that is used regularly by critics in discussing modernist poetry, despite its history, but it has become a catch-word for whatever is vague, suggestive or unresolved in the language of the poem. The instances are too common to need much specification, but I offer one as illustrative of a general tendency: it is from Richard Ellmann's *The Identity of Yeats*:

> These emblems pervade much of Yeats's early verse. Forms so archetypal as the cross and the circle, which the petals of the rose form, have of course a great many implications, some of which we can fix. The four petals are then, chiefly, the four elements. The conjunction of the rose and cross which suggests the fifth element or quintessence is the central myth of Rosicrucianism . . . The conjunction can also be regarded as sexual symbolism, in which Yeats, as comparative mythologist and occultist was well versed; the masculine principle, the cross, merges with the feminine principle, the rose. The cross has the apparent connotation of Christ and Christianity, while the rose, although a Christian symbol too, sometimes implies, as in his dream, a kind of pagan beauty. These associations help to clarify one of the more cryptic of Yeats's early poems.[15]

What Ellmann does is to argue that Yeats's poetry is intended to provoke a multiplicity of meanings or suggestions, but then to try to fix those meanings by uncovering for us what the images might have meant to the poet himself through relating the poem to Yeats's occult reading. The 'associations', therefore, are not, as Yeats was asking they should be, the result of the reader's meditation on the symbols, his 'suspension of the critical faculty', but precisely the tracking down to specific and single meanings of what, theoretically, is being asserted to have many meanings. The associations do not require of the reader 'agility' of mind, but merely the translation of the given terms of the poem into less obscure terms offered by the critic. The critic, in other words, provides one meaning while gesturing, by the word 'association', to the fact that we ought to read it as though it had many meanings.

The other context in which we use 'association' is that of 'free association', a concept given impetus by its use in Freudian psychology. Again, what the concept allows us to do is to give an apparent fixity to a process the very nature of which is its refusal of such fixity. If we describe a poem's structure as that of free association, then we give definition to the totality of that which refuses the logic of definitions and release ourselves from the need to fully experience its alogicality. Defining its nature incorporates it back into the world it sought to refuse, and our critical procedure with poems the structure of which we assume to be free association involves an insistent effort to bring them back into line with 'normal', logical sequences of thought, to make them conform to those categories of the conscious mind which they claimed to defy. Freud's description of how he reads a dream in terms of its *manifest* and its *latent* content is the model for such interpretations:

> we ask the dreamer, too, to free himself from the impression of the manifest dream, to divert his attention from the dream as a whole on to the separate portions of its content and to report to us in succession everything that occurs to him in relation to each of these portions — what associations present themselves to him if he focuses on each of them separately . . .
>
> . . . If one listens to these copious associations, one soon notices that they have more in common with the content of the dream than their starting-points alone. They throw surprising light on all the different parts of the dream, fill in gaps between them, and make their strange juxtapositions intelligible. In the end one is bound to become clear about the relation between them and the dream's content. The dream is to be seen as an abbreviated selection from the associations, a selection made, it is true, according to rules that we have not yet understood.[16]

If we think of the kind of structure we are offered by *The Waste Land* or the *Cantos* or Yeats's 'Nineteen Hundred and Nineteen', we can see the appeal of the language of association as derived from Freud. The critic, like the analyst, remains outside the process he is investigating, untouched by its refusal of logical sequence, assuming that by careful attention the pieces can be fitted together till the manifest surface reveals its latent structure. Instead of psychoanalytical expertise, what the critic brings to the poem is his barrage of scholarship, his knowledge of all the background writing and reading of his chosen poet, so that he can 'fill in gaps' and 'make strange juxtapositions intelligible'. What we are engaged in when we study *A Vision*, or search out allusions in Pound or Eliot, is the provision of the missing associational connections that will make coherent and sensible what the poet has actually given us. We normalise the poem, but in the end the question which Freud was forced to confront in his own technique is the question that faces all such criticism:

> we fill in the hints, draw undeniable conclusions and give explicit utterance to what the patient has only touched on in his associations. This sounds as though we allowed our ingenuity and caprice to play with the material put at our disposal by the dreamer and as though we misused it in order to interpret *into* his utterance what cannot be interpreted *from* them. Nor is it easy to show the legitimacy of our procedure in an abstract description of it.[17]

At least the psychoanalyst has the recovery of the patient as a test of his procedure: the literary work submits eternally to the long disease of its interpretation by techniques the legitimacy of which it is not easy to prove.

There does not seem to be much to choose between 'association' as an outworn eighteenth-century notion and 'association' as a legitimising device for critical paraphrase, for the reduction of the multi-meaninged symbol to its 'demon allegory', as Anna Balakian described it.[18] Both are, as it were, mechanical processes, ways of fixing and defining, of limiting and constraining, the real powers of the mind or of the poem, and Eliot was perhaps right to be hesitant about using the term. And yet the theory of association as a central conception of the mind's working — especially in the field of language — is not as dead as either our literary histories or those critics who wish to assimilate modernist poetry to romantic models would like to claim.[19] The empiricist theory of language which takes the principle of association, the forging of a connection between two terms such that when one appears in consciousness it calls up the other, as its foundation has been a potent element in twentieth-century philosophy: association is the basis of all the stimulus-response theories which characterised behavioural psychology,[20] and remains, despite Chomsky's critique of it,[21] an element within much contemporary linguistic theory. Even within the new linguistically-oriented criticism of the past twenty years, association has been held to be the fundamental principle of all literary language:

> there is a whole area of contemporary linguistics which deals with the definition of words less by their meaning than by their syntactic associations, according to which they take up their position; very

broadly speaking, associations between words occur according to a certain scale of probability: dog is fairly straightforwardly associated with barking, but pretty improbably with 'meowing'; even though syntactically there is nothing to forbid the association of verb and subject. This kind of complementary syntax of signs is sometimes given the name of *catalysis*. Catalysis is closely linked with the special character of literary language. Within certain limits . . . the more abnormal the catalysis, the more patent the literary character . . . Literary messages can thus be defined as deviant associations between signs.[22]

Such a conception must give more substance to Yeats's or Eliot's use of 'association' in their criticism than has been allowed so far by critics,[23] and the principle which governs the epistemology underlying their work, I want to argue, and which provides the fundamental dynamic of their conception of the poem's relation with its society, is 'association'. What distinguishes their poetry from romantic models is precisely the fact that they do not accept the overthrow of association by transcendental theories of the imagination; what distinguishes them from symbolist poets is that they are operating within an essentially secular and psychologistic tradition of speculation about the nature of aesthetics based on the principle of association. To establish this we have to make a historical detour into aesthetic and philosphical history.

Hartley, in his *Observations on Man* attributes 'the word association, in the particular sense here affixed to it'[24] to Locke. Locke, of course, was the villain of Blakean and Yeatsian mythologies of man's fall from intellectual grace —

> Locke sank into a swoon;
> The Garden died;
> God took the spinning-jenny
> Out of his side.[25]

— because he had denied the validity of imaginative modes of cognition. Locke's rationalism led him to denigrate whatever failed to correspond to the observable truths of science, and his philosophy is an attempt to bring to mental phenomena parallel formulations to those that had proved so successful in the physical sciences. Locke's theory of association is developed primarily as an account of what prevents men fulfilling the rationality that ought to be their distinctive characteristic. Thus Locke posits two different kinds of relations that ideas can have with one another: either they have 'a natural Correspondence and Connexion', in which case they are the business of Reason, or,

> Ideas that are not at all of kin, come to be so united in some Men's Minds, that it is very hard to separate them, they always keep in company and the one no sooner at any time comes into the Understanding but its Associate appears with it; and if they are more than two which are thus united, the whole gang always inseparable shew themselves together.[26]

'Gang' points Locke's feelings about this process: it is the method of thinking of those fanatics who deviate from the norms of reason – and from Locke's own political principles. However, as the idea is developed Locke finds more and more that has to come under the heading of Association, though he continues to refuse to allow it under the aegis of the commendatory term 'natural':

> to this, perhaps, might be justly attributed most of the Sympathies and Antipathies observable in Men, which work as strongly, and produce as regular Effects, as if they were Natural, and are therefore called so, though they at first had no other Original but the accidental Connexion of two Ideas, which either the strength of the first Impression, or future Indulgence so united, that they always afterwards kept company together in that Man's mind, as if they were but one idea.[27]

For Locke the expectations and the connections produced by the principle of association are a blindfold which prevents us seeing the world in its true relations. Primarily, of course, the true relations in which Locke was interested were the relations of cause and effect, those that could be uncovered by science and made available for men's use. It was precisely upon Locke's fundamental belief in reason's ability to disentangle causality, however, that Hume was to pounce and completely reverse Locke's metaphysic. For what Hume demonstrated was that the law of causality itself was no more than a 'constant conjunction', as he described it, which inclined us to a psychological expectation of uniform causality in nature but did not in any way prove it: what he did, in effect, was to make the principle of association the sole determinant of all our mental processes, and, in the course of doing so, gave a new and added force to the role of imagination:

> Reason can never show us the connexion of one object with another, tho' aided by experience, and the observation of their constant conjunction in all past instances. When the mind, therefore, passes from the idea or impression of one object to the idea or belief of another it is not determined by reason, but by certain principles, which associate together the ideas of these objects, and unite them in the imagination.[28]

For Hume no faculty of the mind can rise above the processes of association to see the true connections that are part of the world beyond: all our science is the following out of associative connections in our own minds, it is the creation of a very un-Coleridgean imagination.

The associationist theory of art which derives from this inversion of Locke is usually traced to the influence of Hartley — and this primarily because of Coleridge's apostasy from Hartley's philosophy. But to put Hartley's conception of association at the centre of eighteenth-century associationism is profoundly to distort its real development. Hartley wanted not only to explain all mental phenomena by the principles of association — usually accepted as being contiguity, similarity and causality — but to trace those in turn to physical stimuli, to neural mechanics. Hartley's theories, however, were not widely known until the 1780s, although published in the 1740s shortly after Hume's,[29] whereas theories developing Hume's work made no postulate of a material basis to mental phenomena at all. The Hume tradition in associationist thinking culminates in the work of Archibald Alison which, as Walter J. Hipple has noted,[30] is Platonist rather than materialist in bias. Within this tradition mind is the primary reality and association is an account of those principles by which the mind orders itself — not an account of how the mind is ordered by mechanical forces.

Associationist theory could not have given rise to the organicist theory of art for several reasons: first, it was largely secular, empirical in its orientation and could never have postulated that correspondence between human and divine upon which Coleridge's theory rested; secondly, it was directed not at the poet's act of creation, but at the reader's reception of a literary work. Associationist theory is not an account of how art comes into existence, but of how our experience of art is different from our experience of anything not art. The theories which were developed within this context, however, and especially by

Alison in his *Essays on the Nature and Principles of Taste* of 1790, have a dynamism just as significant as Coleridge's, for what they do is to make the real locus of creativity not the poet but the reader, what they imply is a radically subjective aesthetic which, as several critics have noted,[31] prefigures much twentieth-century discussion.

For Alison all aesthetic experience, whether of art or of nature, is the product of the mind's following out its own inherent patterns of association. The mind is a storehouse in which the various connections between objects, and between objects and emotions, lie available to be activated by any new object of perception:

> When any object, either of sublimity or beauty, is presented to the mind I believe every man is conscious of a train of thought being immediately awakened in his imagination, analogous to the character or expression of the original object. The simple perception of the object, we frequently find, is insufficient to excite these emotions, unless it is accompanied with this operation of the mind, unless, according to common expression, our imagination is seized and our fancy busied in the pursuit of all those trains of thought, which are allied to this character or expression.[32]

We can see or read a work of art, but we will not experience it as art unless it succeeds in generating in us a train of associated thoughts and feelings. It is this play of the mind, free from the restrictions of pragmatic considerations, that constitutes the essential attribute of aesthetic experience rather than any quality of the work itself. Indeed, the source of our aesthetic experience will often be inadequate to the experience itself:

> we are conscious of a variety of images in our minds, very different from those which the objects themselves can present to the eye. Trains of pleasing or of solemn thought arise spontaneously within our minds; our hearts swell with emotions, of which the objects before us seem to afford no adequate cause; and we are never so much satiated with delight, as when, in recalling our attention, we are unable to trace either the progress or the connection of those thoughts, which have passed with so much rapidity through our imagination.[33]

The aesthetic object has no power of its own, but is entirely dependent on associative capacities of the imagination that is 'seized' by the excitement of its own rapidity in recalling and uniting elements from past experience. Thus for Alison the imagination is truly the domain of the reader of literature rather than the creator: 'the first lines we meet with take possession of our imagination and awaken in it such innumerable trains of imagery, as almost to leave behind the fancy of the poet.'[34] The connection with Yeats's description of the reading process — 'images pass before you linked by certain associations'[35] — is clear, and Alison, too, considered criticism as inimical to the fundamental experience of a work of literature:

> The mind, in such an employment [criticism], instead of being at liberty to follow whatever trains of imagery the composition before it can excite, is either fettered to the consideration of some minute and solitary parts; or pauses, amid the rapidity of its conceptions, to make them the objects of its attention and review. In these operations, accordingly, the emotion . . . is lost, and if it is wished to be recalled, it can only be done by relaxing this vigour of attention, and resigning ourselves again to the natural stream of our thoughts.[36]

For an example of such associative reading we can do no better than return to Yeats and his record of how he 'reads' a poem in his essay 'The Philosophy of Shelley's Poetry':

> Though I do not think that Shelley needed to go to Porphyry's account of the cold intoxicating cup, given to souls in the constellation of the Cup near the constellation Cancer, for so obvious a symbol as the cup, or that he could not have found the wolf and deer and the continual flight of his Star in his own mind, his poetry becomes the richer, the more emotional, and loses something of its appearance of idle fantasy when I remember that these are ancient symbols, and still come to visionaries in dreams. Because the wolf is but a more violent symbol of longing and desire than the hound, his wolf and deer remind me of the hound and deer that Oisin saw in the Gaelic poem chasing one another on the water, before he saw the young man following the woman with the golden apple; and of a Galway tale that tells how Niamh, whose name means brightness and beauty, came to Oisin as a deer; and of a vision that a friend of mine saw when gazing at a dark blue curtain . . .[37]

The casual contingency, the purely personal nature of Yeats's recall of the 'dark blue curtain', finally completes the passage to pure associational

recall, and away from the pretended scholarship of the initial connections. Yeats's reading of the poem is a matter of filling out, completing
if you like, what is given on the page with a chain of linked associations
of his own. He never, in fact, returns to Shelley's image: the experience
is not of the poet's imagery as such, but of the poet's imagery in the
context of Yeats's own associational potentialities.

The parallels between Yeats — self-confessed 'last romantic', and
the first, none the less, of the moderns — and Alison — avowedly neo-
classical in taste and yet arguably, both for the revolutionary nature
of his theories and for their effect on Wordsworth,[38] the first romantic — will allow me to indicate the general structure and consequences
of an associationist aesthetic and the continuity between Alison's
late-eighteenth-century conceptions and those of the early twentieth
century. At the core of both writers' theory is the assumption that the
unity of a work of art derives from its single emotional impulse, while
its diversity is a function of the quantity of associations invoked and
held within one unified chain. A single emotional tone links together
a multiplicity of particulars that would otherwise have no connection
with each other: 'all those trains of thought which are allied to this
character or expression', as Alison expresses it in the passage already
quoted; or, as he writes elsewhere, 'the only subjects that are in themselves proper for the imitation of these Arts are such as are productive
of some species of Simple Emotion.'[39] Yeats, too, insists on the
emotional basis of art — 'All sounds, all colours, all forms, either because of their preordained energies or because of long association,
evoke indefinable yet precise emotions'[40] — and sees single emotions
fusing together in extended works of art to form a new, engrossing
unity: 'A little lyric evokes an emotion, and this emotion gathers
others about it and melts into their being in the making of some great
epic.'[41] However, the reverse process characterises the reader's perception of the poem, for in him the writer's achievement of emotional
unity provokes associational diversity: 'the object itself appears only
to serve as a hint, to awaken the imagination, and to lead it through
every analogous idea that has a place in memory.'[42] Yeats was to call
this centrifugal movement of the mind 'the emotion of multitude',
distinguishing by that phrase both the unity and the multiplicity of
the process:

> The Shakespearean drama gets the emotion of multitude out of the
> sub-plot which copies the main plot, much as a shadow on the
> wall copies one's body in the firelight. We think of *King Lear* less

as the history of one man and his sorrows than as the history of a whole evil time. Lear's shadow is in Gloucester, who also has ungrateful children, and the mind goes on imagining other shadows, shadow beyond shadow, till it has pictured the world . . . Ibsen and Maeterlinck have, on the other hand, created a new form, for they get multitude from the wild duck in the attic, or from the crown at the bottom of the fountain, vague symbols that set the mind wandering from idea to idea, emotion to emotion.[43]

The artist's task is to structure his work so that it will at once focus for us a specific emotion and yet imply the direction of that centrifugal movement of the mind in which the reader or spectator will inevitably be involved, that movement outwards 'from idea to idea, emotion to emotion'.

In his excellent study of Yeats's aesthetic, Edward Engelberg has argued that 'the emotion of multitude' must not be taken to imply any quantitative dimension. Yeats's art, he suggests, intends 'like a puppeteer' to hold 'all the strings, no matter how multitudinous they become' and to ensure that 'all contemplation must be directed towards the object, not away from it';[44] that, in effect,

It cannot be too much stressed that by 'emotion of multitude' Yeats never meant a multitude of emotions. Multitude was no mere summary of diversified emotions or events, no quantitative measure at all. Through the choice of proper symbols, art attained a qualitative richness which, on the stage for instance, would be more successful proportionate to the economy of physical props.[45]

Engelberg wants to place Yeats in the line of romantic symbolists, but what he fails to see is that within the tradition of aesthetic theory which Yeats is drawing on the quantitative measure is precisely the one the artist is seeking: indeed, the simplification of the art itself is essential in order to maintain that unity of tone which will prevent the breaking of the associative chain that depends upon it. The 'emotion of multitude' means precisely what it says: it is an emotion with multitudinous ideas and subsidiary emotions melting into it. It is what Yeats was to call, in the 1890s, a 'mood':

Literature differs from explanatory and scientific writing in being wrought about a mood, or a community of moods, as the body is wrought about an invisiable soul; and if it uses argument, theory, erudition, observation, and seems to grow hot in assertion or denial, it does so merely to make us partakers at the banquet of the moods.[46]

The singleness of the body or soul leads us to the multiplicity, the excess, of the 'banquet of moods'. Alison emphasises that the artist must strive after purity because only thus will his work continue to hold associational force beyond his own time and its specific associational expectations:

> In all those Arts, therefore, that respect the Beauty of Form, it ought to be the unceasing study of the Artist, to disengage his mind from the accidental Associations of his age, as well as the common prejudices of his Art; to labour to distinguish his production by that pure and permanent expression, which may be felt in every age . . .[47]

Yeats's taste is very different from Alison's, but his recommendations are for a similar concentration on the 'permanent': 'It is only by ancient symbols, by symbols that have numberless meanings besides the one or two the writer lays emphasis on, or the half-score he knows of, that any highly subjective artist can escape from the barrenness and shallowness of a too conscious arrangement, into the abundance and depth of Nature.'[48] The artist's concentration is on those enduring symbols so that his work will always be capable of producing 'numberless' meanings in the minds of future as well as present readers.

The condition in which the receiving mind can generate associations most easily and fully is called, by both Yeats and Alison, 'reverie'.[49] In reverie the mind is freed from any practical purpose, suspended in the flow of its own images and ideas, unguided by the conscious will; the ideas, as it were, are themselves determining their progression. 'It is then, indeed, in this powerless state of reverie', Alison writes, 'when we are carried on by our own conceptions, not guiding them, that the deepest emotions of beauty and sublimity are felt.'[50] The purpose of reverie is an inward journeying, a discovery of the logic that has been secretly stored by the mind in the patterns of its own associational resources, in the memory. Yeats describes the same state in 'The Symbolism of Poetry':

> The purpose of rhythm, it has always seemed to me, is to prolong the moment of contemplation, the moment when we are both asleep and awake, which is the one moment of creation, by hushing us with

an alluring monotony, while it holds us awake with variety, to keep us in that state of perhaps real trance, in which the mind liberated from the pressure of the will is unfolded in symbols.[51]

He could, however, see that unfolding as a much more personal process, something closer to our individual memories than to archetypal symbols:

> nor when the tragic reverie is at its height do we say, 'How well that man is realised! I should know him were I to meet him in the street,' for it is always ourselves that we see upon the stage, and should it be a tragedy of love, we renew, it may be, some loyalty of our youth, and go from the theatre with our eyes dim for an old love's sake.[52]

The recovery of memory is reverie's essential aim, and yet it is an aim that can only be fulfilled on the condition that one's memory is suited to the possibility of sustained associational meditation. In an essay of 1904, Yeats distinguished between two different definitions of 'thought' in two Irish writers, allying himself with the one who,

> though in actual life he is the most practical man I know, meant as Pascal, as Montaigne, as Shakespeare, or as, let us say, Emerson, understood it [thought] — a reverie about the adventures of the soul, or of the personality, or some obstinate questioning of the riddle. Many who have to work hard always make time for this reverie, but it comes more easily to the leisured, and in this it is like a broken heart, which is, a Dublin newspaper assured us lately, impossible to a busy man.[53]

The connection of leisure with the potentiality for reverie is not merely based on having the time, as Yeats's description makes clear. It is that leisure allows the acquisition of kinds of memory which are themselves undeflected by pragmatic considerations and therefore suited to the associational recall which operates when the practical will is dormant. Alison argues that the

> man of business, who has passed his life in studying the means of accumulating wealth, and the philosopher, whose years have been employed in the investigation of causes, have both not only acquired a constitution of mind very little fitted for the indulgence of

imagination, but have acquired also associations of a very different kind from those which take place when imagination is employed . . .[54]

and the inevitable result is, therefore, a deterministic relationship between the kind of life one leads and the possibility of substantial aesthetic experience:

> the diversity of tastes corresponds to the diversity of occupations . . . It is only in the higher situations accordingly or liberal professions of life, that we expect to find men of delicate or comprehensive taste. The inferior stations of life, by contracting the knowledge and affections of men, within very narrow limits, produces insensibly a similar contraction in their notions of the beautiful and sublime.[55]

The associations fostered by the 'inferior stations in life' are neither of the right kind — being largely practical — nor of a sufficient quantity for imaginative reverie; it is a point Yeats makes in 'Discoveries' in relation to 'Those learned men who are a terror to children and an ignominious sight in lovers' eyes, all those butts of traditional humour where there is something of the wisdom of peasants, are mathematicians, theologians, lawyers, men of science', for these are the occupations that encourage an 'abstract reverie'.[56] Alison's division of the social classes into different potentialities for associational response is also echoed by Yeats in his essay of 1901, 'What is Popular Poetry?':

> Go down into the street and read to your baker or your candlestick maker any poem which is not 'popular poetry'. I have heard a baker, who was clever enough with his oven, deny that Tennyson could have known what he was writing when he wrote, 'Warming his five wits, the owl in the belfry sits,' and once when I read out Omar Khayyam to one of the best of candlestick-makers, he said, 'What is the meaning of "I came like water and like wind I go"?' Or go down into the street with some thought whose bare meaning must be plain to everybody; take with you Ben Jonson's 'Beauty like sorrow dwelleth everywhere', and find out how utterly its enchantment depends on an association of beauty with sorrow which written tradition has from the unwritten, which had it in its turn from ancient religion.[57]

Such 'association of beauty with sorrow' cannot be had by those who have not escaped the practical deformation of the mind that Yeats obviously connects here with the urban lower classes.

The principal achievement of associationist theories of art, as far as the eighteenth century was concerned, was that it accounted in an apparently empirical way for the 'diversity of tastes': a man's taste was related to the kind of associations he was capable of, and a culture's taste was founded upon the associations of its landscape and history. There was no intrinsic difference in the mode of experiencing of 'the man of taste' and those from the lower stations — only a superior capacity for sustaining that associational reverie which was the very essence of art and beauty. Thus the educated are not superior by their greater insight or perception, only by the greater quantity of associational material which they can bring into play at any given time. All the art we experience, therefore, feeds back into later aesthetic experience by giving us further associations upon which to draw; we derive a kind of cumulative interest upon the depositis of our experience. Similarly, the beauties of art and nature borrow from our experience of the other:

> the time when nature began to appear . . . in another view than as something useful to human life, was, when [we] were engaged in the study of classical literature . . . The beautiful forms of ancient mythology with which the fancy of the poets peopled every element, are now ready to appear in [our] minds upon the prospect of every scene. In most men, at least, the first appearance of poetical imagination is at school, when their imaginations begin to be warmed by the descriptions of ancient poetry, and when they have acquired a new sense, as it were, with which they can behold the face of nature.[58]

Yeats might almost be carrying out Alison's conception programmatically in the following description from 'The Symbolism of Poetry':

> If I watch a rushy pool in the moonlight, my emotion at its beauty is mixed with memories of the man I have seen ploughing by its margin, or the lovers I saw there a night ago; but if I look at the moon herself and remember any of her ancient names and meanings, I move among divine people, and things that have shaken off our mortality, the tower of ivory, the queen of water . . .[59]

Alison, of course, emphasises the importance of the ancient classics because his own class and culture treat those as central, but as his theory depends on quantitative and not qualitative addition to our associational potential, it obviously leaves itself free to accept any other source of literary material at all. The shift from a quantity of association based on classical education to one based on 'natural' experience, or experience of nature, was one that Wordsworth was to make,[60] but what associationism offered Yeats was a justification for his use of Irish material because its associational efficacy was the only criterion of success.

Alison has pointed out that we often find places of purely personal interest provide us with emotions of beauty or sublimity — the place of our childhood experiences, for instance,[61] but the same effect can be perceived where the broader values of our culture and our history are involved:

> The scenes which have been distinguished by the residence of any person, whose memory we admire, produce a similar effect . . . The scenes themselves may be little beautiful; but the delight with which we recollect the traces of their lives, blends itself insensibly with the emotions which the scenery itself excites; and the admiration which these recollections afford, seems to give a kind of sanctity to the place where they dwelt, and converts everything into beauty which appears to have been connected with them.[62]

The obverse, however, will also be true, and any place that does not have vivid connections with one's personal recollections will be incapable of generating aesthetic experience. Alison's classicism does not prevent his setting limits to the ways in which we can read ancient literature, limits defined by the necessarily personal nature of our associations: 'The fine lines which Virgil has dedicated in his *Georgics* to the praise of his native country, however beautiful to us, were yet undoubtedly read with a far superior emotion by an ancient Roman.'[63] Yeats, in the 1890s, saw the same relation as working to the advantage of Irish writers; since there was 'no feeling, except religious feeling, which moves masses of men so powerfully as national feeling', and national feeling was spread throughout all classes in Ireland, he felt that it 'would give us just that help which men of letters have lacked for similar attempts elsewhere'.[64] Yeats was of course implying that it provided an audience, but it was an audience which would share a set of common feelings and therefore a set of common emotions. The emotions of nationalism would generate associational potential because it would encourage the memory of the national past, and, in the dialectical pattern that is typical of both Yeats's and Alison's conception of the relation of literature with the world around it, in encountering the national past the audience would be in touch with the creation of previous writers:

> A nation can only be created in the deepest thought of its deepest minds — the literature that makes it (and this making takes a long time) — who have first made themselves fundamental and profound and then realized themselves in art. In this way they rouse into national action the governing minds of their time — few at any one time — by an awakening of their desire towards a certain mood and thought which is unconscious to these governing minds themselves. They create national character.[65]

It was on the basis of such a conception that Yeats had proclaimed, in 1886, that he held it 'the duty of every Irish reader to study those [legends] of his own country till they are familiar as his own hands'.[66]

At every level, therefore, within the associationist scheme in aesthetics, there is an interaction between the immediate experience of the art before one and the personal recollections, the cultural context and the whole of one's past experience of art. In that centrifugal movement outwards from the given work of art, the mind must be able to bring continuously into play a wider and wider range of memories, but those memories, once activated, will themselves return to inhabit one's ordinary life, to change the emotions of everyday experience, and both the new experience of art and those changed emotions will, in turn, become the material of recollection which will make further associative, and therefore aesthetic, experience possible. Therefore, Yeats's use of Irish mythology always has a double intent: it both recalls into the present those figures that are part of a national memory, and adds to their memorability, thus creating national consciousness as well as drawing upon it. For Alison the validity of the universality of the classics rested not, as in earlier eighteenth-century views, in their correspondence with 'nature', their original discovery of the true forms of poetic excellence based on their direct apprehension of the world, but on the cultural memory in which people are trained in their youth. Education is the primary enforcement of associative connections on which we draw for the rest of our lives and the classical material, therefore, for the educated classes, represents the common stock of association. This remains a purely contingent precedence, however, and Yeats's constant effort was to make the local associatively significant in terms that concur with what Alison describes in the following passage (which is almost a prophecy of Wilde's reversal of art's imitation of nature):

> Even the unfamiliar circumstance of general nature, which pass unheeded to the common eye, the cottage, the sheep-fold, the curfew, all have expressions to them, because, in the compositions to which they [people of taste] have been accustomed, these are all associated with peculiar characters or rendered expressive of them; and leading them to the remembrance of such associations, enable them to behold with corresponding dispositions, the scenes which are before them, and to feel from their prospect, the same powerful influence, which the eloquence of poetry has ascribed to them.[67]

In March 1889, Yeats was writing to Katharine Tynan that she should read a story about a character of her 'own neighbourhood at Tallaght' and write a poem about him. 'A great many poems should be written on him' because, as he explained in the following letter, 'It would be a fine thing to write a poem that always would be connected with Tallaght in people's minds. All poetry should have a local habitation when possible.'[68] It was that 'local habitation', that fund of associative memory connected with his own countryside, that Yeats had sought in his trips to the West of Ireland and in his browsings in the British Museum, 'some symbolic language reaching far into the past and associated with familiar names and conspicuous hills that I might not be alone amid the obscure impressions of the senses.'[69] The work of the whole literary renaissance he saw as making the Irish at home in their own associations, particularly the Anglo-Irish, whose education and background might divorce them from the traditional memory that inhabited their landscape:

> When I asked the little boy who had shown me the pathway up the hill of Allen if he knew stories of Finn and Oisin, he said he did not, but that he had often heard his grandfather telling them to his mother in Irish. He did not know Irish, but he was learning it at school, and all the little boys he knew were learning it. In a little while he will know enough stories of Finn and Oisin to tell them to his children some day. It is the owners of the land whose children might never have known what would give them so much happiness.

But now they can read Lady Gregory's book to their children, and it will make Slieve-na-man, Allen, and Ben Bulben, the great mountain that showed itself before me every day through all my childhood and was yet unpeopled . . . as populous with memories as her Cuchulain of Muirthemne will have made Dundealgan . . .[70]

'Populous with memories': mind and landscape are joined in that phrase in fulfilment of the associational principle which Alison had brought to the climax of its eighteenth-century development, and which Yeats was carrying forward into the twentieth, and nowhere more fully than in that set of great essays in the period 1900 to 1906 to which the modernist theories of poetry of a decade later were to owe so much.

Yeats, of course, had not read Alison. The parallels in their conceptions of poetry are testimony not to the vitality of Alison's writings – his taste would have appalled any late-nineteenth-century acolyte of Pater and Wilde – but to the continuity of a tradition, to a sustained effort at understanding art, not from the point of view of transcendental idealism, but from that of psychological empiricism. Histories of associationist theory almost all end with the Romantic overthrow of the associationist model;[71] thereafter associationist elements in any writer's thought are regarded as leftovers, as deposits of outmoded conceptions that the writer has failed fully to transcend.[72] But nineteenth-century associationist thinking is no archaeological relic somehow lingering into another age. It is, in fact, the central tradition of nineteenth-century investigation into the workings of the mind, for it is from the experimental work of the associationists that modern psychology develops in the English-speaking world, and if it was to be overtaken by a new romanticism with the arrival of Freudian and Jungian psychology, its survival of previous romantic incursions was to be no less a pointer to future developments.

Alison's work was to have no widespread influence immediately after its publication in 1790; its success dates from the counter-romanticism of Francis Jeffrey's *Edinburgh Review*, and particularly from a review Jeffrey himself wrote of Alison's work in 1811 on the publication of the second edition.[73] Alison's influence probably owes much of its effect to Jeffrey, for that article was to become the basis of the *Encyclopaedia Britannica*'s entry on beauty from 1824 to 1875, but its primary mode of transmission to the late nineteenth century was through the publications of psychologists and philosophers such as Dugald Stewart, Thomas Brown and, most importantly, James Mill.[74]

Mill's study of psychological workings, *The Analysis of the Phenomena of the Human Mind*, drew heavily on Hartley for its materialist assumptions, but when it came to discussing aesthetic theory Mill constructed his whole argument by citations of Alison's work which he had first read as a student in the 1790s.[75] It is through the Mills, father and son, that the associationist theory was kept in the centre of Victorian thinking about poetry, for when, in the famous 'Thoughts on Poetry and its Varieties', John Stuart Mill was to ponder the crucial romantic question, 'Whom, then, shall we call the poets?', his answer accepts the romantic glorification of the creative principle but analyses its workings back into associationist terms: 'Those so constituted that emotions are the links of association by which their ideas, both sensuous and spiritual, are connected together.'[76] The point that Wordsworth had adopted from Alison in the 'Preface to *Lyrical Ballads*', that the poems are intended 'to make these incidents and situations interesting by tracing in them ... the primary laws of our nature: chiefly as regards the manner in which we associate ideas in a state of excitement',[77] becomes identical with the very nature of poets themselves, for they are the possessors of a consciousness which operates on the basis of continual emotional excitement and associational recall. The associative process is transferred from the state in which the reader is experiencing the work of art, to the state of mind which can produce a work of art.

For the romantics, of course, the characteristic of the creative mind was its ability to unify, to see wholeness where before there had only been discrete atomistic elements: it is the basis of Coleridge's distinction between fancy's fixed and definite counters derived entirely from memory, and the dissolving, diffusing and dissipating that allowed imagination to create some new idealised unity. But John Stuart Mill felt that his father had already shown that an associationist psychology could also deal with the transformation of quantity into quality, and cited as an instance the wheel of seven colours which, when spun, appeared white;[78] the son, however, had his own analogy from the new science of chemistry and argued that, 'when impressions have been so often experienced in conjunction that each of them calls up readily and instantaneously the ideas of the whole group, these ideas melt and coalesce into one another, and appear not several ideas, but one. . .'[79] The application of this model to poetry allows Mill fully to adopt Coleridge's insights into the nature of art without departing from strict associationist principles:

Thoughts and feelings will be linked together, according to the similarity of the feelings which cling to them. A thought will introduce a thought by first introducing a feeling which is allied with it. At the centre of each group of thoughts or images will be found a feeling; and the thoughts or images will be there only because the feeling was there. The combinations which the mind puts together, the pictures which it paints, the wholes which Imagination constructs out of the materials supplied by Fancy, will be indebted to some dominant *feeling*, not as in other natures to some dominant *thought*, for their unity and consistency of character, for what distinguishes them from incoherences.[80]

The poet, thus, is accorded his Imagination, but the Imagination is described in terms that accord with Alison's description of the aesthetic experience — it is a series of thoughts and feelings linked together by a dominant feeling which gives unity to what would otherwise be mere incoherence. The pattern here displayed, of appropriating romantic notions to associationist theory, was one that Mill was to use regularly and was to applaud when used, for instance, by his fellow associationist Bain in analysing Ruskin's work. Ruskin is generally regarded as having nailed the coffin lid upon Alison's associationism,[81] but the much proclaimed death of associationist theory was to be prevented yet again:

Mr. Ruskin would probably be astonished were he to find himself held up as one of the principal apostles of the Association Philosophy in Art. Yet, in one of the most remarkable of his writings, the second volume of 'Modern Painters', he aims at establishing, by a large induction and searching analysis, that all things are beautiful or sublime which powerfully recall, and none but those which recall, one or more of a certain series of elevating and delightful thoughts.[82]

Delivered of its metaphysical postulates, its adherence to what Mill described as the *a priori* school that derived from Coleridge, Ruskin's description of the artist's workings and of aesthetic experience is revealed to conform with associationism's empirically established theories of mental process.

It was the advances in empirical psychology achieved by people such as Bain and Herbert Spencer, and the general turn towards a scientific and materialist philosophy in the wake of Darwinian evolu-

tionary theory, that was to bring associationist theory back into prominence in aesthetics. By 1859 Mill was writing to Bain on their success
in getting the *Edinburgh Review* to publish work on their side of the
question[83] and by 1869 he felt that the new temper of the age justified
the reissue of his father's *Analysis*, with additional notes and information by himself and Bain to bring it up to date with contemporary
advances in psychological theory. What is striking, as Isobel Armstrong
comments in her study of Victorian criticism,[84] is not that associationism died with Coleridge's apostasy from Hartley, but that the idealist
theory of art made such little headway against moral or – as
associationism was known in the Victorian period – sensationalist
concepts of criticism. Idealist theories were most prominent during the
period of Carlyle's dominance of the literary scene, but with the
publication of his *Latter Day Pamphlets* in 1859 that particular source
of Germanic influence began to wane. In the second half of the nineteenth century, what Ruskin had objected to in Alison's theory – that
it was metaphysically and morally neutral, that it made no transcendental demands upon the artist – was precisely what brought it back to
the attention of poets who wished to escape the mantle of the prophet
and to leave intellectual, political and social baggage to journalists.
Not that associationism was the motor force of the art for art's sake
movement – although Hume's theories had had a significant influence
on Pater, mentor to the aesthetes and the decadents of the 1890s[85] –
but associationism was on hand to justify and to stimulate the poetic
direction of the age. The symbolist emphasis on a poetry of suggestion,
emanating initially from a transcendentalist conception of a truth
beyond language, gradually incorporated and was transformed by
associationist principles: that transformation was in many ways
responsible for poetic modernism.

The source from which Yeats acquired his associationist theories is
an essay which Isobel Armstrong has pointed to as a striking prefigura-
tion of many of Eliot's critical theories,[86] Arthur Hallam's 'On Some
Characteristics of Modern Poetry', first published in 1831 as a defence
of Tennyson's work. Hallam's argument was intended to justify what
critics had taken to be Tennyson's unnecessary obscurity. Hallam's
reply was that Tennyson's was a poetry of 'sensation', as opposed to
a poetry of 'reflection' like Wordsworth's, the characteristic of sensa-
tional poetry being that it linked together a series of images in an
unusual and unusually rapid chain of associations. The difficulty which
readers found in Tennyson, and which many also found in Shelley,
was due to the fact that the poet's associative process was much less

stereotyped, and therefore much less predictable, than the reader's. For the reader to grasp the meaning and development of the poem he had to make a mental leap into a different awareness of the possible connections which the mind could make between objects in the world; for,

> since the emotions of the poet during composition, follow a regular law of association, it follows that to accompany their progress up to the harmonious prospect of the whole, and to perceive the dependence of every step on that which preceded it, it is absolutely necessary to start from the same point, i.e. clearly to apprehend the leading sentiment in the poet's mind, by their conformity to which the host of associations is arranged. Now this requisite is not willingly made by a large majority of readers.[87]

Like Mill, who may well have drawn the notion form Hallam, Hallam sees the essential unity of the work to depend on our recognition of the underlying emotion that binds together 'the host of associations'. The poem has incorporated Alison's theory of aesthetic experience into its own being: instead of offering a simple and unified emotional tone from which the reader may derive a host of associations, the poem becomes the record of a mind whose ability to generate such a host of associations outstrips the reader's ability to follow. The pleasures of poetry are necessarily, Hallam believes, limited to the few, because only the few can achieve that act of identification with the poet's mental processes that will allow them to understand his work. Where Alison had implied that only a few could fully participate in aesthetic experience, because of the inappropriate nature of their associational recall, Hallam's few is based not only on sufficiency of associations, but on the mind's innate capacities for intensely personal combination of ideas.

Later in his development Yeats was to find Hallam's analysis of poetry, which he had praised several times in the 1890s —

> If one set aside Shelley's essay on poetry and Browning's essay on Shelley, one does not know where to turn in modern English criticism for anything so philosophic — anything so fundamental and radical — as the first half of Arthur Hallam's essay.[88]

— too narrowly constricting, too little engaged with 'traditional statement of certain heroic and religious truths.'[89] Hallam's essay, however, seems to have been influential not only on Yeats, but on Yeats's friend Symons. Arthur Symons's *The Symbolist Movement in Literature* is the work which introduced the new poetry of France (much of it already fifty years old when the book was published in 1899) to English speaking readers, and its influence on Eliot is often noted as justifying our view of his poetry, at least, as deriving from symbolist models. Symons dedicated the book to Yeats — 'the chief representative of that movement [symbolism] in our country[90] — but his analysis of symbolism is rarely carried through in terms of symbolist conceptions of poetry: he applies to it associationist conceptions. In order to explain Mallarmé, for instance, Symons does not offer a critical exegesis of the poetry, but a psychological analysis of the poet's methods of composition. He begins by recalling Mallarmé's essential principle, 'to name is to destroy, to suggest is to create', but thereafter Symons provides us with an imaginary account of how Mallarmé begins with 'a mental sensation', which is then painstakingly translated into words, each word, however, a violation of the original purity of the sensation. At this point, Symons tells us, most poets would stop, the point at which the poem,

> In its very imperfection, it is clear . . . shows the links by which it has been riveted together; the whole process of its construction can be studied. Now most writers would be content; but with Mallarmé the work has just begun. In the final result there must be no sign of the making, there must only be the thing made . . . By the time the poem has reached, as it seems to him, a flawless unity, the steps in the progress have been only too effectually effaced; and while the poet, who has seen the thing from the beginning, still sees the relation of point to point, the reader, who comes to it only in its final stage, finds himself in a not unnatural bewilderment.[91]

What Mallarmé has done, in Symons's reconstruction, is to deny the reader any possible entry to the only point from which the development of the poem's associational progression can be viewed — that of the poet's own emotional state. If there is only 'the thing made', it is impossible to follow the pattern of the images by reconstructing the associations which bound them together in the poet's own mind, even if the writer himself can still see the 'relation of point to point'. In effect, the only thing the reader can do, is to allow his own associations to play over and drift away from the images provided by the poet:

Alison's theory which claimed to account for how we actually do experience language as poetic becomes, because of shifts in poetic style (to which Alison's theory might be an unconscious contributor), the only possible method by which we can read at all.

Neither Symons nor Yeats, I would suggest, was significantly influenced by French writers into developing new aesthetic principles: what they did was to interpret French poetry inside the already-existing principles of an associationist aesthetic. Yeats utilised his occultism to give a spiritualistic ontology to his thinking, as opposed to the materialist emphasis of empirical psychology in general, but in so far as he was following French predecessors in this he was, in fact, going against the current of contemporary developments in France. Indeed, the emphasis that we usually place on the influence of French nineteenth-century literature on late-nineteenth- and early-twentieth-century English literature has obscured a counter-movement of some importance. By the late 1880s and early 1890s in Paris the 'symbolistes' — inheritors of the tradition that is constituted by the writers in Symons's study — were struggling to disavow the occult elements of which Yeats was to make so much. As James Webb, in his study *The Flight from Reason*, notes, Gustave Khan, leading theoretician of this new generation of 'symbolistes', 'found it necessary to dissociate himself and the Symbolists from the occult movement. They were mystics of a sort, he admitted, but not occultists'.[92] The reason for the denial of occultism lay in Khan's essentially empirical attitude to poetry; as A.G. Lehmann describes it, Khan held that,

> all processes of thought are rigidly determined by facts to which he gave the approximate name of laws of association: laws which brooked no interference by the individual choice of the thinking subject, for whom, therefore, poetry was nothing more than a plucking out on the emotional strings of his readers those chords which the association laws sanctioned, and whose work was directed to securing conditions in verse writing in which these virtually impersonal laws should be least impeded by outward conventions.[93]

What Khan's theory bears witness to is the introduction of empiricist theory from psychology into aesthetics, empiricist theory largely derived from the British tradition.

The writer to whom both Eliot and Pound pay regular homage in their early criticism, Remy de Gourmont, was at the very centre of this shift in critical perspective. De Gourmont was the major theoretician of symbolism, but after an initial period in which he accepted a trans-cendental metaphysic he turned to the British tradition because he wanted to connect poetry to science, to give it a value unconnected with religious belief; thus, in the sacred book of modernism's early period, *Le Problème du Style*, he insists that, '*Nihil in intellectu quod non prius fuerit in sensu*: les senses sont la porte unique par où est entré ce qui vit dans l'esprit . . .'[94] Only from the senses does knowledge derive. De Gourmont retreats from idealism and symbolism to the most basic British empiricism:

> La sensation est la base de tout, de la vie intellectuelle et morale aussi bien que de la vie physique. Deux cent cinquante ans après Hobbes, deux cents ans après Locke, telle a été la puissance destruc-tive du kantisme religieux, qu'on en est réduit à insister sur d'aussi éleméntaires aphorismes . . .[95]

De Gourmont was, however, not only making a return to the senses as the source of all knowledge, but to association as the fundamental determinant of the mind's relationship with the world it perceives. As in Alison and other eighteenth-century associationists, language itself has its effect on us in an aesthetic context by the transfer of emotion through association:

> Les mots n'ont de sens que par le sentiment qu'ils renferment et dont on leur confère la représentation. Les propositions géomét-riques même deviennent sentiments, a dit Pascal . . . Un théorème peut être émouvant et, résolu, faire battre le coeur. Il est devenu sentiment, en ce sens qu'il n'est plus perçu qu'associé à un senti-ment . . . Les mots les plus inertes peuvent être vivifiés par la sens-ibilité, peuvent 'devenir sentiments'.[96]

It is through associational connection that any form of language, the specialised form of mathematics, the precise form of poetry, or the dead language of ordinary discourse gains its emotive power. From de Gourmont Eliot and Pound did not learn a symbolist aesthetic, they reacquired an empiricist one.

Eliot's essay, 'The Perfect Critic', the essay he placed first in *The Sacred Wood* in 1920, nominates de Gourmont for the accolade of its title. On the other hand, however, Eliot presents us with the failed critic, Arthur Symons, whose criticism is 'impressionistic' because it allows the work of art to play upon his 'sensitive and cultivated mind — cultivated, that is, by the accumulation of a considerable variety of impressions from all the arts . . .'[97] Symons, in other words, is taken by Eliot to represent the 'associationist', his criticism offering us the suggestions which the work of art arouses in him:

> Some writers are essentially of the type that reacts in excess of the stimulus, making something new out of the impressions . . . Their sensibility alters the object, but never transforms it. Their reaction is that of the ordinary emotional person developed to an exceptional degree. For this ordinary emotional person, experiencing a work of art, has a mixed critical and creative reaction. It is made up of comment and opinion, and also new emotions which are vaguely applied to his own life. The sentimental person, in whom a work of art arouses all sorts of emotions which have nothing to do with that work of art whatever, but are accidents of personal association, is an incomplete artist.[98]

To rest within 'the accidents of personal association' is, for Eliot, to fail to come into contact with the 'object as its really is'.[99] But when we examine Eliot's description of an appropriate form of reading the attack on associationism takes on a very different complexion:

> For in an artist these suggestions made by a work of art, which are purely personal, become fused with a multitude of other suggestions from multitudinous experience, and result in the production of a new object which is no longer purely personal, because it is a work of art itself.[100]

Yeats's 'multitude' returns; Mill's 'fused' returns; the work, in fact, has ceased to be the original creator's work at all: it incorporates both what the poet offers and the multitude of suggestions it arouses in its appropriate reader — we are back with Alison. The difference between the ordinary sentimental person, or his superior version 'the impressionistic critic', and the 'perfect' critic is in the quantity of his association — 'multitude of other suggestions from multitudinous experience' as opposed to 'a considerable variety of impressions from all the arts' — and in his capacity to turn them into a 'new object', 'a work of art itself'. The perfect critic, in other words, does not actually encounter the work he claims to be examining, but creates a new work of art out of his own multitudinous associations. Only the artist, and one of enormous associative recall, can be an adequate critic.

An image, in our sense, is real because we know it directly. If it have an age-old traditional meaning this may serve as proof to the professional student of symbology that we have stood in the deathless light, or that we have walked in some particular arbour of his traditional paradiso, but that is not our affair. It is our affair to render the image we have perceived or conceived.[112]

The emphasis is on making sure the rendering of the conception is exact, but where are those rushing ideas to come from if not from the reader's mind, from some sort of associative process?

Pound's practice as a poet reflects interestingly on Alison's demand that the artist offer a simple and unified emotional focus so that it can sustain a single unified train of emotion. What Pound does is to provide two images which, by their disjunction, generate two contradictory trains of association whose resolution into unity is left to the efforts of each individual reader. The contradictory poles of association generate more associational activity than would a single unified tone:

> The apparition of these faces in the crowd,
> Petals on a wet, black bough.

Pound's comments on 'In a Station of the Metro' and how to read it take us back to Hallam's demand that we 'clearly ... apprehend the leading sentiment in the poet's mind': 'I dare say it is meaningless unless one has drifted into a certain vein of thought. In a poem of this sort one is trying to record the precise instant when a thing outward and objective transforms itself, or darts into a thing inward and subjective.'[113] It is not, of course, the thing itself that darts inward; one image provokes or invokes another, and the connection between them is something that can only be grasped if one has 'drifted' – as in 'reverie' – into a vein – or train – of thought. The connections which I am suggesting between Pound's Imagism and Yeats's associationism, both being versions of an empiricist and psychologistic theory of poetry, are given substantial confirmation by the pattern that Wallace Martin has found in the intellectual interchange between Britain and France in this period:

In practice, however, *image* (in French) was employed to render such varied English words as 'impression', 'picture', 'recept' and 'portrait'; and in one French work on psychology that was translated into English and read by Hulme, the 'impressions', 'recepts', and 'portraits' of English psychologists returned to their native language as 'images'. Of these terminological mutations, the most significant involves the word 'impression', a central term in British empiricism. Translated into French as 'image' and retranslated into English as 'image', the 'impression' of Locke and Hume, retaining its associationist implications, left unmistakable traces of its influence in the aesthetic of Hulme and Pound.[114]

The shift from organicist or Kantian conception to empiricist and associationist ones in French psychology allowed Imagism to offer, under a new and more modern guise, a theory which had been directly engaged in British aesthetic theory for nearly two hundred years. The success of Imagism was perhaps due as much to its familiarity as to its novelty.

In his essay on 'The Metaphysical Poets', Eliot was to give an analysis of Donne's imagery that might have applied equally well to Pound's Imagist poems:

> some of Donne's most successful and characteristic effects are secured by brief words and sudden contrasts:
>> A bracelet of bright hair about the bone
> where the most powerful effect is produced by the sudden contrast of associations of 'bright hair' and of 'bone'. This telescoping of images and multiplied associations is characteristic of the phrase of some of the dramatists of the period which Donne knew . . .[115]

It is precisely such 'telescoping of images and multiplied associations' — an implosion of the chain of associations rather than its extension — that is characteristic of Imagist poetry at its best. And the fact that there is no conflict between concrete image and the multitudinousness of association is revealed by other passages in Eliot's criticism. In fact, it was his complaint against Pound that he failed to maintain the balance between these two equally necessary dimensions of the poetic effect: 'His eye is indeed remarkable; it is careful, comprehensive and exact; but it is rare that he has an image of the maximum concentration; an image that combines the precise and concrete with a kind of almost indefinite suggestion.'[116] The same failure of balance is implicit in Eliot's distinction between Swinburne and Dryden in 1921; Swinburne's words, Eliot judges, 'are all suggestiveness and no denotation; if they suggest nothing it is because they suggest too much', whereas

Dryden's words 'are precise, they state immensely, but their suggestiveness is often nothing'.[117] In other words, if the danger of symbolism was allegory, then the danger of Imagism was literalism, a stripping away of suggestiveness till there was nothing that the 'perfect critic' could fuse into a new object. The poem would be, as a reading experience, dead.

The problem that the essay 'The Perfect Critic' struggles with, however, is one that had all along haunted the associationist aesthetic, the problem that it turned aesthetic experience into a private act utterly severed from the author's original conception or even from any public comparison. Each successful reader creates a new object, a new work of art: agreement and disagreement between critics becomes irrelevant. The implication of 'The Perfect Critic' is that we are, at least within the realms of aesthetic experience, solipsists, trapped within our own consciousnesses whether they be 'sentimental' or 'multitudinous'. Eliot's effort to free himself from this dilemma was the 'objective correlative', a theory which was given its first, and as yet unnamed expression, in *The Egoist* in 1917:

> it is unmistakably human to attach the strongest emotions to definite tokens. Only, while with the Russian the emotion dissolves in a mass of sensational detail, and while with Wordsworth the emotion is of the object and not of human life, with certain poets the emotion is definitely human, merely seizing the object in order to express itself . . . (With Donne) the feeling and the material symbol preserve exactly their proper proportions. A poet of morbidly keen sensibilities but weak will might have become absorbed in the hair to the exclusion of the original association which made it significant; the poet of imaginative or reflective power would endow the hair with ghostly or moralistic meaning. Donne sees the thing as it is . . .[118]

Donne's 'seeing the thing as it is' because he has incorporated 'the original association which made it significant' exactly repeats in the poet the situation of the critic, for how is that association conveyed to the reader? The object may have been seized on by the poet because of an associative connection in him, in his emotional experience, but he can only give the reader 'the thing as it is', the thing without his associations; he can only offer it, therefore, in the hope that it will somehow stimulate the same emotion, or, rather, that it will find a critic who can fuse it with a different set of associations to form a new and different work.

The purpose of the objective correlative is to create a bridge that will save the poet from this act of hope and the critic from his isolation, for what it asserts is the direct and automatic transference of emotion from poet to reader, a transference in which questions of the personal nature of the associational connection disappear; or at least are intended to disappear. What Eliot fails to tell us, however, is in whom — given that we do not all get the same emotional transference from works of art, or we would never disagree about what they mean — such a transference is likely to be so efficient that they could act as an adequate test of a work's success:

> The only way of expressing emotion in the form of art is by finding an 'objective correlative'; in other words, a set of objects, a situation, a chain of events which shall be the formula of that particular emotion; such that when the external facts, which must terminate in sensory experience, are given, the emotion will be immediately evoked.[119]

Since when the 'facts' are presented 'the emotion will be immediately evoked', any failure of the work to evoke an emotion cannot be the failure of the reader: it can only be the fault of the poet. Equally, if emotion is evoked, it cannot be an emotion deriving purely from the reader, it can only be the same emotion that the poet had, directly and immediately transferred. How we are to test such propositions, to compare the transferred emotion with the original or the emotions of two readers each claiming such a transference, remains unstated. The success which the term has had in our critical vocabulary points, however, to our need for it to conceal the abyss between poet and reader which modernist poetry creates. The term implies that accuracy of presentation of the object is identical with the accuracy of its transference of emotion to the reader: *the* emotion is as definite as the formula in which it is asserted to be contained, and all the indefiniteness of 'suggestion', 'association', 'multitudinousness' is cast aside.

Eliot's definition of the objective correlative is, however, only given in the context of a negative instance. He wants to justify his apparently rather eccentric position that *Hamlet* is a failed play, and what the theory allows him to do is to set aside any question that the failure might be his as a reader. If the work does not succeed in transfering a precise emotion it has not achieved the status of an objective correlative, of a successful work of art; and it is not a matter of the critic's failure to fuse his associations into a new unity. What

Eliot sees in Hamlet (the man), however, is a character in whom the failure of *Hamlet* (the play) is dramatised:

> The artistic 'inevitability' lies in this complete adequacy of the external to the emotion; and this is precisely what is deficient in *Hamlet*. Hamlet (the man) is dominated by an emotion which is inexpressible, because it is in excess of the facts as they appear. And the supposed identity of Hamlet with his creator is genuine to this point: that Hamlet's bafflement at the absence of objective equivalent to his feelings is a prolongation of the bafflement of his creator in the face of his artistic problem.[120]

What has actually happened in Eliot's *Hamlet*, however, is that Hamlet has become an image for Eliot's own bafflement in the face of his critical problem, the problem of how an associational connection that makes some object an expression of an emotion for the author can by its associations produce the same emotion in the reader, a reader whose whole context of associational experience may be entirely at variance with the author's. Hamlet is like the critic in the face of a poem: his response is always 'in excess of the facts as they appear' because it includes 'multitudinous suggestion' not embodied directly in the work but provided from his own multitudinous experience. Hamlet lost among the conflicting possibilities of his situation mirrors Eliot, not Shakespeare, as he struggles to find a way to connect the authorial emotion to the reading emotion through the necessarily personal medium of associations. The problem of *Hamlet* is not that it is a failed objective correlative, but that the objective correlative fails to prevent all works being as *Hamlet* is in Eliot's description of it.

The famous 'impersonal theory' of art that Eliot was to make such an influential part of modernist critical vocabulary was a parallel attempt to bridge the abyss between associative contexts in poet and reader, but in the end it is always the poet who is the best critic, because he is the only one whose associations are integral with the creative process that happens not in the poet himself, but in the 'tradition'. The multitudinous potential of a work will be defined not in terms of the poet or reader's associative abilities — though it can be realised only through those — but in the associative potential that is embedded in the very nature of and history of the language and its literature. As Eliot put it in his essay of 1942, 'The Music of Poetry',

The music of a word is, so to speak, at a point of intersection:

it arises from its relation first to the words immediately preceding and following it, and indefinitely to the rest of the context; and from another relation, that of its immediate meaning in that context to all the other meanings which it has had in other contexts, to its greater or lesser wealth of association.[121]

Eliot was only asserting in that essay, written while he was at work on 'Four Quartets', what Yeats had insisted on in 1901 in 'What is "Popular Poetry"?' when he argued that Longfellow's poetry was a failure 'because he tells his story or his idea so that one needs nothing but his verses to understand it. No words of his borrow their beauty from those that used them before . . .'[122] The thread that ties the modernists together in their poetic is the thread of associationism, the concept of a poem that 'borrows its beauty' from the memories our minds have stored, or that have been stored in the transpersonal memory of the tradition.

3 OPENINGS

Wherever we find a poetics of the imagination we find a fundamental opposition: on the one hand there is the world as perceived by Reason, abstract, mechanical, dead, systematic, and on the other the vital, organic, particular world of the imagination. And it is not only reason that is placed on the side of the enemies of the living, memory belongs there too; memory, indeed, is even more dangerous in some ways than reason because it can be mistaken for imagination. If a work of art is produced out of the memory only it will achieve nothing but – to use Coleridge's term – 'fancy'. Even Wordsworthian recollection in tranquillity is recollection of a moment of imaginative insight into the unity and vitality of the universe that disproves the adequacy of the reason. The conflict embodied in this duality of mental activities was summed up by Yeats in one of his essays on Blake:

> If 'the world of imagination' was 'the world of eternity', as this doctrine implied, it was of less importance to know men and nature than to distinguish the beings and substances of imagination from those of a more perishable kind, created by the fantasy, in uninspired moments, out of memory and whim; and this could best be done ... by flying from the painters who studied 'the vegetable glass' for its own sake, and not to discover there the shadows of imperishable beings and substances, and who entered into their own minds, not to make the unfallen world a test of all they heard and saw and felt with the senses, but to cover the naked spirit with the 'rotten rags of memory' of older sensations.[1]

The 'rotten rags of memory' are the preserve, like Coleridgean fancy, of the associationist theory, for associations are entirely the product of our recall of past experiences and states of consciousness. If art can conceive of memory only as 'rotten rags' then association is the least creative of our faculties, the most dependent on a dead, determined, mechanical world.

And yet memory is the obsession of the moderns: they cannot think of the imagination without invoking into it, or incorporating it within, the powers of memory:

And send imagination forth
Under the day's declining beam, and call
Images and memories
From ruin or from ancient trees

(Yeats, CP, p. 219)

Frank Kermode has taught us to see in Yeats's tree imagery one of those symbols 'which have nothing to do with the intellect of the scientists, nothing to do with time',[2] but here, at least, it is precisely the trees' continuous existence through time that makes them interesting to 'imagination'; and later in the same poem, 'The Tower', Yeats submits himself to a hypothetical questioning by one of his own creations, Hanrahan ('And I myself created Hanrahan'), but submits to him because he has endowed him powerfully: 'I need all his mighty memories'. It is the might of memory that is the constant concern of the modernist poets rather than the power of imagination,[3] for the Muses, as Pound remembers from his days as Yeats's secretary,

'Are' as Uncle William said 'the daughters of Memory'

(Canto 95, p. 645)

Eliot, in his essay on Coleridge, is equally concerned to have memory included within imagination:

> Fancy may be 'no other than a mode of memory emancipated from the order of space and time'; but it seems unwise to talk of memory in connexion with fancy and omit it altogether from the account of imagination. As we have learnt from Dr. Lowes's *Road to Xanadu* (if we did not know it already) memory plays a very great part in imagination, and of course a much larger part than can be proved by that book; Professor Lowes had only literary reminiscences to deal with, and they are the only kind of reminiscence which can be fully traced and identified: but how much more of memory enters into creation than only our reading.[4]

There is, as Eliot puts it later in the same essay, 'so much memory in imagination',[5] and the reason for the efforts of all three poets to re-habilitate the memory was, I suggest, that they were working within an associationist framework which made memory the central faculty in aesthetic experience. Where the symbol had sought to integrate different ontological layers of the universe, as for instance in Carlyle's definition which stated that, 'In the Symbol proper ... there is ever, more or less distinctly and directly, some embodiment and revelation of the Infinite; the Infinite is made to blend itself with the Finite, to stand visible, and as it were, attainable there',[5] the associationists were concerned with linking past and present. For the associationist aesthetic the poem's essential existence was not as an intermediary between finite and infinite, but between different historical epochs. As Yeats wrote in 1901, it should be impossible to read a poem without seeing it 'as if moving before a half-faded curtain embroidered ... with holy letters and images of so great antiquity that nobody can tell what god or goddess they would commend to an unfading memory'.[6] 'Unfading memory' is both the origin and the requirement of associationist poetry: it sets itself defiantly against the exclusive power of the imagination.

Memory is, as Yeats's quote shows, the necessary requirement of the audience as well as the artist, for without memory the reader cannot provide that multitude of associations that creates, from a single image, a complete world. The result, however, is that the poem itself is radically incomplete: it is not only that it will not communicate properly unless the reader have an appropriate stock of memories, without such memories it cannot come into its full existence. The real poem, as Yeats's reverie and Eliot's 'new object' both imply, is not the poem as it is on the page, but the poem on the page in conjunction with the reader's associations. It is not a poem, to turn to Pound's definition, unless it is something 'from which, and into which, ideas are constantly rushing'. In the aesthetic experience, in fact, what the poet has created 'vanishes and returns again in the midst of the excitement it creates',[7] and unless the poet manages this outcome, manages to drive the reader back into his own memory, he has failed to create an effective work of art. The fragmentary becomes the central form of modernist poetry in response to the assumed reading experience into which the poem must enter: the gaps and the lucanae in the poetry are spaces into which the reader's associations are invited, are demanded, that the work can reach the completion after which it strives.

It has long been recognised that 'openness' is one of the primary features of all the modernist arts. Umberto Eco describes it in relation to music in the following comparison of the classical with the modern:

a classical composition ... posited an asemblage of sound units which the composer had arranged in a closed well-defined manner before presenting it to the listener. He converted his ideas into conventional symbols which more or less obliged the eventual performer to reproduce the format devised by the composer. Whereas the new musical works ... reject the definitive, concluded message and multiply the formal possibilities of the distribution of their elements. They appeal to the initiative of the individual performer, and hence they offer themselves not as finite works which prescribe specific repetition along given structural coordinates, but as 'open' works which are brought to their conclusion by the performer at the same time as he experiences them on an aesthetic plane.[8]

The openness of the literary work is, however, much more problematic than that of the musical work as described by Eco. The musician who 'encloses' a work in his performance thereby makes available to an audience a specific univocal experience: the 'openness' of the work can only be experienced through a series of performances each offering a different closure. The fact that the specific performance is only one of a possibly infinite number of shapes the work can take is not a factor in the actual experience of the work in any specific version of it. The poem built on an open structure – and, as Eco points out, such openness has been central to poetry since Mallarmé – has a very different effect because we must at one and the same time be conscious of the shape the author has given on the page and the shape the poem is taking in our individual consciousness. Eco quotes Pousseur to suggest how, for instance, we should read *Finnegans Wake*:

it is up to the listener to place himself deliberately in the midst of an inexhaustible network of relationships and to choose for himself, so to speak, his own modes of approach, his reference points and his scale, and to endeavour to use as many dimensions as he possibly can at the same time and thus dynamize, multiply and extend to the utmost degree his perceptual faculties.[9]

This is exactly like Hallam's demand upon the reader, but it assumes, like Hallam, that we can place ourselves within the pattern of the work in order to realise at least one possible unity that it might have. But in the kind of openness that was developed by Yeats, Eliot and Pound, an openness based on the radical incompletion of the associationist poem, we do not close the work by centring ourselves within one possible set of interconnections that its structure embodies, we enclose the poet's structure, or complete his structure, within the process of our own associative recall. The poem is not so much closed as enclosed, and the tactics of the work itself are to encourage and, as far as possible, control that process of enclosure. This kind of process is much more radically open than either of the ones suggested by Eco, for the shape the experience takes is not only unshareable, it is probably unrepeatable. We cannot perform the organisation of the work, as a musician will perform an open composition or a critic a poem, because the shape the experience takes is dependent on what we cannot control, the drift, or the agile leaps, of our own associative connections in constant interaction with what the poet has provided.

Critical exposition has, for many years, paid lip-service to the fact that the reader must participate in the creation of the work he experiences, while at the same time effectively providing information that can act as a substitute for the reader's effort to play his part. Eliot perhaps encouraged the idea that there could be a single critical closure of the work as much as emphasised its openness when he wrote, in the introduction to St-Jean Perse's *Anabasis*, that,

> Any obscurity in the poem, on first reading, is due to the suppression of 'links in the chain' of explanatory or connecting matter, and not to incoherence, or to love of cryptogram . . . The reader has to allow the images to fall into his memory successively without questioning the reasonableness of each at the moment; so that, at the end, a total effect is produced. Such selection of a sequence of images has nothing chaotic about it. There is a logic of the imagination as well as the logic of concepts.[10]

'Logic' implies, as does 'suppressed connections', something that can be expounded or replaced — an idea obviously going back to Hallam and Symons — but how we are to achieve these replacements is again left unstated. What are the criteria by which we are to know if we have grasped the 'logic of images'? Each of us can only allow the work to fall into our memory and wait to see what pattern emerges. The whole process is an act of faith — in so far, that is, as it expects a single pattern to be possible. And the desire for a single pattern has been equally evident in the case of Eliot's own work: there would not have been the same excitement over the manuscripts of *The Waste Land* had there not been expectations that at last the 'missing links' would appear and the poem would be returned to a proper univocal meaning. Faced by the open poem we seek an ingress to the author's psyche, or his reading, or his personal life, or his unconscious, in order to know that we are providng the poem with its appropriate links. We try to provide the poem with the associative memory to which it has denied us access. Take, for instance, the following lines from *The Waste Land*, which is often seen as Eliot's commentary upon our decline in nobility and creativity since Elizabethan times, a view based in part on Eliot's references to Spenser in the same section of the poem: 'Sweet Thames, run softly till I end my song'.

> Elizabeth and Leicester
> Beating oars
> The stern was formed
> A gilded shell
> Red and gold
> The brisk swell
> Rippled both shores
> Southwest wind
> Carried down stream
> The peal of bells
> White towers

(*CP*, p. 73)

The beauty and purity of the river, the royal procession, the references to songs proclaiming fertility are presented, we are told, for contrast with a contemporary river, a contemporary life, that is polluted and ugly. But in D.H. Lawrence's *The Rainbow* we find the following, describing Ursula's hopes after applying for a job as a teacher:

> And yet, as the afternoon wore away, the sweetness of the dream returned again. Kingston-on-Thames — there was such sound of dignity to her. The shadow of history and the glamour of stately progress enveloped her. The palaces would be old and darkened, the place of kings obscured. Yet is was a place of kings to her — Richard and Henry and Wolsey and Queen Elizabeth. The divined great lawns with noble trees, the terraces whose steps the water washed softly, where swans sometimes came to earth. Still, she must see the stately gorgeous barge of the queen float down, the crimson carpet upon the landing-stairs, the gentlemen in their purple velvet cloaks ... 'Sweet Thames run softly till I end my song.'[11]

There are enough echoes here — the allusion to Spenser, Elizabeth, the river, the barge — to suggest a possible source, but how are we to integrate such an awareness into our reading of the poem? We might see in Ursula a prototype for the Thames maidens, still deluded about the pleasures of life in the city. But we can never be certain of what is implied by the possible connection we have made because we have only the set of events, the object itself, and not the associations that made it significant to Eliot. Its having associations makes it significant, perhaps, but significant of what we cannot know except in ourselves, in the pattern it makes in our own processes of recollection.

Paradoxically, the problem that we face as we search back into the darkness of the poet's inner life for the links in the chain that have been suppressed repeats the dilemma of the poets themselves, for they looked out upon the darkness of their readers' minds, the unknowable processes of association by which their works would be completed and from which they had to elicit connections that would constitute some kind of communication, would achieve, at least, a transference of emotion. To find some way of controlling the associative flow in the reader the poet had to know with what kind of memory his poem would engage, but in the ever-increasing isolation of the poet from his public in the conditions of a mass society it was precisely the surety that there was any significant memory in the darkness of his readers' minds that the poet came to doubt. It might seem that associationism ought to provide the most democratic of all possible aesthetics since every reader experiences the poem free from coercion by the author. Indeed, association theory had begun on the assumption of equality between men's minds, since none had any innate faculties or ideas that established an immediate superiority over his fellows. But that seeming equality only served to make more prominent the effects of social conditioning in creating and sustaining the power of memory, and Yeats, Eliot and Pound were driven to politics in order to maintain the institutions and the patterns of society which preserved and promulgated the kinds of memory on which their poetry relied. The open poem demanded for its completion not the free mind of democratic man, but the rich mind of the privileged within a hierarchical society. The open poem demanded as its counterbalance the closed society.

4 YEATS: THE ART OF MEMORY

Looking back to his poetic apprenticeship in the London of the 1890s among the poets of the Rhymers Club, Yeats decided that they had thought 'it was in the nature of poetry to look back, to resemble those Swedenborgian angels who are described as moving forever towards the dayspring of their youth'.[1] That image, combining a Blakean intensity of vision into the eternal with the retrospective movement of association, sums up not only Yeats's attitude to the poet and his creation, but the experience of the reader of poetry as well: 'A poetical passage,' he wrote in 1916, 'cannot be understood without a rich memory, and like the older school of painting appeals to a tradition, and that not merely when it speaks of 'Lethe wharf' or 'Dido on the wild sea banks' but in rhythm, in vocabulary . . .'[2] Each work of art is necessarily, therefore, the recapitulation and the calling up of an extensive past, and in 'A General Introduction for my Work', written only two years before his death, Yeats was to reaffirm that central tenet of his poetic against the tenor of a new age: 'Some modern poets contend that jazz and music-hall songs are the folk art of our time, that we should mould our art upon them; we Irish, modern men also, reject every folk art that does not go back to Olympus. Give me time and a little youth and I will prove that even "Johnny I hardly knew ye" goes back.'[3] Unless the poem can inspire such a movement back, a reverie carrying the mind into the depths of the past, it is, for Yeats as for all associationist theorists, a failure. The work of art and the reader's mind must mirror each other, the one drawing upon a rich memory of accumulated poetic tradition and the other responding out of a memory equally capable of encapsulating an apparently limitless past: 'A great work of art, the "Ode to a Nightingale" not less than the "Ode to Duty", is rooted in the past, as the Mass which goes back to savage folk-lore.'[4] The memory upon which such an art draws is so extensive that it cannot be the acquisition of a single lifetime, even a lifetime of diligent study. The memory upon which art draws must be, for Yeats, part of a man's being, of his blood: 'no new man' could discover beauty, 'for he could but come to the understanding of himself, to the mastery of unlocking words, after long frequenting of the great Masters, hardly without ancestral memory of the like'.[5]

Such ancestral art was integral with Yeats's politics from the outset of his career. His nationalism was part of that tidal wave that had been running across Europe from the moment when Napoleon's armies began their retreat, but the nationalist desire for political independence had to justify itself by the assertion of its cultural independence, and cultural independence was founded on the discovery — or creation — of a significant literary history that could match the Greeks in age and nobility, if not in artistic achievement. The associationist framework could be integrated with the designs of cultural nationalism without strain, since it was inherently relativistic — and the denial of the primacy of classical tradition was the necessary prerequisite of any culture's independence — and inevitably invoked the most distant past to the experience of the most contemporary work. Associationism provided Yeats with the bridge between Dublin and Paris, between mythic Ireland and contemporary European symbolism. He believed that in Ireland they could 're-create the ancient arts, the arts as they were understood in Judaea, in India, in Scandinavia, in Greece and Rome, in every ancient land',[6] arts that would move 'a whole people and not a few people who have grown up in a leisured class'.[7] In the heady days before the fall of Parnell he saw this coming literature as a recreation of the bardic impulse, singing heroic action and 'appealing to all natures alike, to the great concourse of the people, for it has gone deeper than knowledge or fancy, deeper than the intelligence that knows of difference . . . to the universal emotions that have not heard of aristocracies . . .'[8] The recovery of the ancient legends would not only provide poets with material of ancient lineage that could stimulate endless associative reverie, it would also generate a national consciousness united by its shared memory: myths were 'the mothers of nations',[9] raising men into 'a world of selfless passion in which heroic deeds are possible and heroic poetry credible'.[10] The art that carried the mind back into the national past brought back into the present the moral and communal values which would allow the nation to establish itself again, justifying by its present existence the memories upon which the poet's art was founded and founded upon the memories which the poet's art had made available. The power of memory was also a memory of power.

Just as the recall of the past had essential consequences for contemporary society, and was therefore not purely a flight from the modern world, so Yeats saw in Irish material not a retreat from poetic modernity, but one possible fulfilment of the same principle which underlay the most advanced work of his contemporaries. The Irish legends were valuable because they provided a context of memory, and without such a context the poetry of suggestion of modern writers would be without power. The legendary material was, as it were, the foundation of memory upon which all later poetry was built:

> There is only one kind of good poetry, for the poetry of the coteries, which presupposes the written tradition, does not differ in kind from the true poetry of the people, which presupposes the unwritten tradition. Both are alike strange and obscure, and unreal to all who have not understanding, and both, instead of that manifest logic, that clear rhetoric of the 'popular poetry', glimmer with thoughts and images whose ancestors were stout and wise, 'anigh to Paradise' 'ere yet men knew the gift of corn.' It may be we know as little of their descent as men knew of 'the man born to be king' when they found him in that cradle marked with the red lion crest, and yet we know somewhere in the heart that they have been sung in temples, in ladies' chambers, and quiver with a recognition our nerves have been shaped to by a thousand emotions. If men did not remember or half remember imposssible things, and, it may be, if the worship of sun and moon had not left a faint reverence behind it, what Aran fisher-girl would sing . . . [11]

What links the sophisticated cosmopolitan tradition and the folk tradition is the extent of memory to which they are attached, a memory so integral with the nature of our minds that we respond to them not out of conscious memory but because our very 'nerves have been shaped' by the emotions those memories record. Both, by different routes, can carry the mind back through memory to the very sources of our culture and our communal history.

The associational power of the ancient myths and legends comes from their having been purified through time till they accord only with what is universal in the human mind. All the accidents of local suggestion and of contemporary experience have been winnowed away; as Yeats puts it in 'Poetry and Tradition', the 'sediment has had time to settle':

> Whenever I have known some old countryman, I have heard stories and sayings that arose out of an imagination that would have understood Homer better than 'The Cotter's Saturday Night' or 'Highland Mary', because it was an ancient imagination, where the sediment had found time to settle, and I believe that the makers of literature could still take passion and theme, though but little thought, from

such as he. On some such old and broken stem, I thought, have all the most beautiful roses been grafted.[12]

It is precisely such images as are retained by the peasant imagination, however, that a contemporary art of suggestion is intended to recall in its readers as it carries them into the depths of their own minds and memories:

> If the real world is not altogether rejected, it is but touched here and there, and into the places we have left we summon rhythm, balance, pattern, images that remind us of vast passions, the vagueness of past times, all the chimeras that haunt the edge of trance . . . a style that remembers many masters that it may escape contemporary suggestion.[13]

All great works, Yeats believes, reach back to recover 'the vagueness of past times', and the modern memory in its associational recall and the peasant memory in its purification of the past through many generations share, therefore, the same ground. Their works of art are different in themselves, but one brings to the present the 'vast passions' of a distant past and the other leads us from the present into that past. The effort to 'escape contemporary suggestion' was, Yeats felt, the essence of tragic drama and by 1910, when he wrote this latter passage, he saw tragedy as the only way back to an associational art in a world that had come to be dominated by a pictorial realism which could give no stimulus to the memory. Only through tragedy could the art of memory be revived and the power that belonged naturally to peasant art be recovered for a sophisticated audience:

> Tragic art, passionate art, the downer of dikes, the confounder of understanding, moves us by setting us to reverie, by alluring us almost to the intensity of trance. The persons upon the stage, let us say, greaten till they are humanity itself. We feel our minds expand convulsively or spread out slowly like some moon-brightened image-crowded sea. That which is before our eyes perpetually vanishes and returns again in the midst of the excitement it creates, and the more enthralling it is, the more do we forget it.[14]

The paradox of all associational art is summed up in that final sentence: 'the more enthralling it is, the more do we forget it'. The experience is not of the work itself: we forget the work in the recovery of memories we may not even have suspected we possessed. Peasant art retains memory, modern art (like Yeats's) regains memory: that shared purpose with regard to the powers of memory was what convinced Yeats that Ireland could remain true to its ancient art while still participating actively in the advancement of modern poetry:

> Irish literature may prolong its first inspiration without renouncing the complexity of ideas and emotions which is the inheritance of cultivated men, for it will have learned from the discoveries of modern learning that the common people, wherever civilization has not driven its plough too deep, keep watch over the roots of all religion and all romance. Their poetry trembles on the verge of incoherence with a passion all but unknown among modern poets... like all primitive poetry, they foreshadow a poetry whose intensity of emotion, or strangeness of language, has made it the poetry of the little coteries.[15]

Ancient poetry, in Yeats's description of it, comes to share the characteristics of modern poetry in its apparent 'incoherence': like the poetry of the coteries it is incapable of explaining itself to the generality of readers because it depends upon the acceptance of a use of language not guided by utilitarian principles. The earliest and the latest art share the same basis and, according to Yeats, ancient Irish poetry, like modern poetry, is full of 'self-consciousness', its 'warriors not simply warriors, the kings simply kings, the smiths simply smiths: they all seem striving to bring something out of the world of thoughts into the world of deeds — something that always eluded them'.[16] The characters in ancient literature are thus engaged in the same search for an ineluctable essence of reality that had characterised much nineteenth century poetry: their consciousness, in its striving after some 'beyond', is like work of a symbolist poet.

Part of the 'something that always eluded them' — both in the heroic past and in Yeats's own time — was a fundamental religious truth to replace the Christianity which seemed to have failed modern man. The process of association could carry you back into the depths of the past, but arrived there you found the characters of those ancient memories still striving to reach into another 'beyond'. Association might be the basis of aesthetic experience, but what did the aesthetic experience itself mean, what was revealed by it? It might be that the 'old images, the old emotions, awakened again to overwhelming life, like the gods Heine tells of, by the belief and passion of some new soul, are the only masterpieces',[17] but Yeats the romantic would not be satisfied unless the new masterpiece was also a justification not only of the 'old images, old emotions', but of the belief of which they were a part, belief in the gods:

> Alone among nations, Ireland has in her written Gaelic literature, in her old love tales and battle tales, the forms in which the imagination of Europe uttered herself before Greece shaped a tumult of legend into her music of the arts; and she can discover from the beliefs and emotions of the common people the habit of mind that created the religion of the muses.[18]

The 'religion of the muses' is poised on the ambiguity of its possessive: a religion of art or an art of religion? An art whose reality is the memory of the gods or a memory of the gods which is the reality revealed by art? Yeats's art was based technically on an acceptance of associationist principles, but he wanted that art to be, like romantic art, a revelation of ultimate truth, of the eternal: 'the end of art is the ecstasy awakened before an ever-changing mind of what is permanent in the world.'[19] The difficulty with such a desire was that the associationist conception of art is essentially temporal, is a plunge into never-ending processes of recall, and could not produce the stability of that romantic desire for the permanent. The end of art — in the sense of its purpose — within a conception of art as revelation would be the end of association, since one would have reached some fundamental stasis, but the achievement of such a transcendence of temporal process would be the end of art, its redundancy, since without the associations unfolding in time there could be no aesthetic experience. An art which seeks to record and make possible moments of transcendental insight — like Coleridge's — can record its passing, can record the memory of such experience as a haunting possibility, but an art whose essence is the stimulation of associational patterns in the reader cannot transcend time without denying its own nature. Reaching back to those earliest memories of the communal mind in which the religion of the muses is still alive does not release us from time: the very experience of the art in touch with that religion necessarily projects us back into temporal process as it returns us to our associations. Art cannot, within this schema, negate time; it cannot allow us entry into the eternal: the ancient gods remembered in the peasant mind, the ancient heroes their art celebrates, will always be striving after 'something that always eluded them', because the impulse to the eternal, of which they are symbols, is denied by the very conditions within which such symbols take on their power, conditions that depend on the multitude of associations they are capable of producing. Their essence is not their being eternal, but their having many meanings that can be released in time.

It is the contradictory pulls of the romantic desire to transcend time and the associationist dependence on time that forms the basis of much of Yeats's early poetry. Yeats, of course, named himself among the 'last romantics', and his early poetry is often dismissed as a poetry of romantic longing and escape which fails to connect with the real world. Within that poetry, however, there is a rarely acknowledged degree of self-awareness that is the result, I would suggest, of the conflict between competing conceptions of the powers and purposes of art. The poem as a whole may represent an escape from the modern world – in that it deals with Irish mythic subjects in an archaic manner – but because Yeats's conception of such subjects was that they formed the end point of the memory invoked by modern art, the poems often turn back upon the reader to comment on their own status and to comment on the aesthetic experience of which they are a part. They are, despite their apparent naivete, 'self-conscious'.

Probably the finest of the very early poems is 'The Madness of King Goll'. Yeats presents us with the story of an ancient Irish king, Goll, whose success as a king has been to establish peace and prosperity among his people, a success which perhaps involves a denial of those heroic values which he would wish to live by and for which he is interesting to readers of Yeats's poem:

> I sat on cushioned otter-skin:
> My word was law from Ith to Emain,
> And shook at Inver Amergin
> The heart of the world-troubling seamen,
> And drove tumult and war away.

> (*CP*, p. 17)

'Tumult' was a word Yeats often used to describe ancient art – 'a tumult of legend'[19] – and Goll's success in driving 'tumult and war away', banishing the need for the heroic, mirrors nineteenth-century society's destruction of the 'world of selfless passion in which heroic deeds are possible and heroic poetry credible'. Called again to battle against invaders, however, Goll does not recover his heroic stature, but undergoes a revelation that destroys his own ability to live the heroic life:

But slowly, as I shouting slew
And trampled in the bubbling mire,
In my most secret spirit grew
A whirling and a wandering fire:
I stood: keen stars above me shone,
Around me shone keen eyes of men:
I laughed aloud and hurried on
By rocky shore and rushy fen;
I laughed because birds fluttered by,
And starlight gleamed, and clouds flew high,
And rushes waved and waters rolled.
They will not hush, the leaves a-flutter round me, the beech
   leaves old.

The moment of interaction between the eternal — 'keen stars' — and
the temporal — 'keen eyes of men' — is a source of revelation used regularly by Shelley and a part of Yeats's romantic inheritance. The visionary who has been vouchsafed a sudden insight into the eternal beauty
that occasionally visits itself upon the temporal world is cast out of
human society in search of apocalyptic fulfilment of his vision. Like
Shelley's Alastor Goll becomes a wanderer, and even Yeats's imagery
is an echo of Shelley's, for it is by the mirroring of eyes that Shelley
often symbolises union between different ontological dimensions of
existence: 'yellow flowers / For ever gaze on their own drooping
eyes, / Reflected in the crystal calm'.[20] But in Yeats's mirroring in
'King Goll' there is no revelation of spiritual compatibility between
mind and eternity: the stars mirror the eyes of men in battle, their
exaltation the lust for destruction. Goll is not led to a transcendental
consciousness of time resolved into the eternal, but is trapped in an
awareness of endless, and endlessly destructive time. The poem's
refrain, with its emphasis on decay never resolved by death — 'the
leaves a-flutter round me, the beech leaves old' — posits a world of time
forever in motion and decaying and yet without end. Time itself is
equal with eternity in that it never passes away. Nature, so often the
instantiation of the spirit of eternity for the romantics, is here an
image only of unending process, an eternity not of salvation but of
destruction. Yeats's choice of 'a-flutter' to describe the leaves, its
archaism balancing verbal and adjectival against each other, creates
the sense of motion and stasis conjoined, as the reiterated refrain
balances the sense of temporal process which it describes ('old') against
the stasis which its repetition enacts. No apocalypse will save the world

of time from its own unceasing, endless change, a condition which Goll mirrors in his endless 'wandering':

> And I must wander wood and hill
> Through summer's heat and winter's cold.
> *They will not hush, the leaves a-flutter round me, the beech*
>   *leaves old.*

In Goll's endless wandering, however, we can see an image not only of an eternity of time within which mankind is trapped, but an image of the poem's own conception of the nature of art. Goll's moment of insight comes from 'a whirling and a wandering fire' and passes on into further wandering, just as the associational process reaches through a train of images to some overwhelmingly powerful image that will set the mind wandering again from 'idea to idea, emotion to emotion'. The endless movement of associations around the stasis of the work of art is almost figured in the endless flutter of the beech leaves, as though the refrain mirrors the process by which we experience and give significance to Yeats's image. Goll's exclusion from eternity is identical with the poem's inability to lead our minds to anything but further experiences of temporal process. Such mirroring between Yeats's story and the reader's experience might seem fanciful were it not for the fact that the poem's final stanza presents us with Goll mimicking Yeats's own art, for he finds 'this old tympan' and begins to sing:

> I sang how, when day's toil is done,
> Orchil shakes out her long dark hair
> That hides away the dying sun
> And sheds faint odours through the air:
> When my hand passed from wire to wire
> It quenched with sound like falling dew,
> The whirling and the wandering fire;
> But lift a mournful ulalu,
> For the kind wires are torn and still,
> And I must wander wood and hill.

The 'dying sun' operates here on two different levels, one faithful to Goll's sense of the world and one that refers back upon ours. For Goll it is a metaphor for sunset, or an animistic conception of daily recreation of the universe; for us, 'dying sun' all too accurately describes the realities of our universe as revealed by science. Goll's song of Orchil does the same for him as Yeats's poem is doing for its readership; both hide away the dying sun behind figures who inhabit an apparently timeless realm. For us, however, the timeless figure of Goll re-enacts within his own realm of existence the dilemmas from which we sought escape in art, and reveals the extent to which art itself is no pathway to some ultimate transcendence of our human condition. Art, in its associational recall of the past, has its power only by its recall of a tumultuous past, and like Goll is

> Murmuring, to a fitful tune,
> How I have followed, night and day,
> A tramping of tremendous feet.

It is therefore trapped in an endless process of time, and neither heroic action nor visionary insight will release it into a different ontological status.

The failure of heroism and of visionary insight to offer a romantic access to the Infinite dominates Yeats's early poems: the heroes are never satisfied by their great actions, the visionaries never consoled by their insights. Both are haunted by the sense of time as endless series, denying any value to individual action, and by an eternity which is merely an infinite repetition of the events of time. Thus in 'Fergus and the Druid' (*CP*, p. 36), Fergus the warrior king seeks the 'dreaming wisdom' of the Druid, and to gain it has given up his kingship and become, like Goll, a wanderer, because,

> A king is but a foolish labourer
> Who wastes his blood to be another's dream.

Fergus is thus given by Yeats a consciousness of what he will become as a part of Yeats's poem and our own memory — 'another's dream'. His heroism may give eternity of a kind to his name, but it cannot save him; neither, however, can the wisdom of the Druid, for instead of offering a romantic access to the eternal, what the Druid reveals is a world of boundless repetition of the experience of time, a knowledge which is endless memory rather than the transcendence of a world of time and the need for memory that Fergus sought:

> I see my life go drifting like a river
> From change to change; I have been many things —
> A green drop in the surge, a gleam of light

Upon a sword, a fir-tree on a hill,
An old slave grinding at a heavy quern,
A king sitting upon a chair of gold —
And all these things were wonderful and great;
But now I have grown nothing, knowing all.

Fergus's synoptic view of his life parallels the associational reverie in which he would have been a mere part of another's dream, for each thing has lost its significance to the importance of the process, a process which is endless.

What Yeats is presenting in both Fergus and Goll are images of the tensions within his own art. The romantic artist who is the inheritor of the powers of the magus and the druid would like to offer his art as an entry into eternity, as an escape from time, but the art itself denies any such release, and can lead to no ultimate revelation of what is permanent in the world. Associational process, the continual generation of a train of images moving outwards and away from the work of art itself, is mirrored in Goll surrounded by the endlessly ancient and fluttering leaves, is mirrored in Fergus's discovery of the chain of images of which his being is a part. The romantic demand that art, through the spiritual power of the imagination, should save us from the world of time is undone by the knowledge that art works only through memory and is devoted to the endless recall of the events of time. The characters of the poems act out the failure of the romantic desire, ironically commenting on what we have sought from the poem. The conditions from which we have sought to escape are repeated in the world we escape into, and the tension between our desire for transcendence through art and the real nature of what we can be offered by art is perhaps summed up in an image from another early poem, 'The Indian to his Love':

A parrot sways upon a tree
Raging at his own image in the enamelled sea.

(*CP*, p. 15)

The parrot rages at the more perfect life in the 'enamelled sea', but his image there is only a repetition of the condition in which he already exists.

My point in drawing attention to these early poems is not merely to suggest that some of Yeats's early work is more complex than usually taken to be: the conflict which they reveal between the sense of art as a transcendence of time and of an associationist art's necessary complicity with time was to be a pervasive theme of Yeats's poetry. And the technique of playing off the real nature of the reading experience — 'drifting like a river / From change to change' — against the apparent stasis of the poem and the possible unchanging reality to which it testifies was one which he was to exploit with ever-increasing subtlety. In 1925 Yeats began a revision of the whole body of his early poetry,[21] and the images and tensions in the three poems I have mentioned seeped into one of his greatest poems, 'Sailing to Byzantium', written in the following year. The first stanza recapitulates the sense of a world of endless change in which Goll finds himself, process become eternal in its negation of any other dimension of existence:

> That is no country for old men. The young
> In one another's arms, birds in the tree
> — Those dying generations — at their song,
> The salmon-falls, the mackerel-crowded seas,
> Fish, flesh or fowl, commend all summer long
> Whatever is begotten, born, and dies.

> *(CP*, p. 217)

But opposed to that endless re- and de- generative flux is no longer the transcendental leap from time to eternity, of which Goll's vision is a version, however negative in its consequences, but a Wildean assertion of the death-defeating, time-transcending work of art:

> Caught in that sensual music all neglect
> Monuments of unageing intellect.

The paradox, often ignored by critics, is that the opposition is not between life and art, but between life as unconscious art in time (song) and art as a conscious manifestation of thought's desire to defy time (monument), between life in time shaped as though by art, and art shaping temporal life into stasis.

The second stanza of 'Sailing to Byzantium' offers us Yeats — 'A tattered coat upon a stick' — in the same guise as the Druid whose knowledge could be of no comfort to Fergus:

> Look on my thin grey hair and hollow cheeks
> And on these hands that may not lift a sword,

This body trembling like a wind-blown reed.
No woman's loved me . . .

(CP, p. 37)

Knowledge such as the Druid's cuts him off from the pleasures of active
life; cut off from the pleasures of active life, Yeats sets off after knowledge as compensation for what time has taken from him. But his
journey to Byzantium is paradoxical, poised between real and hypothetical as was the journey of the lovers in 'The Indian to his Love':

> The island dreams under the dawn
> And great boughs drop tranquility;
> The peahens dance on the smooth lawn,
> A parrot sways upon a tree,
> Raging at his own image in the enamelled sea.
>
> Here we will moor our lonely ship
> And wander ever with woven hands,
> Murmuring softly lip to lip,
> Along the grass, along the sands,
> Murmuring how far away are the unquiet lands.

(CP, p. 15)

Like Byzantium the island is beyond time: it 'dreams' its own existence
and the journey towards it is one which, since it is a journey of the
mind, is in effect a stasis. 'Will', at the beginning of stanza two, upon
which the whole of the rest of the poem syntactically depends, could
imply either that they have arrived and will stay, or that they will
arrive in some hypothetic future. And the world that the lovers enter
is, because of this ambiguity, one that is suspended between time and
stasis in the very texture of the poem's language:

> How we alone of mortals are
> Hid under quiet boughs apart,
> While our love grows an Indian star,
> A meteor of the burning heart.

'Are', by its emphatic placing, implies 'being' rather than action, and
the verbal form 'hid' also implies the stasis of a permanent condition
rather than the impetus of action, but both are balanced against the
self-consuming rapidity and impermanence of the 'meteor'. In 'Sailing

to Byzantium' the sense of movement and stasis is equally ambiguous, turning upon the middle lines of the poem —

> And therefore I have sailed the seas and come
> To the holy city of Byzantium

— which are poised between arrival ('I have ... come') and approach ('I have sailed and come towards'), leaving the final two stanzas poised, as in the early poem, between real entry into a world of the imagination, and hypothetical or imaginary entry into an apparently real place.

The echoes between early and late poems continue in the imagery of 'song': in 'King Goll' the mad song allows the goddess to be called up who 'hides away the dying day'; in 'Sailing to Byzantium' the sages are called from the work of art just as the goddess was called from eternity, but are called to be singing masters and asked to

> Consume my heart away; sick with desire
> And fastened to a dying animal
> It knows not what it is; and gather me
> Into the artifice of eternity.

Goll's song puts him in touch with eternity through artifice; the song in 'Sailing to Byzantium' conceals death by incorporating the speaker into artifice. The origins of the golden bird that Yeats decides to take as his form in the afterlife may be in Hans Andersen's clockwork nightingale and Keats's 'immortal bird',[22] but it also takes us back to the parrot, for while in the early poem the bird rages at its aesthetic mirror image, enamelled by the sea, in the later poem the poet crosses into the world of art to become an 'enamelled' golden bird. In 'The Indian to his Love' the voyage of escape to the island turns back upon itself, for the lovers' conversation is of what they have left behind, of 'how far away are the unquiet lands', and in exactly parallel fashion 'Sailing to Byzantium' turns back upon itself, as the artificial bird, released from time and change, sings of 'what is past, or passing, or to come'. That turning back to the world which one has desired to escape has, since its first publication, always presented problems to Yeats's critics. Why should the achievement of an eternal stasis in a perfect world of art be qualified by a return to time in the bird's song? The comparison with the early poems allows us to see, I think, that this is not just an accidental or contradictory element in Yeats's writing of this particular poem, but an essential part of his view of art.

The contradictions from which one seeks an escape through art always repeat themselves within the world of art, and 'Sailing to Byzantium' is no exception. And that internal movement of the poem is related to the formal tension between its apparent stasis — a 'monument of unageing intellect' — and the temporal process of association upon which it depends for its full experience. If the work of art succeeded in defying time it would destroy its own essential power, which comes from the trains of thought it generates in time, from what 'is past, or passing, or to come'. The bird's singing does not mean that it has the gift of prophecy (Yeats cancelled 'future' from the drafts),[23] but that it sings what is always to come, and what dominates the rest of the volume 'The Tower', to which it is the introduction — death and loss and destruction. As a part of a remembered tradition, however, it also introduces what is to be placed against those eternal enemies — the powers of memory.

The problems which 'Sailing to Byzantium' has posed revolve largely around the fact that Byzantium is supposed to be Yeats's ideal city of the imagination — or 'Condition of Fire', as Harold Bloom calls it;[24] it is supposed to be a symbol of the symbolising faculty's ability to carry us into a spiritual eternity. But the desire for such transcendence is set within a concept of art based on invoking into the matrix of the reader's experience a succession of images from the past, and in reading it we are driven necessarily, therefore, to defy the fixity to which the poetic persona aspires. 'Sailing to Byzantium' is not a failed poem of the 'Condition of Fire' or of the romantic imagination, as Bloom, for instance would have us believe, but a poem ironically commenting upon the ways in which poets will create heavens from their art in spite of that art's real nature. Just as the early poem 'The Indian upon God' presents us with a peacock who imagines God 'a monstrous peacock, and he waveth all the night / His languid tail above us, lit with myriad spots of light' (*CP*, p. 15), so the poetic persona in 'Sailing to Byzantium' invents a heaven which the poem itself undercuts as it forces him to turn back to the world of time. And that turning back is something that we, too, are forced to experience as we read the final lines:

Once out of nature I shall never take
My bodily form from any natural thing,
But such a form as Grecian goldsmiths make
Of hammered gold and gold enamelling
To keep a drowsy Emperor awake;

> Or set upon a golden bough to sing
> To lords and ladies of Byzantium
> Of what is past, or passing, or to come.

Where is the golden bird, so much the subject of critical debate? To know the form the speaker will take we have to return to the 'birds in the trees / Those dying generations' of stanza one: we have to make a journey back in memory to the world of time, or, if we are lucky, back in memory to previous descriptions of such artifacts. It is not the golden bird that figures for us Yeats's conception of art, defying time in the perfection of its beauty, but the whole dialectic of the poem. Yeats's art is a combining of the flux of time, to which the art of music is the appropriate correlative, and the sculpted stasis of the monumental image: the time transcending images of the poem recall a world of time in our associations and it is through those associations that the images gain their power and significance. It is the song of the dying generations *and* the fixity of the artistic form together that are the basis of Yeats's concept of art; it is the forward movement of the poem, a song in time, towards an image that is apparently beyond time, as though sculpted, but releasing the reader's mind into an associative reverie that will carry him far into the past, that constitutes the essential structure of Yeats's poetic. And within such a poetic the associations with which we enclose the poem may, from the point in time when the poem was written, be in the future: thus can it sing what is yet 'to come'.

The tension between his inheritance of a romantic idealist epistemology and his adoption of an empiricist-associationist one accounts for the difficulty that Yeats had in finding a workable definition of the symbol. Initially, as Edward Engleberg has stressed,[25] Yeats attempted, in the distinction which was to influence Pound's definition of Imagism, to differentiate between three kinds of symbols: the intellectual, the emotional and the kind which were a combination of both. Intellectual symbols are those which occur only within the context of religious or mystical belief: they are like the symbolist's symbols in being pathways to the Infinite. Emotional symbols, however, are personal and belong to the world of casual everyday experience. The symbols carry the mind either towards the world or towards transcendence of it:

> if one is moved by Shakespeare, who is content with emotional symbols, that he may come nearer to our sympathy, one is mixed

with the whole spectacle of the world; while if one is moved by Dante, or the myth of Demeter, one is mixed into the shadow of God or a goddess.[26]

At times, however, Yeats was less than certain about the status of Shakespeare's 'emotional' symbols: it might be that Richard II was an 'image for an accustomed mood of fanciful, impracticable lyricism' in Shakespeare's own mind,[27] but in another essay he argues that under different historical circumstances those emotional symbols of Shakespeare's might have taken on characteristics closer to those of intellectual symbols:

> Those nobles with their indifference to death and their immense energy seem at times no nearer the common stature of men than do the gods and heroes of the Greek plays. Had there been no Renaissance and no Italian influence to bring the stories of other lands, English history would, it may be, have become as important to the English imagination as the Greek myths to the Greek imagination; and many plays by many poets would have woven it into a single story.[28]

Such a unity would have given England what Yeats himself had thought possible in Ireland, 'the deliberate creation of a kind of holy city of the imagination, a Holy Sepulchre, as it were, or Holy Grail for the Irish mind'. What he has discovered, however, is that he must, in present historical circumstances, be 'content to express the individual',[29] and it would seem, therefore, that the emotional symbol, if wrought into a sufficient body of symbols with an underlying unity, could be transformed into an intellectual symbol. The basic distinction between the emotional and the intellectual is less in their innate characteristics than in whether or not they participate in some publicly ordered system of belief or ritual. The system of symbols defines and orders the associative potential of each so that, as Yeats said in wishing upon Shelley 'a crowd of believers who could put into all those strange visions the strength of their belief', they become 'solid underfoot and consistent enough for the soul's habitation'.[30] The need for such distinctions between symbols evaporated, however, when Yeats realised that all symbols operated by their associative power, and

> Whether their power has arisen out of themselves, or whether it has an arbitrary origin, matters little, for they act, as I believe,

because the Great Memory associates them with certain moods and persons. Whatever the passions of man have gathered about, becomes a symbol in the Great Memory . . .[31]

For Yeats, the universal spirit that animates poetry and mystical insight is no longer the creative godhead uttering its profound 'I AM', as Coleridge has envisaged,[32] but an eternal and all-embracing memory.

It was Shelley who led Yeats to his conception of a memory underlying and integrating all our individual and personal associative contexts, for in Shelley's poetry he found works that seemed to refuse to operate either within the terms of an 'intellectual' symbol, deriving from some public system of belief, or from emotional symbols like Shakespeare's. In reading Shelley's poetry Yeats had to translate it into Irish equivalents with which is own associations would connect:

> I have re-read *Prometheus Unbound* for the first time for many years, in the woods of Drim-na-Rod, among the Echtge hills, and sometimes I have looked towards Slieve na nOg where the country people say the last battle of the world shall be fought . . . And I think this mysterious song utters a faith as simple and ancient as the faith of these country people in a form suited to a new age . . .[33]

The validity of such a procedure was one not easily justified by any view of the symbol based on its having a specific, if unstatable, meaning, but for Yeats the symbol could be shifted from context to context because it was not its meaning that was important, but its ability to generate associational trains of thought, and those trains of thought were able to overleap the boundaries of culture and of nationality because, at the deepest levels of our reverie, we are given access not just to our own forgotten experience, but to a memory to which nothing is lost:

> Anyone who has any experience of any mystical state of the soul knows how there float up in the mind profound symbols, whose meaning, if indeed they do not delude one into the dream that they are meaningless, one does not perhaps understand for years. Nor I think has anyone, who has known that experience with any constancy, failed to find some day, in some old book or some old monument, a strange or intricate image that had floated up before him, and to grow perhaps dizzy with the conviction that our little memories are but a part of some great Memory that renews the

world and men's thoughts age after age, and that our thoughts are not, as we suppose, the deep, but a little foam upon the deep.[34]

The individual memories of artist and audience, of nation and culture, are united in the Great Memory, so that even the work with which we have no shared associational context can suddenly open up for us vistas of memory of which we are unconscious in our daily lives. Through contact with the Great Memory infinite associational potential is leased to us: it may be contingent and personal memories which inaugurate our trains of association, but the depths we reach in the course of our reverie will be depths not of our own mind's associations, but those which have formed around symbols in the Great Memory:

> The symbols are of all kinds, for everything in heaven or earth has its association, momentous or trivial, in the Great Memory, and one never knows what forgotten events may have plunged it, like the toadstool and the ragweed, into the great passions.[35]

Personal and universal are fused together, and for those who manage to make contact with the resources of the Great Memory the problems posed by Hallam's aesthetic disappear. There is no need for direct communication between poet and reader: the poem is a communion rather than a communication, a joint meditation in which, through what the poet offers, we reach down to into an infinite potentiality for recall in the memory from which our personal memories are fed. The poem thus, paradoxically perhaps, gives us access to the associational potential by which it can be completed and experienced fully, by which it can transcend the limitations of its creator's own personal associations.

Awareness of the central role of memory in the effect of poetry fed back into the thematic concerns of Yeats's poetry, and as he revised his early poetry he brought the theme of memory into ever greater prominence. 'The Lamentation of the Old Pensioner', for instance, is a poem almost entirely rewritten in the 1920s, and what was originally a rather feeble version of 'King Goll', presenting the pensioner as wanderer outcast, turns into something very different. The 1890 version contains the following complaint:

> The road-side trees keep murmuring:
> Ah, wherefore murmur ye,
> As in the old days long gone by,

Green oak and poplar tree?
The well-known faces are all gone
And the fret lies on me.[36]

The endless youthfulness of the natural world, its constant repetition, is no consolation to the being whose individual life is, like the road, linear. But in the final version of the poem, a version again produced in the rewriting that much of Yeats's early poetry went through after 1925, the destructive losses of the processes of time are to be balanced against its gains:

Though lads are making pikes again
For some conspiracy,
And crazy rascals rage their fill
At human tyranny,
My contemplations are of Time
That has transfigured me.

There's not a woman turns her face
Upon a broken tree,
And yet the beauties that I loved
Are in my memory;
I spit into the face of Time
That has transfigured me.

(*CP*, p. 52)

The poem turns on a double sense of transfigured: on the one hand he has been degraded and reduced by the physical effects of time, on the other he has transcended the limitations of time. The last two lines are poised between both the desire to be young again, to have back the active life from which physical decay has excluded him, and the recognition that the 'beauties' he once loved are not lost to him, but preserved in memory. Indeed, within the terms of an associationist conception those beauties are only beautiful because they are remembered, and their beauty increases, therefore, with his old age, with the accumulation of associations that give them their significance. The paradox of the associationist conception of beauty is dramatised in the tensions of the old pensioner's attitude to time, for that which is directly present to us can be beautiful only by virtue of the memories which it invokes as associations. To have back those beauties as they were in his youth would be a loss as well as a gain, for their beauty increases with the accumulations of memory. Beauty is thus integral to loss and destruction: we cannot know it until it has to be retrieved from memory, a paradox upon which much of Yeats's late poetry was to be founded.

A similar change occurs in the revision of one of the best of Yeats's early poems, 'The Two Trees', the trees imaging the conflict between the two poles of the traditional romantic dualism, one, as Kermode puts it, symbolising the 'creative and redemptive imagination and the second all barrenly discursive and prudential knowledge'.[37] Kermode notes one or two of Yeats's revisions to this poem, but does not quote the section which shows most decisively the shift away from the Blakean antitheses upon which it was originally based. The 1895 version of the poem presents the truths of the heart as open to direct introspection, and the poet's beloved is asked to pay heed to their creative potential:

> There, through bewildered branches, go
> Winged Loves borne on in gentle strife,
> Tossing and tossing to and fro
> The flaming circle of our life.
> When looking on their shaken hair,
> And dreaming how they dance and dart,
> Thine eyes grow full of tender care . . .[38]

The crucial term is 'dreaming', but by the 1920s it is only memory that can direct the beloved towards a redemptive view of the world and of the potential of their love:

> There the Loves a circle go,
> The flaming circle of our days,
> Gyring, spiring to and fro
> In those great ignorant leafy ways;
> Remembering all that shaken hair
> And how the wingèd sandals dart,
> Thine eyes grow full of tender care . . .

(CP, p. 55)

The replacement of 'looking' and 'dreaming' by 'remembering' points to Yeats's developing doubts about the value of dream and of imagination: both come to imply illusion and deception as his poetry realises more fully the implications of his poetics. The romantic division between the two kinds of awareness symbolised by the trees remains, but access to the creative view of life is achieved now through memory. What had been true, for Yeats, of the way in which the poet wished his poem to be read, has come to be equally true of the emotional life of the beloved whose beauty he celebrates.

Memory's crucial role to love as to art, the foundation of natural as well as invented beauty on the past, is best revealed, among the early poems, by 'The Lover asks Forgiveness because of his Many Moods' from 'The Wind Among the Reeds':

> If this importunate heart trouble your peace
> With words lighter than air,
> Or hopes that in mere hoping flicker and cease;
> Crumple the rose in your hair;
> And cover your lips with odorous twilight and say,
> 'O Hearts of wind-blown flame!
> O Winds, older than changing of night and day,
> That murmuring and longing came
> From marble cities loud with tabors of old
> In dove-grey faery lands;
> From battle-banners, fold upon purple fold,
> Queens wrought with glimmering hands;
> That saw young Niamh hover with love-lorn face
> Above the wandering tide;
> And lingered in the hidden desolate place
> Where the last Phoenix died,
> And wrapped the flames above his holy head;
> And still murmur and long:
> O Piteous Hearts, changing till change be dead
> In a tumultuous song':
> And cover the pale blossoms of your breast
> With your dim heavy hair,
> And trouble with a sigh for all things longing for rest
> The odorous twilight there.

(*CP*, p. 73)

The poem belongs to Yeats's ornate 'symbolist' style and contains almost all of the words that Yeats came to dislike in the diction of his early poetry, 'dove-grey', 'glimmering', 'dim heavy'. But the poem is still a considerable achievement in its uniting of poet and his beloved in a single syntactic movement that reflects an underlying union between them even though she wishes to refuse his overtures. Like many of Yeats's poems in this period the beloved is provided by the poet with her gestures — 'Crumple the rose in your hair'; such constitutions of the beloved's actions and speech emphasise the fact that her beauty is not truly hers, or hers alone, but is a function of all the associations it invokes in him, that he provides for her. What she is given — hypothetically — to say is, in effect, an apostrophe to the memories that congregate around her, focused by her beauty but contributing to it at the same time. Attributing to her an awareness of the sources in him of her own beauty, the speaker seeks to deflect the urgency of his passion by making himself conscious of the fact that it is self-inflicted. The dismissive words and actions that he attributes to her, however, do not still the 'winds' that carry memorable images to congregate around her: whatever she does can only stimulate further trains of association and keep in motion those 'things longing for rest' which are the source of beauty in the present. The beloved's complaint mirrors the paradox of the artist in his effort to transcend time: just as her pity only troubles to continued movement the associations which she wishes to quiet, so the artist generates through his beautiful creations not an apocalyptic escape from time, but a further troubling of the processes of time. The various associated images which the poem calls up as the constitutive elements of the beloved's beauty are themselves moments of beauty that have tried to transcend time, but, as with all beauty, their destiny — like Fergus's as a man of action — is to become participants in the chain of association that makes something else beautiful. They are trapped, 'changing till all change be dead', forever contributing to other focuses of beauty that will continue to dream the escape from time that would deny the very source of their power.

Yeats was to use the same conception of the relationship between the poet-lover and the object of his affections in 'Old Memory'. Again the two are intertwined in the fact that it is the lover's own associations which contribute to the power of the beloved over him and to his suffering, but that fact is here turned to a plea that she recognise and accept the creator of her beauty rather than reject him:

O thought, fly to her when the end of day
Awakens an old memory, and say,
'Your strength, that is so lofty and fierce and kind,
It might call up a new age, calling to mind
The queens that were imagined long ago,

Is but half yours: he kneaded in the dough
Through the long years of youth, and who would have thought
It all, and more than it all, would come to naught,
And that dear words meant nothing?'

(*CP*, p. 86)

The beauty of Maud Gonne calls up 'queens that were imagined long ago', but it does so in part because of the associations with which Yeats has endowed her in others' minds. The strength of her beauty – and some portion of her political influence – is the result of the associations he has 'kneaded in the dough', associations which lead men to expect of her queenly achievements. The poem demands not only that she remember their shared youth, but remember his share in creating the memory by which her beauty is made potent. Precisely because beauty is a function of memory, however, time will be no healer of the poet's own suffering: just as the old pensioner was transfigured by the addition, through time, of increasing powers of memory, so, in 'The Folly of being Comforted', Yeats discovers that,

Time can but make her beauty over again:
Because of that great nobleness of hers
The fire that stirs about her, when she stirs,
Burns but the more clearly.

(*CP*, p. 86)

Like the sages in 'Sailing to Byzantium', Maud Gonne lives in the midst of art's purifying fire, but does so not because of an imagination that can leap beyond the boundaries of time, but because her beauty gathers about it a multitude of images from the past. Time is overcome not by rising above it, but by collaborating with it.

The poem in which the conflict of these two modes of overcoming time is most manifest is Yeats's famous elegy, 'In Memory of Major Robert Gregory'. In the context I have been outlining even the title takes on an added significance, but it is one that has been generally ignored by critics because they believe Yeats to stand by an apocalyptic romantic view of the perfection of art and its relationship with the world. They have tended to read the poem with Gregory as hero, an instance of the 'unity of being' Yeats felt to be impossible in the modern world. Graham Martin summed up the general view when he took Robert Gregory to be 'a heroic apotheosis of the human activities that make life valuable'. D.J. Gordon and Ian Fletcher echo the same thought: 'For the Gregory of the poem, sharp and early death was the only imaginable end . . . The revelation of complete mastery is the sharp flare: consummation is extinction; extinction that is a condition of triumph.'[38] And yet most critics, while accepting this as one of Yeats's great poems, feel compelled to quibble with the Gregory the poem offers us: Frank Kermode sees Gregory as the archetypal artist, escaping the antinomies of life, but can do so only by ignoring stanza eight as an insertion made at Lady Gregory's request to make the virtues of her son more clear;[39] Dudley Young, on the other hand, feels that Yeats is ambivalent to Gregory because he will not fit into the pattern of history Yeats had, at the time of writing the poem in 1918, just established to his own satisfaction;[40] Bloom, less convinced by Yeats's elevation of his friends to heroic stature, sees Gregory as just too weak a candidate for such an apotheosis.[41] The quibbles point to a nagging sense of doubt about the poem, a doubt which has, however, led few critics to follow Marjorie Perloff's suggestion that the 'speaker or persona of the poem is consistently presented as the one who has heroically survived the turmoil and temptation of the fledgling artist to achieve the unity of being denied to Robert Gregory in his lifetime.'[42] Perloff's view, I want to argue, is substantiated by seeing Yeats as implementing not a romantic aesthetic of apocalypse, but an art of memory, and what the poem dramatically instantiates is the superiority of the man committed to the slow process of acquiring power over time through collaboration with it, through memory, to the man who wishes to outleap the bounds of time altogether.

'In Memory of Major Robert Gregory' opens not with Gregory but with Yeats, and his wife of less than a year, settling into their new house, the symbolic tower to figure so largely in the later poetry:

> Now that we're almost settled in our house
> I'll name the friends that cannot sup with us
> Beside the fire of turf in th'ancient tower,
> And having talked to some late hour
> Climb up the narrow winding stair to bed:
> Discoverers of forgotten truth
> Or mere companions of my youth,
> All, all are in my thoughts to-night being dead.

(CP, p. 148)

The tone is of a man almost weary with the problems of establishing his new domestic life — a new life that will contrast vividly with the death that came upon Gregory. And for the speaker marriage has come as no rekindling of the passions of youth, but rather a necessary acceptance of the limitations that time has imposed on him. Like the tower itself he can be accommodated to these new arrangements only with difficulty. The bed to which they climb is given to us as no joyful consummation of life's potentialities, but the end point of life's restrictions, a seeming afterthought to conversation about his youth. The rhythms of 'Climb up the narrow winding stair to bed' are constantly anticlimactic, toiling over the heavy stresses to a conclusion which, syntactically, only opens again upon the past — 'Discoverers of forgotten truth' — rather than leading forward into the new truths of the future. 'The fire of turf' symbolises a way of life which will be contrasted with a very different fire in the stanza which is the crux for any interpretation of this poem, stanza eleven:

> Some burn damp faggots, others may consume
> The entire combustible world in one small room
> As though dried straw, and if we turn about
> The bare chimney is gone black out
> Because the work had finished in that flare.
> Soldier, scholar, horseman, he,
> As 'twere all life's epitome.
> What made us dream that he could comb grey hair?

Perloff draws the parallel between this stanza's use of the fire and a passage from *The Trembling of the Veil* about Yeats's companions in the Rhymers Club:

> They had taught me that violent energy, which is like a fire of straw, consumes in a few minutes the nervous vitality, and is useless in the arts. Our fire must burn slowly, and we must constantly turn away to think, constantly analyse what we have done, be content even to have little life outside our work . . .[43]

Despite the apparent connection between the two passages, critics have continued to insist, as does Daniel Harris in a recent book, that 'the smolder, like "the fire of turf", is the speaker's life, his imagination: mere survival, an art without creative passion'.[44] That the poem we are reading makes nonsense of such a claim might seem to be just another of those Yeatsian denials that he can write the poetry he is writing — 'but a thought / Of that late death took all my heart for speech' — but it goes much deeper: critics are continually drawing Gregory back into the centre of the poem's focus because he fits romantic conceptions of the artist's tragic fight with his times. It is precisely those conceptions that Yeats is opposing: it is 'imagination' that will, in the end, have been supplanted by 'memory'.

That Yeats saw in Gregory the assertion of an individualism which was in conflict with his true role as an aristocrat is not, I think, difficult to establish. The poem that follows the great elegy in *Collected Poems* is 'An Irish Airman Foresees his Death' (*CP*, p. 152), a poem whose existential values have concealed from many its underlying critique of Gregory, for the airman's values are a denial of all but self:

> Those that I fight I do not hate,
> Those that I guard I do not love
> . . .
> Nor law, nor duty bade me fight,
> Nor public men, nor cheering crowds,
> A lonely impulse of delight
> Drove to this tumult in the clouds.

The 'tumult' is not the 'tumultuous past' Yeats so often invokes: Gregory has reversed the process in which the multitudinous comes to encircle the individual by setting off on an individual search for 'tumult'. In doing so he has denied the past — 'A waste of breath the years behind' — and therefore denied the culture that has shaped him and of which he ought to be the finest product. Yeats's doubts about the appropriateness of Gregory's fighting for the British have to be seen in the context of the Irish rising, only recently over, with its deaths of those from the lower orders, the Catholic middle classes, fighting for Ireland, while Gregory fights for no one but himself. The doubts were made explicit in a poem Yeats chose not to publish, 'Reprisals', written during the Black and Tans' marauding of the Irish countryside:

> We called it a good death. Today
> Can ghost or man be satisfied?
> Although your last exciting year
> Outweighed all others, you said,
> Though battle joy may be so dear
> A memory, even to the dead,
> It chases other thought away,
> Yet rise from your Italian tomb,

Flit to Kiltartan cross and stay
Till certain second thoughts have come
Upon the cause you served, that we
Imagined such a fine affair:
Half-drunk or whole-made soldiery
Are murdering your tenants there.

(*Var.*, p. 791)

Gregory's personal values are weighed, here, in a scale that includes the values of his community, of the people he ought to have been defending from attack. His only 'memory' is that of his 'last exciting year'; the cause he fought for, the British cause, with which Yeats had little sympathy, was 'Imagined such a fine affair': such deceitful 'imagining' was possible only because 'memory' had been restricted to the immediate past, because it had lost its true function. Compare Gregory with Alfred Pollexfen, whose elegy is contained in the same volume: Pollexfen was buried 'near the astrologer', his brother George, who had been Yeats's childhood companion:

Yesterday in the tenth year
Since he who had been contented long,
A nobody in a great throng,
Decided he would journey home,
Now that his fiftieth year had come,
And 'Mr. Alfred' be again
Upon the lips of common men
Who carried in their memory
His childhood and his family.

(*CP*, p. 176)

Pollexfen's commitment is to the value of the common memory; Gregory's a destruction of it because with him dies his family name and his lineage. He who, as an aristocrat, should most be concerned with passing on his family values from the past to the future, has turned his back upon family, country, continuity and memory: and all for that 'lonely impulse of delight'. Such delight is not a Yeatsian virtue. Just as the beloved is beautiful by virtue of the associations she calls to mind, so the hero, for Yeats, calls the past into the present: indeed, can only be heroic because he fulfils some possibility already instantiated in the art of the past. Thus in an essay of 1903, of which some of the language is echoed by 'An Irish Airman', Yeats writes:

I do not think these country imaginations have changed much for
centuries, for they are still busy with those two themes of the
ancient Irish poets, the sternness of battle and the sadness of parting
and death ... It is not a difference in the substance of things that
the lamentations that were sung after battles are now sung for men
who have died on the gallows. The emotion has become not less,
but more noble, by the change, for the man who goes to death with
the thought —

It was with the people I was,
It was not with the law I was,

has behind him generations of poetry and poetical life.[45]

Gregory, who ought to have had behind him 'generations of poetry and
poetical life', is given no such context in the poems about him: he is
a denier of the people and of the past. He brings to his heroism no
accumulations of time and memory, no responsibility to the values
of memory, and it is not he, but Pearse, leader of the 1916 uprising,
who is accorded by Yeats the right, in the late poem 'The Statues',
to have 'summoned Chuchulain to his side', Cuchulain whom it had
been Yeats's life work to make an integral part of the Irish mind.

In writing his elegy for Gregory, Yeats was, of course, performing
a public duty for his old friend and patron Lady Gregory, and no
such thoughts could be put directly into the poem. The poem had to be
a celebration of Gregory's life, a mourning at his death, but in its implicit contrasts it draws a very different picture from that apotheosis
of artist or hero which would make Gregory a symbol of the imagination's self-consuming and self-transcending energy. The poem opposes
to each other two men who have both inherited Irish tradition and
memory: Yeats, who has renovated the 'ancient tower', who by his
marriage has committed himself to the future of his country and its
values as well as the past; and Gregory, who dies without issue and who
could 'so well have counselled us / In all lovely intricacies of a house',
but not only cannot assist in rebuilding the tower, but has left his own
house, the house of Gregory, in ruins. The man of memory, living by
the values of time, opposes the man of imagination, who will be shown
trapped in the values of space. The poem opens as an exercise in
memory, recalling the participants in Yeats's youth: the appropriation
of the national past through the symbolic ancient tower is therefore
matched with a reappropriation of the personal past, and both
emphasise the poet's task of integrating his own life with the life of
his community, his own memory with the memory of his culture.

These figures from Yeats's past are generally discussed as prefiguring the virtues of which Gregory is to be the consummation: even Marjorie Perloff sees them in these terms with each of the three remembered men exemplifying one facet of Gregory's personality. 'Gregory sums up these three virtues: he is "soldier" (like Synge); "scholar" (like Johnson), and "horseman" (like Pollexfen).'[46] The three figures much more fully, however, sum up the stages of Yeats's own career as an artist: from 1890s decadence and dreaminess, like Johnson, to nationalist individualism, like Synge, to occult speculation, like Pollexfen. Their relationship to Gregory can only be a function of Yeats's choice of them to illustrate his life; their relationship to Yeats himself is that they are distinct elements in his own nature — they remain in his memory because they have helped shape the person he has become and the culture he has come to inhabit. The three characters face in both directions, towards Gregory and towards Yeats, and their deaths are symptomatic of their failure to sustain the tensions of their personalities. Significantly, in terms of the poem's opening, they are none of them married, and that is what links them to Gregory and separates them from Yeats. But they are also men who have destroyed themselves in the search for pattern and order: they are representative of those potentialities for self-destruction that Yeats himself has avoided while retaining the value of what they had to teach.

The pattern that is inscribed in the descriptions of the three men is that of a conflict between the values of time and the values of space; of a conflict they have been unable to resolve. Johnson's dream was of a 'measureless consummation', an apocalyptic end to time (as well as a denial of mundane sexuality), but the reality of his life was 'much falling', both physical and moral; Synge travels long before he reaches the race that allows him to express himself, but he reaches them only when he is no longer able to participate in life, when the living world has become for him only a 'text'; Pollexfen, like Synge an isolate, attempts to shape all the patterns of time upon geometrical space: he

> could have shown how pure-bred horses
> And solid men, for all their passion, live
> But as the outrageous stars incline
> By opposition, square and trine;

For each of them fulfilment can only come with the end of time, whereas Yeats's tower with its spiralling stair is an instantiation of continuous development through time in the same place. The tragedy

of all three men that the poem invokes lies, however, in the fact that
they have been the guardians of some form of memory: Johnson had
his 'Greek and Latin learnings'; Synge's plays are memorials to a
peasantry Yeats had seen pass away; Pollexfen retains the secret knowledge of the occultists. What each has been unable to do, however, is
to bring that memory to any fruition in contact with the modern
world. All have retreated: Johnson to drink and dreams; Synge to the
West of Ireland; Pollexfen to a 'sluggish and contemplative' old age
when he is no longer the companion of 'Mayo men'. Their memory
has distanced them from the modern world and isolated them from
action. By retaining them within his own memory and the memory of
his poem, Yeats is attempting to maintain the forms of knowledge that
they preserved and make them integral to modern Ireland.

Gregory's memory is what the poem itself is devoted to, but he goes
unnamed within it: indeed, his memory seems to be fading even from
the mind of his memorialist — 'and where was it / He rode a race without a bit?' — for it has failed to inscribe itself in the common mind of
the place. Gregory may have been a painter of the landscape, but his
'delighted eye' sees in purely spatial terms,

> The tower set on the stream's edge;
> The ford where drinking cattle make a stir

and not in the mythological terms, landscape married to memory, that
Yeats wished:

> Have not all races their first unity from a mythology that marries
> them to rock and hill? We had in Ireland imaginative stories, which
> the uneducated classes knew and even sang ... Perhaps even these
> images, once created and associated with river and mountain, might
> move of themselves and with some powerful, even turbulent life,
> like those painted horses that trampled the rice-fields of Japan.[47]

Gregory's 'mind outran the horses' feet', gathering none of the associative power that would add temporal depth to his depictions of 'cold
Clare rock and Galway rock and thorn'. Yeats, of course, had to write
a poem to which Lady Gregory could subscribe, but the descriptions
of Gregory's achievements are always ambiguous. Gregory is 'our
Sidney and our perfect man' — 'our' implying that he would not have
had those qualities for anyone else? Yeats and Lady Gregory 'dreamed
that a great painter had been born' in Gregory — 'dreamed' implying

that their hopes would have been nothing but dreams even had he lived?

> Soldier, scholar, hoseman, he,
> And yet he had the intensity
> To have published all to be a world's delight.

What is significant is what is missing: landowner, artist, father? And would he have published to delight the world or that the world might be delighted with him? Yeats balances syntactic and semantic ambiguity to allow himself to perform his public gesture for Gregory while implying, without self-congratulation (the temptations to self-destruction, as symbolised by Synge, Johnson and Pollexfen have been too great for that) or immodesty, that Gregory will be significant only because he is inscribed in Yeats's art of memory. For Gregory death must be an annihilation of the whole world —

> Some burn damp faggots, others may consume
> The entire combustible world in one small room

— because he has committed himself to a life like that Yeats describes of John F. Taylor:

> His articles are nothing, and his one historical work ... is almost nothing, lacking the living voice; and now, though a formidable man, he is forgotten but for the fading memory of a few friends ... Did not Leonardo da Vinci warn the imaginative man against preoccupation with arts that cannot survive his death?[48]

Gregory's delight is in arts that do not offer themselves to the memory.
    In the final stanza Yeats reveals the tripartite division of our faculties which underlies his poem:

> I had thought, seeing how bitter is that wind
> That shakes the shutter, to have brought to mind
> All those that manhood tried, or childhood loved
> Or boyish intellect approved,
> With some appropriate commentary on each;
> Until imagination brought
> A fitter welcome; but a thought
> Of that late death took all my heart for speech.

Throughout the poem mind has been repository of memory – 'all that come into my mind are dead', 'comes the first to mind', 'a portion of my mind and life' – and has been balanced against the heart as seat of the emotions – 'In the affections of the heart'. The poem has been made from memory when the heart is lost for speech. 'Imagination' is suspended between the two, and suspended too between Yeats and Gregory. 'Until imagination brought / A fitter welcome' can be read as referring to Yeats, who has written the poem at a low point of his imaginative vitality when only personal memories remain to him; or it might imply that imagination has been revitalised by the subject of Gregory's death, firing Yeats to use his whole 'heart for speech'. On the other hand, it might be that Gregory is fitted for the welcome of the imagination, because the imagination is a destructive flame, and that Yeats remains waiting in the world of memory. Gregory, who 'might have been your heartiest welcomer', is representative of the imagination that would consume the world, and failing, consumes itself; Yeats's mind is entirely taken up with memory, and though the poem cannot assert as much, what we are witness to is the victory of those who would rebuild the world in continuity with the past, opposing the bitter wind of history with the preserving powers of memory. The bitter wind is made the more so by the destruction of the Anglo-Irish aristocracy for the 'Anglo' part of itself in defiance of its Irish heritage, but the poem reincorporates Gregory to the world he has denied, offering him a place in the 'slow fire' with such consummate skill that it is an act of courtesy to the mother of one who did his people the discourtesy of dying for a cause that could contribute nothing to their lives, nor fulfil any image in their communal memory.

The airman symbolises the desire to outleap the bounds of life, a heroism made irrelevant because enacted without consciousness of the past. Revelation is no longer for Yeats a trascendence of time and an entry into eternity, but access to all the accumulations of time:

I know now that revelation is from the self, but from that age-long memoried self, that shapes the elaborate shell of the mollusc and the child in the womb, that teaches the birds to make their nest; and that genius is a crisis that joins that buried self for certain moments to our trivial daily mind.[49]

The eternal is not something we aspire to by escaping time; it is something from which we take inspiration because it contains all time, and is contained within us as our 'buried self'. The wandering that Goll was committed to because excluded from a transcendence of time becomes, metaphorically, the very medium by which we transcend our trivial daily selves, for it is the mind wandering through its associations that will bring us to the uncovering of our deepest self:

> Such thought, that in it bound
> I need no other thing,
> Wound in mind's wandering
> As mummies in the mummy-cloth are wound.
>
> (*CP*, p. 259; 'All Souls' Night')

Our associations gathered in the Great Memory are our eternity and preserve all that time takes from us. The symbol which gives us entry into such funds of memory is neither a pathway to the eternal nor a thing with a life of its own, organic and self-defining; it is that which, by its ability to stimulate innumerable associations, allows us to recall the whole of the past as an intensification of the present. Robert Gregory, who would abolish the world with his death, wishes to consume past and future with himself; Yeats, who remembers Gregory, wishes to link past with future through himself, to keep unbroken the chain of association that can carry us into the depths of the past, the depths of the buried self.

Placing memory at the centre of his thematic concerns was, given his romantic inheritance, sufficiently difficult for Yeats; finding a poetic form capable of acting as a stimulus to memory in the reader that he might fulfil the demands of an associationist aesthetic was even more problematic. Yeats's earliest effort in this direction were the 'Rose' poems in which the symbol of the rose was intended, by its innumerable meanings, to form, for both poet and reader, 'the only pathway from which he may hope to see beauty and wisdom with his own eyes'.[50] Yeats's rose symbol has its multitude of meanings, certainly, for it represents, as Harold Bloom remarks, not only the 'Eternal Rose of Beauty and Peace' as well as Shelley's 'Intellectual Beauty', but also 'Maud Gonne, Ireland (Dark Rosaleen), a central symbol of the Rosicrucian Order of the Golden Dawn, a sexual symbol, the sun, and much else'.[51] Bloom concludes that the symbol is incoherent, but that is because Bloom, like Northrop Frye, looks for symbolism to establish a second-order language with a distinct, if not definite, semantic system.[52] But for Yeats the symbol was not part of a language, but the entry through reverie into the multitudinous associations of the Great Memory. The trouble with the rose symbolism was that it attempted to include within itself, by authorial fiat, the plenitude of associations which could properly only arise through the symbol's interaction with the memory of its audience:

> Thy great leaves enfold
> The ancient beards, the helms of ruby and gold
> Of the crowned Magi; and the king whose eyes
> Saw the Pierced Hands and Rood of elder rise
> In Druid vapour and make the torches dim;
> Till vain frenzy awoke and he died; and him
> Who met Fand . . .
>
> (*CP*, p. 77; 'The Secret Rose.')

The poem is providing us with Yeats's associations for the rose, but it is a list that is potentially endless, because it represents the end to which all other symbols strive, represents an entry into eternity. The problem posed by the rose as a symbol is perhaps described in an essay of 1898, 'A Symbolic Artist', dealing with the drawings of Althea Gyles: 'If one imagine a flame burning in the air, and try to make one's mind dwell on it, that it may continue to burn, one's mind always strays immediately to other images; but perhaps, if one believed that it was a divine flame, one's mind would not stray.'[53] The desire to prevent 'mind's wandering' is a desire to bring to a conclusion the associational recall: later, Yeats's concern will not be with the single, unwavering flame, but with

> Flames that no faggot feeds, nor steel has lit,
> Nor storm disturbs, flames begotten of flame

that appear on the streets of Byzantium.[54] But even in 1898, Yeats cannot hold to his intent of unwavering concentration on the single flame: symbol turns rapidly to narrative:

The Knight upon the Grave of his Lady tells much of its meaning to the first glance; but when one has studied for a time, one discovers that there is a heart in the bulb of every hyacinth, to personify the awakening of the soul and of love out of the grave. It is now winter, and beyond the knight, who lies in the abandonment of his sorrow, the trees spread their leafless boughs against a grey winter sky; but spring will come, and the boughs will be covered with leaves . . .[55]

No unwavering flame here, but a drift into unravelling the story and turning it into what Yeats claimed to dislike, 'subject pictures', rather than a drawing with 'patterns and rhythms of line'.[56] And the picture does the same as Yeats's early symbolist poems: having become conscious of its symbolical nature it takes as its *theme* the end – religious awakening, raising of the buried self, entry into eternity – that ought to be a function of its *form*. It becomes an allegory of the workings of symbol rather than a symbol producing its appropriate effect on the audience.

The vagueness of such a symbol is a function of its lack of real associative potential for its audience: in trying to contain so many meanings it effectively stimulates no train of images. The same, in a slightly different way, is true of Yeats's use of Irish names in his early poetry: for most of his audience such names must have been 'blanks' with merely the hint of Celtic twilight to them to give them significance. And yet just as the poet has somehow to find a way of stimulating sufficient associations in the reader to carry him down into the multitudinous associations of the Great Memory, so Yeats had to use his Irish names until they gained, from their contexts within his poems and the works of Lady Gregory and others of the Renaissance, a significant place in the reader's memory. The difference it made in the technique of the later Yeats can be seen again in the revisions. The original version of 'Cuchulain's Fight with the Sea' presents the enchanted Cuchulain, sent to challenge the sea so that he will not turn on his companions his anger at having slain his own son, in the following terms:

> In three days' time, Cuchulain with a moan
> Stood up, and came to the sands alone:
> For four days he warred with the bitter tide;
> And the waves flowed above him, and he died.

> *(Var.*, p. 105)

The poem's dying fall is in part the result of its need to tell the story. The revision of the 1920s could, because of the success of Yeats's own poetry, take that for granted and imply, rather than state the conclusion:

> Cuchulain stirred,
> Stared on the horses of the sea, and heard
> The cars of battle and his own name cried;

And fought with the invulnerable tide.

(CP, p. 40)

The tide is invulnerable and Cuchulain will be destroyed, and yet that defeat is also a victory because he remains eternally a symbol in the national mind. The end of the poem dramatises both the victory and the defeat, because it leaves us with Cuchulain in the midst of the conflict that is the ultimate revelation of his significance. He is caught there, eternal, and yet forever demanding that we continue and complete the narrative. Our continuations can never, like the tide he fights, defeat him, because it is a sea that flows out from him, an emotion of multitude forever completing what remains forever incomplete on the page. The single image does not need to assert its multiple meanings; it leaves them to the associations that emanate from it into the time by which it was once defeated, but with which it is now in endless collaboration.

It was by the technique of the climactic image that Yeats learned to use and to control the associative reverie which he assumed to be the condition of the reading mind in the act of aesthetic appreciation. We can see its development most clearly, perhaps, in 'He Remembers Forgotten Beauty', from *The Wind Among the Reeds*. It is a poem which begins, like so many of the early poems, in a description of associative process, of the associations which constitute the beauty of the beloved:

> When my arms wrap you round I press
> My heart upon the loveliness
> That has long faded from the world;
> The jewelled crowns which kings have hurled
> In shadowy pools, when armies fled;
> The love-tales wrought with silken thread
> By dreaming ladies upon cloth
> That has made fat the murderous moth;

(CP, pp. 69-70)

The beloved's beauty, through the associations it inspires, saves in memory what has been destroyed in time; but equally, her beauty consists of the memories which gather around it. Through that gathering up of time into a single focus of beauty, however, the speaker — still a romantic — seeks entry into eternity, seeks access to Eternal Beauty in her essence:

For that pale breast and lingering hand
Come from a more dream-heavy land,
A more dream-heavy hour than this;
And when you sigh from kiss to kiss
I hear white Beauty sighing, too,
For hours when all must fade like dew,
But flame on flame, and deep on deep,
Throne over throne, where in half sleep,
Their swords upon their iron knees,
Brood her high lonely mysteries.

Eternity, however, is no single divine flame, but a multitude which, like the associational process, like the paradoxical union of destruction and preservation in the lover's recall of all that 'has long faded from the world', demands that we see in beauty no single focus of transcendence of time, but a patient and brooding accumulation of all the losses that time entails. To say even this much, however, is to deflect the climactic power of the poem's ending, for those enigmatic figures are left to the reader, and it is we who must, by passing into a 'slight trance' in which 'images pass rapidly before you . . . linked by certain associations', brood beauty's 'high lonely mysteries', allowing Yeats's image to complete itself from our own reverie. The poem is constructed so that the speaker's associative train rises to an image which is at once an emblem of the associative process and a climactic release of further association in the reader: there is an unspoken second half to the poem mirroring, in our associations, the associations which brought us to that climactic image. The poem's closure on the page is also its opening in our minds, its eternal refusal of finality.

The climactic image allowed Yeats to turn his poems outward upon the reader. Where the Rose symbol had acted as a kind of transcendental vacuum cleaner, sucking all associations up into itself in order to transcend time, the climactic image turns towards the reader, turns back into time, in order to project a flow of associations over which the poet claims no real control, but without which his poem could not be experienced as a poem. The dramatic structure of the poem involves the presentation of the poet's chain of associations as they rise – or rather, as they descend – towards the Great Memory, and it is when some image is released from the Great Memory that it is turned loose to find its own significance in the reader. The poem on the page is the poet's half of a shared meditation, and the other half is demanded of the reader, or, if the poet is particularly confident that the Great

Memory influences events in the world, is demanded of the world itself:

> Surely some revelation is at hand;
> Surely the Second Coming is at hand.
> The Second Coming! Hardly are those words out
> When a vast image out of *Spiritus Mundi*
> Troubles my sight: somewhere in sands of the desert
> A shape with lion body and the head of a man,
> A gaze blank and pitiless as the sun,
> Is moving its slow thighs, while all about it
> Reel shadows of the indignant desert birds.
> The darkness drops again; but now I know
> That twenty centuries of stony sleep
> Were vexed to nightmare by a rocking cradle,
> And what rough beast, its hour come round at last,
> Slouches towards Bethlehem to be born?
>
> (*CP*, p. 210; 'The Second Coming')

The image has no specific meaning: coming from the buried self it sets in motion associative connections over which not only the poet, but possibly we ourselves, have no control, we reel, like the shadows of the desert birds, from this intrusion into our consciousness (if we read it as Yeats presumed). The final rhetorical question — and the rhetorical question is a regular Yeatsian device to produce a climactic conclusion — directs a path for our associations, but its frightening quality resides in its implication that the world itself is ordered like a chain of associations: when this image has been given, a series of others, not in the mind but in reality, will flow from it, a series occurring through us but over which we have no control. Where in the earlier poems Yeats had sought a presiding symbol that would channel all associations to a specific end, in 'The Second Coming' he plays upon the poem's lack of finality to enforce our fearful apprehension of the uncontrollable future. The mixture of joy and horror with which Yeats himself envisages his climactic image is the result of fear of what is to come, but exultation that what is to come will be shaped, however terribly, by the buried self to which the poet has given us access. The poet is gatekeeper not to eternity, but to the forces that drive through us towards the future from the past: the art of memory is, paradoxically, through the associations it releases in us, also the moulder of the future:

We can deliberately refashion our characters, but not our painting or poetry. If our characters also were not unconsciously refashioned so completely by the unfolding of the logical energies of art, that even simple things have in the end a new aspect in our eyes, the arts would not be among the things that return forever.[57]

They return forever because every poem is a recall of many past works of art, the re-enactment of old memory in each new associational pattern provoked by the poem; but the new associations will also shape the events of the future, and shape them upon the model of the past that they recall. All art is a second coming opening into a future of eternal returns.

5 ELIOT, POUND AND THE MEMORY OF ART

In 1919, under the title of 'A Foreign Mind', which given its author's nationality seems somewhat ironic, T.S. Eliot reviewed W.B. Yeats's volume of essays *The Cutting of an Agate*:

> Mr. Yeats sometimes appears, as a philosopher of aesthetics, incoherent. But all his observations are quite consistent with his personality, with his remoteness. His remoteness is not an escape from the world, for he is innocent of any world to escape from; his procedure is blameless, but he does not start from where we do. His mind is, in fact, extreme in egotism, and as often with egotism, remains a little crude; crude, indeed, as from its remoteness one would expect.[1]

What Eliot attacks in Yeats were the qualities he found in all romantic art: isolation from some central tradition of culture leads to an overvaluation of the personal and an inflation of the poetic ego at the expense of a true awareness of the world. Eliot's 'we' places him at the centre of a culture to which Ireland — 'There is something of this crudity, and much of this egoism, about what is called Irish literature'[2] — is peripheral. As a result the Irish writer, whether Joyce or Yeats, is unable to maintain the balance between self and outside world which Eliot constantly sought in great art. For Eliot, Yeats's writing never achieves objectivity: like Arthur Symons, as described in 'The Perfect Critic', or Hamlet in the account of the play given in connection with the objective correlative, Yeats never finds objects that are adequate to his feelings:

> Very powerful fooling *is* crude: the fault of Mr. Yeats's is that it is crude without being powerful. The weakness of his prose is similar to that of his verse. The trouble is not that it is inconsistent, illogical or incoherent, but that the objects upon which it is directed are not fixed; as in the portraits of Synge and several other Irishmen we do not seem to get the men themselves before us but feelings of Mr. Yeats projected.[3]

Like Hamlet, Yeats is a man whose feelings can find no adequate objects in the world upon which to fix themselves. But Eliot's review of Yeats was published in July 1919, and his essay on Hamlet in September of the same year, and in the essays of Yeats's that Eliot was reviewing we find the following passage, written in 1905 or 1906:

> It is not possible to separate an emotion or spiritual state from the image that calls it up and gives it expression. Michelangelo's *Moses*, Velasquez' *Philip the Second*, the colour purple, a crucifix, call into life an emotion or state which vanishes with them because they are its only possible expression . . .[4]

The difference between an 'image' that calls an emotion into life because it is 'its only possible expression', and the 'set of objects, a situation, a chain of events which shall be the formula of that *particular* emotion' is slight enough to suggest that the one is an echo of the other, to suggest, in other words, that Eliot was judging Yeats by standards and theories that Yeats had himself developed and passed on to his younger contemporaries.

Eliot may well have owed more to that remote Irish mind than he realised or cared to admit. In 1917, the year when many of Eliot's central critical principles were in gestation, he reviewed – and reviewed enthusiastically – the little book of J.B. Yeats's letters that W.B. Yeats had had printed in 1916. What Eliot picks out for quotation is revealing, and perhaps was a revelation to Eliot:

> He is quite literal too when he says, 'In every great poet is a Herbert Spencer', or, 'the poet does not seek to be original, but the *truth*, and to his dismay and consternation, it may be, he finds the original, thereby to incur our hostility and misunderstanding.' . . . This last statement, in fact, is a thought which takes very deep roots; it strikes through the tangle of literature direct to the subsoil of the greatest – to Shakespeare and Dante and Aeschylus. Ordinary writers of verse deal either in imagination or in 'ideas'; they escape from one to the other, but neither one nor the other nor both together is truth in the sense of poetic truth. Only old ideas, 'part and parcel of the personality' are of use to the poet.[5]

Ordinary verse writers use 'imagination', great writers deal in 'truth', and truth is constituted by 'old ideas'; in Yeats's 'Discoveries' there is the following distinction:

The artist stands between the saint and the world of impermanent things, and just in so far as his mind dwells on what is impermanent in his sense, on all that 'modern experience and discussion of our interests,' that is to say, on what never recurs, as desire and hope, terror and weariness, spring and autumn, recur, will his mind losing rhythm grow critical . . . He will think less of what he sees and more of his own attitude to it.[6]

Yeats, too, insists on the avoidance of the casual and the modern, and insists on the 'impersonality' of the poet, his setting aside of his own 'attitude' in favour of concentration on the recurring in human experience. Yeats's language is very different from Eliot's; it is 'remote' from modern criticism; and yet the underlying pattern of the ideas which were to be given memorable formulation in well-turned generalisations by Eliot, were already present in Yeats's writings at the beginning of the century. Eliot, much more than is generally acknowledged, was developing the work of Yeats, even if it was a Yeats filtered through Pound, and what joins them is their effort to found their poetry on a different basis than that of the romantic imagination. For Yeats, the conflict was between his associationist aesthetic and his romantic conception of the purposes of art; for Eliot the issue was clearer, a rejection of an outmoded poetic style that he saw as integral with romantic escapism.

The poem in which these issues are centrally present is 'Prufrock', a poem which we cannot help seeing perhaps, because of Hugh Kenner's formulation of it, as a parody of the style of effete romanticisim, a style not too distant from Yeats's:

The phenomenon of sound obscuring deficiencies of sense from writer and reader is often observed in English poetry; the Romantics may be said to have elevated it into a method. Mr. Eliot's originality consisted in allowing the deficiency to be concealed only from the speaker.[7]

And yet this probably sees Eliot's early work too much through the lens of the later criticism, in particular through the essay on Swinburne: 'he uses the most general word, because his emotion is never particular, never in direct line of vision, never focused; . . . it is not merely the sound that he wants, but the vague associations of idea that the words give him.'[8] To see Prufrock as merely an instance of such poetic failure transposed into a character misses the extent, however, to which we see Prufrock equally in relation to the society of which he is a part, and in terms of that society our evaluation of him might be very different. As Stephen Spender has said,

> Prufrock, considered as a consciousness, or imagination, situated in a world that has become phantasmagoric to him, negates negation. He has, after all, a positive aspect. He is more than the inhabitants of the drawing room precisely because he knows that he is much less than they are. He knows what he lacks . . . He suffers . . .[9]

Spender ascribes to Prufrock precisely what Kenner denies him – a consciousness of himself that raises him above his environment. This too reads back into the early poetry a later essay – the essay on Baudelaire.[10] What is common to both views, however, is that they are trying to account for the intensely literary atmosphere of the poem: Prufrock tempts us to see in him a parody of literary fashion because his language is not poetic language masquerading as someone's real thought – as one might expect of earlier dramatic monologues – but thought deliberately presenting itself as poetry:

> And indeed there will be time
> For the yellow fog that slides along the street
> Rubbing its back upon the window-panes;
> There will be time, there will be time
> To prepare a face to meet the faces that you meet;
> There will be time to murder and create,
> And time for all the works and days of hands
> That lift and drop a question on your plate.
>
> > (*CP*, p. 14)

Prufrock's thoughts are not being presented through the medium of poetry: the medium is the very nature of his thought, as the opening image, in its deliberate challenge to our normal ways of reading metaphor, insists:

> Let us go then, you and I,
> When the evening is spread out against the sky
> Like a patient etherised upon a table.

Prufrock's failings as a human being are the result of his inability to act, to pose his question: the opening image suggests, however, that

Prufrock's whole being is suspended, separate from the ordinary course of life, and that the action of the poem is not a mimesis of a presumed reality, but rather a hypothetical, etherial, disembodied series of fictions. What Prufrock has in common with his language is that, just as it draws attention to its status as literature, so he tries to see himself constantly through the medium of art: his actions are not imitations in the poem of a reality beyond it, but his imitation in imagination of characters in art.

The prototypes whose dramatic gestures are thrown on the screen of Prufrock's consciousness — Hamlet (and the Fool), Lazarus, John the Baptist — repeat on the level of action what we are conscious of in the language. They turn Prufrock's social self-consciousness into an aesthetic self-consciousness: the women who 'come and go / Talking of Michelangelo' see Prufrock as a failed *homme do monde* — '(They will say: "How his hair is growing thin!")' — and his only defence is to adopt a gesture from a more significant narrative than his own. The gestures, however, are all gestures in the face of death: each is a pose preserved because of the significance that someone has extorted from his confrontation with death, whether Hamlet, Lazarus or John the Baptist. Prufrock invokes such gestures because what he suffers from is endless life in which time is seemingly suspended. The repetitions, the verb tenses referring always to what 'might be' or 'might have been', enforce our sense of a life in which action and change are impossible: time will bring neither fulfilment nor release:

> In a minute there is time
> For decisions and revisions which a minute will reverse.

Prufrock invokes images of significant death because they insist upon the reality of time in a world where time has become like furniture, to be encountered repeatedly:

> For I have known them all already, known them all —
> Have known the evenings, mornings, afternoons.

Instead of 'knowing' the women he encounters, he knows only lumps of time, and if the sexual potentialities that the language constantly implies is thereby denied him, he is freed from the terrors of time too: within this society time has been domesticated, its claws drawn:

> And the afternoon, the evening, sleeps so peacefully!

Smoothed by long fingers,
Asleep . . . tired . . . or it malingers,
Stretched on the floor, here beside you and me.

The social patterns have become eternal:

And I have seen the eternal Footman hold my coat, and snicker,
And in short, I was afraid.

Death will take our bodily garments only as part of social etiquette,
subdued to the irresistible decorum which enforces Prufrock's sense
of social inferiority. At the same time, Prufrock's fear raises him above
his society because he is aware, as no one else seems to be, that there
is something beyond it. The translation of his fears into those archetypal encounters with death is an acknowledgment of what cannot
be spoken or known within his society. In its polite perfection the
society has reified time, become unconscious of death. Prufrock's
consciousness of death, as shown by his recollection of Hamlet and the
others, is the sign of his superiority: he knows there is significance to
be gained in the face of death that neither he nor his society will
find in a life in which death is denied. It is, however, an impotent
superiority, for those archetypal efforts to find meaning in death can
succeed only because they too exist in unreal time. Their confrontation
with death is a confrontation in imagination, the reality of it lost to
us: they, as you and I ('let us go then, you and I') are not, were 'meant
to be', and Hamlet's existential questioning — 'to be or not to be' —
is undone by Eliot's poem, for what it insists upon is that Hamlet *is*,
continues in being, even through death.

Prufrock is trapped, therefore, between two kinds of eternity, the
eternity of the unceasing 'times' of the social world in which death does
not figure, and the eternity of art, in which a significant confrontation
with death can take place only because it is not truly a part of life.
The work of art as a pure structure of meaning can present death as
meaningful only by its being hypothetical, repeatable, eternally present.
Such deaths cannot be translated into our ordinary human world as
models for our own awareness, for in our ordinary world meaning is
not given as part of our being:

Would it have been worth while,
To have bitten off the matter with a smile,
To have squeezed the universe into a ball

> To roll it towards some overwhelming question,
> To say, 'I am Lazarus, come from the dead,
> Come back to tell you all, I shall tell you all' —
> If one, settling a pillow by her head,
>   Should say: 'That is not what I meant at all.
>   That is not it, at all.'

Prufrock, in attempting to find a suitable stance to make engagement in life possible, looks for prototypes in art, but his imagination over-leaps the demands of his specific situation, and finds archetypes for his real question, the question that his society cannot frame. The dramatic models for his poses, however, are as false to the real nature of time as the 'eternity' of the social world, for they have 'squeezed the universe into a ball' to make it 'roll towards some overwhelming question' — the universe for them is self-contained, comprehensible. Those deaths are significant only by being in a realm where death is unreal, because it was 'meant to be'. The fundamental irony, of course, the irony that makes Prufrock superior and not inferior to us, is that when he says 'No! I am not Prince Hamlet nor was meant to be' the words of Prufrock, envisaged by us as a human being sharing our existential dilemmas, conflict with the Prufrock who is a piece of art, whose very being is in the meaning of his name. Prufrock, that prudish, effeminate, socially inadequate person is no person but a dramatic character, 'meant to be'. Contrasting himself with Hamlet, Prufrock sides with us, contingent, time-bound, death-bound, but as a piece of art he opposes us, standing on the other side of the footlights, on the other side of death. His declension from Hamlet reveals his inadequacies as a hero, but he does not decline so far as to join the audience:

> Am an attendant lord, one that will do
> To swell a progress, start a scene or two,
> Advise the prince; no doubt, an easy tool,
> Deferential, glad to be of use,
> Politic, cautious, and meticulous;
> Full of high sentence, but a bit obtuse;
> At times, indeed, almost ridiculous —
> Almost, at times, the Fool.

But not the fool of time, for he is, as a piece of art, out of time. That is why the jaunty little couplet that follows affects us as an unreal *cri de coeur* at the processes of time:

I grow old . . . I grow old . . .
I shall wear the bottoms of my trousers rolled.

He can return into the 'eternity' of his social world with a comfort he
cannot bequeath to us, with whom he cannot share his 'meaning':
he is ageless.

Compare the progress of Prufrock to Yeats's King Goll. Goll suffers
a moment of insight into the interconnection of the eternal with the
temporal that leaves him a wanderer in a world of endless regeneration,
a world of time become, like himself, eternal; Prufrock suffers an
ironic version of such a moment of insight, a moment when the heavens
reveal their complete refusal of meaningfulness to human life —

When the evening is spread out against the sky
Like a patient etherised upon a table;

— an interconnection between heaven and earth based only on unconsciousness. Goll seeks meaning in myth though he is, himself, to
us, part of a myth; Prufrock seeks meaning in art though he is, himself,
to us, a piece of art: Goll's song of Orchil, who hides away 'the dying
day', enacts within the poem what the poem itself is doing for its
audience; Prufrock's hope that the mermaids might sing to him enacts
within the poem what the poem itself does for its audience:

I shall wear white flannel trousers, and walk upon the beach.
I have heard the mermaids singing, each to each.

I do not think that they will sing to me.

I have seen them riding seaward on the waves
Combing the white hair of the waves blown back
When the wind blows the water white and black.

We have lingered in the chambers of the sea
By sea-girls wreathed with seaweed red and brown
Till human voices wake us, and we drown.

Prufrock escapes from his dilemmas into a world of pure imagination,
though it is a world which can no more offer him, through its female
characters, an answer to the problems of sex, than the world of art
could, through its male characters, provide answers to the question of

death. The final line, however, turns to incorporate the reader into Prufrock's dilemma: we too, in reading the poem, have lingered in a world of the imagination, a place where everything has become eternal, but from which we are shut out. The human voices of our ordinary world intervene and we drown. Prufrock, as the representation of a person, drowns in a world for which he is unfitted, but as Stephen Spender's comments implied, he is also saved. As representation, mimesis, he is capable of stepping outside the boundaries of his society and yet incapable of confronting fully the questions that he is conscious it suppresses, but as character in an art world he shares the eternity of Hamlet or the mermaids, and is forever saved from the world of time in which we live. The failure of art to give significant shape to his own world is a failure which we have to apply to ourselves in relation to his world; as Prufrock is to the women from whose self-possession he quails, but whose possession he desires, so we are to Prufrock, whose failings we might mock, but whose eternity mocks us. We, in reading the poem, engage ourselves in the timeless world of the imagination, but what we find there is a character who reveals the impossibility of that timeless world connecting with our ordinary lives and dilemmas, reveals that all art is a hiding of the dying day. Prufrock may be drowned out by human voices, but those human voices will drown in time as he will not. Art, for us even more than Prufrock, is self-deception; the values of the imagination are not transferable from the realm of art, because it cannot help but conceal the reality of those fundamental questions it seems to pose.

Prufrock and Goll are both the inheritors of a theory of art as our salvation from time, whether, in symbolist fashion, by allowing us to transcend it, or whether, in Pateresque fashion, by offering us an intensity of perception of the moment. Both utilise the ethos that such theories encourage, but use them to undercut the end to which they are directed. Imagination will not save us; it is an evasion of the fundamental conditions under which our lives have to be lived. For Yeats the problem was to harmonise his technique with his associationist principles, but for Eliot the technique was established from the writing of 'Prufrock': what he sought in his theories was a means of escaping the endless self-irony that Prufrock implied and for which Laforgue offered a stylistic model. Memory, however, in the early Eliot is almost as self-defeating as imagination. 'Rhapsody on a Windy Night' presents us with an exploration of the powers of the memory, but one in which the memory, like Coleridge's 'fixities', cannot be infused with 'organic' life:

And through the spaces of the dark
Midnight shakes the memory
As a madman shakes a dead geranium.

(CP, p. 26)

Just as for Prufrock no work of art could be a presentation of the
reality of death, so here no *dérèglement de tous les sens* will make of
memory a means to the revitalisation of the past. All that memory can
achieve is the illusion of meaning for our past existence:

The memory throws up high and dry
A crowd of twisted things;
A twisted branch upon the beach
Eaten smooth, and polished
As if the world gave up
The secret of its skeleton,
Stiff and white.
A broken spring in a factory yard,
Rust that clings to the form that the strength has left
Hard and curled and ready to snap.

What memory gives us back from the depths is something artificial —
'polished' — which seems to offer significant insight but remains only
an 'as if'. Whatever comes back in memory is a skeletal version of a
once living reality, and it is the process of memory itself that is a
rusted spring, incapable of bearing the pressure it seems to have been
designed for.

Grover Smith has suggested that 'Rhapsody on a Windy Night'
presents 'a dreamlike process, the quintessence of the non-intellectual',
and that it 'works by free association rather than by logic';[11] but a
poem which asserts the inadequacy of memory can hardly adopt a
method utterly dependent on memory for its effectiveness. Rather
than being a process of association the poem is an examination of the
working and relevance of association: it does not 'dissolve the floors
of memory' in order to produce a 'total synthesis' from the 'kaleidos-
copic images',[12] but reveals the memory's incapacity to reach the real
depths of experience because its operation is mechanical:

I have seen eyes in the street
Trying to peer through lighted shutters,
And a crab one afternoon in a pool,

An old crab with barnacles on his back,
Gripped the end of a stick I held him.

The crab grips the stick as the mind grips a memory: the image operates as a reflexive commentary on the very process from which it emanates, emphasising memory's failure to provide spiritual insight into the depths of our consciousness. Without such spiritual insight, however, the whole world is reduced to mechanical responses to external stimuli: we peer into windows for an inner life which always escapes us:

So the hand of the child, automatic,
Slipped out and pocketed a toy that was running along the quay.
I could see nothing behind that child's eye.

We have no 'key' to consciousness.

In the second half of the poem, however, the personal loss of significance which the first four stanzas have presented is extended on to a more universal scale:

The lamp hummed:
'Regard the moon,
La lune ne garde aucune rancune,
She winks a feeble eye,
She smiles into corners.
She smooths the hair of the grass.
The moon has lost her memory.

Instead of the prostitute who emerges from hidden depths —

Who hesitates toward you in the light of the door
Which opens on her like a grin

— and who was the prelude to the first uprush of memories, her 'eye' that 'Twists like a crooked pin' fishing for the depths, the moon presides over a degraded urban world where there is no significant memory, only casual reminiscence:

She is alone
With all the old nocturnal smells
That cross and cross across her brain,'
The reminiscence comes

Of sunless dry geraniums
And dust in crevices,
Smells of chestnuts in the streets,
And female smells in shuttered rooms,
And cigarettes in corridors
And cocktail smells in bars.

The degraded memory that can encompass only a congerie of artific-
ialities, of the natural trapped within the urban, have the effect of
turning us back to the earlier images and finding in them a potentiality
for real significance which the speaker has refused. Compared to the
'reminiscence' that comes from this decrepit moon the 'twisted branch
upon the beach' is a pointer to the fact that there are depths to be
encountered, depths which the moon has lost as she is removed from
the 'sea' over which she ought to rule. The initial encounter with the
prostitute opens up memories which are all close to the sea and if they
do not reveal its depth they at least point towards those depths in
which the world conceals the 'secret of its skeleton'. The progress of
the poem is toward an ever more etiolated conception of what memory
gives access to, until memory becomes our means of locking ourselves
back into our mundane shallowness:

The lamp said,
'Four o'clock,
Here is the number on the door.
Memory!
You have the key,
The little lamp spreads a ring on the stair.

The lines point, however, in two different directions. Memory locks
us into the room where 'The bed is open; the toothbrush hangs on the
wall' and where we will 'sleep, prepare for life', but on the other hand
it has indeed been the key to a depth we have refused to enter, the
depth beyond mere reminiscence. The 'little lamp' on the stair is the
personal memory, and though Eliot may not allow us access to a
Yeatsian sea of the Great Memory, we can at least reach as far as beach
or rock pool, though what we find there is only the remnants of what is
going on in the depths of the mind.

Twenty years after writing 'Rhapsody on a Windy Night' Eliot was
to return to similar experiences in *The Use of Poetry and the Use of
Criticism*, when he argued the importance to the poet of the mind's

automatic storing of 'material — an image, a phrase, a word — which may be of use to him later. And this selection runs through the whole of his sensitive life. There might be the experience of the child of ten, a small boy peering through sea-water in a rock-pool . . .'[13] The sea returns insistently when Eliot discusses memory: his memories are of the sea, but the sea is also the memory to which one seeks access:

> What seas what shores what grey rocks and what islands
> What water lapping the bow
> And scent of pine and the woodthrush singing through the fog
> What images return
> O my daughter.
>
> ('Marina'; *CP*, p. 115)

Unlike Yeats, Eliot seems without confidence in our access to a total body of memory beyond conscious recall: it remains 'Under sleep, where all the waters meet' (*CP*, p. 115), but individual memories do still point beyond themselves to the unknowable reservoir from which they emanate:

> Why, for all of us, out of all that we have heard, seen, felt, in a lifetime, do certain images recur, charged with emotion, rather than others? The song of one bird, the leap of one fish, . . . six ruffians seen through an open window playing cards at night at a small French railway junction where there was a water-mill: such memories may have symbolic value, but of what we cannot tell, for they come to represent the depths of feeling into which we cannot peer.[14]

The significance of the images remains an 'as if', for it is not in themselves that they are significant, revealing the world's secret, but in what they gesture towards. Prufrock found the imagination self-defeating; 'Rhapsody on a Windy Night' finds memory no escape, but it is the value of memory that comes to dominate Eliot's thinking as he seeks to find a means to manage his imagery so that, for his readers as well, the poem will provide an access to those 'depths of feeling into which we cannot peer'.

The phrase 'depths of feeling' connects back from Eliot's essay of 1933 to his early criticism, with its technical distinctions between 'emotion' and 'feeling',[15] and from there to F.H. Bradley and the thesis Eliot wrote on Bradley in Oxford in the early years of the First

World War. It was in part through Bradley's philosophy that Eliot developed his associationist poetics, paradoxical as this might seem since Bradley's work, the most complex product of English Idealism,[16] is often taken to be the antithesis of empiricist psychology. Indeed, in choosing a passage to illustrate the virtue's of Bradley's prose Eliot, in his essay of 1927, chose one in which Bradley is conducting an attack on the theories of Mill and Bain.[17] However, Eliot goes on to make the point that Bradley was not, in fact, determined to destroy associationist psychology, but only to overthrow the Benthamite philistinism with which it was often joined:

> People are inclined to believe that what Bradley did was demolish the logic of Mill and the psychology of Bain. If he had done that, it would have been a lesser service than what he has done; and if he had done that it would have been less of a service than people think, for there is much that is good in the logic of Mill and the psychology of Bain . . . Anyone who reads his own *Principles* will see that his force is directed not against Mill's logic as a whole but only against certain limitations, imperfections and abuses. He left the structure of Mill's logic standing, and never meant to do anything else.[18]

By allowing that Bradley had incorporated rather than refuted Mill, Eliot was maintaining his distance from the kinds of Coleridgean *a priori* idealism to which Bradley's philosophy might seem to commit him. Indeed, what Bradley had done was to do the same to Mill as he had done with Coleridge, for just as Mill had reinterpreted Coleridge's insights into the artist in terms of associationist theory, so Bradley incorporated associationism back into idealist theory.

There are two important strands in Eliot's work on Bradley which are relevant to my discussion here. The first is his qualification of the theory of association itself. Bradley's attack was essentially directed at what he saw as the psychological atomism of the associationists, their reduction of mental experience to individual units, bonded together in a chain and yet each retaining its separate and individual character, so that a recalled impression returned in exactly the same form in which it had first been experienced. Bradley, however, argued that it was not a specific atom of perception that returned, but rather some universal element recognised as being common to two different impressions, and because it is the ideal connection of a universal which causes the recall, the element recalled will not return in exactly the

the same form under which it was first perceived, but will be modified by the new context into which it enters. For Bradley, any impression is always part of a greater whole, and any impression recalled from the past is part of the whole which modified our perception of it, but, equally, enters into a new whole by which it is modified in our present experience. This process Bradley called 'redintegration',[19] association operating by fusing an element from one past totality of experience into a new totality. Associations are therefore no longer subsequent to one another, forming a 'train' or 'chain', but a fusion in a new 'gestalt' which incorporates both new and old experiences in a whole which is not to be separated into its individual elements again. And rather than the mind allowing itself to wander through its associations until it comes upon some particularly significant or overwhelming image — as Yeats suggests — Eliot sees the poet's mind as 'a receptacle for seizing and storing up numberless feelings, phrases, images, which remain there until all the particles which can unite to form a new compound are present together'.[20] Rather than forming a track along which the mind moves, Eliot's associations lurk in the mind unnoticed until they suddenly, and of their own volition — by the recognition of some common universal, in Bradley's terms — fuse together into a new whole. In traditional associationist theory the work of art is always appearing and disappearing in the train of associations it inspires; in Eliot's theory the work is always a new fusion of past and present, both together in the same act of creation and of apprehension. Thus, perhaps, is Eliot's use of allusion justified theoretically, for it fuses a past and a present experience together, but not because of some casual connection in the poet's mind, but by virtue of a real universal which the two wholes, the past work of art and the present experience embodied in the new work of art, share. And thus, too, is the conception of the complete recreation of the work of literature by the critic, as described in 'The Perfect Critic', justified, because the work as experienced by the critic is a fusion into a new whole, as complete and integral as a work of art itself, of the elements provided by the poet and the associations it generates in the critic. These associations are not merely subsequent upon or consequent to the object he is experiencing, but fused with it so that they are themselves a part of what he is experiencing, a part of the object itself.

The term 'object' takes us to the second important aspect of Bradley's theory, in so far as it affects the development of a poetics of memory. For Bradley, as an idealist, the world is entirely phenomenal, and thus he envisages the world as being made up, fundamentally, of 'feeling', an undifferentiated mass of experience which gradually separates itself out into subject and object. The two poles of our dualistic view of mind's relation with matter therefore turn out to be essentially the same: all objects are essentially 'feeling', and all 'feelings' are attached to objects. Feeling, however, is not entirely passive, but always trying to integrate itself into larger and more complete 'wholes', striving towards the Absolute in which everything will be fused in a single totality:

> Every mental element (to use a metaphor) strives to make itself a whole or to lose itself in one, and it will not have its company assigned to it by mere conjunction in presentation. Each struggles to develop itself by the weapon of identity, which gives strength by coalescence and enlargement by recall. And this effort to succeed by association with like characters may bring loss of life to the single member. To speak more strictly, each element tends (that is, moves unless prevented) by means of fusion and redintegration to give itself a context through identity of content, and in the result which is so made the element may not survive in distinguishable form. It is also a fact that the collision, which results in great part from this movement, causes pain and unrest; and I think we may see that the unrest cannot cease as long as the elements given are unable to form a whole possessed throughout of such a content that it suggests nothing out of harmony with anything else.[21]

Eliot's 'dark embryo' from which the poem is hatched is exactly such a restless movement towards a new harmony from discrete and discordant elements.[22] What is more important, however, is that in this Darwinian struggle to achieve coherence the workings of the mind, as it forms new wholes, and the working of the world, as it forms 'feeling' into objects, mirror each other. The process of the world is like the process of the mind and strives always to integrate individual elements into larger and more coherent wholes. What is 'objective' for Bradley is thus not what is opposite to mind: 'objectivity' is defined by the coherence which elements of feeling have achieved, and 'truth' is not a matter of accurately reporting what is objectively beyond the mind, but of forming a coherent view of the world or of the aspect of the world under discussion: 'Everything, from one point of view, is subjective; and everything, from another point of view, is objective; and there is no absolute point of view from which a decision may be pronounced.'[23]

The elements which are forever struggling, in Bradley's philosophy, to find themselves whole or to lose themselves in a greater whole, can thus, like everything else in Bradley, be regarded from two different aspects: we can see them either from the point of view of their internal coherence, assimilating discrete elements into their own unity, or we can see them from their external aspect, as participants in some greater totality. It is a distinction Eliot employs constantly in his early criticism. The work of art, as it fuses its numberless feelings into a new whole, achieves a unity of point of view which is 'objective' because it is as self-contained and coherent in its unification of feelings as anything in the world we usually see as being outside of ourselves. What we have to remember when Eliot uses the term 'objective' is always that, as he says in *Knowledge and Experience in the Philosophy of F.H. Bradley*, 'the objective world is only actual in one or another point of view, but . . . each point of view intends to be, not a point of view, but the world one and impersonal.'[24] Thus, Eliot wrote of Conrad that he 'has no ideas, but he has a point of view, "a world"; it can hardly be defined, but it pervades his work and is unmistakeable'.[25] The work of art is not 'objective' by being entirely divorced from the authorial consciousness, but by being a completely coherent amalgamation of feelings: it is a whole into which many elements have been subsumed. Eliot's main examplar of such 'objectivity' is Ben Jonson: Jonson's drama is, for Eliot, a 'world', one that is 'sufficiently large; it is a world of the poetic imagination':[26]

> The immediate appeal of Jonson is to the mind; his emotional tone is not in the single verse, but in the design of the whole. But not many people are capable of discovering for themselves the beauty which is to be found only after labour . . . When we say that Jonson requires study, we do not mean study of his classical scholarship or of seventeenth-century manners. We mean intelligent saturation in his work as a whole . . .[27]

The whole that is Jonson's work has to be studied in order to be made whole within our own point of view: it does 'not so much require the power of putting ourselves into seventeenth century London as it requires the power of setting Jonson in our London'.[28]

The view of art which emerges from Eliot's use of Bradley in relation to Conrad and Jonson would be the antithesis of an art of memory, for the work would be a self-subsistent entity whose wholeness we would remake by integrating it into our own contemporary experience.

However, in discussing Jonson Eliot marks out something that Jonson does not possess, what he calls the 'third dimension'. Jonson's is a wholeness entirely of its internal elements: the third dimension is the relationship of the work to an external totality of which it is to form a part. Initially Eliot distinguishes this as a matter of the depth of emotion to which the work gives access: the third dimension is 'not the difference between feeling and thought, or superior insight, superior perception, on the part of Shakespeare, but his susceptibility to a greater range of emotion, and emotion deeper and more obscure'.[29] The distinction is made more clear later in the essay: 'the polished veneer' of Jonson's work, Eliot says, 'reflects the lazy reader's fatuity; unconscious does not respond to unconscious; no swarms of inarticulate feelings are aroused'.[30] Essentially, therefore, what Jonson prevents is that process of personal association which is the fundamental element in the response of the ordinary sentimental person or the impressionistic critic, and yet without such association, it would appear, something is missing. The work has its internal coherence, but it does not point out beyond itself; the work can be integrated by us into the whole that is our awareness in the present, but it does not imply in its own operation its place within the larger organisation that is the literary tradition. That, too, is a Bradleian whole in which the elements strive to fuse themselves into a single harmonious unity:

> When we assume that a literature exists we assume a great deal: we suppose that there is one of the five or six (at most) great organic formations of history. We do not suppose merely 'a history', for there might be a history of Tamil literature, but a part of History, which for us is the history of Europe. We suppose not only a corpus of writings in one language, but writings and writers between whom there is a tradition; and writers who are not merely connected by a tradition in time, but who are related so as to be in the light of eternity contemporaneous, from a certain point of view, cells in one body.[31]

The contrast between 'History' and 'history' is the contrast between elements which remain — like personal associations — merely accidental, and those which — like the critic's impersonal associations — are fused together with a multitude of others in a new unity. Just as, within the poet's mind, unrelated experiences which remain in the ordinary man 'chaotic, irregular, fragmentary' are 'always forming new wholes', so in the whole body of literature there are writings which remain, however internally coherent, isolated and fragmentary, as opposed to those which form part of an enlarging and developing totality we call a tradition. The work which participates in a tradition will do so because the poet has allowed the material of the tradition to combine significantly with his own experience in the formation of his own new work. It is as though the tradition is forming its own new and more inclusive wholes by using the individual writer's mind, though at the same time this can only occur because the individual is able 'to write not merely with his own generation in his bones, but with a feeling that the whole literature of Europe from Homer and within it the whole literature of his own country has a simultaneous order and a simultaneous existence'.[32] 'Tradition and the Individual Talent', in its famous description of the dialectical relationship between the past and the present in the creation and the appreciation of art is nothing more, in some respects, than an application of Bradley's redintegrative conception of association: the whole tradition becomes the material, the elements, which lurk in the dark, awaiting their opportunity to find new universal connections through which they can suddenly fuse and come to consciousness in a new totality; equally, our consciousness of the new totality of the individual work changes the nature of the totality of the tradition to which it relates externally. The work which is created out of the tradition changes the tradition by its creation.

The importance of the external relations of the work lies not only, however, in the larger coherence of which it is thereby made a part: that larger coherence gives it access to associations that stretch back to the very beginnings of history, associations that reach down, therefore, to the deepest elements in the individual psyche. Like Conrad, whose *Heart of Darkness* made such a profound impression on him,[33] Eliot saw the human mind as containing 'all the past':[34] to travel back in time was the same as to delve into the depths of oneself. Thus,

the poet should know everything that has been accomplished in poetry (accomplished, not merely produced) since its beginnings – in order to know what he is doing himself. He should be aware of all the metamorphoses of poetry that illustrate the stratifications of history that cover savagery.[35]

The savage does not disappear, but is merely covered, and the poet, despite the fact that he 'is, in an impersonal sense, the most conscious of men', is 'the most and the least civilized and civilizable; he is the most competent to understand both the civilized and the primitive.'[36]

The reason for the paradoxical union of the cultivated and the savage is that the poet's multitudinous associative processes carry him to the very heart of darkness, to the depths of the self and the depths of the past. Shakespeare and the Jacobeans are greater than Jonson because,

> Their words have often a network of tentacular roots reaching down to the deepest terrors and desires. Jonson's most certainly do not; but in Beaumont and Fletcher we may think at times we find it. Looking closer, we discover that the blossoms of Beaumont and Fletcher's imagination draw no sustenance from the soil, but are cut and slightly withered flowers stuck into the sand ... the evocative quality of the verse of Beaumont and Fletcher depends upon a clever appeal to emotions and associations which they have not themselves grasped; it is hollow.[37]

In plumbing the depths of the mind through its associative processes, the poem links the savage and the civilized to an end which Eliot, in 1925, defined as identical with the purposes of psychoanalysis: 'what analytic psychology attempts to do for the individual mind, the study of history — including language and literature — does for the collective mind. Neglect of Greek means for Europe a relapse into unconsciousness.'[38] It is a relapse into unconsciousness because we would have lost control over part of the chain that connects us with the beginning of time; we would be able to integrate less of the historical experience of mankind into the whole which our tradition and our individual works of art strive to make as total as possible. We would be less able to reach the margins of those 'depths' into which we cannot peer. From its cultural tradition it is the business of the work of art 'to bring to convergence' — as Eliot described it in isolating the poetic qualities of a sermon — 'a multitude of fleeting but universal feelings' so that the words 'echo and linger in the mind'.[39] In the appropriate mind those echoing and lingering associations 'can be made to insinuate the whole history of a language and a civilization'.[40] The poem opens up the past through its associations, but opens it up so that we can see its wholeness. That is why the poet's essential task is 'a continual surrender of himself as he is at the moment to something which is more valuable',[41] for it is a submission to the 'accumulated wisdom of time'.[42] That wisdom, however, is inscribed in the history of a culture's art: poetry is, essentially, a memory of art, and thus 'the most individual part of [the poet's] work may be those in which the dead poets, his ancestors, assert their immortality most vigorously.'[43] The personal memories that constitute the domain of reminiscence are irrelevant to the associational process, because they represent no differentiation of feeling, no integration of an increased number of elements into a new totality. They play no part in History, though they may be participants in history, and thus, for Eliot, the poetry that depends upon personal memory, on the kinds of memory that show no increase in complexity through time, can never be successful: it draws on entirely inadequate depths of memory:

> It does not occur to Mr. Blunden that this love of one's own childhood, a passion which he seems to share with Lamb and Vaughan, is anything but a token of greatness. We all know the mood, and we can all, if we choose to relax to that extent, indulge in the luxury of reminiscence of childhood; but if we are at all mature and conscious, we refuse to indulge this weakness to the point of writing and poetizing about it; we know that it is something to be buried and done with though the corpse will from time to time find its way up to the surface . . .[44]

Compared to the sea of memory, our personal reminiscence is a floating corpse, and attention to that merely personal fund of memory is what Eliot takes to be typical of romanticism: in its concentration on the imagination it fails to develop the powers of memory and the sense of History that goes along with it, and it therefore requires no historical depth, no memory of its reader:

> To appreciate Herbert's sensibility we have to penetrate the thought and emotion of the time; we should know Andrewes and Hooker. In short, the emotion of Herbert is clear, definite, mature and sustained; whereas the emotion of Vaughan is vague, adolescent, fitful and retrogressive . . .[45]

Vaughan's art looks forward to romanticism as Eliot was to define and castigate it, an art without memory.

What Eliot asserted in the essays he wrote between 1917 and the mid-1920s was a sophisticated, more philosophical version of what Pound had been thrusting upon literary London in the years before Eliot's arrival on the scene. In 1914, Pound had announced in *Blast* that, 'All the past that is vital, all the past that is capable of living into the future is pregnant in the VORTEX, NOW.'[46] In the context of *Blast*'s explosive attack on the establishment, this might have been taken to mean that only the Vorticists were truly alive, but they were the only 'vital' ones because they were the only ones truly in touch with the past: 'The scientist does not expect to be acclaimed as a great scientist until he has discovered something. He begins by learning what has been discovered already. He goes from that point onward.'[47] The need for memory is, for Pound, a much more technical need than for Eliot: it is to know what has been done so that one can advance upon it that drives Pound back to the study of past art, rather than the need to know the 'stratifications of civilization' as matters of 'feeling'. But for Pound, much more than for Eliot, technique is itself an index of civilisation:

> It is not to be expected that knowledge of the human consciousness, or its most efficient registering material, language, can dispense with progress in method at least par with that of the particular sciences, nor that any one individual can escape the limitations of his confreres. No biologist expects to formulate a WHOLE NEW biology.[48]

Progress in technique is equivalent to progress in other areas of scientific knowledge and a general indicator of the vitality of a culture, but what the technique is there to fulfil is the specific historical instantiation of something that takes us back to Yeats: 'great works of art [are] lords over fact, over race-long recurrent moods.'[49] Each onward progress in technique only provides a means of recapturing something that goes back to the very beginnings of human consciousness. The associationist theory demanded that each forward movement of the mind in reverie was a return to the depths of the past, and Pound's insistence on making the past contemporary, on making it new, performs the same pattern:

> A return to origins invigorates because it is a return to nature and reason. The man who returns to origins does so because he wishes to behave in the eternally sensible manner. That is to say, naturally, reasonably, intuitively. He does not wish to do the right things in the wrong place, 'to hang an ox with trappings', as Dante puts it. He wishes not pedagogy but harmony, the fitting thing.[50]

And despite the ethos of scientific rationalism which Pound used as part of his propaganda for a new kind of poetry, what the poetry is intended to bring into the present is a transpersonal mind like the sea on which, for Yeats, our little minds are but a foam:

If Plato's ideas were the paradigms of reality in Plato's personal thought, their transmutation into phenomena takes us into the unknown. What we can assert is that Plato periodically caused enthusiasm among his disciples. And the Platonists after him have caused man after man to be suddenly conscious of the reality of the *nous*, of mind, apart from any man's individual mind, of the sea crystalline and enduring, of the bright as it were molten glass that envelops us, full of light.[51]

If Pound is still to be credited with 'modernising' Yeats's style — though Pound's style remains for several years a long way behind Yeats's in its modernity — then Yeats must be given credit for introducing Pound to that congeries of occult and anthropological speculation, particularly in the work of Allen Upward, which plays a significant part in the *Cantos*.

The paradox of Pound's writing, and of the critical attitudes which have developed in response to them, is that they insist on objectivity, on clarity, on precision, on the avoidance of all that might count as symbolic or suggestive, and that yet they are as obscure, as incomplete as the work of his modernist contemporaries who were less concerned to avoid the symbolic. There has been a persistent — and insistent — effort to separate Pound from Yeats and Eliot and to attach him to the so-called 'objectivist' school. Donald Davie has put this point of view most firmly: he quotes Pound's own comments on 'In a Station of the Metro', to the effect that he was trying to record 'the precise instant when a thing outward and objective transforms itself or darts into a thing inward and subjective', and comments:

Here once again one sees the traffic being run all the other way from the *symbolistes*. For to Pound it is the outward that transforms itself into the inward, whereas to the devotee of the objective correlative it is always the inward (the poet's mood or state of feeling) that seeks in the outward world something to correspond to itself.[53]

Davie is given support by Herbert Schneidau in his detailed study of the relations between Pound and Yeats on the question of symbolism. Schneidau takes a passage of Pound's from 1913 as pointing the direction in which his poetry was to move:

Mr. Yeats has been subjective; believes in the glamour and associations which hang near the words. 'Works of art beget works of art.'

He has much in common with the French symbolists. Mr. Hueffer believes in an exact rendering of things. He would strip words of all 'association' for the sake of the precise meaning.[54]

It is important to note the terms here, however: what Pound is distinguishing are the associations 'which hang near words': only a year later he was to be giving a more positive view of Yeats in answering the question, 'Is Mr. Yeats an Imagiste?':

No, Mr. Yeats is a symbolist, but he has written *des Images* ... There have always been two sorts of poetry which are, for me at least, the most 'poetic'; they are firstly, the sort of poetry which seems to be music just forcing itself into articulate speech, and secondly, the sort of poetry which seems as if sculpture or painting were just forced or forcing itself into words. The gulf between evocation and description, in this latter case, is the unbridgeable difference between genius and talent. It is perhaps the highest function of art that it should fill the mind with a noble profusion of sounds and images, that it should furnish the life of the mind with such accompaniment and surrounding. At any rate Mr. Yeats' work has done this in the past and continues to do so.[55]

Yeats is praised for his images that are like sculpture or painting coming over into words. Pound is drawing attention to the change in Yeats's style with which he himself has often been credited, but at the same time that sculptural poetry is successful in so far as it is not description but evocation. It is directed towards the evoking of emotion in the reader in exactly the same way that the objective correlative was — no matter what differences we might see in the genesis of the poem. And Pound's insistence that the end of poetry is the filling of the mind 'with a noble profusion of sounds and images' is something that sounds much closer to Yeats's 'emotion of multitude' than it does to the ascetic concentration on the singleness of the Image. It does not tend in the direction, at any rate, of attention to the values of the 'outer world as it existed in its own right'.[56]

The reason for the confusion lies, I suggest, in Pound's careful distinction between the role of association in relation to language and its role in relation to images. Pound's debt to Ford Madox Ford (or Hueffer, as he was until the War) lay in Ford's insistence on the *mot juste* because, as Pound paraphrases the doctrine of Conrad, 'all English words are instruments for exciting blurred emotions.'[57] This does not mean, however, that he wants to direct our attention to objects in separation from their power of evoking emotion: it is to get a precise evocation of emotion that one must have a precise description of the object. Description without evocation, however, is not great art. In the *ABC of Reading* he included association as one of the three elements the writer has to deal with in shaping a language, because 'the words have meanings which have "grown into the race's skin" . . . and the good writer chooses his words for their "meaning", but that meaning is not a set cut-off thing like the move of a knight or pawn on a chess board. It comes up with roots, with associations, with how and where the word is familiarly used or where it has been used brilliantly or memorably.'[58] In fact, in the definition of his three principles of poetry — phanopoeia, melopoeia, and logopoeia — in the *ABC of Reading*, Pound seems to make association — logopoeia — an over-arching concept that can subsume both of the others: the three principles involve:

I   throwing the object (fixed or moving) on to the visual imagination.
II inducing emotional correlation by the sound and rhythm of the speech.
III inducing both effects by stimulating the associations (intellectual or emotional) that have remained in the receiver's consciousness in relation to the actual words or word groups employed.[59]

That Pound was not primarily concerned with logopoeia — that that was Eliot's domain — he readily admitted,[60] but the real issue lies in the workings of phanopoeia, the throwing of images on the visual imagination, which Pound took to be central Imagist tenet.

Pound's belief that juxtapositions of images could convey ultimate truths about nature derives from Ernest Fenellosa's work on Chinese poetry, which suggested to Pound that the poetic image is 'a general equation of real knowledge'[61] and that 'everything is there, not merely by "suggestion" but by a sort of mathematical process of reduction.'[62] But in his later writings we find Pound reverting to the 'suggestive' view: 'There is a limited gamut of what will come over from Chinese verse without the rigours of Chinese technique — acoustic technique over and above the universal technique of matter and of visual suggestivity.'[63] The image may be turned towards the world in order to 'suggest some fundamental relation'[64] between objects, or it may be turned towards the reader's mind and to the evocation of emotion. In either case, the end which Pound seeks is probably best revealed by his definition of civilization in *Guide to Kulchur*:

> To define it ideogramicly we may start with the 'Listening to Incense'. This displays a high state of civilization. In the Imperial Court of Nippon the companions burnt incense, they burnt now one perfume, and now another, or a mixture of perfumes, and the accomplishment was both to recognize what had gone materially into the perfume and to cite apposite poems.
> The interest is in the blend of perception and association.
> It is a pastime neither for clods nor for the illiterate.[65]

It is the 'blend of perception and association' that Pound seeks; but what he hoped for from Fenellosa was exactly what Yeats and Eliot, in their different ways, had also been seeking — a means of justifying the connection between the associative connections of the poet and those of his audience. If the image was truly a configuration of the real the audience's associations do not count: the poem is teaching them the structure which they ought to perceive in the world. But if the image can still only 'suggest some fundamental relation', then the poem still needs its associative impact in order to focus the reader's attention on what cannot actually be stated directly in language.

It is Pound's failure to find an appropriate method of communication that has been the strongest charge against his work, and one that has been seen by Yvor Winters precisely in terms of an associationist conception of the mind: he writes of the *Cantos* that,

> The structure appears to be that of more or less free association, or progression through reverie. Sensory perception replaces idea. Pound, early in his career, adopted the inversion derived from Locke by the associationists: since all ideas arise from sensory impressions, all ideas can be expressed in terms of sensory impressions. But of course they cannot be: when we attempt this method, what we get is sensory impressions alone, and we have no way of knowing whether we have had any ideas or not.[66]

Donald Davie has tried to combat this by accepting its terms but making our inability to express ideas the essence of Pound's design:

> this state of not knowing whether we have ideas or not, may be

precisely the state of mind that Pound aimed to produce – and for good reasons. Perhaps by his arrangement of sensory impressions (that is to say, of images) Pound aimed to express, not 'ideas', some of which admittedly cannot be expressed in this way, but rather a state of mind in which ideas as it were tremble on the edge of expression . . . What we get in Canto XVII is not quite the idea of Venice held in the mind of the Venetian builder before he began to build; rather we have expressed the state of mind in the builder immediately before the idea crystallizes. In fact, the idea crystallizes only in the process of building, and the achieved building is the only crystallization possible.[67]

What Davie does here is the same as Eliot does with Hamlet in defining the objective correlative: he makes of the character in the poem the image of the state of mind of the author or reader. The builder will only know his emotion or idea when it is expressed (crystallised) in the completed building, as Hamlet could only know his emotion by objectifying it. The poet's job is to catch the state of mind of the emotion about to be objectified, and that state of mind is also the state of mind of the reader confronted with the images of the poem. Davie has turned Winters' criticism of the overall form of the poem by referring us to a specific element of content, from what the poem is doing as a structure to what it refers to in the world. But the dramatic presentation of the builder's state of mind before his idea has crystallised can be no justification of a poem which has failed to crystallise, no matter how many of its moments are descriptions of such crystallisation. Davie insists that there are moments when the apparently random pattern is drawn together, moments when the *forma*, the essential lines of force, are revealed. But it is in precisely those passages that Pound is offering us an idea, and an idea we can usually only come at through his prose. The poem cannot carry the burden of its own meaning by itself because we need the rest of the poet's writings to explain the specific associational patterns which the images emerge from.

Another critic who has tried to turn Winters' criticism is Daniel Pearlman, who has seen the *Cantos* as based on the same technique as the 'stream of consciousness' novel, the thoughts and images being 'causally determined by significant associations rather than by objective causal connections in the outside world'.[68] There is an enormous difference, however, between 'stream of consciousness' in a novel like *Ulysses* and 'stream of consciousness' in a poem like the *Cantos*. In the novel there is still a defined world of various points of view whose associative processes can be measured against each other in order to imply a 'real' world beyond. As a method of narration, 'stream of consciousness' still leaves us with a definite (if less immediately apprehensible) set of events narrated. In the *Cantos* there is nothing against which we can measure the associative connections of the poem: they are the world, one and only, that we encounter through the poem. We cannot compare the process of association between different characters, as in a novel, but can only refer to the poet himself for their elucidation.

Neither of these views takes account of the fact that associational poetry is not necessarily an account of the poet's associations, but is directed at the reader's: it is not reverie in the poet that is important, but the controlling of the inevitable reverie in the reader. Pound gives us an instance of his own reading experience in *Guide to Kulchur*:

> If I have, a few pages back, set a measure for music, I set another for poetry. No man can read Hardy's poem collected but that his own life, and forgotten moments of it, will come back to him, a flash here and an hour there. Have you a better test for true poetry?[69]

True poetry revitalises personal memory, and equally its acceptance by the memory is the standard of the truly valuable in culture. *Guide to Kulchur*, as Donald Davie has pointed out, makes a distinction between two kinds of memory, between what needs to be searched out from a book, and those that 'are in one as one's stomach or liver, one doesn't have to remember them, though they now and again make themselves felt'.[70] Culture is, for Pound, 'what is left after a man has forgotten all he set out to learn';[71] it is whatever has 'resisted the erosion of time and forgetfulness'.[72] And the business of the poet in learning the whole of what has been achieved by his predecessors is a matter of uncovering what cannot be allowed to be forgotten. The poet, in subject, in cadence, in the very texture of his technique – as Hugh Kenner has so brilliantly demonstrated in 'Blood for the Ghosts'[73] – calls back to the memory the works of the past. The layers of Canto 1, Andreas Divus's Renaissance Homer recreated through Pound's stylistic imitation of Anglo-Saxon epic, enact in the texture of the multiple imitations what Pound believed of all great poetry, that its ancestry stretches back through the tradition to 'god knows what "hidden antiquity"'.[74] In 1913 Pound had thought he was distinguishing himself from Yeats by insisting that Yeats believed that 'works of art beget works of art', but within a few years he had given that theory much more radical instantiation in his poetry than ever Yeats was to do. Pound's poetry operates not by quotation and by word association, as Eliot's does, but by the associations generated out of events retold and a style remade, each a recalling and a renewal of the past.

As memory became integral to Pound's technique it also became central to his conception of the purpose of poetry. The tradition which Pound identified in 1913 in his essay of that title was a poetic tradition:

> The two great lyric traditions which most concern us are that of the melic poets and that of Provence. From the first arose practically all the poetry of the 'ancient world', from the second practically all that of the modern.[75]

The same tradition, in 'Terra Italica' of 1931, had, however, come to be the underground current not only of a genre or a style or an art form, but of a memory with deeper implications:

> It may be arguable that Eleusinian elements persisted in the very early Church, and are responsible for some of the scandals. It is quite certain that the Church later emerges riddled with tendencies to fanatacism, with sadistic and masochistic tendencies that are in no way Eleusinian.
>
> It is equally discernible upon study that some non-Christian and inextinguishable source of beauty persisted throughout the Middle Ages maintaining song in Provence, maintaining the grace of Kalenda Maya.
>
> . . . the cult of Eleusis will explain not only general phenomena but particular beauties in Arnaut Daniel or in Guido Cavalcanti.[76]

The best art not only recalls previous art, making it new, it renews itself from some fundamental and lasting source of beauty: the literature of this tradition maintains the memory of the mysteries of Eleusis, and those mystic elements give beauty to the art that remembers them. Thus for Pound as for Yeats, at the back of the poetic memory is the memory of the gods: 'without gods, no culture'.[77] The process of memory is not merely one of value accruing to that which survives; something which survives does so because it is in harmony with the ultimate nature of reality, representing our essential relation with the world about us. Fenellosa's conception of the image as an indicator of forces actually at work in the world may not have been accurate for the individual image itself, but in terms of the memory to which poetry gives us access it is true for Pound, for the memory of art is also the memory of the gods, gods who symbolise man's proper relations with the natural world:

> There is a truce among the gods,
> Korè is seen in the North
> Skirting the blue-gray sea
> In gilded and russet mantle.
> The corn has again its mother and she, Leuconoë,
> That failed never women,
> Fails not the earth now.
>
> The tricksome Hermes is here;
> He moves behind me
> Eager to catch my words,
> Eager to spread them with rumour;
> To set upon them his change
> Crafty and subtle;
> To alter them to his purpose;
> But do thou speak true, even to the letter:
>
> 'Once more in Delos, once more is the altar a-quiver.
> Once more is the chant heard.
> Once more are the never abandoned gardens
> Full of gossip and old tales.'
>
> ('Surgit Fama'; *CSP*, p. 99)

The first and second stanzas represent here a conflict between the two impulses of poetry; on the one hand there is the principle of preservation and rebirth, symbolised by Korè and Leuconoë, goddesses of spring returning from the underworld, and on the other the principle of change, of the new not as renovation but as novelty – Hermes. The poem's conclusion is an assertion of ancient and repeatable truth, the return of fertility in the garden, but a garden that contains 'gossip and old tales' – the new and the old. Within the eternally recurrent is contained the temporal and ephemeral: the poem is an obeisance to the power of memory and the memory is of the powers that do not forget to return to fertilise the world. Art remembers not only the traditions of art, but a primitive and abiding truth of the human condition.

'Surgit Fama' asserts a continuity it only minimally enacts, but in 'Envoi', from 'Hugh Selwyn Mauberley', the poem in its textured allusiveness forms a matrix of associations which do contrive to suggest that they encompass the whole tradition:

Tell her that sheds
Such treasure in the air,
Recking naught else but that her graces give
Life to the moment,
I would bid them live
As roses might, in magic amber laid,
Red overwrought with orange and all made
One substance and one colour
Braving time.

Tell her that goes
With song upon her lips
But sings not out the song, nor knows
The maker of it, some other mouth,
May be as fair as hers,
Might, in new ages, gain her worshippers,
When our two dusts with Waller's shall be laid,
Siftings on siftings in oblivion,
Till change hath broken down
All things save Beauty alone.

(CSP, p. 215)

The poem's initial allusion is to Waller's 'Go Lovely Rose', whose form it imitates, but the poem's insistence is parallel to all those love poems of Yeats's in which the beloved's beauty is formed in part of the associations the poet brings to her, except that, for Pound, both girl and poem are equally carriers of a memory of Beauty from past into future. The poet's desire to make the passing beauty eternal — 'in magic amber laid' — is a falsification of its essence, a reduction of it to uniformity, for its real beauty lies not in 'braving time', but in collaborating with the time which 'sifts' perfection from passing experience even as it blends beauty into a 'sifting' of dust. Eternity is not transcendence of time, but an acceptance of its accumulations and a continual renewal of those in time. The aesthetic experience is generated, in the appropriate mind, out of the multiple — or multitudinous — echoes of past lyrics that the poem encloses; for, as John

J. Espey says, 'the echoes of the long line of English poets from Chaucer down are so varied and interwoven as to make a complete unravelling almost impossible.'[78] The poem is truly a vortex into which all of the living past is constantly rushing, and from which, in our minds, the echoes are constantly spreading out.

In the context of a poem like this it is less easy, I think, to claim that Pound's is, as D.S. Carne-Ross has argued, a poetry of 'simplicity' in which we 'feel that something is missing there; the whole reverberating dimension of inwardness', for there 'is no murmurous echo chamber where deeps supposedly answer to deeps . . .'[79] Carne-Ross, like Davie, would like to place Pound with those whom Eliot would describe as lacking the 'third dimension', through whose work 'unconscious does not respond to unconscious; no swarms of inarticulate feelings are aroused'. Kenner's analyses of the 'echoing' effect of Pound's language refutes this claim, I think, but we have to remember, if we use such apparent simplicity as a means of distinguishing Pound from Eliot and Yeats, that Yeats's original formulation of the 'emotion of multitude' was not offered at the level of verbal echo, of word association or allusion, nor even primarily at the level of symbol, but of plot:

> The Shakespearean drama gets the emotion of multitude out of the sub-plot which copies the main plot, much as a shadow upon the wall copies one's body in the firelight. We think of *King Lear* less as the history of one man and his sorrows than as the history of a whole evil time. Lear's shadow is in Gloucester, who also has ungrateful children, and the mind goes on imagining other shadows, shadow beyond shadow, till it has pictured the world. In *Hamlet*, one hardly notices, so subtly is the web woven, that the murder of Hamlet's father and the sorrow of Hamlet are shadowed in the lives of Fortinbras and Ophelia and Laertes, whose fathers, too, have been killed. It is so in all the plays, or in all but all, and very commonly the sub-plot is the main plot working itself out in more ordinary men and women, and so doubly calling up before us the image of multitude.[80]

For Yeats, the use of symbols to set 'the mind wandering from idea to idea, emotion to emotion' is only a variation on the traditional plot devices by which a dramatist such as Shakespeare set the audience's mind towards that outward flow of reverie. It was precisely such qualities that Pound thought he had found in Wyndham Lewis's series of paintings, *Timon*: the sequence, Pound wrote, suggested 'a complete world', making Lewis appear 'as a painter with an apparently unlimited subject-matter, a capacity for suggesting unlimited subject-matter'.[81] Lewis's paintings, according to Pound, were based on a 'pattern unit ... so simple that one can bear having it repeated many times'.[82] As Ronald Bush has commented, such a description is 'tantalizingly similar to the encyclopaedic inferno of the Cantos'.[83] Through the connection of the emotion of multitude, association at the level of phanopoeia rather than logopoeia, we can see how Pound's epic is derived from an associationist theory. Just as the drama must multiply plot to imply a world which we will create as we pass beyond the play into our associations, so Pound's central themes, the Descent and the Metamorphosis,[84] are — at least initially in the *Cantos* — echoed and shadowed until we have called up before us 'the image of multitude', 'an unlimited subject-matter'.

For the opening Canto, Pound goes back to the oldest memories of European culture, to Odysseus's descent and to the traditions recorded in Ovid's *Metamorphoses*. The poem seems to programmatically enact, therefore, Eliot's assertion that the poet is 'the most and the least civilized and civilizable', that through poetry we 'illustrate the stratifications of history that cover savagery'.[85] Both men saw the essence of art as memory, but what memory did for the human mind was very different for each of them. For Eliot the art of memory was the power of holding at bay primitive impulses always on the doorstep of modern man: poetry kept us conscious of the distance we had come and prevented us falling back into the abyss of a world of undifferentiated feeling, into the savage. For Pound, the art of memory kept alive what civilisation kept trying to conceal, to cover, to lose, a harmony with nature which was symbolised by the gods and had been the essence of the Eleusinian cults. But for both, loss of the historical depth of consciousness provided by the memory is a loss of our grasp upon the reality of the present. But because their poems are incomplete without our memories, our associations, they are like the Tiresias whom both incorporate into their major works: he can offer no more than a guide to the wisdom of which he is keeper; he opens the way to our descent into the underworld, the past, the depths of ourselves, but it is we who must make the journey. The open poem is turned towards us for its completion, to our memories for its fulfilment. It can never have the kind of coherence of structure we expect of other forms of poetry, because its real totality is composed not on the page, but in the fusing of what the poet offers with the multitudinous suggestions it generates in us. It journeys through us as we journey through it, and we are all sailors, like the Odysseus of Canto 1, on an 'ocean flowing backward', our only chart the memory of the tribe inscribed in the traditions of past art.

6 CLOSURES

The changes in poetic style which we describe as 'modernism' were rooted in the apparently stable world of the years before the First World War. The great works of modernism, however, are the products of the war's aftermath, as though to encompass the enormity of the historical experience a completely new scale, a new ambition was required of the writers. Whether we are looking at *The Waste Land* or the *Cantos* or *The Tower* (or even *Ulysses* or *Women in Love* or *Mrs. Dalloway*) what we find are experiments originally directed at capturing the subtlety of individual thought, the fleeting movement of sensibility, states of consciousness to be saved from the destructive passage of time, turned upon the effort to match themselves against the destructive processes of history. 'Tradition', wrote Eliot in 1919 in 'Tradition and the Individual Talent', 'involves, in the first place, the historical sense'.[1] The historical sense is the core of modernism's burgeoning achievement after 1918: it is a change wrought by history and by the effort to incorporate history into the patterns of art. The moment of that transformation is dramatised in Yeats's 'Meditations in Time of Civil War':

> I climb to the tower-top and lean upon broken stone,
> A mist that is like blown snow is sweeping over all,
> Valley, river, and elms, under the light of a moon
> That seems unlike itself, that seems unchangeable,
> A glittering sword out of the east. A puff of wind
> And those white glimmering fragments of the mist sweep by.
> Frenzies bewilder, reveries perturb the mind;
> Monstrous familiar images swim to the mind's eye.

> (*CP*, p. 231)

The calm unchanging scene, measured by the lines that move firmly to their rhymes, is both familiar and 'unlike itself'; a 'puff of wind' and the whole pattern is suddenly altered, for instead of seeing the landscape through the mist, the mist is suddenly in focus, and the landscape a mere background; a 'puff of wind' and suddenly we are in the midst of 'monstrous familiar images', images we had locked into the background of our mind because we thought them irrelevant to the ordered world we had created. It is not just another shift in awareness to be recorded by the delicate instruments of the perfected art; it is a transformation which challenges the very foundation of the art, turning the tower from aesthetic and symbolic artifact back into military stronghold, turning history back upon itself.

That turning back of history was what Spengler's *Decline of the West* gave voice to: 'We no longer believe in the power of reason over life,' wrote Spengler in 1919, 'we feel that life governs reason.'[2] Throughout the nineteenth century, European ideologies had placed history at the very centre of their conception of the world and whether it was Hegel's Christian *logos* unfolding itself in time, or Marx's class conflict in dialectical progression, or even Darwinian evolution through struggle, all conceived of history as essentially open to rational investigation, and justifying, by its patterns, the rational progress of mankind. What gave Spengler his popularity, however, was not just his pessimism about the future of the West, his return to a cyclic rather than a linear conception of historical process, it was that while reversing the pattern of nineteenth-century ideologies of history he maintained the centrality of history in our experience, and maintained the belief that we could understand it rationally, even if we could not control it rationally. But within nineteenth-century historiography there had been developing a very different attack on history, an attack not on 'progressive' theories of history, but on the validity of the historical discipline upon which such theories were based. Almost as soon, indeed, as history had been raised to the level of First Mover by Hegel, the foundations of history's claim to truth was challenged by Schopenhauer, who argued that it could know only particulars, and that any general conclusions it drew were no more than a misuse of language, treating abstract terms as though they were equivalent to the general laws of the physical sciences. History, Schopenhauer insisted, was essentially literature: its value lay in its fulfilment of the same criteria we apply to works of literature, and it had to stop, therefore, trying to unpack the significance of events by tracing chains of cause and effect, and had to begin to find significance where literature found it, in an event's expression of a unique personality, in its revelation of 'the depths of the human heart'.[3] The historian, like the poet or dramatist, must regard the figures in his narration for their own sake, and not for any end to which they contributed. If, however, history is essentially an art rather than a science, and if literature is a higher, more accurate, form of awareness of the past than historical narration, then the history of literature and of art must represent a higher form of

history, of the true development of mankind, than the history of
political or economic events. It was this transition that Burckhardt was
to make: 'history finds in poetry not only one of its most important
but also one of its purest and finest sources.'[4] Understanding the past
is not, for Burckhart, a matter of charting economic and political
changes, but of achieving sympathetic insight into the 'spirit' of the
past by way of its creative legacy. Like literary interpretation, however, the historian's construction was his own: there was no truth by
which it could be measured, no way of disproving it. Its value was a
literary value, resting on the insight it allowed us into the relations
between characters and events, to be criticised only as one might
criticise an author's insight into his own characters.

Hegel's heir in nineteenth-century historiography is Marx, insisting
that historical consciousness is the means towards realising the true
nature of the struggle to create the future; Schopenhauer's heir is
Nietzsche, asserting that historical consciousness is the cause of modern
man's decline, his collapse into *aboulie*. Nietzsche carries Schopenhauer's attack on history beyond a merely intellectual debate about
its value as truth, to a moral debate about history's effect on our
capacities as human agents. For Nietzsche, action is born out of 'forgetfulness', because an awareness of historical time inevitably saps
man's capacity to believe in the significance of his own actions:

> even a happy life is possible without remembrance, as the beast
> shows; but life in the true sense is absolutely impossible without
> forgetfulness. Or, to put my conclusion better, there is a degree . . .
> of rumination, of 'historical sense', that injures and fatally destroys
> the living thing, be it a man or a people or a system of culture.[5]

An excess of the 'historical sense' was, for Nietzsche, the central
flaw, the corrupting disease of modern consciousness:

> Let me give a picture of the spiritual events in the soul of modern
> man. Historical knowledge streams on him from sources that are
> inexhaustible, strange incoherences come together, memory opens
> all its gates and yet is never wide enough, nature busies herself to
> receive all the foreign guests, to honour them and put them in their
> places. But they are at war with each other, violent measures seem
> necessary, in order to escape destruction of one's self . . . The
> modern man carries inside him an enormous heap of indigestible
> knowledge stones that occasionally rattle together in his body . . .[6]

Having so much knowledge at his disposal man ceases to be an actor in the world and comes to regard himself as an on-looker: the aesthetic character of historical awareness turns modern man into an aesthete of human drama: 'modern man . . . is continually having a world panorama unrolled before his eyes by the historical artists. He is turned into a restless dilettante spectator and arrives at a condition when even great wars and revolutions cannot affect him beyond the moment.'[7] But one cannot escape from historical consciousness into more than a momentary forgetfulness, and Nietzsche's response to the modern condition is not to seek the overthrow of history, but to counteract its aestheticising effects through aesthetic experience, by using literature to produce a life-enhancing rather than life-denying sense of the past. Nietzsche's prescription is for a history that recognises its function as literature, and whose objectivity is that of the artist, not the scientist:

> We understand by [objectivity] a certain standpoint in the historian, who sees the procession of motive and consequence too clearly for it to have an effect on his own personality. We think of the aesthetic phenomenon of the detachment from personal concern with which the painter sees the picture and forgets himself . . . But it is only a superstition to say that the picture given to such a man by the object really shows the truth of things. Unless it be that objects are expected in such moments to paint or photograph themselves by their own activity . . . To think objectively, in this sense, of history is the work of the dramatist: to think one thing with another, and weave the elements into a single whole . . .[8]

The business of the historian is the same as the business of the artist: it is to raise and ennoble events, taking the banal and turning it into a universal symbol: 'its real value lies in inventing ingenious variations on a probably commonplace theme, in raising the popular melody to a universal symbol and showing what a world of depth, power and beauty exists in it.'[9] Hayden White has summed up Neitzsche's position as being,

> the dissolution of the dream of a method by which history-in-general can be endowed with any sense at all. The historian is liberated from having to say anything about the past; the past is only an occasion for his invention of ingenious 'melodies'. Historical representation becomes once more all story, no plot, no explanation,

no ideological implication at all — that is to say, 'myth' in its original meaning as Nietzsche understood it, 'fabulation'.[10]

The historian is replaced by the artist and through the artist man is given a 'myth' by which action can again become purposive, through which we can be released from the destructive effects of historical consciousness. The value of history is the same as the value of art: its value in enhancing life, in directing us towards the future, encouraging creative activity.

Nietzsche's conception of history was the most radical challenge to nineteenth-century ideologies of history, because it challenged their ability to know the past at all. In transferring value back to the artist, however, Nietzsche was saving the poet, particularly, from the marginality into which developments in science, in technology, even in the novel, had cast him. If history was shaped by the myth-maker, both in the sense of his shaping the past and in the sense that that shaping shaped the future, then the poet was situated again at the very centre of historical process. The effete spectator, the *flaneur*, the passive aesthete, the decadent, all those models of the poet alienated from the sources of power in his society could be cast aside: the controller of myths was the true source of power in his society. The challenge of the new mythic history was, according to Nietzsche, that it should reverse the implicit motto of the older history — 'let the dead bury the — living'[11] — by showing how much of the past could be assimilated into a truly healthy historical awareness, one that recognised its creative relation to action in the future. The index of the health of a culture is, for Nietzsche, precisely its capacity to incorporate history without submitting to the debilitating historical sense of the modern world:

> To fix this degree and the limits to the memory of the past, if it is not to become the gravedigger of the present, we must see clearly how great is the 'plastic power' of a man or a community or a culture. I mean the power of specifically growing out of oneself, of making the past and strange one body with the near and the present, of healing wounds, of replacing what is lost, repairing broken moulds ... The deeper the roots of a man's inner nature, the better will he take the past into himself; and the greatest and most powerful nature would be known by the absence of limits for the historical sense to overgrow and work harm.[12]

It is the challenge of Nietzsche's conception of history — implicitly if not explicitly[13] – which Yeats, Eliot and Pound try to meet through their poetry of memory: it is a poetry which seeks to test itself against the measure of an 'absence for the historical sense to overgrow and work harm', which seeks to incorporate all of the past into its own inner nature. Indeed, Nietzsche's conception of the 'historical sense' is echoed in 'Tradition and the Individual Talent', for Nietzsche's 'past and strange' that is 'one body with the near and present', becomes Eliot's 'perception, not only of the pastness of the past, but of its presence'; and Eliot's 'sense of the timeless as well as the temporal and of the timeless and the temporal together',[14] repeats Nietzsche's demand that we know 'the right time to forget as well as the right time to remember, . . . when it is necessary to feel historically and when unhistorically'.[15] By 1914, Nietzsche had ceased to be fashionable in Britain,[16] but it was Nietzsche's conception of history which offered, in the midst of the historical crisis of the war, a new conception of the role of the poet that gave him back a sense of power equal to the scale of the historical events by which he was surrounded.

Theoretically, Nietzsche's conception of history was as 'open' as the associationist conception of poetry, for history was there to be 'played' in as many different melodies as there were historians and artists to perform it, but in effect it was precisely its own theoretical openness which the mythic conception of historical knowledge had, in performance, to deny: the myth which art offered us had to be believed in as the one and only relevant myth if it was to save us from the 'inexhaustible, strange incoherences' that are offered when 'memory opens all its gates'. The philosopher's consciousness of the real nature of historical knowledge must not be allowed to intervene to prevent our acceptance of the presiding myth that will save us from too much unassimilable knowledge: 'the unrestrained historical sense,' Nietzsche asserts, 'pushed to its logical limits, uproots the future, because it destroys illusions',[17] and our recovery, despite our knowledge of their real nature, lies in recovering our illusions about history. It is within this paradoxical awareness that the modernist poet operates, on the one hand conscious of history (the discipline) as an illusion, and on the other knowing his own centrality to the creation of the illusions that make history (the lived experience), and yet, at the same time, having to believe his own illusions that history may be shaped to an acceptable pattern. Thus the poet has to close the theoretical openness of history (the past) in order to impose himself upon history (the future). And the closure of the past into a single myth is also the closure of memory. It was because they were developing an art of memory that Yeats,

Eliot and Pound could see themselves as central to the historical crisis they were living through: their theory answered Nietzsche's demand for a healthy incorporation of the past, it reconnected past and future in a situation in which other theories of history seemed to have collapsed before historical fact, but the need to shape the future through a myth of the past drew an insistent circle around what could be counted as the relevant past, and what, therefore, could be counted as relevant closure for the open work. In the end they wanted to enclose their poem within the single healthy pattern of memory that would be the chosen history of a society which recognised and promulgated the value of memory itself.

In *Guide to Kulchur* Pound reveals the tensions between the openness of the mythic history that is the creation of the present and the desire to close it into its single 'real' pattern. 'We do NOT know the past in chronological sequence', he asserts; 'It may be convenient to lay it out anaesthetized on the table with dates pasted on here and there, but what we know we know by ripples and spirals eddying out from us and from our own time.'[18] Such relativity of historical consciousness is also his lesson to John Buchan when Buchan had failed to take Cromwell's banking activities sufficiently seriously:

> Buchan has a little mislaid the real reason for writing and reading history, namely that the past should be a light for the future. That the purpose of history is instruction, that is to make people think and to guide their thought toward what will elucidate today and tomorrow.[19]

This 'new' historical sense, however, was to form its own closure in Pound's view of the past, insisting on a single central tradition:

> The 'new' historic sense in our time demands this tradition, as it demands whole slabs of the record in latin of such men as Claudius Salmasius (and at the moment neither I nor Prof. X.Q. nor anyone else really knows their names or their number). We may know that whole beams and ropes of real history have been shelved, overclouded and buried. As in more recent times the thought of Van Buren, A. Johnson, A. Jackson . . .[20]

The meaning of 'real' here? Pound has switched from a relative to a definitive view of history: history's relativity is the means of attacking traditional, deadening history, but one's own history has to have all the certainty of ultimate truth:

No one has claimed that the Malatesta cantos are obscure. They are openly volitionist, establishing, I think clearly, the factive personality, Sigismundo, an entire man. The founding of the Monte dei Paschi as the second episode has its importance. There we find the discovery, or at any rate the establishment, of the true bases of credit, to wit the abundance of nature and the responsibility of the whole people.

As history becomes better understood I think this emphasis will become steadily more intelligible to the general reader.[21]

The *Cantos* are no mystery for Pound: 'they are the tale of the tribe', but the sense of the poet's centrality to history upon which that idea is founded demands that he insist on his own tale as 'history' itself. The same play upon the meanings of 'history' can be seen in Yeats when he describes the moment at which an artist 'fixes the finer elements of national character for generations':

> up to that moment literature has tried to express everybody's thought, history being considered merely a chronicle of facts, but now, at the instant of revelation, writers think the world but their palette and if history amuses them, it is but, as Goethe says, because they would do its personages the honour of naming after them their own thoughts.[22]

The poet plays with the 'history' of the past, but in doing so he truly makes the history to come, and when that new history is established it will see the past as 'real' which the poet made in play. The relativity of historical perspective which these views imply in Yeats and Pound, was already built into Eliot's Bradleian heritage. Bradley's conception of the partiality of all historical understanding is revealed and, at the same time, qualified in the following passage of Eliot's from 1929:

> The materialistic interpretation of history is of course like any other interpretation of history, an aspect of history. It is just as genuine an aspect as any other. Like every other interpretation of history, it asserts itself to be the 'fundamental' interpretation: and if one went into the matter thoroughly, one would question it, not from the point of view of any other interpretation, but from the point of view of an observer who believes that any interpretation of history is merely a selection of a particular abstracted series of causes and effects, and is valid only from a particular point of view.[23]

The implication of a point of view which stands outside of all the interpretive schemas that constitute history is thoroughly unBradleian.[24] When, in 'Tradition and the Individual Talent', Eliot had defined the historical sense as 'a sense of the timeless as well as of the temporal and of the timeless and the temporal together',[25] he was describing what happened within a historical point of view that united past and present in a single, and, as it were, contemporaneous whole. But in 1929 he is asserting the superiority of a point of view which sees the unreality of all historical points of view, their only limited validity. Such an attack on others' historical viewpoints, however, is, like Pound's, the tactic of aggression: the demolition of historical perspectives achieved, the singleness of history insistently returns to justify the particular path towards the future the writer wishes to assert. Thus already, in 1926, Eliot had picked out two sentences from a book he was reviewing which revealed the direction he was moving in: 'Few have had a finer sense of the value of historical tradition than Hooker. To him the unity and continuity of history was neither a phrase nor a fallacy, but a practical truth as well as an inspiration.'[26] Eliot, about to commit himself to the religious tradition of which Hooker is one of the original thinkers, looks back into history and finds the past complimenting him on his choice of tradition by insisting that it is the true medium of historical continuity, historical unity.

In Schopenhauer, Burckhardt and Nietzsche, the poet became the model for the historian; having taken on the mantle of historical arbiters, the poets became defenders of the singleness of history which it had been the philosophers' task to challenge. The incomplete work of art, dependent for its full existence on the reader's associations, demanded an insistent closure of history in order to define the track of memory which linked its present existence with the depths of the past. That closure of the past into a single strand was also, however, a closure of the future, an insistence that society be moulded to the pattern which would be a living embodiment of the continuity of memory upon which the poem was founded. The multitudinous meanings of the literary work must not be released into an equally multitudinous set of historical perspectives, but into a history whose univocal meaning would resolve each of these multitudinous memories back into single shared future. Nietzsche, faced by the sceptical openness of history which was sapping the strength from modern man, asked of the poets a closure through myth that we might regain our certainty in the face of the future; the poets, writing out of a parallel conception of a radically open poetry, demanded of history the enclosing counterbalance to the incompletions of their art.

7 YEATS: THE LOSS AND RECOVERY OF MEMORY

It was Yeats's belief that 'nations, races, and individual men are unified by an image, or bundle of related images, symbolical or evocative of the state of mind which is, of all states of mind not impossible, the most difficult to that man, race, or nation.'[1] Parnell had been such an image to the Irish nation, uniting it by being what was most difficult for it to model itself upon: 'I had seen Ireland in my own time turn from the bragging rhetoric and gregarious humour of O'Connell's generation and school, and offer herself to the solitary and proud Parnell as to her anti-self, buskin followed hard on sock.'[2] By 1907, however, Yeats was to feel that a change had come upon Ireland that had dispossessed it of the barest conditions for such a unity of the whole people:

> Poetical tragedy, and indeed, all the more intense forms of literature, had lost their hold on the general mass of men in other countries as life grew safe . . . I always knew this, but I believed that the memory of danger, and the reality of it seemed near enough sometimes, would last long enough to give Ireland her opportunity. I could not foresee that a new class, which had begun to rise to power under the shadow of Parnell, would change the nature of the Irish movement, which, needing no longer great sacrifices, nor bringing any great risk to individuals, could do without exceptional men, and those activities of the mind that are founded on the exceptional moment.[3]

It is the 'memory of danger' that will make possible still both heroic action and the intense forms of literature — each depends upon and feeds the potentialities of the other — because danger forces every mind to reach to what is fundamental and impersonal in itself, to what it shares with its whole culture and race. In such situations each mind can participate in the kind of intelligence Yeats found in John Shawe-Taylor: 'something simple and impersonal within them which is, as I believe, imaged in the fire of their minds, as in the shape of their bodies and faces . . . It is as though they have sunk a well through the soil where our habits have been built, and where our hopes take root or lie uprooted, to the lasting rock and the living stream.'[4] That potentiality does not exist for Ireland's new class, the class that consisted of Catholic shopkeepers and businessmen, the new urban middle classes. Looking back to the efforts of his own mentor in nationalism, John O'Leary, Yeats realised that his fight had been misplaced — history had deceived them about who their real opponent was:

> John O'Leary had spent much of his thought in unavailing war with the agrarian party, believing it the root of change, but the fox that crept into the badger's hole did not come from there. Power passed to small shopkeepers, to clerks, to that very class who had seemed to John O'Leary so ready to bend to the power of others, to men who had risen above the traditions of the countryman, without learning those of cultivated life or even educating themselves, and who because of their poverty, their ignorance, their superstitious piety, are much subject to all kinds of fear. Immediate victory, immediate utility, became everything, and the conviction, which is in all who have run great risks for a cause's sake, in the O'Leary's and Mazzinis as in all rich natures, that life is greater than the cause, withered, and we artists, who are the servants not of any cause but of mere naked life, and above all of that life in its nobler forms, where joy and sorrow are one, Artificers of the Great Moment, became as elsewhere in Europe protesting individual voices.[5]

The artist is alienated from the purposes of the 'whole people' because the people themselves have lost touch with the images that made them whole, made them heroic. The two pillars of Yeats's early conception of society, the peasant and the educated city person, both of whom have a memory that invigorates their sense of life and gives them, from their literature, models for action and for contemplation, have been supplanted by this new, cultureless class:

> All who have any old traditions have something of aristocracy, but we have had opposing us from the first, though not strongly from the first, a type of mind which had been without influence in the generation of Grattan, and almost without it in that of Davis, and which has made a new nation of Ireland, that was once old and full of memories.[6]

That new class is not merely a political adversary, it is a destruction of the very foundations in the mind of all that makes culture possible, both the poet's and hero's culture, the foundations of old memories.

The dynamics of Yeats's politics, taking him from nationalism in the 1890s to support for the dying Anglo-Irish aristocracy in the years after Ireland had achieved her independence, are provided by his search for a suitable memory, based in the life of the community, for his poetry. In the 1890s Yeats had seen in Ireland, and especially in the peasant, a culture which had not yet been uprooted, where 'civilization has not driven its plough too deep'[7] to destroy the recollections that welded present art to the depths of the past. But the virtues of the peasant were not virtues stemming directly from being 'close to the land'; they were virtues originating in sustained and continuous memory, virtues which Yeats, in 'Poetry and Tradition', when he was moving to an identification with Anglo-Ireland, could transfer directly to the aristocracy. Both were valuable for the same reasons, for they 'look backward to a long tradition' and have therefore 'held to whatever pleased them'.[8] The peasant's value lay in his being the antithesis of the industrial world of modern England, and Ireland as a whole took its significance from its refusal of that commercial world where,

> The mere business of living, of making money, of amusing oneself, occupies people more and more, and makes them less and less capable of the difficult art of appreciation. When they buy a picture it generally shows a long-current idea, or some conventional form that can be admired in that lax mood one admires a fine carriage or fine horses in; and when they buy a book it is so much in the manner of the picture that it is forgotten, when its moment is over, as a glass of wine is forgotten.[9]

That which is 'long-current', but not ancient, survives only because it is so easily forgotten as to seem a novelty when something similar recurs. In Ireland, on the other hand, 'there is no river or mountain that is not associated in the memory with some event or legend'.[10] Even the Catholicism of the peasant makes itself acceptable to Yeats when he sees it not as a set of theological beliefs, but as a system of memory:

> The makers of religions have established their ceremonies, their form of art, upon fear of death, upon the hope of the father in his child, upon the love of man and woman. They have even gathered into their ceremonies the ceremonies of more ancient faiths, for fear

a grain of the dust turned into crystal in some past fire, a passion that had mingled with the religious idea, might perish if the ancient ceremony perished.[11]

Yeats's nationalism in the 1890s is founded on the fundamental opposition between remembering Ireland and forgetful England, but the rise of the new class was to introduce into Ireland a fifth column of that world it seemed to have refused.

In his nationalist commitment Yeats saw the Anglo-Irish as the equivalent in Ireland to the forgetfulness of English culture. It was a class which has divorced itself from the nation and its past, caught in a 'curious imaginative sterility resulting from their antagonism to the life about them, which until recently has cut them off from the foundations of literature, and left their imaginations cold and conventional'.[12] Then Yeats had seen the artists of the new Ireland as people who 'have laboured to be citizens, not merely of that passing and modern Ireland of prosaic cynicism and prosaic rivalries which it may be their duty to condemn, but of that eternal and ancient Ireland which has lived in old times';[13] people, in other words, who were transcending the historical divisions of contemporary Ireland by a return to the past. But the Ireland that was 'old and full of memories' had not fallen to the power of England, but to the power of those who were the sons and daughters of the peasantry, people who, in moving to the towns, had lost the culture that connected them to the past of the folk without gaining the culture that would connect them to the past of the cultivated. In Ireland the poet was left to find his appropriate audience in the same way that Yeats envisaged the Elizabethan dramatist as finding his:

Realism is created for the common people and was always their peculiar delight, and it is the delight to-day of all whose minds, educated alone by schoolmasters and newspapers, are without memory of beauty and emotional subtlety. The occasional humorous realism that so much heightened the emotional effect of Elizabethan tragedy — Cleopatra's old man with an asp, let us say — . . . was made at the outset to please the common citizen standing on the rushes of the floor; but the great speeches were written by poets who remembered their patrons in the covered galleries.[14]

The poets 'remembered their patrons' by remembering the importance of memory to the appreciation of poetry; Yeats would find such memory, in the end, only among an aristocracy in Ireland that was on the point of extinction, but who represented a living tradition of memory that modern Ireland was, in imitation of modern England, trying to stamp out.

The conflict that was having to be fought in two different directions at the same time – against England and against the new classes in Ireland – is given by Yeats in historical disguise in his essay on Edmund Spenser, written in 1902. Yeats sees Spenser as kind of English mirror image of his own condition, for Spenser represents, in England, the last of the old culture that modern business culture is about to exterminate, but represents, in Ireland, precisely that destructive English culture beginning to impose itself on the world, while Yeats, as a young man in England, had represented the exiled spirit of old Ireland, but returned to Ireland discovered the English spirit amongst the Irish themselves destroying the values he wished to preserve. Imagining the scene at Spenser's funeral, and the poets who gathered there, Yeats writes:

> Like him they belonged, for all the moral zeal that was gathering like a London fog, to that indolent, demonstrative Merry England that was about to pass away ... If one of those poets who threw his copy of verses into the earth that was about to close over his master were to come alive again, he would find some shadow of the life he knew, though not the art he knew, among young men in Paris, and would think that his true country. If he came to England he would find nothing but the triumph of the Puritan and the merchant . . . He had lived in the last days of what we may call the Anglo-French nation, the old feudal nation that had been established when the Norman and the Angevin made French the language of court and market.[15]

'Anglo-French', of course, echoes 'Anglo-Irish': the paradox of Spenser's career, for Yeats, was that in Ireland Spenser was involved in the destruction of the culture which, in its memories and its nobility, was closest in spirit to his own Anglo-French, and most opposed to the commercial mentality:

> When Spenser wrote of Ireland he wrote as an official, and out of thoughts and emotions that had been organised by the State. He was the first of many Englishmen to see nothing but what he was desired to see. Could he have gone there as a poet merely, he might have found among its poets more wonderful imaginations than even among those islands of Phaedria and Acrasia. He would have found

among wandering story-tellers, not indeed his own power of rich sustained description, for that belongs to lettered ease, but certainly all the kingdom of Faery, still unfaded, of which his own poetry was but a troubled image.[16]

Spenser, in other words, failed to rescue the Anglo-French from extinction at the hands of the Puritans because he could not do what Yeats had done — go collecting among the believers in 'faery', among those whose memories are 'unfaded'. But if that class and that life was itself being destroyed, if the puritans in their new disguise of the Catholic middle classes were themselves taking over Ireland, then the poet's only choice — if he was not to betray the sources and the ends of his art — was support of the aristocracy that was being ousted as the Celtic world itself had been ousted by England. That Yeats's Anglo-Irish had been responsible for the destruction of Celtic life in its heroic form was no bar to his support of them as an established social form that preserved memory. Would the peasantry have kept their culture if it had not been organised around the stable centre of the 'big house'? Would they ever have become conscious of the memory the past bequeathed to them had it not been for the Protestants who translated their epics and made them available again to the world? As the century wore on Yeats's answer to such questions would be an ever more insistent 'no':

How should the world be luckier if this house,
Where passion and precision have been one
Time out of mind, became too ruinous
To breed the lidless eye that loves the sun?
And the sweet laughing eagle thoughts that grow
Where wings have memory of wings, and all
That comes of the best knit to the best? Although
Mean roof-trees were the sturdier for its fall
How should their luck run high enough to reach
The gifts that govern men, and after these
To gradual Time's last gift, a written speech
Wrought of high laughter, loveliness and ease?

'Upon a House Shaken by the Land Agitation' (*CP*, p. 106) defies all who would overthrow anything based on the acquisitions of 'gradual Time': the Anglo-Irish have become the preservers of memory, their superiority founded on their consciousness of the past — 'wings have memory of wings'. Such graces can only exist where 'time' is 'out of mind' and where mind is the product of time. No personal memory could equal that range, and it is the poet's duty to preserve memory whatever its form, to preserve the pattern of life that embodies continuity with the past, those roofs that grow as naturally from the past as a tree. Once, the Anglo-Irish might have had to learn from the peasantry the memories they preserved of an almost forgotten Ireland, but who would preserve the peasantry against the seductive power of a commercial world losing memory as it gained in strength?

For the romantics it was loss of contact with the shaping spirit of the universe, the formative spirit of the imagination, that led to a sense of alienation from the world and from the best of oneself. It is loss of memory that is the equivalent and haunting fear of the poet who bases his work on associationist principles. In the years after 1900, Yeats was confronted everywhere by what he saw as the erosion of memory: Ireland was no longer a bulwark against the amnesia of the modern world, but 'pure poetry' he no longer saw as a viable possibility. Aestheticism ceded the world to the enemy but, more importantly, it destroyed the preconditions of its own success, for it shut itself off from the communal mind which operated as the test of the poet's escape from mere 'idle fantasy', a purely subjective pattern of association. Poetry had to mix with the world if it was to continue to appeal not only to this present world, but to the future, and in mixing with the world had to find other means of expression than the pure 'sensationalism' of Hallam and the aesthetic school. In 'Art and Ideas', in 1913, Yeats records his shift away from his earlier principles – 'those of Arthur Hallam in his essay upon Tennyson'[17] – to a new aesthetic, but it is one designed to incorporate more and more varied forms of experience into the art of memory than Hallam's conceptions would allow; it is no denial of the past:

> The arts are very conservative and have a great respect for those wanderers who still stitch into their carpets among the Mongolian plains religious symbols so old they have not even a meaning. It cannot be they would lessen an association with one another and with religion that gave them authority among ancient peoples. They are not radicals, and if they deny themselves to any it can only be to the *nouveau riche*, and if they have grown rebellious it can only be against something that is modern . . .[18]

Art is rebellious only in defence of its relationship with the past, even if what it seeks is 'the spontaneity of gesture or of some casual emotional phrase'.[19] The refusal of the contemporary world and its debates that had been the escape of Yeats and his friends in the 1890s, had in fact been a denial of serious art, because it had been a denial of the traditions of art. Even ideas could be contained — indeed, were perhaps necessary — to the associative recall of the past:

> We knew that system of popular instruction was incompatible with our hopes, but we did not know how to refute it and so turned away from all ideas. We would not even permit ideas, so greatly had we come to distrust them, to leave their impressions on our senses. Yet works of art are always begotten by previous works of art, and every masterpiece becomes the Abraham of a chosen people. When we delight in a spring day there mixes, perhaps, with our personal emotion an emotion Chaucer found in Guillaume de Lorris, who had it from the poetry of Provence; we celebrate our draughty May with an enthusiasm made ripe by more meridian suns; and all our art has its image in the Mass that would lack authority were it not descended from savage ceremonies taught amid what perils and by what spirits to naked savages.[20]

Without ideas as well as emotions, that associational chain that connects our poetic experiences back to the most distant past, that makes our poetic experience out of the connection with the past, would be impossible. Art must inevitably oppose 'systems of popular instruction', 'the nouveau riche', all those who are in their very being deniers of the 'high breeding of poetical style where there is nothing ostentatious, nothing crude, no breath of parvenu or journalist'.[21] Art's rebellion is paradoxical, because it is a rebellion against change; the only insurance against the disruption of the continuity of memory is in an environment where memory is hereditary, a part of the process of breeding. It was this Yeats thought he had discovered in the Japanese Noh plays, an art form based in a social system encouraging and sustaining a hereditary memory:

> 'Accomplishment' the word Noh means, and it is their accomplishment and that of a few cultivated people who understand the literary amd mythological allusions and the ancient lyrics quoted in speech or chorus, their discipline, a part of their breeding.[22]

The play could only be made by and for an aristocracy, a memory bred in the bone.

Yeats's hatred of realism, in novel or play, and his contempt for the journalist, are both aspects of his fear of the loss of memory. From the early years of the century the journalist features in his prose as the poet's anti-type; 'The imaginative writer differs from the saint', he comments in 1906, 'in that he identifies himself – to the neglect of his own soul, alas! – with the soul of the world and frees himself from all that is impermanent in that soul, an ascetic not of women and wine, but of the newspapers'.[23] The language of journalism is, for Yeats, the language of realism, a form of art in which he can only find significance by a personal effort of association which the art itself seeks to deny:

> In watching a play about modern educated people, with its meagre language and its action crushed into the narrow limits of possibility, I have found myself constantly saying: 'Maybe it has its power to move, slight as that is, from being able to suggest fundamental contrasts and passions which romantic and poetical literature have shown to be beautiful.' A man facing his enemies alone in a quarrel over the purity of water in a Norwegian Spa and using no language but that of the newspapers can call up to our minds, let us say, the passion of Coriolanus.[24]

Yeats's own associations manage to endow the play with some of the power its journalistic language denies it, but for an audience whose minds have been taught that the language of journalism and the methods of realism are the only true forms of communication and art, the associative art which Yeats wants will be, quite literally, incomprehensible. The mind of the new Ireland,

> distrusts all that is not plainly organised and determined, all that is not plainly logical work. A play with a purpose, or a moral, let us say, is as much part of social organization as a newspaper or a speech ... It loves rhetoric because rhetoric is impersonal and pre-determined, and it hates poetry whose suggestiveness cannot be foreseen.[25]

Suggestion is an art of self-discovery, because our associative connections as they unfold beyond our control uncover what we did not know was contained in our own minds: it is an art reminding us of what we have forgotten, maintaining memory. But realism encourages our forgetfulness, shutting us into those opinions and ideas which are the common currency of the day. That such distinctions are not merely aesthetic but involve the whole bases of our social life is revealed in the same diary entries:

> One thought must be continually pressed upon all free souls — here in Ireland above all — to resist ill-breeding in thought as our fathers in their more leisurely lives — alike in country poverty, where most of all they brooded on this one thing, or in great houses — resisted ill-breeding in manners. These are associated, and even though we be called the worst names, the hardest to bear, we must keep the fountains pure. Education, newspapers, a thousand impersonalities have filled the world with the imitation of what was once gold — an imitation worse than the ill-manners of the parvenu.[26]

It may be that memory and manners are sustained equally among poor and rich, but the new minds 'hate the freedom of the rich and the high-bred more bitterly than the fantasy of the poor',[27] and almost as a reflex against that hatred, it might seem, Yeats takes the side of the rich. But clearly the metaphor of 'ill-breeding' is one which easily returns to its genetic origins, and only those who are truly 'high-bred' will also be capable of the kinds of memory that can cope with suggestive art. Yeats's interest in the Noh was not lessened by his discovery that the 'players, unlike the despised players of the popular theatre, have passed on proudly from father to son an elaborate art, and even now a player will publish his family tree to prove his skill'.[28] Culture belongs to those who inherit or create 'a rich world of memories and habits of thought',[29] but the possibility of such memory would not exist but for its assurance through continuity of breeding, for it 'requires a certain amount of wealth to ensure continuity from generation to generation, and to free the mind in part from other tasks'.[30] Thus does it come about that Yeats sees art as integral with aristocratic lineage: 'Is not all charm inherited?', he asks in his diary on 22 January 1909, ' — whether of the intellect, of the manners, or of character, or of literature? A great lady is as simple as a good poet. Both possess nothing that is not ancient and their own . . .'[31]

Such a definition of culture cut out, as it was no doubt intended to do, all of Catholic Ireland: the peasant might have had his ancient memory but he was 'low-born', and his sons and daughters who had moved to the city had no claim upon an ancient lineage whatsoever. Yeats found justification for his emerging politics in the effects upon the peasant mind of organisations, like the Gaelic League, with whose nationalist and Celtic principles he had been in sympathy in the 1890s. In a comment on MacDonagh, later to be memorialised in 'Easter 1916', Yeats wrote:

> He was very low-spirited about Ireland. He is managing a school on Irish and Gaelic League principles but says he is losing faith in the League. Its writers are infecting Irish not only with an English idiom but with the habits of thought of current Irish journalism, a most un-Celtic thing. 'The League,' he said, 'is killing Celtic civilization.' I told him that Synge about ten years ago foretold this in an article in the *Academy*. He thought the national movement practically dead, that the language would be revived without all that he loved it for. In England this man would have become remarkable in some way, here he is being crushed by the mechanical logic and commonplace eloquence which gives the most power to the most empty mind . . .[32]

There is almost a transposition, here, in Yeats's original mythologies of Ireland and England: it is now Ireland, in 1909, that is the country of 'logic', of 'mechanical thought . . . crushing as with an iron roller all that is organic', while it is England that would have allowed Mac-Donagh to fulfil himself. History was to hold a very different fulfilment for MacDonagh, but in 1909 Yeats was at the lowest point in his faith in the power of memory. The society around him was destroying the very bases of his art in its destruction not only of a common memory, but of all memory. The bitterness of his rejection of the contemporary world was founded on the awareness that 'all creation requires one mind to make and one mind for enjoyment; the theatre can at rare moments create this one mind for an hour or so, but this grows always more difficult.'[33] The poet is like 'an old peasant telling stories of the great famine or the hangings of '98 or from his own memories'; his art is a recovery of the past, and he needs an audience that can enter equally into 'the depth of the mind',[34] an audience which contemporary society makes almost impossible.

 Two more of Yeats's journal entries for 1909, entries about plays he was helping put on at the Abbey Theatre, reveal Yeats making explicit to himself the sources of his conflict with his time and with its realistic art forms:

> In the four morning papers *Time* is cursed or ignored and *The Crossroads* given great praise . . . They prefer mere logic, even when they

do not understand it, to suggestion, which alone is the foundation of literature. State a logical proposition and the most common-place mind can complete it. Suggestion is richest to the richest and so art grows unpopular in a democracy like this.[35]

Only in the mind that has been stocked by 'gradual time' can the in-complete work find its fulfilment: the mind's riches upon which the literature of suggestion depends are dependent in turn upon material riches:

I see that between *Time*, suggestion, and *Cross-roads*, logic, lies a difference of civilization as well as of art. The literature of sugges-tion, richest to the richest, does not belong to a social order founded upon argument, but to an age when life conquered by being itself and the most living was the most powerful. What was leisure, wealth, privilege but a soil for the most living?[36]

'Richest to the richest': that the riches of the memory be sustained the soil of wealth and privilege and power must be maintained. The power of memory in a society will be evidenced by the power assigned to those who embody in their lineage a continuous memory, the power assigned to those whose riches makes possible a richness of associa-tive recall: 'And in suggestive drama there must either be enough loosening and slackening for meditation and the seemingly irrelevant, or a chorus, and neither is possible without rich leisurely minds in the audience, lovers of Father Time.'[37] That his art can exist Yeats needs those 'rich leisurely minds', and it is the dynamics of his search for and attempt to preserve such minds that guides his politics: democracy, mass education, industrialisation, are no doubt hated because they were alien to the world Yeats grew up in, but they are hated with a bitterness that springs from their being an attack on memory, on the associative art that is 'richest to the richest'. Only in the Anglo-Irish aristocracy could he find a continuing social location for that kind of memory, and it was one facing annihilation: Yeats's politics were to become, as the possible sources of memory were eroded or overthrown, a willful desire for the victory of the enemy that it might come the quicker to self-destruction, to the next turn of the wheel: 'After our present industrialism will come reaction and the more decisive the industrialism can be forced to be, the sooner will come reaction.'[38]

The loss of memory which Yeats saw in the world around him was enforced, in its effect on his poetry, by two events in his own life. In

1903 Maud Gonne finally destroyed Yeats's long-maintained hopes of winning her by marrying Major MacBride, another who was later to die in the Easter Rising. In the same year, the Order of the Golden Dawn,[39] the occult organisation to which Yeats devoted so much of his energy, went through a crisis which deprived Yeats of many of his closest confrères in the magical arts. Since Maud and the occult had been among the primary sources of its inspiration, this double blow was deeply to affect his art. He wrote little poetry in the years between 1903 and 1912, turning his attention to the drama. His concentration, as the above passages show, on developing a theatre of suggestion was the application to the stage of those principles he had been trying to develop in his poetry: in the theatre, perhaps, even if only momentarily, the communal mind of the people could be reawakened. The effect of his engagement in the theatre, however, was to turn his poetry into a medium for argument and statement rather than suggestion. It is as if, having concentrated his attention on the drama as the focus of an associative art, he finds poetry liberated from the burdens of suggestion and able to engage more directly and fully in ordinary communication. The poetry is used by Yeats to carry his argument with his time's failure of memory rather than as the medium through which memory is to be reactivated. It is a 'prose' poetry, in Yeats's terms, that he now writes, and we should remember when we praise Yeats's increasing realism and directness, that they were his response to the collapse of the context which he saw as necessary to true poetry, the poetry of suggestion. When we read 'The Fisherman', for instance, often taken as a statement of his aesthetic credo, with its hope that,

> Before I am old
> I shall have written him one
> Poem maybe as cold
> And passionate as the dawn

> (*CP*, p. 167)

we should remember that it is written out of loss of an actual audience that might share a memory with the poet. The poet has to imagine his audience, 'Imagining a man,/ . . . /A man who does not exist, / A man who is but a dream.' Rather than the rebirth of his poetic style, what this man bears witness to is the death of poetry, the power of suggestion, and since Yeats is still to write this man his 'one poem' whatever we read now is not itself poetry. The one mind that Yeats sought was possible, in debased Dublin, only at the racecourse, where 'Delight makes all of the one mind', but it is mind no longer responsive to the true sources of beauty:

> We, too, had good attendance once,
> Hearers and hearteners of the work;
> Aye, horsemen for companions,
> Before the merchant and the clerk
> Breathed on the world with timid breath.
>
> ('At Galway Races'; *CP*, p. 108)

The racecourse calls up the memory of the real horsemen of the past, of whom the crowd know nothing, those who, though 'they ride upon horses' are also 'hearteners' for poets.

The tension between the associative and non-associative modes in Yeats's poetry in this period are summed up in a poem of dejection written in 1915, when this phase of Yeats's career was about to come to an abrupt conclusion:

> When have I last looked on
> The round green eyes and the long wavering bodies
> Of the dark leopards of the moon?
> All the wild witches, those most noble ladies,
> For all their broom-sticks and their tears,
> Their angry tears, are gone,
> The holy centaurs of the hills are vanished;
> Banished heroic mother moon and vanished,
> And now that I have come to fifty years
> I must endure the timid sun.
>
> ('Lines written in Dejection'; *CP*, p. 163)

The images are turned upon us in deliberate blankness, for their meanings, given the disappearance of 'heroic mother moon', which Yeats saw as the principle of the poetic, the subjective, must remain beyond our knowledge. The associative blankness of the Irish names in his early poetry Yeats could compensate for with notes, because he was building up a memory that he believed would someday be active and complete, but these images retain their obscurity because they are only tokens of a memory to which we have no access whatsoever. The poet has been reduced to a merely personal memory which can be given no public or shared significance: even the overwhelming experience of Yeats's life, his relationship with Maud Gonne, is no longer one that he can look upon as an image of the poetic faculty, the poet creating through associations the beauty everyone else will perceive, even if he is allowed no possession of it. That beauty is now a forgotten thing:

> Although crowds gathered once if she but showed her face,
> And even old men's eyes grew dim, this hand alone,
> Like some last courtier at a gypsy camping-place
> Babbling of fallen majesty, records what's gone.
>
> ('Fallen Majesty'; CP, p. 138)

In 'Poetry and Tradition' in 1907, Yeats could still assert that the writer was 'like some mystic courtier who has stolen the keys from the girdle of Time, and can wander where it please him amid the splendours of ancient Courts',[40] but by 1912 the poet is no mystic traveller of time, but an outcast, a wanderer preserving the memory of what the world has forgotten. With the passing of memory, beauty too has gone, and heroic individualism, both of which require the memory of past greatness, past beauty as their foundation. The madness of those who are shut out from transcendence returns, but now the mad wanderers are shut out from memory and can only show defiance in their isolated opposition to the forces of history:

> Bred to a harder thing
> Than Triumph, turn away
> And like a laughing string
> Whereon mad fingers play
> Amid a place of stone,
> Be secret and exult,
> Because of all things known
> That is most difficult.
>
> ('To a friend whose work has come to nothing'; CP, p. 122)

In the greatest, perhaps, of the poems of this middle period, Yeats turns his occult learning, his personal memory, all that had been the foundation of his art against himself in a resurrection of the powers of memory that is a grotesque parody of the renewal from the buried self which he imaged as the essence of poetic inspiration. In 'The Cold Heaven' (*CP*, p. 140), Yeats presents us with the sudden intrusion of memory upon his quotidian awareness, an intrusion utterly desolating in its consequences, and this reversal of the value of memory is mirrored in the structure of the poem, which begins with the climactic

image on which Yeats usually ends his poem, and then unpicks the unconscious process of association that has led to this sudden revelation:

> Suddenly I saw the cold and rook-delighting heaven
> That seemed as though ice burned and was but the more ice,
> And thereupon imagination and heart were driven
> So wild that every casual thought of that and this
> Vanished, and left but memories, that should be out of season
> With the hot blood of youth, of love crossed long ago;
> And I took all the blame out of all sense and reason,
> Until I cried and trembled and rocked to and fro,
> Riddled with light. Ah! When the ghost begins to quicken,
> Confusion of the death-bed over, is it sent
> Out naked on the roads, as the books say, and stricken
> By the injustice of the skies for punishment?

The purification of casual thought, the recovery of memory, which
ought to be a salvation from time, can only cast the speaker into a
sense of the afterlife in which there is no redemption from past suffering, and no renewal from the buried self. The afterlife will be lived
under these selfsame unjust skies, with the unresolved memory of loss.
The poem, in its syntactic structure, enacts the dissolution of time
that memory allows, for in its middle section different points in the
speaker's life are conflated in 'should be out of reason / With the hot
blood of youth': on the one hand, memories are not appropriate to our
youthful experience which ought to be casual and forgettable; on the
other, he has, from his present point in time, been carried back into
the past so vividly as to be young again, and yet still to suffer from the
memory of loss, a memory he should be protected from by his 'hot
blood'. With time overthrown what Yeats presents is an experience of
suffering which has become eternal: the same suffering that was his
then, as a young man, returns now to the middle aged man, and will
return to his ghost after death. The time transcending symbol that
allows recovery of the past, wrapping all the past into the present, may
have failed in the world, but it has become the appalling inner truth of
Yeats's own condition in his utter isolation before that 'rook-delighting'
but humanly horrifying 'heaven' of 'ice'. In seeing that icy heaven Yeats
has been given a revelation, an image thrust from his memory of what
'the books say', but rather than defusing the horror of the image, the
qualification of the rhetorical question only intensifies it, because it
shows us Yeats trying to place back in the past, in the safety of his

own reading, the associative connection that has revealed to him the true condition of his life: he may still be a part of our quotidian world of time, but he is in effect a ghost in the afterlife, because the loss which the poem returns to in memory has deprived him of all that was truly vital in life. The 'confusion of the death bed' images his present feelings, for it is as though he had died, but those feelings are the recall of the 'love crossed long ago' that was, he discovers, truly his death.

What is interesting about the form of 'The Cold Heaven' is that it refuses to leave its climactic image to the audience. Memory having become the poet's private domain —

> All day in the one chair
> From dream to dream and rhyme to rhyme I have ranged
> In rambling talk with an image of air:
> Vague memories, nothing but memories.
>
> ('Broken Dreams'; *CP*, p. 172)

— the poem deflects us from any personal reverie by tracking down the source of the associations in Yeats himself. The concluding rhetorical question, rather than opening the poem out upon our own associations, turns the poem back to its beginning, enacting the cyclic trap of memory in which the speaker is caught. The poem, therefore, has used all the elements of an associational art, but used them entirely within the confines of the poet's associational powers. It assumes, as it were, that the audience will be lacking in the appropriate memories. And it is such an ironic tension between the form of the poem and the assumed reading response that becomes the structural device in many of Yeats's most powerful poems from the period when he has lost confidence in a communal memory. A public poem which offers a parallel false resurrection to the private one of 'The Cold Heaven' is 'To a Shade' (*CP*, p. 123), a poem which invokes Parnell's ghost to judge the spirit of a city that can refuse the gift of a collection of paintings, paintings that would have 'given their children's children loftier thought / Sweeter emotion, working in the veins / Like gentle blood'. By recalling — both in memory and as a ghost — Parnell, Yeats is enforcing his condemnation of that Catholic class whose hounding of the nationalist leader is at one, for Yeats, with their philistinism over Hugh Lane's paintings. The memory which makes such a judgement of their attitudes possible, however, is precisely what Yeats's opponents lack: those who are capable of memory and wish, through art, to encourage the memory that can be passed on from 'generation to generation' like 'gentle blood', must suffer a society committed to cultural amnesia. Parnell is warned that it is not yet time for a resurrection of his values or of his memory:

> Go, unquiet wanderer,
> And gather the Glasnevin coverlet
> About your head till the dust stops your ear,
> The time for you to taste of that salt breath
> And listen at the corners has not come:
> You had enough of sorrow before death —
> Away, away! You are safer in the tomb.

In consigning Parnell's memory and spirit again to the grave, Yeats is acknowledging the fact that his society has cut itself off from the most heroic values of even its recent past, but ironically, of course, the poem preserves the memory its speaker despairs of, for every reading of the poem brings Parnell's ghost back to inspect and judge the failures of Dublin. We are forced to retain as a part of our living memory what Yeats, as speaking voice of the poem, insists will no longer be remembered. The heroic figure it consigns to the dust it has, in effect, resurrected.

It is that ironic conflict between the poem as an inevitable supporter of memory by virtue of its formal repeatability, its apparent stasis, and the dramatic situation of a speaker who cannot force his society to maintain the values of memory that is enacted in both 'September 1913' and 'Easter 1916'. Here Yeats finds a method of using the tension between the associative effect of the poem and its actual structure, between its dramatic situation in history and its place in an enduring cultural memory, that allows him to return to his associative art while operating within an apparently forgetful society. 'September 1913' (*CP*, p. 120) opens in famous denigration of modern, unheroic Ireland:

> What need you, being come to sense,
> But fumble in a greasy till
> And add the halfpence to the pence
> And prayer to shivering prayer, until
> You have dried the marrow from the bone?

The unheroic have lost all recollection of the 'names' that once stilled 'childish play', for to remember those values would be to confront their own failure:

Was it for this the wild geese spread
The grey wing upon every tide;
For this that all that blood was shed,
For this Edward Fitzgerald died,
And Robert Emmet and Wolfe Tone,
All that delirium of the brave?
Romantic Ireland's dead and gone,
It's with O'Leary in the grave.

At its conclusion the poem seems reconciled to the loss of such hero-ism, which was, after all, a form of delirium, something unacceptable in a peaceable society. The reconciliation of the speaker is, however, refused by the poem as a formal structure, since those names are recalled with each reading of the poem, and are made as permanent in the national memory as the words in which they are contained:

They weighed so lightly what they gave.
But let them be, they're dead and gone,
They're with O'Leary in the grave.

The paradox of the speaker's casting aside what the poem retains is enacted semantically in the ambiguity of 'Let them be': for the speaker they are to be allowed to rest in the grave; through the poem, however, they are remade, allowed 'to be' a part of our minds again. Thus the dramatic forward movement of the speaker's thought, distancing him-self from the values of the past, is reversed in our reading of the poem, because it makes the past vivid, sustains its place in our minds: the poem insists, despite its avowed statements, that we 'let them be', reinforcing the memory of what it despairs and renewing the associa-tions that time seems to have eroded.

The recovery of an implicit memory in the poetic form, in despite of its social context, which is enacted in 'September 1913', was to suffer an ironic reversal at the hands of history, for the Rising of 1916 struck so deeply into Yeats's awareness because it challenged his assumption that the focus for societal amnesia lay in the rise of the Catholic middle class. It was that class which provided the martyrs, and which had retained a sense of the heroic, a commitment to national ideals, of which Yeats himself had despaired. 'Easter 1916' (*CP*, p. 202) rehearses Yeats's equivocal acceptance that a rebirth of Irish values has occurred, that the old heroic stance had not been forgotten. His ambivalence, however, found its appropriate expression by an inversion of the terms of the form-content tension of 'September 1913': where the earlier poem, by its form, retains what its speaker accepts as cast aside, the later poem moves towards an acceptance of what history has made permanent in the memory no matter what the feelings or the thoughts of the speaker himself, an acceptance based on the fact that poetry is committed by its form to whatever is powerful in the memory. The chant of names at the poem's close is Yeats's recognition that these — however he might feel about them as a man — have become symbols in the national mind, and that, as a poet, he must accept those locuses of associational potential that history gives to him. Whereas 'September 1913' attempted to maintain associations which were in the process of being lost, 'Easter 1916' is driven to an unwilling acceptance of those that history has created.

The dramatic design of 'Easter 1916' therefore entails the presentation of the speaker as one who belongs in the memoryless world of 'casual comedy', accepting the social conditions of his time. That this is not the 'real' Yeats we have seen from the embittered poems he was writing in the years immediately before 1916: the poem dramatises not the Yeats who, as poet, was struggling against the failures of his time, but Yeats the citizen of a modern country where heroism, and all the nobility that comes from the memory of a great past, has been laid aside:

> I have passed with a nod of the head
> Or polite meaningless words,
> Or have lingered awhile and said
> Polite meaningless words,
> And thought before I had done
> Of a mocking tale or a gibe
> To please a companion
> Around the fire at the club,
> Being certain that they and I
> But lived where motley is worn:
> All changed, changed utterly:
> A terrible beauty is born.

The final two lines, to be echoed twice in the course of the poem (and many times since), imply at this point the speaker's despair in the face of what has occurred. It is a despair founded on the fact that he who, of all men, should have been able to recognise the potentiality for nobility, has seen only the comic surface of life, but a despair, too, that what had been only a part of the art work — tragedy — has become all too real in life:

> This other man I had dreamed
> A drunken vainglorious lout.
> He had done most bitter wrong
> To some who are near my heart,
> Yet I number him in the song.

Yeats the dreamer has utterly failed to penetrate the reality of the world he has been living in, and is forced to accept into his art what his art could not accept as a possibility of the world in which it has operated. Thus the central sections of the poem present us with a banal world being turned into 'song' because it has revealed its tragic potential, and a 'poetic' world, the world of the Irish countryside as opposed to the urban world of Dublin, being used to question the validity of such tragic action:

> Hearts with one purpose alone
> Through summer and winter seem
> Enchanted to a stone
> To trouble the living stream.
> The horse that comes from the road,
> The rider, the birds that range
> From cloud to tumbling cloud,
> Minute by minute they change;
> A shadow of cloud on the stream
> Changes minute by minute;
> A horse-hoof plashes within it;
> The long-legged moor hens dive,
> And hens to moor-cocks call;
> Minute by minute they live:
> The stone's in the midst of all.

It has often been pointed out that Yeats's description here is closely based on his comments on Ireland, in his essay on Synge, as a land

> that has given itself to agitation over much; abstract thoughts are raised up between men's minds and Nature, who never does the same thing twice or makes one man's mind like another, till minds, whose patriotism is perhaps strong enough to carry them to the scaffold,

cry down natural impulse with the morbid persistence of minds unsettled by some fixed idea.[41]

The connection between this passage and the imagery of the poem would imply the unnatural fixity of the rebels in a world whose essence is flux and change, and we have to read the poem as a condemnation of the state of mind that made their heroism possible. Such a reading is given confirmation by a similar passage in *Autobiographies*: 'The Nationalist abstractions were like the fixed ideas of some hysterical woman, a part of the mind turned into stone.'[42] The poem, however, is much more complex in its attitude than such passages, for it is precisely these typifications of the Nationalist mind that the rebels had, by their heroism, disputed: instead of the derogatory 'fixed ideas of some hysterical woman' their sacrifice implied the recovery of the heroic virtue, the tragic nobility which Yeats, as a poet, had sung so often and so often bemoaned the loss of in the modern world. If the rebels are wrong in their sacrifice then there is something wrong too in the values of Yeats's poetry. And it is precisely this identification upon which the poem plays: the stone in the midst of all is not only the fixities of the nationalist ideology, it is the poem which, in spite of its fixed structure, continues to trouble the living stream. The rebels are not merely like 'stones', they 'seem /Enchanted to a stone': it is from the perspective of the casual comedy, perhaps, that such fixity seems stony, because the casual comedy is afraid of the capacities of tragedy. But it is also from the world of nature that their fixity is like a stone, because it is, like the work of art, a defiance of time. Yeats in questioning the values of the rebels' refusal of the natural world is also questioning his own refusal of it as an artist. The ordinary Yeats, part of the comic world, questions the poet Yeats who by his art, has helped create the values which are embodied in the tragedy:

Men who are imaginative writers to-day may well have preferred to influence the imagination of others more directly in past times. Instead of learning their craft with paper and a pen they may have sat for hours imagining themselves to be stocks and stones and beasts of the wood, till the images were so vivid that passers-by became but a part of the imagination of the dreamer ... Have not poetry and music arisen, as it seems, out of the sounds the enchanters made to help their imagination to enchant, to charm, to bind with a spell themselves and passers-by?[43]

The 'enchantment' of the rebels is parallel to the enchantments of art: it is modern art reverting to its traditional role, undoing the careful distinctions which an ageing Yeats has been constructing between his art and his life.

In effect, the 'symbolic' section of 'Easter 1916' is a means of uniting the effect of art and the effects of heroism in life upon a single image, an image which casts doubt on both, but also forces an awareness of their value and their interdependence as well. The stone, like the poem, is the fixity without which the multitudinous flow of the associative process would have no centre, no stimulant; as the beloved in an earlier poem could not but 'trouble . . . all things longing for rest' despite her desire for peace, so all things here that are in movement cannot help being seen as centred on the stillness of the stone. Another passage from *Autobiographies* implies that the fixed and the flowing are integral to each other, for a nation is structured like the 'emotion of multitude', a flow of many associations around a single focus:

> Is there a nation-wide multiform reverie, every mind passing through a stream of suggestion, and all streams acting and reacting upon one another, no matter how distant the minds, how dumb the lips? A man walked, as it were, casting a shadow, and yet one could never say which was man and which was shadow, or how many shadows he cast. Was not a nation, as distinguished from a crowd of chance comers, bound together by this interchange among streams or shadows; the Unity of Image, which I sought in national literature, being but an originating symbol?[44]

In the stream of the national life that has lost touch with its sources in the memory it is, perhaps, only the 'terrible beauty' of such sacrifice that can recreate the unity of image. The fixity of the 'hearts with one purpose alone' which is destructive in life is, once pushed to the fixity of death, creative, for it is the image from which all those 'streams acting and reacting on one another, no matter how distant', will take their shared character. The rebels have passed beyond the questions which the time-bound, disenchanted citizen will ask --

> Too long a sacrifice
> Can make a stone of the heart.
> O when may it suffice?

-- because they have become focuses of associational value, and the poet has to accept them because he is the servant of such richness:

> And what if excess of love
> Bewildered them till they died?
> I write it out in verse —
> MacDonagh and MacBride
> And Connolly and Pearse
> Now and in time to be,
> Wherever green is worn,
> Are changed, changed utterly,
> A terrible beauty is born.

The double meaning of 'September 1913' is repeated: the rebels 'are now' despite their deaths, and are 'in time' to come into their essential being, 'to be'. The living stream of the future will be troubled — and united — by the multiple associations their names will generate no matter what the actual meaning of their action, the real nature of their commitments. Their fixity and their meaningfulness, however, is something the poem contributes to as it instantiates them in the formal structure of its language: the poet does not get to choose his symbols, but bows to those which will have, in his audience's mind, the greatest associational effect.

If 'Easter 1916' reflects Yeats's increasing distrust of the imagination that can enchant and destroy, it also reflects his recovery of confidence in the power of memory in the world around him. The loss of memory, or its dwindling to a personal and incommunicable minimum, is the theme of much of Yeats's poetry between *In the Seven Woods* of 1904 and the earliest poems of *The Wild Swans at Coole* volume of 1919.[45] The Rising of 1916 coincided, however, with Yeats's gradual recovery of belief in and commitment to the occult, giving surety again to his sense of a universal memory which made the losses and failures of social memory insignificant. In *Responsibilities* he had published a poem which seems to advertise his loss of contact with the Rosicrucianism of his youth: 'The Mountain Tomb' opens cheerfully enough, and the end of the first stanza plays on the implications of 'is' in the same way that 'September 1913' plays on 'be':

> Pour wine and dance if manhood still have pride,
> Bring roses if the rose be yet in bloom;
> The cataract smokes upon the mountain side,
> Our father Rosicross is in the tomb.

(*CP*, p. 136)

By the end of the poem, however, the tone has changed to one of hope-lessness despite the 'sleep' which implies the possibility of a resurrec-tion:

> In vain, in vain; the cataract still cries;
> The everlasting taper lights the gloom;
> All wisdom shut into his onyx eyes,
> Our father Rosicross sleeps in his tomb.

It is a sleep which will not be broken to give us access to the 'everlast-ing wisdom', a sleep closer to its euphuistic implication of death than to imminent awakening. The bitterness of Yeats's conflict with the Ireland of his day and the decay of social forms of memory stems from this loss of any contact with a fundamental source of memory tran-scending any specific hisstorical circumstances. However, on 10 April 1912, Leo Africanus had made his first visit to Yeats, claiming to be his attendant spirit, and that by 'association with one another' they 'should each become complete'.[46] Where before Yeats had seen the Great Memory as a sea to which all our associations went back, he conceives it now as made up of active spirits, each one using the life of some living person to make complete its own incomplete experience. The other world of the spirit perfectly mirrors Yeats's aesthetic: just as the poem brings its symbols to us for completion through our associa-tions, so the spirit comes to us to complete its associations – having nothing left but the pattern of its memories – through the symbols it releases into our minds. Spirit and poem are identical in the way they interact with our associations, leading us on to confront those overwhelming images by which our actions and our futures will be shaped.

Yeats's spirit world is, since it is pure mind, shaped on the pro-cesses of association by which our minds work when freed of practical concern:

> Swedenborg has written that we are each in the midst of a group of associated spirits who sleep when we sleep and become the *dramatis personae* of our dreams, and are always the other will that wrestles with our thought shaping it to our own desire.[47]

That group of 'associated' spirits who perform in our dreams are themselves engaged in purifying their memories until 'all that was accidental or habitual dies away':[48]

The dead, as the passionate necessity wears out, come into a measure of freedom and may turn the impulse of events, started while living, in some new direction, but they cannot originate except through the living. Then gradually they perceive, although they are still but living in their memories, harmonies, symbols, and patterns, as though all were being refashioned by an artist . . .[49]

There is thus a continual interaction between the associations in dream or reverie of the living man and the memories of the dead gradually purifying themselves into the shape of art. From the work of art our associations spiral out or down into the depths of the communal mind, while from within that mind, individual memories are finding the harmonies and patterns that will resolve the multiplicity of their memories into unity, unity like that of the work of art. It is not, there-fore, that we step over a certain threshold which suddenly releases us from personal into universal memory: that universal memory is directed at us through our attendant spirits, and there is, in effect, no distinction to be made between our associations and the memories of the spirits in the other world. Our associations are spirits in the other world: psychology, as always in Yeats, becomes ontology:

> Communication with the *Anima Mundi* is through association of thoughts or images or objects; the famous dead and those of whom but a faint memory lingers, can still − and it is for no other end, that all unknowing, we value posthumous fame − tread the corridor and take the empty chair.[50]

Associations at their most intense points of interaction with the spirit world manifest themselves as ghosts, but they can do so because there is no real distinction between the psychological data of our reverie and the real nature of the outside world. For Yeats, 'all our mental images no less than apparations (and I see no reason to distinguish) are forms existing in the general vehicle of *Anima Mundi*',[51] and Berkeley's philosophy was to justify this occult speculation by proving conclusively that 'to be is to be perceived.' The associative process becomes the true reality of the universe:

> though images appear to flow and drift, it may be that we but change in our relation to them, now losing, now finding with the shifting of our minds. Henry More speaks by the book, in claiming that those images may be hard to the right touch as 'pillars of

crystal' and as solidly coloured as our own to the right eyes.[52]

The poem which intends to provoke an associative reverie is thus no retreat from the real world into the vagueness of personal meditation: the world itself is nothing but a process of association working through the interaction of those images we receive from the spirit world, from the dead, and those that seem to belong to the material. They are, in effect, like the mind which produces a poem and the mind in which it finds its completion, two intersecting trains of association, and the images which are released to us in the depths of our reverie are images whose consequences are not merely psychological, but may set in motion another train of association in the 'real' world:

> I am persuaded that a logical process, or a series of related images, has body and period, and I think of *Anima Mundi* as a great pool or garden where it moves through its allotted growth like a great water plant or fragrantly branches in the air. Indeed, as Spenser's Garden of Adonis:
>> There is the first seminary
>> Of all things that are born to live and die
>> According to their kynds.
> The soul by changes of 'vital congruity', More says, draws to it a certain thought, and this thought draws by its association the sequence of many thoughts, endowing them with a life in the vehicle meted out according to the intensity of the first perception. A seed is set growing, and this growth may go on apart from the power, apart even from the knowledge of the soul.[53]

'Intensity of perception' is the only distinction between images, between those we think of as 'real' and those we think of as psychological: association completes itself in the world if it begins in the mind, in the mind if it begins in the world.

By returning to the study of Swedenborg in 1911 or 1912, Yeats rediscovered that total memory which had been his assertion in the essay 'Magic' in 1901, but which had withered in his thought in the intervening years. In 'Swedenborg, Mediums and the Desolate Places' of 1914, he takes his first steps towards a total vision of an occult universe, but what most catches his enthusiasm is Swedenborg's description of the first stage of the soul's progress after death, one in which the soul is still surrounded by an 'earth resembling life':

This earth-resembling life is the creation of the image-making power of the mind, plucked naked from the body, and mainly of the images of memory. All our work has gone with us, the books we have written can be opened and read or put away for later use, even though their print and paper have been sold to the buttermen; and reading his description one notices, a discovery one had thought peculiar to the latest generation, that 'the most minute particulars which enter the memory remain there and are never obliterated', and there as here we do not always know all that is in our memory, but at need angelic spirits who act upon us there as here, widening and deepening the consciousness at will, can draw forth all the past . . . all the pleasures and pains of sensible life awaken again and again, all our passionate events rush up about us and not as seeming imagination, for imagination is now the world.[54]

Imagination is also returned to its original meaning, 'image making', and the images derive from the memory. But this description of the afterlife, more importantly, matches exactly with Yeats's description of associative reverie, and the process of association is again, for Yeats, integrated into the whole pattern of the world so that, no matter how much society may deny the continuity of memory, no matter how much may be forgotten and cast aside, it all takes its place in the un-conscious mind, the Great Memory, and Yeats can find the notion of the buried self a pathway again to regeneration, because,

The dead living in their memories, are, I am persuaded, the source of all that we call instinct, and it is their love and their desire, all un-knowing, that makes us drive beyond our reason, or in defiance of our interest it may be; and it is the dream martens that, all unknow-ing, are master-martens to the living martens building about church windows their elaborate nests . . .[55]

Memory is the essential creative force of the universe, whether in the martens or in the poet, but it is a memory that no longer requires completion only in the reader's associations, but that completes itself in action or in reverie alike, for there is no essential difference between the two.

Yeats's occultism is often regarded as an absurdity in a 'modern' poet, but it was his means to tapping the unconscious, or rather, to developing a theory of the unconscious, and then the means towards situating his poetry at the centre of a universe which was integral with the workings of his art. Because the whole process of the world, of the afterlife, of matter, of history, imitated the workings of his poetry, as he conceived them, the poetry could cope with a subject matter that was nothing less than the totality of human experience. The extension of the power of Yeats's poetry after 1914 was not based primarily on his achievement of a new hard, direct style, but on discovering that the poem, even in its incompletion, was a microcosm of the workings of the universe, was the very channel through which the power memory shaped history. The poem, in finding pattern and harmony and revelatory symbol, completes one process of association emerging from the Great Memory through the poet's mind, and, in engaging the associations of the reader's mind, re-enters the flow of events that we think of as history. The individual moments of revelation that this process brings about in the reader are, microcosmically, what occurs when some overwhelming formative image enters history to set in motion a pattern of events, a train of connected images, that will last for an epoch. And whatever is destroyed materially returns to the Great Memory, to be brought back time and again, like our own lost emotions and forgotten experiences, when some flow of association picks them up from the darkness into which they have been cast. This renewed faith in memory is summed up in 'Under Saturn', addressed to his wife, whose automatic writings were the final proof of the recovery of the powers of memory:

> Do not because this day I have grown saturnine
> Imagine that lost love, inseparable from my thought
> Because I have no other youth, can make me pine;
> For how should I forget the wisdom that you brought,
> The comfort that you made? Although my wits have gone
> On a fantastic ride, my horse's flanks are spurred
> By childish memories of an old cross Pollexfen,
> And of a Middleton, whose name you never heard,
> And of a red-haired Yeats whose looks, although he died
> Before my time, seem like a vivid memory.
> You heard that labouring man who had served my people. He said
> Upon the open road, near to Sligo quay –
> No, no, not said, but cried it out – 'You have come again,
> And surely after twenty years it was time to come.'
> I am thinking of a child's vow sworn in vain
> Never to leave the valley his fathers called their home.

> (*CP*, p. 202)

The return home has been made by way of loss, the loss of Maud, but is, in its recovery of a memory that seems to stretch beyond the bounds of actual recollection — the 'red-haired Yeats whose looks . . . seem like a vivid memory' — the completion of a childish vow, of the circle of his life. The occult learning his wife has renewed for him is itself the culmination of his 'childish memories' of Pollexfen, and gives comforts for past losses and for all the lost past than can now return in memory. Memory has been so renewed that he is bound to grow saturnine thinking of past suffering, but the return of memory is more than compensation for any pain it causes: the 'open road' becomes cyclic, and like the open poem brings back what has been forgotten. Yeats prefaced *A Vision* with a letter to Ezra Pound, and quotes an early poem of Pound's which sums up the purpose of the poetry of memory in both their works:[56]

> See, they return; ah, see the tentative
> Movements, and the slow feet,
> The trouble in the pace and the uncertain
> Wavering!
>
> See, they return, one, and by one,
> With fear, as half-awakened;

That the forgotten can be recovered is consolation against all suffering and all loss: the destructive resurrection of 'The Cold Heaven' is, with his return amongst his own people and his marriage, with the situation recorded at the beginning of 'In Memory of Major Robert Gregory', annulled, because the return of memory is no longer purely the recurrence of unbearable suffering, but proof that, despite the suffering of individual losses, nothing of the past is lost.

It is part of the paradoxical effect of the associationist theory, that only what is past or lost or has been forgotten is truly effective in creating aesthetic experience. Beauty is always a recovery in memory, and aesthetic experience is integrally related with loss and destruction:

> Man is in love and loves what vanishes,
> What more is there to say? That country round
> None dared admit, if such a thought were his,
> Incendiary or bigot could be found
> To burn that stump on the Acropolis,

Or break in bits the famous ivories
Or traffic in the grasshoppers or bees.

('Nineteen Hundred and Nineteen'; *CP*, p. 234)

What makes Yeats's envisaging of the destructive impulses in mankind so intense is that he knows it integral to his own view of art. What 'Nineteen Hundred and Nineteen' presents as a physical destruction of the work of art is only the mirror image of the psychological effect of our reverie in which the work 'perpetually vanishes and returns again in the midst of the excitement it creates, and the more enthralling it is, the more do we forget it'.[57] The work of art before us is annihilated that we can enter fully into our experience of it, but that annihilation is also the recovery, through our memory, of past works of art. Equally, in action, we are committed to destruction of what exists that we may have the pleasure of creation again, a pleasure in which the memory of what has been destroyed will participate. We love what vanishes and we are therefore committed to destruction, in politics as in art:

All teeth were drawn, all ancient tricks unlearned,
And a great army but a showy thing;
What matter though no cannon had been turned
Into a ploughshare? Parliament and king
Thought that unless a little powder burned
The trumpeters might burst with trumpeting
And yet it lack all glory.

The aesthetic pleasures which recall past violence as a purely picturesque thing turns, in time, back into life again, and 'The guardsmen's drowsy chargers' of the opening section of 'Nineteen Hundred and Nineteen' are transformed:

Now days are draggon-ridden, the nightmare
Rides upon sleep: a drunken soldiery
Can leave the mother, murdered at her door,
To crawl in her own blood, and go scot-free.

The connection between the aesthetic and violence is enacted within the poem itself, however, as it reaches its climactic final images:

Violence upon the roads: violence of horses;
Some few have handsome riders, are garlanded

On delicate sensitive ear or tossing mane,
But wearied running round and round in their courses
All break and vanish, and evil gathers head:
Herodias' daughters have returned again,
A sudden blast of dusty wind and after
Thunder of feet, tumult of images,
Their purpose in the labyrinth of the wind;
And should some crazy hand dare touch a daughter
All turn with amorous cries, or angry cries,
According to the wind, for all are blind.

It is a conclusion whose combination of violence and beauty has posed problems for several critics; Dudley Young sums up the feeling congently:

> To put it crudely, is this poetry about hysteria or is the writing itself hysterical? As a set piece of gothic fantasy it certainly differs markedly from the preceding sections; for all its violence no one is in pain ... the objection to section vi must be that it abandons five sections of sustained high seriousness for an apocalyptic fantasy which may be to some extent pornographic.[58]

Yeats may be posing the problem of the relationship between the desire for beauty and the need for destruction, but is he also exploiting it in ways which violate our expectations of art?

The question is poised, I think, upon the nature of our understanding of Yeats's images and their function. Young finds the previous five sections of the poem to display 'high seriousness', but two of them, which offer images of how we are to see the pattern of history, and which are often taken as real statements of Yeats's beliefs, have to be seen, I want to suggest, as the false aestheticism of the poet. Section I of the poem had asked, 'But is there any comfort to be found?' and found nothing but man's love of destruction for answer. Section II, however, sets out to make sense of history:

When Loie Fuller's Chinese dancers enwound
A shining web, a floating ribbon of cloth,
It seemed that a dragon of air
Had fallen among the dancers, had whirled them round
Or hurried them off on its own furious path;
So the Platonic Year

Whirls out new right and wrong,
Whirls in the old instead;
All men are dancers and their tread
Goes to the barbarous clangour of a gong.

The Platonic Year turns barbarism to dance, the contingency of history into the pattern of art, but the way in which the image is introduced is itself contingent, the dance troup a deliberately personal memory of Yeats's. The emphatically personal nature of that image effectively undercuts the value of the universalising image of the Platonic Year, which, like the 'floating ribbon of cloth' constructs from artifice the illusion of a superior and controlling force beyond what men make of themselves. It is a comfort forged by art, as is the image of noble fortitude against overwhelming odds with which Yeats identifies himself in the third section of the poem:

Some moralist or mythological poet
Compares the solitary soul to a swan;
I am satisfied with that.
Satisfied if a troubled mirror show it,
Before that brief gleam of its life be gone,
An image of its state;
The wings half spread for flight,
The breast thrust out in pride
Whether to play, or to ride
Those winds that clamour of approaching night.

The image is again a memory which the language reveals as chosen by the poet, deliberately shaping a consolation in the sense either, as in the first, of being part of a total pattern, or, in the second, being a significant individual challenging the ultimate forces of the universe. The swan may offer the consolations of tragic nobility, but it does so only because art has suspended time in the moment of confrontation; the swan does not remain in that statuesque pose:

The swan has leaped into the desolate heaven:
That image can bring wildness, bring a rage
To end all things.

Such dreams are 'crack-pated' and bring a reaction of destruction more intense than the urge to creation and form which they reveal. After such illusion there is only nihilism, 'for we / Traffic in mockery'.

It is against the background of the failure of the creative imposition of form and order upon experience that we have to read the final section. And the crucial difference is that the image is not one that is chosen by the poet: it is given, and it refuses, like the earlier ones, to be reduced to a neat paradigm, for it is, and intends to be, multitudinous. According to Thomas Whitaker, we ought, in reading this section, to be conscious of Symons, Pater, Mallarmé, Heine, Jacob Grimm and Charles Leland — to name but a few.[59] It is a daunting background of explication for 18 lines, and Yeats knew that its symbols were uncommunicative when he provided a note to explain elements of it in the legends of country people. But the pattern is, I think, clear: the shapes we have found to make ennobling sense of history collapse — the 'garlanded' horses are 'wearied running round and round in their courses' — and what returns is 'Thunder of feet, tumult of images'. The purpose of Herodias's daughters is the same as the purpose of the poem, the unleashing of an uncontrollable, tumultuous train of images, because we are neither outside of time and history, able to see its whole pattern, not sure of our own role within it and the gesture that is required of us. We are in the middle of events, and participation in the tumult that we can perhaps discover 'Their purpose in the labyrinth of the wind' is all that is left to us. When Yeats makes this submission he is given his revelation:

But now wind drops, dust settles; thereupon
There lurches past, his great eyes without thought
Under the shadow of stupid straw-pale locks,
That insolent fiend Robert Artisson
To whom the love-lorn Lady Kyteler brought
Bronzed peacock feathers, red combs of her cocks.

We have our climactic image; there can be no explication of it because it ends one process of association and begins another, just as it stands between different historical epochs. We may see in it if we choose a horrific inversion of Yeats — art's son — and his patron Lady Gregory, but the sense of joyous acceptance of violence comes not from indulgence in the violence as such, but in the fact that if memory gives forth its image then violence, destruction and loss are the illusions — not the imaginative forms by which we try to tame history. Memory has held even the horrific in waiting for this moment of revelation, and no matter what horrific train of events or associations the poem releases, no matter what destruction ensues, all will be retained by the preserving power of a universal memory so that what is destroyed becomes an element in the recollections which will contribute their share to our future experience of beauty. We cannot know the total pattern, but we know our image has been given and there is consolation — indeed, joy — in the knowledge it brings as well as horror at what it prophesies. By its form it consoles us that all will return; in its content it warns us we are to suffer violence and destruction in ignorance of any sense of pattern.

'Nineteen Hundred and Nineteen' repeats the structure of 'The Second Coming' as it rises to its climactic image. Both offer an initial image of elemental power and significance — Herodias's daughters, the walking sphinx — which leads on to a second image, rough beast or insolent fiend, which is like the first step of our associations as they flow out from the initial image. The second image is one of movement, thrusting outwards upon the world a flow of images which will enact the character of the new age that the first image has announced. Our fear of the unknown future is matched by the openness of the associative potential of the image upon which we have to meditate. But although memory has not let us down in 'Nineteen Hundred and Nineteen', art has not found its focal image which will unify the emotion of multitude. The concluding images are of tumult, rather than merely inspiring tumult, and it is as if the loss of those Greek statues at the poem's opening has left the emotion of multitude severed from the unified image that ought to be their source. What returns to us from memory is an image of formless and anarchic violence because all our form-giving images have failed. Yeats wishes upon himself Chinese or Greek unities because the Irish have failed to create their own central emblem which, in seeming 'sheer miracle to the multitude', will give order to the tumult of images it inspires. Without that emblem there is only the 'tumult of images'; we are lost under the 'thunder of feet'. The return of memory is one kind of salvation, but it is no salvation for Ireland unless, like the Greeks, it can match its dionysiac multitude to an apollonian image; unless its multitude can be subdued to the power of the significant individual. The terms can be transferred directly to politics. The recovery of memory by the poet and the return of the 'memory of danger' upon which, according to Yeats, all the intense forms of literature depend, prefigure a new opportunity for Ireland, if only the 'multitude' can be brought to order upon a single focus, a focus found by the poet and acted out by the heroic individual, by the politician of sufficient strength and individuality to subdue the tumult of the world to a new order without losing the vitality which it gives access to. The new political order will weld together again, both in people's social relations and in their aesthetic experience, apollonian and dionysiac, focal image and emotion of multitude.

At the opposite pole from the anarchic centreless flux of contemporary Ireland, Yeats envisaged the perfect stasis of Byzantium, a political order fulfilling part at least of his aesthetic demand, a place where the sundered poles of image and multitude could be fused together again. 'Byzantium' is almost programmatically an account of Yeats's aesthetic theories as they join psychological and occult elements in the context of an appropriate political framework. The poem is also, of course, a summation of Yeats's symbolism, its images, as Gordon and Fletcher describe them, being 'encyclopaedic in the sense that they represent a compendium of Yeats's system of images'.[60] *A Vision*, systematising Yeats's thought, and his increasingly self-conscious use of a limited number of symbols, encourages the idea of an 'encyclopaedia' in which their meanings can be defined and fixed. But if we allow ourselves to adopt this procedure we do violence to the essential openness that he required of image as of poem. The development of Yeats's art is towards integrating images into his poems or into the whole body of his poetry so that they acquire an ever-increasing associative potential for his audience. Dragon, horse or weasel, for instance, in 'Nineteen Hundred and Nineteen', gain in intensity as repeated useage adds to their conglomerate connections in our minds, as do the birds, towers, or wandering madmen in the whole oeuvre. The poem and the book are made carriers of their own memories which we acquire as we read, but this is still just the first stage in the opening up of the unspoken series, like Shakespeare's shadowing plots, which continue beyond everything the poet provides. Such a principle may neither be true nor workable, but we must still resist the effort to turn associative plenitude into allegoric unity. And yet 'Byzantium', above all, encourages us to just that because its narrative implies so directly that it is an account of how symbolism works rather than a use of the symbolism itself, that Byzantium is the city in which art and afterlife mingle in a mutually purifying fire of all Yeats's central symbols:

Where blood begotten spirits come
And all complexities of fury leave,
Dying into a dance,

An agony of trance,
An agony of flame that cannot singe a sleeve.

(CP, p. 281)

But 'Byzantium' remains as structurally problematic as Yeats's ultimate transcendence of time and history by art as 'Sailing to Byzantium' did as a journey towards such transcendence. Bloom, for instance, complains that,

> The function of this stanza [three] has not yet been defined satisfactorily by any Yeats critic, in my judgment, and one can wonder how the poem would suffer if the stanza were to be omitted . . . another [problem] is presented by the sequence of the two remaining stanzas. Winters has rightly observed that 'the fourth stanza deals with the purification of the entering spirits, and the fifth with the struggle to enter: as far as the mere logic of the discussion goes, these stanzas ought to be in reverse order.'[61]

As with 'Sailing to Byzantium', I want to suggest, the problems are based on a mistaken notion of what the 'logic' of the discussion is: 'Byzantium' as symbol of Yeats's conception of how art purifies the material of life is based on the mirroring relation between his aesthetic and his ontology, and both are structured by the principle of association.

The first three stanzas of 'Byzantium' set up the three terms of the mirroring cosmology: in the foreground, but being winnowed away in this place of art and magic are the 'unpurged images of day', our common material world. Since matter, as we must not forget, is no reality for Yeats, these, no less than the fictions of art or the apparitions of ghosts, are only 'images':

> The unpurged images of day recede;
> The Emperor's drunken soldiery are abed;
> Night resonance recedes, night-walker's song
> After great cathedral gong;
> A starlit or a moonlit dome disdains
> All that man is,
> All mere complexities,
> The fury and the mire of human veins.

The logic of stanzas two and three is provided in line five of the first stanza — 'A starlit or a moonlit dome' — because the 'fury and the mire' of our unpurged lives suffers the contempt of two different versions of eternity, the eternity of the heavens' starlit dome and the perfection of art's moonlit cathedral dome, each mirroring the other. From the first of these, stanza two derives its version of a transcendent image, a ghost – 'more image than shade' – whose business is the purification of memory, undoing the past so that it can begin to complete what has been left incomplete in its previous experience. What it requires, however, is our life: we stand breathless before the sudden revelation of an image from our buried self, but it comes to breathe upon us new potentialities of future existence:

> For Hades' bobbin bound in mummy-cloth
> May unwind the winding path;
> A mouth that has no moisture and no breath
> Breathless mouths may summon;
> I hail the superhuman;
> I call it death-in-life and life-in-death.

The eternity of art projects its image in the 'Miracle bird or golden handiwork' which, in its refusal of time,

> Planted on the star-lit golden bough
> Can like the cocks of Hades crow,
> Or, by the moon embittered, scorn aloud
> In glory of changeless metal
> Common bird or petal
> And all complexities of mire and blood.

Both are out of time; both are 'superhuman', yet within Yeats's aesthetic both can have their power only through their interaction with our associations. The bird may scorn ordinary mortals, but it calls back the dead, like the cocks of Hades releasing them from their underworld. The dead return, however, only through us, through the 'I' to which they call and by which they are recalled. The 'death-in-life' of the changeless metal calls back to life the dead; the 'death-in-life' of the ghost gives life to the dead metal of the bird by endowing it with associative energy. The spirits bring back to us our dead, and the work of art carries beyond death something of ourselves but we need both of them: the bird may scorn change, but only the shifting images of our associations make it meaningful and those associations are identical with the memories of the dead as they purify their past experience.

Bird and ghost endow each other with life, but it is a life they can only acquire through us, through the 'mire of human veins' that they seem to transcend.

The order of stanzas four and five is, within this scheme, perfectly logical. The fourth stanza presents us with the emotion of multitude as it is resolved into pattern, the associations of poet or reader — the memories of the dead — discovering the single image that will allow access to the buried life or that will stimulate, at the end of reverie, a new stream of events in life:

> At midnight on the Emperor's pavement flit
> Flames that no faggot feeds, not steel has lit,
> Nor storm disturbs, flames begotten of flame,
> Where blood-begotten spirits come
> And all complexities of fury leave,
> Dying into a dance,
> An agony of trance,
> An agony of flame that cannot singe a sleeve.

The flames, like associations, beget one another: the associations are the purifying fire for spirits, but it is a fire which, like a work of art, may be 'agonising' and yet touches no one. Throughout his career Yeats had linked 'flames' with the 'moods' instantiated by the art work; as he put it in the 1890s:

> Time drops in decay,
> Like a candle burnt out,
> And the mountains and woods
> Have their day, have their day;
> What one in the rout
> Of the fire-born moods
> Has fallen away?

('The Moods'; *CP*, p. 62)

The 'rout' of the moods is the emotion of multitude transferred from the psychological to the ontological plane, and Yeats's first effort to envisage a world structured as a spiritual fabric mirroring the processes of his art. The same pattern appears in the poem he used as a preface to his 1895 collection:

> While I wrought out these fitful Danaan rhymes,

My heart would brim with dreams about the times
When we bent down above the fading coals
And talked of the dark folk who live in the souls
Of passionate men, like bats in the dead trees;
And of the wayward twilight companies
Who sigh with mingled sorrow and content,
Because their blossoming dreams have never bent
Under the fruit of evil and of good:
And of the embattled flaming multitude
Who rise, wing above wing, flame above flame,
And, like a storm, cry the Ineffable Name,
And with the clashing of their sword-blades make
A rapturous music . . .

('To some I have talked with by the fire'; CP, p. 56)

The poem rises through casual conversation to a universe that consists of an 'embattled flaming multitude': it is that sense of an ontology of spirits identical with the self-begetting, purifying process of association that Yeats's system allowed him to recover, so that the universe itself is an associative process, 'wing above wing, flame above flame', preserving in its memory the 'fire-born moods'. The conception in 'Byzantium' is much more dynamic, for rather than being the essential universe, in the face of which our own unpurged world is mere illusion, it is the interaction of these different dimensions of experience and existence which is now the focus of Yeats's concern. The work of art calls into existence those 'flames begotten of flames', that from their recovery and extinction in the process of association we may find pattern and order for our experience: that is why they 'die' into a dance, their individual being lost in the new shape which cannot singe a sleeve, but may set in motion other agonised flames; or may set in motion some action in the world again.

It is for this reason that stanza five is placed last: it recounts, as all associational art must, the turning back to life and time which is the purpose of the reverie. We do not transcend time in Yeats's Byzantium, except momentarily when we identify ourselves with one or other version of eternity that is at the opposite pole from ordinary life. But those eternities need time, need 'The fury and the mire of human veins', and release their power back into time through our associations. Thus stanza five, in its first half, shows the spirits being called to Byzantium, to death, to the perfection of art, for purification, in order to show us art turning the flow of its energy back into life at the poem's end:

> Astraddle on the dolphin's mire and blood,
> Spirit after spirit! The smithies break the flood,
> The golden smithies of the Emperor!
> Marbles of the dancing floor
> Break bitter furies of complexity,
> Those images that yet
> Fresh images beget,
> That dolphin-torn, that gong-tormented sea.

As several critics have noted 'break' has two opposed meanings in line two: it can imply 'interrupt, halt' or it can imply 'set loose, unleash', and those two meanings sum up the double focus of the unified image and the emotion of multitude upon which Yeats's aesthetic is based. The golden work of art interrupts the flow of time, the flood of un-purged images, by producing a time-transcending, death-defying object; the dancing floor similarly turns time into pattern and interrupts and reduces the fury and complexity of ordinary life to produce shape and harmony. But at the same time, those time-transcending unities 'break' loose upon the world new trains of association, new sequences of events in time: 'those images' (works of art) beget 'fresh images' (associations, historical events), while 'those images' in turn (historical events, associations) beget fresh images (works of art, ghosts), and both derive from and return to the sea that is both the sea of life and time (dolphin-torn) that Cuchulain opposed, and the sea of the Great Memory that transcends time and to which the 'great cathedral gong' calls. Yeats's eternity is no denial of time, but a space, like the work of art, into which images from our past life crowd, and from which other images flow back into time. 'Byzantium' attempts to perform in narrative what Yeats saw as the function of the artist's symbol, time's endless incorporation and regeneration of past into present, nothing forgotten or destroyed, but all called back again to be purified in the mind, or in the universal mind after death, that it could re-enter the flow of events and seek its completion. And as we read the poem we have to allow both those directions in which the work of art faces to have their place in our mind: we must see the poem's resolu-tion of life into pattern, the kind of pattern I have been expounding, but we also have to allow it to turn back upon our associations, allow-ing our memories to engage in the 'agony of flame' that its image may 'yet / Fresh images beget.'

It is on the dialectic of the ordered pattern of 'Byzantium' and the anarchic multitude of 'Nineteen Hundred and Nineteen' that Yeats's politics, as well as his aesthetics, is founded. 'Byzantium', as focus of aesthetic order, is also a place of political stability, its social world shaped to the rigidity of sculpture. It is a politics turned towards death, however, rather than towards life, and it is the dynamic of multitude that Yeats requires of society, but a multitude whose incessant movement is but the shadowing from one to another of a shared and single focus. Byzantium, if anything, is a place whose rigidity is too severe; we turn back with relief to the 'gong tormented sea' just as in 'Nineteen Hundred and Nineteen' we look back with nostalgia upon the Greek perfection that was 'sheer miracle to the multitude'. The relationship between the work of art and its emotion of multitude is, for Yeats, the same as the relationship between the state or nation and its people; the multitude has to be given its direction by the image which imposes on us from without, by the memory which preserves those images for future use: 'how shall we arouse the multitude,' he asks in 1930, 'if we admit our truths are partial?'[62] At the same time, to seek the answer we must 'speak of things that come out of the common consciousness, where every thought is like a bell with many echoes'.[63] A people must be bound together by what is a powerful emblem of its past, because such emblems have associative strength, and by a system of government that ensures the effectiveness of those emblems in uniting the multitude: images producing the emotion of multitude, a multitude resolved into unity by an image – upon that dialectic Yeats's politics are woven. That is why he found Swift's analysis – 'All States depend for their health upon a right balance between the One, the Few, and the Many'[64] – so satisfying; it accorded both with his aesthetics and his politics.

When Yeats expounds a theory of society based on activating the irrational commitment of the multitude through images with effective associational impact he is at one with the central strand of Fascist ideology. From Gustave Le Bon Sorel and Mussolini had both taken the lesson that

> Crowds being only capable of thinking in images are only to be impressed by images. It is only images that terrify or attract them and become motives of action.[65]

It is from the deliberate attempt to excite and sustain political motivation through the irrational power of the image that Fascist politics takes its style, and the most effective images, justifying the nationalist ideology of Fascism, were those to which people were long accustomed as the emblems of their nationality. Nationalism was, for Fascism, a pragmatic political theory based on their understanding of group psychology: the leaders of the nation were those who could be identified in the popular mind with the images which bonded the people into a single group. Thus for Yeats,

> The will of the State, whether it build a cage for a dead bird or remain in the bird itself, must always, whether interpreted by Burke or Marx, find expression through some governing class or company identified with that 'bent or current', with those 'elemental forms', whether by interest or training.[66]

Those elemental forms were what defined national spirit: the power of the ruling elite was not theirs directly, but theirs because they were associated directly with the images which had the greatest motivational impact on the multitude. Yeats's love of aristocrats and their houses is, therefore, no mere nostalgia for the eighteenth century: it is the medium through which the past offers to our memory those images which can unite the nation. To make what is already a part of the common memory rich in associational impact, as Yeats's poetry strove to do, is to make it an effective political instrument for mass motivation.

Yeats's turning to Fascism, however, is the result of his bitter realisation that the Anglo-Irish aristocracy was being destroyed as the peasants had been — or rather, was destroying itself in its inability to realise its true values. Robert Gregory, Maud Gonne, the proud and the beautiful inheritors of past riches fail to maintain their inheritance, bartering the 'rich horn' for individual 'delight' or 'an old bellows full of angry wind'.[67] 'Coole Park and Ballylee, 1931' tells the loss that has ensued:

> A spot whereon the founders lived and died
> Seemed once more dear than life; ancestral tree,
> Or gardens rich in memory glorified
> Marriages, alliances and families.

> (*CP*, p. 276)

The loss of what was 'rich in memory', however, is but the prelude to the creation of a new unity out of the old material: 'Both Sorel and Marx, their eyes more Swift's than Vico's, have preached a return to a primeval state, a beating of all down into a single class that a new civilisation may arise with its Few, its Many, and its One.'[68] As with all loss, Yeats could accept that beating down when he thought how whatever was remade was built from the same sources in the memory to which what has been destroyed has been returned. Thus 'Meditations in Time of Civil War' places against the decay of aristocracy Yeats's own tower:

> Two men have founded here. A man-at-arms
> Gathered a score of horses and spent his days
> In this tumultuous spot,
> Where through long wars and sudden night alarms
> His dwindling score and he seemed castaways
> Forgetting and forgot;
> And I, that after me
> My bodily heirs may find,
> To exalt a lonely mind,
> Befitting emblems of adversity.

(CP, p. 227)

At the beginning, the man of action, 'forgetting and forgot', but imposing order on 'this tumultuous spot'; at the end, Yeats, preserving in memory the values of the tower that it may gather the multitudinous present again to a single focus. From the real tower came one aristocracy, from the symbolic tower, with its commitment to memory, will come another. The mantle of the old aristocracy will, through Yeats himself and those like him, pass to new men of action when it is possible for the state to be again complete, and not 'half dead at the top.' Thus Yeats's marching songs for the Blueshirts march to the future in recovery of the past:

> Justify all those renowned generations,
> Justify all that have sunk in their blood,
> Justify all that have died on the scaffold,
> Justify all that have fled, that have stood,
> Stood or have marched the night long
> Singing, singing a song.
>
> . . .
>
> Fail, and that history turns into rubbish,
> All that great past to a trouble of fools;

Those that come after shall mock at O'Donnell,
Mock at the memory of both O'Neills,
Mock Emmet, mock Parnell:
All the renown that fell.

(*CP*, p. 322)

When Yeats rewrote the poem in 1938, when the action of Irish marching men seemed less urgently a part of contemporary politics, he
changed 'Justify' to 'Remember'. Without memory history — future
as well as past — turns to 'rubbish'.

The poem in which the dialectic of image and multitude is brought
most clearly to focus in its historical implication is 'Leda and the Swan'.
The genesis of the poem in specific historical circumstance is well
known; Yeats's own note makes it clear:

> I wrote 'Leda and the Swan' because the editor of a political review
> asked me for a poem. I thought 'After the individualist, demagogic
> movement founded by Hobbes and popularized by the Encyclo-
> paedists and the French Revolution, we have a soil so exhausted
> that it cannot grow a crop again for centuries.' Then I thought,
> 'Nothing is now possible but some movement from above pre-
> ceded by some violent annunciation.' My fancy began to play with
> Leda and the Swan for metaphor, and I began this poem; but as I
> wrote, bird and lady took such possession of the scene that all
> politics went out of it, and my friend tells me that his 'conservative
> readers would misunderstand the poem.[69]

Conor Cruise O'Brien quotes this passage in his famous essay on Yeats's
politics, and asks,

> How can that patter of Mussolini prose 'produce' such a poem?
> How can that political ugly duckling be turned into this glorious
> Swan? It is in a sense like the transmutation, in 'Easter 1916', of
> those whom Yeats had thought of as commonplace people.[70]

In the rhetoric of transmutation, however, O'Brien is doing what he
has, earlier in his essay, criticised others for doing — acting as though a
good poem must necessarily be antipathetic to an 'unacceptable'
politics. Fascism, whether as a political theory or an element in the
implication of art, is not necessarily inimical to human sympathy, and
it is surely the sense of sympathetic identification with Leda, her

terror and brutalisation, that gives the poem its force: we see in her the plight of every individual in a century when history has picked up and cast aside so many millions who knew nothing and wished to know nothing of its purposes. In the face of the immensity of our historical experience, we are all Leda:

> A sudden blow: the great wings beating still
> Above the staggering girl, her thighs caressed
> By the dark webs, her nape caught in his bill,
> He holds her helpless breast upon his breast.
>
> How can those terrified vague fingers push
> The feathered glory from her loosening thighs?
> And how can body, laid in that white rush,
> But feel the strange heart beating where it lies?
>
> A shudder in the loins engenders there
> The broken wall, the burning roof and tower
> And Agememnon dead.
>
>   Being so caught up,
> So mastered by the brute blood of the air,
> Did she put on his knowledge with his power
> Before the indifferent beak could let her drop?

(CP, p. 241)

The sense of historical determinism in which we are trapped and by which we are used is what the sudden transition from the 'shudder in the loins' to its consequences enforces, and what has happened to Yeats's original thought is that it is less the 'violent annunciation' of 'some movement from above' that concerns him than the response to such an annunciation from below. Yeats the artist, who seems in the prose to regard himself as in touch with the powers that come from above, projects himself in Leda as the medium which is violated that those powers can achieve their ends.

The tension between the real event which 'took possession of the scene' and a purely metaphoric event has not, in fact, been dissolved in Yeats's final poem, for the image remains ambiguous about its status: are we witness to an event we are to conceive of as real, or an image in art, like the sculpture of Leda and the Swan we know Yeats had seen in the British Museum, or are we to read it mythically, a metaphor for other experiences? The poem's language refuses to let us settle for one or the other, for its present tense verbs could imply either the immediacy of an actual event or the timelessness of art and myth, and the wings that are 'beating still' resolve themselves differently depending on which reading you emphasise: they are, existentially, in the act of beating during the course of the rape; aesthetically, they are actually still but with the appearance of motion; mythically, they beat still above our heads now as then. The consequences of the rape as the poem presents them share the same ambiguity: are they predestined by Zeus, or foreseen in a sudden access to divine omniscience by Leda, or merely recalled by the narrator as what actually occurred? We know the destruction, but we do not know what pattern of history's causation makes sense of that destruction: is all worth while because of the unspoken event that stands between violation and destruction — the birth of Helen? The questions which the poem poses about the nature of history are turned, equally, on the nature of the poem itself: has all been justified by the fact that the characters, their suffering and deaths, have been transformed to mythic figures in our memory?

The fact that the poem can thus maintain the contradictory tensions of different possible responses to the event does not mean, however, that it has somehow transferred itself to an apolitical realm. These ambiguities arise from the central tension of the poem, one also instantiated in the ambiguities of its language: do the 'loosening thighs' imply coercion or acceptance? Is the heart of Zeus 'lying' physically within the swan's body, or is it deceitful, not only in its disguise but in its intentions towards humanity? Underlying the sympathy with Leda's violation there is an undertow of identification with her based not on compassion but on desire — desire for the elevation that such participation has conferred on her. Yeats's awe-struck question — 'Did she put on his knowledge with his power'; — dramatises the desire that drives us, indifferent to suffering as the bird, to be made a part of a purpose so superior to the contingent and accidental actions of our individual lives. To play a part, even a suffering part, in such a divine intervention is to be granted some part of a divine omniscience, to be at the fulcrum of the passage between past and future. What happens to Leda is, metaphorically, what happens to the artist, as Yeats conceives him, and his sympathetic identification derives from his awareness that such knowledge and power speaks through him as well, speaks through him perhaps in the very act of writing this poem, which announces a new turn of the historical cycle. The poet's desire to control those images which will be the driving force of history, the ordinary man's desire to be taken up by the processes of history and have new significance, grander meaning, accorded to his life – these are not antipathetic to the 'patter of Mussolini prose'. They are the essence of the historical philosophies to which Fascism is attached and they are central to the emotions upon which Fascism called. The desire to accept suffering, reduction of selfhood, death, that one can play one's part upon the historical stage; the desire to be mastered by history even in the moment of terror: as we read the poem we should perhaps ask whether it is its knowledge or its power that we wish to put on?

'Agamemnon dead' brings us up against a terrifying existential full stop, but death for Agamemnon is also perpetual life in the memory. As it was for Cuchulain, for the rebels of 1916, death is life. The history that destroys them also preserves them as long as history remains in the memory: they are, like Leda, 'caught up' into a superior realm of existence. It is a transformation Yeats accords to Kevin O'Higgins, the justice minister of the Irish State – and often compared with Mussolini[71] – who was assassinated in 1927:

> A great man in his pride
> Confronting murderous men
> Casts derision upon
> Supersession of breath;
> He knows death to the bone –
> Man has created death.
>
> (*CP*, p. 264)

The unreality of death is a function of the universality of memory –

> Though grave-diggers' toil is long,
> Sharp their spades, their muscles strong,
> They but thrust their buried men
> Back in the human mind again.
>
> ('Under Ben Bulben'; *CP*, p. 398)

– but what comes back from the memory is not the 'murderous men', but the 'great man in his pride'. The poet, like Zeus as swan, drives his time to terror that it may achieve the memorability of tragedy, that the individual may define himself against the multitude, apollonian form requiring the assent of the dionysiac rout even at the moment of its extinction, knowing that, whatever is forgotten, it will be among the things that always return. The recovery of the power of memory by the poet justifies all those whose memory of power drives them to confront and dominate the anarchic multitude of the modern world: like the work of the poet they are and will be committed to memory.

8 ELIOT, POUND: MEMORY'S BROKEN BRIDGE

In 'Edmund Spenser', in 1902, Yeats had argued that English culture had undergone a radical break with the rise of the Puritans and their commercial spirit, a break to which Spenser was witness:

> In the time of Chaucer English poets still wrote much in French, and even English labourers lilted French songs over their work; and I cannot read any Elizabethan poem or romance without feeling the pressure of habits of emotion, and of an order of life, which were conscious, for all their Latin gaiety, of a quarrel to the death with that new Anglo-Saxon nation that was arising amid Puritan sermons and Marprelate pamphlets.[1]

Spenser's *Faerie Queen*, according to Yeats, 'was written in Merry England, but when Bunyan wrote in prison the other great English allegory, Modern England had been born',[2] a modern England full of 'joyless earnestness'. Spenser ('Sweet Thames, run softly till I end my song') was to play his part in Eliot's creative memory, but the rupture of history to which Yeats pointed was to become, in Eliot's theory, the dissociation of sensibility, and Yeats's sense of a culture which was continuous with the past was to be focused not on Spenser, but on Marvell:

> The seventeenth century sometimes seems for more than a moment to gather up and to digest into its art all the experience of the human mind which (from the same point of view) the later centuries seem to have been partly engaged in repudiating ... Marvell's best verse is the product of European, that is to say Latin, culture.[3]

And against such 'Latin' culture, Eliot too sets 'the flock of Zeal-of-the-land Busy or the United Grand Junction Ebenezer Temperance Association'.[4] Marvell's achievement, like those Yeats approved, was one that stems from 'an educated mind, rich in generations of experience'.[5] Eliot's is also an art that is 'richest to the richest' and depends upon an unbroken and unfading memory in history. The superiority of English as a literary language — 'the reason why it is the richest language for poetry'[6] — lies in its inheritance of the whole spectrum of European traditions in poetry in many different languages, and also, according to an essay of 1928, derives from the fact that Britain is not only the bridge between the major cultural traditions of Europe, but equally between Europe and the outside world:

> To our mind, the peculiar position of Britain is this: that she is on the one hand a part of Europe. But not only a part, she is a mediating part: for Britain is the bridge between Latin culture and Germanic culture, in both of which she shares. But Britain is not only the bridge, the middle way, between two parts of Western Europe: she is, or should be, by virtue of the fact that she is the only member of the European community that has established a genuine Empire — that is to say, a world wide Empire as was the Roman empire — not only European but the connection between Europe and the rest of the world.[7]

The English language and the British Empire offer the poet that continuity of history upon which a continuous train of association to the earliest times is founded, or rather, they would do so had it not been for the tragedy of the dissociation of sensibility.

The term 'dissociation' is Eliot's creative adaptation of a phrase of Remy de Gourmont's, intended to define a particular process of thought in which one sets out to break the habitual bonds of association between ideas and so allows oneself a new perspective on any question.[8] Pound continued to use de Gourmont's term in its original sense throughout his writings on economics,[9] but in Eliot's hands it underwent a shift which was related to his development of an associationist aesthetic. He uses the word several times in de Gourmont's sense, as, for instance, when he says of Charles Whibley that 'he has no dissociative faculty',[10] or when he suggests in 'Seneca in Elizabethan Translation' that 'progress was made, not by rejection, but by dissociating this type of verse into products with special properties.'[11] In *The Dial*, however, he attributed Virginia Woolf's art to what he saw as her powers of dissociation:

> A good deal of the charm of Mrs. Woolf's shorter pieces consists in the immense disparity between the object and the train of feeling which it has set in motion. Mrs. Woolf gives you the minutest datum, and leads on to explore, quite consciously, the sequence of images and feelings which float away from it ... The book is one of the most curious and interesting examples of the process of dis-

sociation which in that direction, it would seem, cannot be exceeded.[12]

Eliot's description — 'a train of feeling', 'the sequence of images and feelings which float away from it' — is of a process of association, but one so untypical and so conscious that it amounts to a breaking down of our habitual patterns of association. Dissociation ruptures common conjunctions in our thought and it is in this sense that Eliot uses the term in his essay on the Metaphysicals in which he announces the seventeenth century's fracture of its sensibility. Having pointed out the 'richness of association' in the work of the Metaphysicals, Eliot suggests that Samuel Johnson had

> hit, perhaps by accident, on one of their peculiarities, when he observes that 'their attempts were always analytic'; he would not agree that, after the dissociation, they had put the material together again in a new unity.[13]

Eliot's Metaphysicals, in this description, sound very like the Imagists, and Eliot's presentation of their quality of mind, or rather, the poet's quality of mind of which they are exemplars, insists on the ability to dissociate our habitual connections between events and so produce new and interesting totalities:

> When a poet's mind is perfectly equipped for its work, it is constantly amalgamating disparate experience; the ordinary man's experience is chaotic, irregular, fragmentary. The latter falls in love, or reads Spinoza, and these two experiences have nothing to do with each other, or with the noise of the typewriter or the smell of cooking; in the mind of the poet these experiences are always forming new wholes.[14]

Such dissociations and reconstitutions are, and this is the implication in de Gourmont's conception as well, synchronic: it is a capacity to 'devour any kind of experience'.[15] There is a point in history at which such a capability passed away, but the capability itself is not presented as resting on a foundation of historical continuity.

The essay on Marvell, however, begins to make a division between different kinds of Metaphysicals. 'Donne would have been an individual at any time and place',[16] but Marvell's verse is founded on a 'quality of civilization, of a traditional habit of life'.[17] The wit of Marvell is not a product of synchronic dissociations of different simultaneous, but usually unconnected, elements in present experience; it depends on 'a recognition, implicit in the expression of every experience, of other kinds of experience which are possible',[18] a recognition which involves an essentially historical perspective and a consciousness of the different ways in which an emotion would be expressed at different points in time. Marvell's dissociations are not of the common habits of association in his own historical epoch, but wrought from the conflict between different possible habits of association in different historical epochs. Quoting lines from 'To his Coy Mistress', Eliot comments: 'A whole civilization resides in these lines.'[19] The dissociations which the line achieves are diachronic, resulting for the reader in a consciousness of the whole literary tradition: 'The verse of Marvell has not the grand reverberation of Catullus's Latin; but the image of Marvell is certainly more comprehensive and penetrates greater depths than Horace's.'[20]

Penetration to greater depths is the outcome of the poem's ability to send its associations 'reverberating' back through the whole of history, an effect only possible because it has previously managed a dissociation of the habits of thought of other cultures. Such a range of association is, for Eliot, entirely 'impersonal', existing in the tradition and not in the individual. His displacement of Donne from the centre of his concerns rests upon his decision that there is too much in Donne which may be 'a curious personal point of view',[21] a failure of Donne's poetry to 'gather up and to digest into its art all the experience of the human mind': in fact, Donne's synchronic dissociations, powerful as they are, are themselves a part of the dissociation of sensibility that destroys the historical perspective of our habits of emotion. After the dissociation of sensibility the capacity for significant dissociations within the tradition withers; the break in the continuity of associative memory which the dissociation of sensibility involves makes impossible that play of wit which works by harnessing together discordant trains of feeling.

The capacity for dissociation rests, therefore, for Eliot, on the foundation of an unbroken pattern of association connecting the present with the depths of the past, and that in turns rests on the continuity of history. To know the continuity of history one must have a mind, like Marvell's, rich in generations of experience: thus H.G. Wells, we are told,

has not a historical mind; he has a prodigious gift of the historical imagination, which is comparable with Carlyle's, but this is quite a different thing from the understanding of history. *That* demands a degree of culture, civilization and maturity which Mr. Wells does not possess.[22]

Those same qualities — culture, civilization, maturity — are what is required for the production of great art. As Eliot put it in 'What is a Classic?',

> A classic can only occur when a civilization is mature; when a language and a literature are mature; and it must be the work of a mature mind. It is the importance of that civilization and of that language, as well as the comprehensiveness of the mind of the individual poet, which gives the universality.[23]

And as he says later in the same essay, 'The maturity of a literature is the reflection of that of the society in which it is produced', and that depends on 'a consciousness of history'.[24] There is thus a mutually buttressing relationship between belonging to a mature and continuous history and having the historical consciousness which makes one a mature writer. And the reason for that dependence lies on Eliot's underlying insistence that each work of art's power depends on its ability to stimulate an associational richness echoing back through all the 'stratifications of history': American literature, like works from any new or peripheral culture, was bound to be impoverished: 'Poe and Whitman, like bulbs in a glass bottle, could only exhaust what was in them. Hawthorne, more tentacular and inquisitive, sucked every actual germ of nourishment out of his granite soil; but the soil was mostly granite.'[25] Such minds cannot be 'rich in generations of experience' and the writer cannot, therefore, imply awareness 'of the predecessors behind his work' who 'should themselves be great and honoured'.[26]

The need for an unbroken bridge from present to past is not, for Eliot, a merely aesthetic loss, it is a moral loss, for it prevents the writer grasping the true depths of human experience. Eliot's insistent analogy throughout his writings is the equation of depth of historical consciousness with consciousness of the real depths of human nature: associative richness is a means of achieving a 'network of tentacular roots reaching down to the deepest terrors and desires'.[27] Thus, of Marvell's 'The Nymph and the Fawn', Eliot writes:

These verses have the suggestiveness of true poetry; and the verses of Morris, which are nothing if not an attempt to suggest, really suggest nothing; and we are inclined to infer that the suggestiveness is the aura round the bright clear centre, and that you cannot have the aura alone. The daydreamy feeling of Morris is essentially a slight thing; Marvell takes a slight affair, the feeling of a girl for her pet, and gives it a connection with that inexhaustible and terrible nebula of emotion which surrounds all our exact and practical passions and mingles with them.[28]

The associational 'aura' is our means of bringing to consciousness the 'inexhaustible and terrible nebula of emotion' which each of us carries within us, and can only be grasped by a mind with a historical consciousness. To lose the sense of history, or to be cut off from history's continuous development, is to relapse to the savage. Yeats and Pound had both seen continuity of memory as a means of getting back to a lost source of knowledge and harmony with the world: for Eliot memory is essential because it maintains the bridge that allows us to keep our distance from the beginnings of human history, from the savage. Eliot, like Conrad, had taken his lessons from Frazer: the rituals and the beliefs of the savage are still there within modern man, and only 'civilization', 'maturity' will protect us from them. Eliot's argument with romanticism was precisely that it sought to destroy this distance by destroying the importance of memory. As he said in response to Middleton Murry's argument that all morality rests not upon principle but on an 'inner voice':

> My belief is that those who possess the inner voice are ready enough to harken to it, and will hear no other ... possessors of the inner voice ride ten in a compartment to a football match at Swansea, listening to the inner voice, which breathes the eternal message of vanity, fear and lust.[29]

Without the conscious culture that maintains our distance from the roots of memory by maintaining our awareness that they are still in us, we revert to the primitive, we are taken over by the eternal message that speaks through the species unredeemed by history. Associative processes reaching back to the beginnings of our culture reach down, at the same time, to those depths in ourselves from which only the memory of culture and the differentiation of feeling within history can save us.

The implication that the lower classes live in the depths of such a

memory is one that Eliot, while accepting the analogy of classes to
levels of consciousness in the mind, was to reject in *Notes towards the
Definition of Culture*, when he argued against what he saw as,

> our tendency to think of culture as a group culture exclusively,
> the culture of the 'cultured' classes and elites. We then proceed
> to think of the humbler part of society as having culture only in
> so far as it participates in this superior and more conscious culture.
> To treat the 'uneducated' mass of the population as we might treat
> some innocent tribe of savages to whom we are impelled to deliver
> the true faith, is to encourage them to neglect or despise that culture
> which they should possess and from which the more conscious part
> of culture draws vitality . . .[30]

The lower orders form, in relation to conscious culture, the same kind
of hinterland that memory and maturity of civilisation form for the
conscious artist, and unless that bridge too is held intact the conscious
culture will wither. Indeed, there was a point when Eliot, like Yeats,
seemed to find the culture of the lower orders the only part of culture
which had maintained the continuity of memory through its self-
conscious adherence to its own culture. In his essay on the death of
Marie Lloyd he wrote:

> I have called her the expressive figure of the lower classes. There
> is no such expressive figure for any other class. The middle class
> are morally corrupt. That is to say, their own life fails to find a
> Marie Lloyd to express it . . . The middle classes, in England as
> elsewhere, under democracy, are morally dependent on the aristoc-
> racy, and the aristocracy are subordinated to the middle class, which
> is gradually absorbing and destroying them. The lower class still
> exists; but perhaps it will not exist for long.[31]

What was significant, for Eliot, in this disappearing lower-class world
was that the working man 'who went to the music-hall and joined in
the chorus and saw Marie Lloyd was himself performing part of the
act; he was engaged in that necessary collaboration of the audience
with the artist which is necessary in all art.' The collaboration of the
audience in the art of poetry was more complex, but the destruction
of memory was, for conscious culture, exactly such a destruction as
Eliot foretold was about to descend upon the lower classes as well:
they would soon, like other classes, be made memoryless, unconscious

by the 'senseless music and action too rapid for the brain to act upon'
of the cinema, and would 'receive, without giving, in that same listless
apathy with which the middle and upper classes regard any entertain-
ment of the nature of art'.[32]

Eliot's attitude to the 'humbler part of society' was, however, to be
more influenced by the analogy of the depth of the mind, the depths
of time, and the depths of society as equivalent retreats from the
conscious maintenance of the sense of history and maturity than these
two extracts imply. In 1927 in a description which is perhaps not
unconnected with the General Strike of the previous year, Eliot finds,
in a piece called 'The Latest Muscovite Menace', that the artistic participation of the lower orders is not an 'expression' of their own
appropriate culture, but a threatening return to primitive ritual:

> Readers of an interesting German book, entitled *Geist und Gesicht
> des Bolshevismus* . . . will remember a photograph of a proletarian
> conductor, with a couple of railway flags, directing some 'com-
> munity singing' from the top of a factory. Of late, whenever any
> very large number of Britons is assembled in one place for holiday
> enjoyment, a Cup Final or Test Match, we find that a large part of
> the excitement consists in their singing all together. We have not
> witnessed such a sacrifice, and do not know whether it is as yet
> merely a newspaper wheeze, or whether it has really taken hold
> of the British *Massenmensch*. If it has really caught on we should
> like our social philosophers to tell us what it means . . . We are
> already accustomed to seeing, from time to time, immense numbers
> of men and women voting all together, without using their reason
> and without enquiry; so perhaps we have no right to complain
> of the same masses singing all together, without much sense of tune
> or knowledge of music; we may presently see them praying and
> shouting hallelujahs all together, without much theology or know-
> ledge of what they are praying about. We cannot explain it. But it
> should at present be suspect: it is very likely hostile to Art . . .[33]

The savage sacrifice of Art by the *Massenmensch* represents the collapse
of the ordered progression of history and the ordered relation between
the conscious and the unconscious elements in society. The lower
orders can no longer act as an 'unconscious' for 'high' culture because
they have lost the consciousness of their own culture and reverted to an
unconsciousness that is like savagery itself. The same will happen to
'high' culture if it loses its relationship with the past or with the lower

elements in its own society. Without all these 'tentacular roots' the plant of culture withers, and the central commitment, therefore, for any artist is 'to preserve the continuity of life',[34] for we may discover at any moment 'the relation of a modern Englishman to Shakespeare . . . to be that of a modern Greek to Aeschylus'.[35] The first moral of artistic and of political life is thus identical, and it is one Eliot found promulgated by the French historian Fustel de Coulanges, a hero of the *Action Française* and subject of a *Criterion* article translated by Eliot in 1928, who wrote that 'true patriotism is not love of the soil, it is love of the past, it is respect for the generations which have gone before us.'[36] The bridge that connects us with the past is defended by the few against the forgetting many, for 'the forces of deterioration are a large crawling mass, and the forces of development half a dozen men.'[37]

Eliot's early criticism had seemed to insist that literature must be separated from all other aspects of life, and it could do so because the memory upon which Eliot wished literature to draw was a memory contained within the tradition of literature, a tradition he seemed to assume had a kind of independent and self-sustaining existence. Thus in his essay on Blake — an interesting example of Eliot's very personal form of criticism, one which works by judging the artist's life in terms of an implicit contrast with Eliot's own to reveal the conditions which prevented his becoming a truly impersonal artist[38] — despite acknowledging the limitations placed on Blake by his 'being a humble engraver', Eliot insists that 'we are not really so remote from the continent, or from our own past, as to be deprived of the advantages of culture if we wish them.'[39] Such a voluntarist view of the acquisition of culture can operate only because the 'monuments' of the cultural tradition are, as 'Tradition and the Individual Talent' explains, 'ideal': they are a pattern in the mind only, and any mind which acquires them is identical with the 'European mind' itself. What Eliot came quickly to see, however, was that the ideal memory had to be sustained in the context of a continuity embodied in social patterns which preserved an unbroken memory for other than literary reasons. The tension reveals itself in 'Burbank with a Baedeker: Bleistein with a Cigar', for the poem develops a technique that is parallel to Yeats's in works like 'September 1913', except that instead of dramatising a speaker whose assertions are denied by the poem's formal qualities, the form in Eliot's poem asserts a memory in defiance of the characters whose life it narrates. The American for whom Europe is a cultural tourist trip and the American whose genealogy cuts him off from all the continuity of culture which Europe represents, are opposed by the verbal texture of the poem itself, a texture which, in its multiple echoes of past literature, insists on its development directly out of the tradition, despite the fact that it is written by an American:

> Burbank crossed a little bridge
>   Descending at a small hotel;
> Princess Volupine arrived,
>   They were together, and he fell.
>
> Defunctive music under sea
>   Passed seaward with the passing bell
> Slowly: the God Hercules
>   Had left him, that had loved him well.
>
> The horses, under the axletree
>   Beat up the dawn from Istria
> With even feet. Her shuttered barge
>   Burned on the water all the day.
>
> But this or such was Bleistein's way:
>   A saggy bending of the knees
> And elbows, with the palms turned out,
>   Chicago Semite Viennese.
>
> A lustreless protrusive eye
>   Stares from the protozoic slime
> At a perspective of Canaletto.
>   The smoky candle end of time
>
> Declines. On the Rialto once.
>   The rats are underneath the piles.
> The Jew is underneath the lot.
>   Money in furs.

(CP, p. 42)

Burbank 'fell', seduced by a Europe which is decadent, the remnant of a great tradition. But Burbank is prepared for his fall by the analogy with Bleistein, emblematic of the American experience of mixed cultural inheritance. Bleistein, product of no single culture, blood of the alien, inheritor of modern industrial civilisation, stares with an atavistic eye at the perspective of the past, uncomprehending. The ordered development of European tradition to which Burbank might have been an appropriate inheritor is undone by the deracinated, but is undone because the European tradition itself has already been corrupted by the same racial and cultural confusion: 'The Jew is underneath the lot'. By his cultural refusal of integration, the Jew undoes the continuity of culture and Burbank's and the Princess's fall is prepared for them by the succumbing of their cultures to the same infection.

The poem itself enacts a memory, however, by which we judge the characters. The situation is both given its sense of significance and judged as a decline by comparison with the situations to which the richly allusive texture of the verse points. That memory is also turned upon us as readers, however, challenging us to a mastery of the past, judging us by our almost inevitable failure. The tradition which we watch in decline in the characters is remade if we can rise to effect the associative totality which the allusions leave us to perform. The impurity of the characters is thus challenged by the 'purity' of the art emotions in which their actions are encased; the decline of the tradition by its reconstitution in the mind of the appropriate reader. Where Prufrock had found the world of imagination that refused itself to life (or death) — the gestures of art being without application in our contingent reality — Eliot, in 'Burbank with a Baedeker: Bleistein with a Cigar', strives to present an amnesiac world in art despite its antipathy to his medium; he strives to engender in his readers those depths of memory which his characters have denied. But the 'little bridge' by which we cross to the past to construct the perspective of the 'ideal monuments' of tradition rests upon rotten piles if the society of which we are a part has already lost its continuity. History, the pattern of the 'great organic formations'[40] of human life, may always have its ideal existence, but its pattern need not pass through any particular individual culture: only a local history which keeps its own memory and tradition intact can be a carrier of the whole tradition, a bridge between past and future for the whole European mind. Thus by 1928, although still insisting on the error of 'confusing literary questions with others, such as moral, philosophical or religious', Eliot was to qualify it by adding that 'it is not that these matters are unconnected, but that we must keep them separate to see their connections.'[41] In an early essay he had ascribed George Wyndham's failure as a writer to the fact that 'his literature and his politics and his country life are one and the same thing'; they are not expressions of the developing pattern of the tradition, but of 'this peculiar English type, the aristocrat, the Imperialist, the Romantic'.[42] But it was only through the social life of such peculiar English types that memory could, in the 1920s, be sustained in the face of a far more dangerous threat than 'riding to hounds across one's prose', the threat of the oblivion of the whole tradition; 'For the Russian Revolution has made men conscious of the position of Western Europe as (in Valéry's words) a small and isolated cape on the western side of the Asiatic continent.'[43] The threat from without was matched by the threat from within the 'civilised countries'[44] of Europe.

The world of collapsing historical perspectives and cultural amnesia Eliot dramatised in Sweeney, the archetypal antagonist of the quatrain poems written at the end of the War:

(The lengthened shadow of a man
   Is history, said Emerson
Who had not seen the silhouette
   Of Sweeney straddled in the sun.)

                          ('Sweeney Erect'; *CP*, p. 45)

Emerson's naivety about history is the result of his not having encountered the challenge to culture posed by the flow of 'mixed immigration'[45] of which Sweeney is, like Bleistein, a product. But in a later poem Sweeney is allowed an awareness of what threatens even his part in the modern world, the ever imminent incursion of the 'eternal message' of the species:

I knew a man once did a girl in
Any man might do a girl in
Any man has to, needs to, wants to
Once in a lifetime, do a girl in.

                      ('Sweeney Agonistes'; *CP*, p. 134)

It is the essence of Eliot's theory of poetry that by reaching down through memory to those 'deepest terrors and desires' beyond the 'stratifications of history that cover savagery', we prevent the possibility of a return in action of such impulses: art cathartically releases into the conscious mind and into conscious control that incursion of the savage 'which an age of prudence can never retract'.[46] The tension between descent into the savage and control of it through memory is enacted in the conflict between Eliot's poetic style and the memoryless animality of the world Sweeney inhabits – 'Gesture of orang-outang / Rises from the sheets in steam' (*CP*, p. 44). It is a world in which

Sweeney is knowingly at home —

> Sweeney addressed full length to shave
>   Broadbottomed, pink from nape to base,
> Knows the female temperament
>   And wipes the suds around his face.

(*CP*, p. 45)

— but which the poem can only handle with a linguistic scrupulousness that keeps it securely at arm's length. Sweeney and his companions live in a world which, in its unconsciousness of the past, walks through the dark of the savagery from which civilisation is our only salvation.

Nowhere is the tension between the memoryless recurrence of the primitive and civilised memory more dramatically presented than in 'Sweeney Among the Nightingales', a poem whose insistent attention to surface presentation and suggestion of narrative continuity tempt us to believe that we can close its openness:

> The person in the Spanish cape
> Tries to sit on Sweeney's knees
>
> Slips and pulls the table cloth
> Overturns a coffee-cup,
> Reorganised upon the floor
> She yawns and draws a stocking up;
>
> The silent man in mocha brown
> Sprawls at the window-sill and gapes;
> The waiter brings in oranges
> Bananas figs and hothouse grapes;
>
> The silent vertebrate in brown
> Contracts and concentrates, withdraws;
> Rachel *née* Rabinovitch
> Tears at the grapes with murderous paws;

(*CP*, p. 59)

The concentration on surface is so assiduous as to seem conciliatory to those — 'such as stockbrokers, politicians, men of science'[47] — who need to approach art through human rather than art emotions, even if the human emotions (reduction of people to animals — 'silent verte-

brate', murderous paws') are unpleasant. But it is precisely the delibera-
tion of surface that makes the poem opaque: characters are trapped by
their gestures, action is suspended out of the flow of time, suggesting
a multitude of possibilities none of which the poem will confirm or
deny. What is the relationship between the characters? Is 'Rachel
née Rabinovitch' suspect because of her racial origins or because
of her being 'in league' with the 'lady in the cape'? Is Sweeney about
to be murdered in some love triangle — or is he, as some critics have
maintained, asleep and dreaming the whole performance? Equally,
the large poetic allusions which frame the action are entirely vague:

> The circles of the stormy moon
> Slide westward toward the River Plate,
> Death and the Raven drift above
> And Sweeney guards the hornèd gate.

Just as there are no actions in the poem to concretise the relations
between the characters, there is no common poetic memory to which
these symbols can be attached to acquire significance: the multitudinousness of suggestion is a function of their total decontextualisa-
tion, as though challenging the reader with his failure to sustain a
significant memory.

The poem's conclusion, however, unleashes an entirely different
order of significance:

> The host with someone indistinct
> Converses at the door apart,
> The nightingales are singing near
> The Convent of the Sacred Heart,
>
> And sang within the bloody wood
> When Agamemnon cried aloud
> And let their liquid siftings fall
> To stain the stiff dishonoured shroud.

The change of tense marks the release of memory into the present-
tense world of Sweeney and his narrator. The verse acquires an associative depth which is not that of mere vagueness, because the concrete
immediacy of the image enforces a sense of the temporal gap between
Sweeney and Agamemnon, a gap which has to be filled from memory
as the mock-heroic symbols of the earlier part of poem did not need

to be since they shared the same moment of time as Sweeney himself. From being a poem whose openness depended upon its narrative obliquity, the poem suddenly reaches a climactic image whose openness is that of allowing its reverberations to echo and linger in our minds — a diachronic rather than a synchronic dissociation. Paradoxically, therefore, as we move forward in the poem's implied narrative we seem to be moving ever nearer to an act of violation or violence about to be committed, but the poem's conclusion reverses the forward thrust of narrative and turns back to the beginnings of our cultural memory. This double movement enacts, I suggest, Eliot's double conception of the power of memory: for those with memory, such violence returns as a recall of the past already controlled by art; for those without memory such barbarism will return in deed. Sweeney's companions will re-enact in reality the drama they have failed to remember as art. As Harry says in *The Family Reunion*, which also unites the contemporary world with the world of Greek tragedy:

> When I remember them
> They leave me alone: when I forget them
> Only for an instant of inattention
> They are roused again, the sleepless hunters
> That will not let me sleep.[48]

Memory protects us by keeping the horrific potentialities of our minds in consciousness; forgetfulness releases those secreted memories into action again. As we read the final stanza of 'Sweeney Among the Nightingales' we know both with equal force: the potentialities of barbarism and also the means by which we have controlled it. In ancient Greece the horror was kept at bay by the balance of the apollonian and the dionysiac, but that balance itself is the embodiment, for us, of the horrors to which failure of memory will return us.

'Sweeney Among the Nightingales' is the poem which, in Eliot's collected poems, immediately precedes *The Waste Land*. Originally, Eliot intended to preface *The Waste Land* by 'Gerontion', the poem which now opposes 'Sweeney Among the Nightingales' from the other end of the 'Poems 1920' section of *Collected Poems*. The two, I suggest, are deeply related and form the dialectic within which *The Waste Land* will operate. For in 'Sweeney Among the Nightingales' the current of memory still flows, but flows only to uncover as its foundation the horrific and ritual violence embodied in Greek tragedy; in 'Gerontion' the bridge of memory is down: it is a poem exploring the condition of a mind capable of memory, but operating within a culture which offers that memory no pathway to the past, no pathway even to the dubious salvation of tragic irony:

> Neither fear nor courage saves us. Unnatural vices
> Are fathered by our heroism. Virtues
> Are forced upon us by our impudent crimes.

(*CP*, p. 40)

The ironic reversals upon which tragedy was built and which offered some foundation to memory in 'Sweeney Among the Nightingales' can provide no basis for the world Gerontion inhabits, because it is one in which association is infinite, but meaningless: 'After such knowledge, what forgiveness?' The question baffles response because 'knowledge' has no referent but explodes into all its possible connotations in the English language. The past weighs enormities of suggestion in every word of the poem, but we, like Gerontion, will toil in vain to release from it a unitary meaning:

> These with a thousand small deliberations
> Protract the profit of their chilled delirium,
> Excite the membrane, when the sense has cooled,
> With pungent sauces, multiply variety
> In a wilderness of mirrors.

We are trapped, in 'Gerontion', in the region Yeats called Hodos Chameliontos, where 'image called up image in an endless procession, and I could not always choose among them with any confidence; and when I did choose, the image lost its intensity, or changed into some other image . . .'[49] For in 'Gerontion' the assertive rhetoric of 'Tradition and the Individual Talent', promulgating its confident sense of an ideal tradition through which our associations are channelled back into the past in a single stream, finds its terrifying anti-self, a mind in which all memory is an endless echoing of an unstable present, multitude without pattern, memory without history, incapable even of the horror of the revelation that 'Sweeney Among the Nightingales' provides.

'Gerontion' is memory detached from any answering pattern in history. It opens in negation of direct involvement in history — 'I was neither at the hot gates / Nor fought in the warm rain' — as significant action, and continues by dissolving the very word 'history' into the multiplicity of its possible meanings — the discipline of research, the narration of events, the actual events of the past, the significant events of the present: all are and are not, 'history':

> History has many cunning passages, contrived corridors
> And issues, deceives with whispering ambitions,
> Guides us by vanities. Think now
> She gives when our attention is distracted
> And what she gives, gives with such supple confusions
> That the giving famishes the craving. Gives too late
> What's not believed in, or is still believed,
> In memory only, reconsidered passion.

With each of the possible meanings of 'history' all the other words — 'passages', 'corridors', 'issues' — change meaning. Instead of a rich life of accumulating memory, we look into 'Gerontion' and find the fear that history has by-passed us. Where, in 'Prufrock', it was the certainty of art that could not be brought into life, in 'Gerontion' it is the certainty of a single 'history' and therefore a justification of univocal memory that cannot be brought into life: 'The word within a word, unable to speak a word / Swaddled with darkness'. Only some kind of revelation can release us from this endless uncertainty, grounding memory in history, but the meanings we have tried to live by will, in their turn, be transformed in the 'point of view' — or rather, 'points of view' — of the future, and thus we are to

> Think at last
> We have not reached conclusion, when I
> Stiffen in a rented house.

Action, like language, will echo to meanings we have not envisaged when we committed ourselves to it.

In Hodos Chameliontos memory attaches to no reality, and therefore, according to Yeats, we 'never long escape the shape-changers', for 'the dead no longer remembering their own names become characters in the drama we ourselves have invented'.[50] Yeats's ghosts become inconsistent, but Gerontion's drama, too, is enacted by characters who have lost their identities to the gestures they perform in the speaker's own drama:

> In depraved May, dogwood and chestnut, flowering judas,
> To be eaten, to be divided, to be drunk

Among whispers; by Mr. Silvero
With caressing hands, at Limoges
Who walked all night in the next room;
By Hakagawa, bowing among the Titians;
By Madame de Tornquist, in the dark room
Shifting the candles; Fraulein von Kulp
Who turned in the hall, one hand on the door. Vacant shuttles
Weave the wind. I have no ghosts.

Yeats needs ghosts who remember their own names: Gerontion needs ghosts. If Eliot's poetry fearfully recovers the memory of savagery as the horrific end point of memory, what it seeks, like all associationist poetry, as salvation, is the calling up of a ghost. A ghost is the sustained presence of the past made visible to us, it is a buried memory resurrected. Associationist poetry always finds its appropriate metaphor in the ghost which symbolises access to a continuity of memory beyond the individual and his capacity to recall the past: the past recalls itself to us in the ghost.[51] Trapped in the entropic world of modern physics —

De Bailhache, Fresca, Mrs. Cammel, whirled
Beyond the circuit of the shuddering Bear
In fractured atoms.

— Gerontion is visited by no ghosts, and his memories are only

Tenants of the house
Thoughts of a dry brain in a dry season.

Gerontion's associations are like the arch of a bridge leaning out into space with no arch on the other side to buttress them.

In Gerontion's ghostless existence Eliot was possibly dramatising his response to the draft of three cantos published by Pound in 1917. There, Pound examines Browning's misuse of history in *Sordello*, but finds it, in the end, of no consequence:

And half your dates are out, you mix your eras;
For that great font Sordello sat beside —
'Tis an immortal passage, but the font? —
Is some two centuries outside the picture.
Does it matter?

> Not in the least. Ghosts move about me
> Patched with histories.[52]

History is only our fragmentary knowledge of the past, fragmentary rags of the living memory that appears as ghosts. Eliot wants History to be the ontological justification of memory, separating the personal and accidental into universal associations and traditions, and with the failure of history there is only an endless echoing passageway, that leads neither to the future nor to the depths of the past. Pound, however, like Yeats, sees the past directly; it is a memory offering itself to him:

> Dordoigne! When I was there,
> There came a centaur, spying the land
> And there were nymphs behind him.
> And going on the road by Salisabury
> Procession on procession —
> For that road was full of peoples,
> Ancient in various days, long years between them.
> Ply over ply of life still wraps the earth there.[53]

The ghosts — though Pound was to remove them from the early Cantos — are no melodrama of the poetic imagination, but the only means of visualising — in both of its senses — a memory lingering on beyond physical life, and one which remains entirely separate from the perceiving consciousness. The dissociation of sensibility was to seem so significant to Eliot because he had no such ontology to give justification to memory beyond its instantiation in history. For Yeats and Pound memory was significant because it took us back to an awareness of the reality of memory in the past: if we lost the way back that memory continued none the less, but for Eliot it was the elements contained in the pattern of our memory that was important, because it was our distance from the past, not our incorporation of it, that he wanted to achieve. The distinction can be seen clearly in the three men's attitudes to what constitutes the power of a tradition. Yeats, for instance, attributes some of the effect of Shakespeare to his continued access to a memory in which gods and goddesses were real:

> Maive (Medb is the Irish spelling) is continually described as the
> queen of all the western fairies, and it is probably some memory
> of her lingering in western England, or brought home by adventurers

from Ireland, that gave Shakespeare his Queen Mab. But neither Maive, nor any of our Irish faeries is like the fairies of Shakespeare; for our faeries are never very little, and are sometimes taller and more beautiful than mortals. The greatest among them were gods and goddesses of ancient Ireland, and men have not yet forgotten their glory.[54]

Eliot also regrets the loss of those ancient and primitive deities, but only because their loss breaks up the continuity, the richness, of a memory that has no other justification but its unbroken plenitude:

> We may speculate, for amusement, whether it would not have been beneficial to the north of Europe generally, and to Britain in particular, to have had a more continuous religious history. The local divinities of Italy were not wholly exterminated by Christianity, and they were not reduced to the dwarfish fate which fell upon our trolls and pixies. The latter, with the major Saxon deities, were perhaps no great loss in themselves, but they left an empty place; and perhaps our mythology was further improverished by the divorce from Rome. Milton's celestial and infernal regions are large but insufficiently furnished apartments filled by heavy conversation; and one remarks about Puritan mythology its thinness. And about Blake's supernatural territories, as about the supposed ideas that dwell there, we cannot help commenting on a certain meanness of culture.[55]

For Eliot there is no glory to the beliefs of the past, as there is for Yeats, but lack of them impoverishes the memory to which present art is heir. Eliot's conception is echoed, with more positive intent, however, by Pound, for he, like Yeats, sees in memory a means to reconstituting a pagan religion integral to the needs of poetry: 'What we believe is really the pre-Christian element which Christianity has not stamped out. The only Christian festivals having any vitality are welded to sun festivals, the spring solstices, the Corpus and St. John's eve, registering the turn of the sun . . .'[56] For Pound, Christianity retains unintentionally the memory required by poetry, as for Eliot, later, Christianity would provide the only continuous memory on which the tradition could rely.

In the early 1920s, however, before his conversion to Christianity, ontological foundation was what Eliot — as compared with Yeats or Pound — lacked in his conception of memory. Perhaps that is why the draft Cantos of 1917, with their insistence upon the reality of the ghost, were to linger so powerfully in Eliot's mind. Meditating still on Browning, Pound asks the purpose of our projections into the past:

> what were the use
> Of setting figures up and breathing life
>   upon them
> Were't not *our* life, your life, my life,
>   extended?
> I walk Verona. (I am here in England)
> I can see Can Grande. (Can see whom you will)
>   You had one whole man?
> And I have many fragments, less worth?
>   Less worth?
> Ah, had you quite my age, quite such a
>   beastly and cantankerous age?
> You had some basis, had some set belief.[57]

Without set beliefs Pound is not, however, quite reduced to 'shoring fragments against ruin', because he has with him the memory of a time when memory revealed itself as still living, still vital: he describes his 'chosen and peninsular village' on a festival day, a place where 'some old ghost eats smoke':

> And the place is full of spirits.
> Not *lemures*, not dark and shadowy ghosts,
> But the ancient living, wood-white,
> Smooth as the inner bark, and firm of aspect,
> And all agleam with colors – no, not agleam,
> But colored like the lake and like the olive
>   leaves
> Glaukopos, clothed like the poppies, wearing
>   golden greaves,
> Light on the air.[58]

Though the social and historical forms by which we recover the past are 'all but truth and memory / Dimmed only by the attritions of long time', what such experiences speak is the message the ghost brings – 'But we forget not.'[59] And therefore, for Pound, the place in which such an experience is possible is home: 'This is our home, the trees are full of laughter'.[60] That home was to be recovered by

Eliot in 'Burnt Norton', first of the *Four Quartets*, when he steps

> Into our first world.
> There they were, dignified, invisible,
> Moving without pressure over the dead leaves.

> (*CP*, p. 190)

and he finds that

> the leaves were full of children
> Hidden excitedly, containing laughter

The ghosts Gerontion did not have reveal themselves, and the associations which lost themselves in a 'wilderness of mirrors' can find their ontological justification in a living memory:

> And what the dead had no speech for, when living,
> They can tell you, being dead: the communication
> Of the dead is tongued with fire beyond the language of the living.

> ('Little Gidding'; *CP*, p. 215)

When Yeats, at the beginning of *A Vision*, took Pound's 'The Return' not as a poem announcing 'some change of style',[61] but as prefiguring his own occult discoveries, he was in turn prefiguring Eliot's allusion to Pound's poem in the concluding section of 'Little Gidding':

> We die with the dying:
> See, they depart, and we go with them.
> We are born with the dead:
> See, they return, and bring us with them.

> (*CP*, p. 222)

Four Quartets rediscovers memory out of the collapse of Europe in the Second World War: the bridge they establish to the past is the undoing of the collapse of memory which the First World War betokened, and of which *The Waste Land* is the fundamental expression: 'London Bridge is falling down falling down falling down'. In 'Little Gidding', however, when the real London is being bombed, memory is resurrected to confirm that the bridge is unfallen; the ghost walks:

After the dark dove with the flickering tongue
  Had passed below the horizon of his homing
  While the dead leaves still rattled on like tin
Over the asphalt where no other sound was
  Between three districts whence the smoke arose
  I met one walking, loitering and hurried
As if blown towards me like the metal leaves
  Before the urban dawn wind unresisting.
  And as I fixed upon the down-turned face
That pointed scrutiny with which we challenge
  The first met stranger in the waning dusk
  I caught the sudden look of some dead master
Whom I had known, forgotten, half recalled
  Both one and many; in the brown baked features
  The eyes of a familiar compound ghost

(*CP*, p. 217)

In the 1930s Eliot's poetry had turned away from a style involving multiplicity of association because the world had lost its memory: the poetry, like Yeats's in the period between 1903 and 1916, has to accept that it must argue for the values of memory without being able to use them. Thus in 'Choruses from *The Rock*' repetition replaces recall as the central means of poetry, because, for the audience, the bridges are down that would connect them with their past:

The world turns and the world changes,
But one thing does not change.
In all of my years, one thing does not change.
However you disguise it, this thing does not change:
The perpetual struggle of Good and Evil.
Forgetful, you neglect your shrines and churches

(*CP*, p. 163)

The recovery of shared Christian belief, shared suffering, shared memory in *Four Quartets* is also the recovery of an associational poetic language, one in which the memory which builds up multiple meanings for words and images through the four poems can finally open out into the totality of the Christian tradition, a tradition which includes the totality of the poetic tradition:

Through the unknown, remembered gate

When the last of earth left to discover
Is that which was the beginning;
At the source of the longest river
The voice of the hidden waterfall
And the children in the apple-tree
Not known, because not looked for
But heard, half-heard, in the stillness
Between two waves of the sea.
Quick now, here, now, always —
A condition of complete simplicity
(Costing not less than everything)
And all shall be well and
All manner of thing shall be well
When the tongues of flame are in-folded
Into the crowned knot of fire
And the fire and the rose are one.

$$(CP, \text{ pp. } 222\text{-}3)$$

Out of the sea of memory come the 'unknown, remembered' experiences that join end to beginning, and each word is replete with all the lingering echoes of its many contexts in this particular poem and of 'all the other meanings which it has had in other contexts, to its greater or lesser wealth of association'. 'Rose' and 'fire' bring to focus the many levels of meaning, from the straightforwardly referential to the most highly symbolic, which they have acquired in the course of the poem, and release that multiplicity into the whole past of the tradition to fulfil the 'music of poetry'. It is a gathering of end to beginning which also encompasses, however, the tradition which I have been describing, for we end in 1942 with the fulfilment of Yeats's 'fire' and 'rose' of the 1890s, but ones which no longer need to be turned to narrative, for Eliot, like Yeats, has learned how to order and control the associative accumulation of his language to reach that point at which it can be turned loose upon the memory of the reader.

The loss and recovery of memory between 'Gerontion' and *Four Quartets* is mirror image to Pound's development in the same period. For Pound contact with an ontological realm of memory had remained possible even through the darkening years of the 1930s, when his poetry too takes on the qualities of argument and assertion rather than suggestion. But the collapse, with the end of the war, of his political ambitions, in the purgatory of the prison camp at Pisa, he rediscovered the foundations of his art:

> before the world was given over to wars
> Quand vous serez bien vieille
>> remember that I have remembered
>>
>>>> (Canto 80; p. 506)

The reference to the fifty-eighth of Ronsard's 'Sonnets pour Hélène', translated by Yeats as 'When you are old' in 'The Rose', combines the memory of the tradition with that of London before 1914 which is the basis of the personal memories that haunt the *Pisan Cantos*, a world to which Yeats is muse. Yeats it was who had asked.

> What one in the rout
> Of the fire-born moods
> Has fallen away
>
>>>> (*CP*, p. 62)

in the confident expectation that all would be preserved in an eternal memory; in his old age, recovering the world and the words of the mentor of his youth, Pound has to rediscover that enduring memory in doubt and hesitation:

> But for Actaeon
> of the eternal moods has fallen away
> in Fano Caesaris for the long room over the arches
> olim de Malatestis
>
>>>> (Canto 80; p. 501)

Where in the draft of the first three cantos history was fragmentary and the ghosts whole, in the *Pisan Cantos* it is the fragments of a ghostly past, a purely personal memory, that has to be winnowed till an enduring and impersonal memory, one beyond the fragile world of culture, can be recovered in nature itself, and the ghosts can appear again:

> in the timeless air

> that they suddenly stand in my room here
> between me and the olive tree
>
>>>> (Canto 76; p. 452)

The quest which the *Pisan Cantos* enacts is the archetypal quest of Yeats and Eliot, all of whose poetry is founded in memory. It is a quest for the revelation at the end of memory of an ancient wisdom that makes memory itself the power that endlessly renews the world, ensuring that nothing is lost. Forrest Read has argued that in the *Pisan Cantos* the poet's persona is

> making a journey among the experiences out of which consciousness is being formed, and is seeking a new ordering of three realms: of self (as prisoner of time, infernal); of nature (as time redeemed in its harmony with the process, purgatorial); and of ancient wisdom (as the revelation of the process in the human mind, paradisal).[62]

The process is the underlying order and pattern of recurrence in the world: the journey of the *Pisan Cantos* is thus towards nature as revelation of an order that is itself inscribed in the ancient wisdom Pound seeks to recover from memory's oblivion. As with Yeats and Eliot, the quest only takes on its full significance when the world around has collapsed into total forgetfulness. Like 'The Tower' volume or *The Waste Land*, the *Pisan Cantos* is a poem fulfilling the art of memory out of the despair that memory can be made integral with the world again. It is as though it is only in the collapse of memory in his own experience that Pound's technique at last matches with his subject matter, for throughout the rewritten early Cantos memory remains integral, unbroken:

> I sat on the Dogona's steps
> For the gondolas cost too much, that year,
> And there were not 'those girls', there was one face
> And the Buccentoro, twenty yards off, howling 'Stretti',
> And the lit cross-beams, that year, in the Morisini,
> And peacocks in Koré's house, or there may have been.
> > Gods float in the azure air
> Bright gods and Tuscan, back before dew was shed.
>
> > > > (Canto 3; p. 11)

The personal memory, even if uncertain, leads straight back into an eternal world that is always present. Even in the London of Canto 7, a world that has itself become ghostly, trapped in terrible and repetitive stasis, out of all contact with the buried memory —

> We also made ghostly visits, and the stair
> That knew us, found us again on the turn of it,

Knocking at empty rooms, seeking for buried beauty;
And the sun-tanned, gracious and well formed fingers
Lift no latch of bent bronze, no Empire handle
Twists for the knocker's fall; no voice to answer.

(p. 25)

— Pound's own sense of contact with the eternal world does not fail:

Nicea moved before me
And the cold grey air troubled her not
For all her naked beauty, bit not the tropic skin,
And the long slender feet lit on the curb's marge
And her moving feet went before me,
          We alone having being.
And all that day, another day:
          Thin husks I had known as men,
Dry casques of departed locusts
          speaking a shell of speech

(p. 26)

Canto 7 was the inspiration for much of Eliot's imagery for *The Waste Land*, but the memory which resists the sterile decay of contemporary London in Canto 7 is Pound's own: we are given as narrative his preservation of the past as a living present. In *The Waste Land* Eliot will create a poem which turns to its readers, invoking their memories as the bulwark against decay, and it is that pattern which will be repeated in the *Pisan Cantos*, for in those poems we are forced, as readers, slowly to acquire and make our own the fragmentary past to which the poem gives us access, and as we find our way about those memories, making them cohere, so we find Pound also in the process of uncovering coherence, the coherence of the memory of nature itself. We are forced to engage ourselves directly in the poetic journey, and it was that breakthrough, I suggest, that Eliot had — with Pound's help — made in 1921. *The Waste Land* is, above all others, an associationist poem, for it is turned upon the reader, demanding his associations and his memory that it can be made whole, and as we make it whole, we remake the wholeness of the tradition which it has succeeded in incorporating into itself. The difference between Canto 7 and *The Waste Land* lies in the fact that what Pound asserts or describes —

'Beer bottle on the statue's pediment!

'That, Fritz, is the era, to-day against the past,
'Contemporary.' And the passion endures.

(p. 25)

— Eliot forces us to enact by a technique in which the present's denial
of the past and the poem's insistence on the preservation of memory
are set in conflict in the texture of the verse itself:

But at my back from time to time I hear
The sounds of horns and motors, which shall bring
Sweeney to Mrs. Porter in the spring.

(*CP*, p. 70)

The degradation of the present and the enduring passion of the past
fuse together: as we recall Marvell's poem (which in turn seems 'to
gather up and to digest into its art all the experience of the human
mind') we remake the past in the very instant when what the poem
describes turns the 'present against the past'. We, the readers, can, with
our memories, revitalise the wasted land, or can, with our failure of
memory, contribute to it. The poem is a test of our commitment, and
it is only from our memory that the bridge can be rebuilt which will
perform the archetypal completion of all associationist poetry — the
recovery of memory in the very moment of its apparent loss.

For this reason the critical puzzle of *The Waste Land* is essentially
insoluble. More than any other poem I have looked at, its real existence
is not on the page, but in our completions of it, completions which will
be different for each reader, and different with each reading as the
poem teaches us its memory and acquires, contingently, some of ours.
Critical debate on the poem has concentrated on performing the two
possible modes of reading associationist poetry left us by nineteenth-
century critics: on the one hand we search, through Eliot's reading
or thought, for the 'coherent intellectual thread upon which the items
of the poem are hung',[63] the point of view from which all the links in
the chain will be comprehensible; on the other, we try to construct the
mind of a character, a protagonist, in which all the elements of the
poem will harmoniously cohere — or at least cohabit. The associations
which hold the elements of the poem together, however, in so far as
they are the author's, are essentially unverifiable; and when we make
the various 'I' statements refer to a single character we make an assumption for which the poem gives us no warrant. Some of the fragments
which were already in existence when Eliot began to put *The Waste*

Land together included an 'I' which was dropped in the final version, freeing the images from location in any particular psyche. In the draft the speaker comments upon the fact that his images are the product of a 'chain' over which he has lost control,[64] but in the final version only the images are offered to us and we have to forge — in both senses — whatever connections we can: the images are linked not through the presumed operations in the mind of a dramatic character whose psychological tics we have to unravel, but by whatever gravitational attraction they exert upon the associational habits of our own minds:

> A woman drew her long black hair out tight
> And fiddled whisper music on those strings
> And bats with baby faces in the violet light
> Whistled, and beat their wings
> And crawled head downward down a blackened wall
> And upside down in air were towers
> Tolling reminiscent bells   (*CP*, pp. 77-8)

The possibility of access to a mind which would unfold the logic of such images is precisely what the poem denies us: to manufacture a protagonist whose psyche we have to enter in order to follow the progression of the images is to thrust *The Waste Land* back into the mould of nineteenth-century associationism, defusing its much more radical demand that we enclose the poem only through our own associations. A 'protagonist' would allow us to complete the poem, but it is 'completion' that the poem refuses. Equally, therefore, efforts to see the poem as a continuous parallel between ancient myth and contemporary banality, in the mode of *Ulysses*, can provide no more than moments of interconnection: the fisher king myth is not a scaffold for the structure of the poem, but one node, one cluster of associative potential which can echo and re-echo in our memories. There is no 'reasoned' chain: the search for unity in *The Waste Land* is bound to fail because whatever unity it has is created only temporarily in the completions of each individual reader.

This does not mean, however, that it is without any kind of structure. Just as Yeats's effort was to find ways of controlling and ordering the associative flow that his poem was intended to release, so Eliot's finds ways of organising the impulses of memory, and they are ways, I suggest, which enact for us the stages of the mind's descent through the 'stratifications of history' which cover savagery. Eliot's poem is spatial — as Joseph Frank has argued[65] — but it is spatial in the way that an archaeological site is spatial: it is a configuration of time and history. Our journey through *The Waste Land* is a journey through the layers of memory back to the fundamental elements, the mythic memories, of our cultural inheritance. That recovery is not, however, in itself a regaining of health, a Jungian reintegration of the psyche, but the re-establishing of the conscious distance from the savage sources of our mind that saves us from falling into the re-enactment of the savage which we saw in 'Sweeney Among the Nightingales'. The two forms of memory which that poem fused together in its conclusion are both present in *The Waste Land*, one holding the archetypal violence of our lives at bay, the other submitting to it. And between the two is the casual world of reminiscence, personal and shallow, capable neither of knowing nor of acting out of the horrific depths of consciousness to which memory gives access and from which memory preserves us. The paradox of Eliot's conception is that even Sweeney can acquire significant value, because in comparison with those who live within a minimal personal memory his submission to the forces of the unconscious is, potentially at least, leading him to an awareness of the true depths of life. This is why the Sweeney of 'Sweeney Agonistes' is so different from the Sweeney of 'Sweeney Erect'. Return to savagery may be horrific, but it is a confrontation with the realities of human experience, whereas the voices which dominate the opening section of *The Waste Land* are voices of those who confine memory within the limits of a personal reminiscence that will neither quicken nor destroy.

Pound's editing put memory as the poem's opening statement of its theme:

> April is the cruellest month, breeding
> Lilacs out of the dead land, mixing
> Memory and desire, stirring
> Dull roots with spring rain.
> Winter kept us warm, covering
> Earth in forgetful snow, feeding
> A little life with dried tubers.   (*CP*, p. 63)

Yeats had written in 'Art and Ideas' that 'works of art are always begotten by previous works of art', and that therefore when 'we delight in a spring day there mixes with our personal emotion and emotion Chaucer found in Guillaume de Lorris, who had it from the poetry of Provence'.[66] The interdependence of art and nature which Yeats asserts is dramatised in Eliot's inversion of Chaucer in the first line of *The Waste Land*. What the poem tells us is the pain of reawakened memory, but what it forces us to perform is precisely the recall which will give

give back traditional meanings to the natural cycle. As we recall Chaucer we are also recalling a whole tradition of response to the experience of spring, a tradition which the forgetful world of the poem denies. What Yeats had achieved by setting the repeatable form of the poem against the historically situated statements of his speaker in 'September 1913' or 'Easter 1916', is achieved in *The Waste Land* by the implosion of its individual lines into an echoing recollection of past poetry. Eliot therefore manages what Yeats had thought impossible, combining the banal world of the 'realistic' drama or novel, with its narrow and constricted means of expression, with the expansive movement of the reader's mind into reverie, into the emotion of multitude, and does so by fulfilling what Yeats had asked of the language of poetry, that its words 'borrow their beauty from those that used them before'.[67] The conflict between the mimetic and the associative modes is, indeed, enacted almost allegorically at the heart of the poem when the typist, after the departure of the 'young man carbuncular',

> turns and looks a moment in the glass,
> Hardly aware of her departed lover;
> Her brain allows one half-formed thought to pass:
> 'Well now that's done, I'm glad its over.'
> When lovely woman stoops to folly and
> Paces about her room again, alone,
> She smoothes her hair with automatic hand,
> And puts a record on the gramophone.

Mirror and gramophone are media of re-presentation; they record the moment. The poem itself, however, presents, records and recalls in the same moment, for in its metric and in its allusion to Goldsmith the power of memory asserts what mirror and gramophone deny, the interaction and mutual qualification of past and present.

The memory which is embodied in poem's technique is, however, powerless to transform the world it presents. The nadir of the bestial oblivion which has overwhelmed the modern world is the typist's encounter with her lover, but our sense of its horror lies in the fact that it is mediated through the consciousness of Tiresias, personification of the living memory that unites the very earliest elements of European civilisation with its latest:

> Flushed and decided, he assaults at once;
> Exploring hands encounter no defence;

— faces the memory of Gerontion-Tiresias, losing itself in endless association or incapable of bringing its knowledge of the past to bear upon the present. The journey which the poem offers us is one which will connect ancient and modern together, but connect them at the level of conscious cultural recall and not in unconscious repetition of the past. That is a journey we must make: there is no protagonist but ourselves. But there is an antagonist. Across the desert of *The Waste Land* the temptation which we have to refuse is the path of Nietzsche, an escape into the dionysiac, into tragedy. The poem is haunted by echoes of the tragic — Ophelia, Kyd's Hieronymo, Wagner's Tristan and Isolde, Parsifal, Antony and Cleopatra — and takes place in the world defined by Nietzsche as a world lost to myth because of its critical spirit, a world in need of the myth of tragedy that it can be revitalised:

> It is probable ... that nearly everyone, on close examination, feels so disintegrated by the critical historical spirit of our culture, that he can only perhaps make the former existence of myth credible to himself by learned means through intermediary abstractions. Without myth, however, every culture loses its healthy natural creative power: it is only a horizon encompassed with myths which rounds off to unity a social movement.[68]

The 'arid plain' of Eliot's Fisher King suggests the loss that Nietzsche describes in *The Birth of Tragedy*, as does the poem's search, through Jessie Weston's *From Ritual to Romance*, for a saving myth. Nietzsche's words echo in the poem's final section:

> Who are those hooded hordes swarming
> Over endless plains, stumbling in cracked earth
> Ringed by the flat horizon only

Loss of myth leaves the horizon as the only boundary, and it is such loss that is brought about by the workings of abstract thought and abstract morality, 'the abstract man proceeding independently of myth':

> let us picture to ourselves the lawless roving of the artistic imagination not bridled by any native myth: let us imagine a culture which has no fixed and sacred primitive seat, but is doomed to exhaust all its possibilities, and has to nourish itself wretchedly from other

cultures — such is the Present, as the result of Socratism . . . And now the mythless man remains eternally hungering among all the bygones, and digs and grubs for roots, though he have to dig for them among the remotest antiquities.[69]

Nietzsche's hatred of the 'historical sense' is utterly opposed to Eliot's view of the historical sense as the first prerequisite for the poet, but Nietzsche's description of the modern world and its artistic imagination almost exactly describes not only the world but the method of *The Waste Land*:

> What are the roots that clutch, what branches grow
> Out of this stony rubbish? Son of man,
> You cannot say, or guess, for you know only
> A heap of broken images, where the sun beats,
> And the dead tree gives no shelter . . .

Indeed, the lives of the cultured in 'A Game of Chess' might be intended to illustrate Nietzsche's thesis that modern culture consists only of deadening raids upon the past:

> And other withered stumps of time
> Were told upon the walls; staring forms
> Leaned out, leaning, hushing the room enclosed.

The enclosure of the room conceals the empty horizon by false culture, but the question we might wish to ask is: does the whole poem do any more? Is *The Waste Land* itself only the expression of a 'hungering among bygones', or has it more to offer? Eliot's poem enacts the paradigm journey of Nietzsche's 'free spirit', but does so to find other than Nietzschean solutions:

In the background of his activities and wanderings — for he is restless and aimless in his course as in a desert — stands the note of interrogation of an increasingly dangerous curiosity: 'Cannot all valuations be reversed? And is good perhaps evil? . . .' Such thoughts lead and mislead him more and more, onward and away. Solitude encircles and engirdles him, always more threatening, more throttling, more heart oppressing . . . From this morbid solitariness, from the desert of such years of experiment, it is still a long way to the copious, overflowing safety and soundness which does not care to dispense with disease itself as an instrument and angling-hook of knowledge: — to that mature freedom of spirit which is equally self-control and discipline of the heart, . . . to that excess of plastic, healing, formative and restorative powers, which is exactly the sign of splendid health.[70]

Through the desert to self-control and disicipline of the heart —

> your heart would have responded
> Gaily, when invited, beating obedient
> To controlling hands

— is the journey *The Waste Land* also makes.

Eliot had never anything good to say about Nietzsche, and Patrick Bridgwater comments that he 'could hardly have taken less interest in the most fashionable philosopher of his student years',[71] but the most powerful influences are always the least ascertainable because the most pervasive. Whether Eliot was consciously utilising Nietzsche in writing *The Waste Land* is beyond investigation, but the Nietzschean conception of tragedy and the return of the dionysiac, a refusal of history, is what the poem fears, fearing it has nothing to put in its place. In *The Birth of Tragedy* Nietzsche describes the experience of the audience as they reach the climax of Wagner's *Tristan und Isolde*:

> all of a sudden we see only Tristan, motionless, with hushed voice saying to himself: 'the same old tune, why does it wake me?' And what formerly interested us like a hollow sigh from the heart of being, seems now to tell us how 'waste and void is the sea.' And when, breathless, we thought to expire by a convulsive distention of all our feelings, and only a slender tie bound us to our present existence, we now hear and see only the hero wounded to death and still not dying . . .[72]

The theme of *The Waste Land* is also, of course, the theme of the wounded hero, the living death, but Nietzsche's quotation from Wagner appears, in German, in the crucial hyacinth garden scene of 'The Burial of the Dead', and occurs at a point when the speaker is also bound by 'only a slender tie . . . to our present existence', seeing into the heart of things:

— Yet when we came back, late, from the hyacinth garden,
Your arms full, and your hair wet, I could not
Speak, and my eyes failed, I was neither
Living nor dead, and I knew nothing,
Looking into the heart of light, the silence.
Oed' und leer das Meer.

The Waste Land journey is not one towards, but away from tragic emotion: these lines also echo Conrad's *Heart of Darkness*, from which Eliot originally intended to take his epigraph:

Did he live his life again in every detail of desire, temptation, and surrender during that supreme moment of complete knowledge? He cried in a whisper at some image, at some vision — he cried out twice, a cry that was no more than a breath —
  'The horror! The horror!'[73]

In the hyacinth garden passage, the rise through dionysiac exultation to the apollonian individuality of the tragic hero is undercut by combining with it the descent from noble individuality to horrific barbarity. For Nietzsche the plunge into the dionysiac is essential for modern man if the apollonian is to be released in all its form-giving power again; for Eliot, with Frazer's *Golden Bough* to teach him the nature of savage magic, tragedy's elevation of its hero to noble individuality is only a prelude to the barbarism that demands by his death a return of the dionysiac. To build on the value of tragedy a new future out of the rubble of the past, would be to undo the force of history. Nietzsche is the spirit of Sweeney's world in 'Sweeney Among the Nightingales', but *The Waste Land* is presided over by Tiresias — it has no tragic hero. The Nietzschean transformation of the dionysiac through the apollonian will not be given to this world except as a reversion to primitivism, and yet it is a world held in thrall still to Apollo: the epigraph that Eliot eventually gave to his poem is the answer of the sybil who had been given eternal life but not eternal youth by Apollo when asked what she wants most — 'I want to die'. She cannot be released from life into death any more than we can be released from our living death by the significant death of tragedy: 'I am not Prince Hamlet nor was meant to be.'

The Waste Land takes as its world the aftermath of tragedy, attempting to discover some meaningful stance in a world deprived of apollonian heroism. The poem's progression is modelled on Nietzsche's description of the only way forward for a culture that has been touched by the dionysiac but has lost the equipoise of Dionysus and Apollo as manifested in tragedy:

> If at every considerable spreading of the Dionysian commotion one always perceives that the Dionysian loosing from the shackles of the individual makes itself felt first of all in an increased encroachment on the political instincts, to the extent of indifference, yea even of hostility, it is certain, on the other hand, that the state-forming Apollo is also the genius of the *principium individuatonis*, and that the state and domestic sentiment cannot live without an assertion of individual personality. There is only one way from orgasm for a people – the way to Indian Buddhism.[74]

The Waste Land's journey east is the only way for a world of the failed apollonian, but Eliot's dialogue with Nietzsche is an attempt to transcend the tragic by allowing it as part of a continuous memory whose continuity is more important than any of its elements. We retain the value of tragic art so that we do not need to return to the tragic as a value in life. For Nietzsche, the dionysiac, which is the final and completing moment of tragedy, reintegrates the hero into a primal oneness which is expressed in music: his individuality has been illusory:

> Tragic myth is to be understood only as a symbolisation of Dionysian wisdom by means of the expedients of Apollonian art: the mythus conducts the world of phenomena to its boundaries, where it denies itself, and seeks to flee back again into the bosom of the true and only reality; where it then, like Isolde, seems to strike up its metaphysical swan song:

> > In the sea of pleasure's
> > Billowing roll,
> > In the ether waves'
> > Knelling and toll,
> > In the world breath's
> > Wavering whole –
> > To drown in, go down in –
> > Lost in a swoon – greatest boon![75]

The apollonian is illusion, however necessary, concealing the eternal music of 'the true and only reality', a sea of music. Haunted by music as by tragedy — 'This music crept by me upon the waters' (1. 257) — *The Waste Land* offers a parodic version of the dionysiac wisdom in Madame Sosostris who cannot find a tragic hero — 'the hanged man' — among her cards, but warns against the transforming effects of drowning:

> Here, said she,
> Is your card, the drowned Phoenician Sailor,
> (Those are pearls that were his eyes. Look!)

Death transformed by dionysiac illusion into beauty is what Madame Sosostris warns against, but like everything else she says it is a false remembrance of ancient wisdom. The drowning is essential, but it is not a drowning into the oneness of the dionysiac, a reintegration into the original earth music: it is conducted in the terms by which Eliot will oppose Nietzsche, the terms of remembering and forgetting:

> Phlebas the Phoenician, a fortnight dead,
> Forgot the cry of gulls, and the deep sea swell
> And the profit and loss.
>   A current under sea
> Picked his bones in whispers. As he rose and fell
> He passed the stages of his age and youth
> Entering the whirlpool.

What Phlebas enters is not the sea as transforming power of art, is not a dionysiac drowning into primal darkness and oneness, but a dissolution of personal life, a recapitulation of memory, unpicking his existence from 'age to youth'. What Phlebas allows us, as readers, to do is to enter the deepest layers of memory, that mythic landscape of 'What the Thunder Said'. It is through the recovery of an ancient memory that we will be able to turn back again to our own lives and judge them, and by the recovery of that ancient memory we will also place tragedy as a stage on our development which we have passed, or must strive to pass.

Eliot's 'ideal monuments' in 'Tradition and the Individual Talent' are an application of Nietzsche's 'monumental' mode of history, as defined in *The Use and Abuse of History*; the 'objective correlative' echoes Nietzsche's concept of 'adequate objectification' in *The Birth of Tragedy*, a phrase also applied in defining the failure of *Hamlet* to fulfil the tragic ethos;[76] *The Waste Land* conducts a dialogue with

Nietzsche – who had analysed the 'historical sense' as the source of modern man's sickness – from the point of view of the historical sense, but in the context of the collapse of history. In that context the world before tragedy – we seek 'in vain for one single, vigorously branching root, for a speck of fertile soil: there is dust, sand . . .'[77] – and the world after tragedy are the same:

> Here is no water but only rock
> Rock and no water and the sandy road.

Tragedy, for Nietzsche, revitalises as the dionysiac releases its 'thundering torrent': 'A hurricane seizes everything decrepit, decaying, collapsed, and stunted; wraps it whirlingly into a red cloud of dust: and carries it like a vulture into the air.'[78] But for Eliot the voice of the thunder does not contain, as it does for Nietzsche, 'the mothers of being, whose names are: Wahn, Wille, Wehe' (Whim, Will, Woe),[79] but 'Datta, Dayadhvam, Damyatta' – give, sympathise, control. And thus Nietzsche's vision of the perfection of a society founded on the tragic mythos will be subsumed and altered by *The Waste Land*:

> When the dionysian powers rise with such vehemence as we experience at present, there can be no doubt that, veiled in a cloud, Apollo, has already descended to us, whose grandest beautifying influences a coming generation will behold.
>
> That this effect is necessary, however, each one must surely perceive by intuition. If once he found himself carried back – even in a dream – into an old Hellenic existence. In walking under high Ionic colonnades, looking upwards to a horizon defined by clear and noble lines, with reflections of his transfigured form by his side in shining marble . . .[80]

The 'colonnade' appears in the false rebirth of 'The Burial of the Dead' –

> Summer surprised us, coming over the Starnbergersee
> With a shower of rain; we stopped in the colonnade,
> And went on in sunlight

– to be transformed to the possibility of a real rebirth in 'The Fire Sermon', *The Birth of Tragedy* shaping the poem's second climactic moment of insight as it had shaped its first in the hyacinth garden:

> O City city, I can sometimes hear
> Beside a public bar in Lower Thames Street,
> The pleasant whining of a mandoline
> And a clatter and a chatter from within
> Where fishmen lounge at noon: where the walls
> Of Magnus Martyr hold
> Inexplicable splendour of Ionian white and gold.

The tragic mythos and its perfection have not disappeared: they have been subsumed into the continuity of Christianity, and we may, perhaps, see in the third climactic moment of insight in the poem an echo of Nietzsche's transfigured self-image in the marble column, but again transformed into a Christian context:

> Who is the third who always walks beside you?
> When I count, there are only you and I together
> But when I look ahead up the white road
> There is always another one walking beside you

The Nietzschean apotheosis of the tragic was possible only when apollonian and dionysiac were perfectly balanced; that balance was lost with the rise of the rationalism of Socrates: the art of memory as Eliot conceives it can recapture tragedy's ability to tame the primitive, but by returning to the depths in recollection, not in action. The dialectic of apollonian and dionysiac is replaced, in the very texture of *The Waste Land*'s language, by a continual dialectic between the origins and the ends of our culture, between the mythic ur-memories of the primitive and the personal memories of our private experience, with the cultural tradition as the essential bridge between.

Thus in the final section of the poem *The Waste Land* can perform its moral purpose by allowing us to set the failures of our personal life within the context of that mythic memory which represents the deepest layer of the self. The poem journeys to self-discovery by forcing us to encompass the values we have accepted in our personal life by the memories of our buried self:

> *Datta*: what have we given?
> My friend, blood shaking my heart
> The awful daring of a moment's surrender
> Which an age of prudence can never retract
> By this, and this only, we have existed

Which is not to be found in our obituaries
Or in memories draped by the beneficent spider
Or under seals broken by the lean solicitor
In our empty rooms.

If we are to know and control the impulses that come from the deepest layers of the savage self we can only do so by situating them within the context of a memory equally capable of reaching the depths. We cease, both in action and in remembrance, to be 'each in his prison / Thinking of the key', but unless the return of memory is tamed by the historical sense it can only be a return of tragedy. It is such a return that we are faced with by the poem's conclusion: the collapse of the bridge of culture brings back the tragic mythos that memory of the culture would defend us against:

London Bridge is falling down falling down falling down
Poi s' ascose nel foco che gli affina
Quando fiam uti chelidon — O swallow swallow
Le Prince d'Aquitaine à la tour abolie
These fragments I have shored against my ruins
Why then Ile fit you. Hieronymo's mad againe.

Fragmented memory is what the poem challenges us to complete and make whole so that the tradition can be total, the poem an access to all of history, and therefore a defence against the madness of the dionysiac. If we are to keep the savage at bay we must escape, in reading the poem, from the purely personal memory that traps us in our living death of sentimental reminiscence, but we must also evade the horrific potentialities of our buried self by maintaining the bulwark of history:

'O keep the Dog far hence, that's friend to men,
'Or with his nails he'll dig it up again!
'You! hypocrite lecteur! — mon semblable! — mon frère!'

We are each of us that hypocritical reader when we seek systematic meaning in the poem or seek meaning through the personal life of the poet: we must follow the associations to their roots in our buried memory through all the accumulations of the tradition. It is, of course, an impossible demand. If tragedy, as Hazlitt thought, was committed to the imposing individual who asserted himself against the mass, associationist art, like Eliot's, is no less opposed to the multitude, despite its invitation through its openness of our 'multitudinous suggestions'. The kinds of closure which the poem demands are dependent on 'an educated mind, rich in generations of experience': it is an act of defiance of all who cannot be expected to share its cultural memory. However we actually read it, *The Waste Land* intends to be a test of our memory, a memory which would be our salvation from dessiccation. It is a test by which we are almost bound to be failed, and by which the wasted condition of the land is bound to be proved. Its openness could only be closed and made complete within an ideal tradition of culture which could exist, if anywhere, only in Eliot's mind. It is a bridge always open, always collapsing: there can be no final reading to the poem because it represents an eternal challenge to our inability to make total our memory and therefore to release ourselves from our incomplete existences. Its allusive method aids the illusion, however, that only those who can recognise elements of the tradition can be truly moral human beings, an illusion Eliot himself was to recognise when he sought a source of salvation from, rather than by, historical memory.

The rebirth we ought to experience from reading *The Waste Land* is metaphorical: the tradition grows through us, transforming us as we transform it. Pound, a literalist of the creative mind compared to Eliot, had already presented such rebirth as a reality of the natural world in his poem 'A Girl':

The tree has entered my hands,
The sap has entered my arms,
The tree has grown in my breast —
Downward,
The branches grow out of me, like arms.

Tree you are,
Moss you are,
You are violets with wind above them.
A child — so high — you are,
And all this is folly to the world.

(CSP, p. 75)

We can take this as the metaphorical rendering of 'delightful psychic experience', but it is an account, as Bryan Knox has pointed out, closely based on Allen Upward's conception of the sources of the Osiris myth: 'The attention of primitive man . . . could scarcely ignore the superior richness of the vegetation on soil which had been manured by the process of burial.'[81] For Eliot the richness of poetry lies in its rootedness in the past; for Pound it lies in its rootedness in the processes of the earth itself, in its fidelity to the sources of all the earth's wealth:

> The stone is alive in my hand, the crops
> will be thick in my death year . . .
>
> (Canto 6, p. 21)

Memory remains essential to Pound, however, because it keeps us in touch with the myths by which humanity has recognised its relationship with the earth. To lose touch with the sources of memory is to lose touch with the knowledge of our dependence on the natural economy: poetry's health is an index of the riches of a society, its rootedness in the past, its refusal of the false wealth of usury. Pound's economics and politics have one central postulate, the reality of the 'increment of association', which he defines in *Social Credit: An Impact* in 1935 as, 'the advantage men get from working together instead of each on his own'.[82] The increment of such association, like the increment of the psychological association, is the result of our inheritance from the past: we live on the wealth that is 'a hook up with the accumulations of all past inventiveness'.[83] Douglas's social credit economics were so congenial to Pound because they fulfilled in economics the same principles that his poetry relied on: true wealth is not invented from nothing, as the banks pretended to do in loaning money for interest, but is based on the increment of association that roots us in the natural wealth of the soil.

All associationist art is based on a double movement: the movement forward of the poem in time is matched by the associative movement backwards in time of the reading mind. Projected upon the social world such an aesthetic requires as its complement a politics with an equivalent double movement, a dynamic of innovation and invention matched with a recuperation of the values of the past. 'Make it new', Pound's battle-cry for his generation summed up the dialectic, for what was to be made new was the truth the past had accumulated, the 'facts' contained in 'the one everlasting repository' of the human mind:

> Certain facts must stand in the common tongue. These root facts must go to the PEOPLE, they must go into the one everlasting repository, the MIND of the people. They must go into folklore, into men's proverbs.[84]

The poem which in its modernity, in its 'newness', was also a recovery of all the past found its political model in Fascism: 'The increment of association exists. It is affirmed in every fascio clamped on a public building; in every bundle of rods set up as a symbol.'[85] Fascism provided an identical set of terms for Pound to work with, bridging the false society of usury to recover the true spirit of the past while asserting its aggressive modernity in the march towards the future. Pound believed that in Mussolini he had found a politician who was not only an artist — 'Treat him as *artifex* and all the details fall into place'[86] — but whose political ideals were the same as the memory based art of the modernists: 'The new economics bases value on the cultural heritage.'[87] As all of the past is implied in the modern poem that recognises its true basis in the power of memory, so the politics which will be truly modern is one which brings all of the past to bear on its action in forging the future. And Fascism claimed such an inheritance.

For Eliot, the needs of politics were similarly based on an acknowledgment of our reliance upon the past: 'our problem being to form the future, we can only form it on the materials of the past; we must use our heredity, instead of denying it.'[88] Having no ontological foundation for memory, however, Eliot's politics are not based on a radical recovery of the past and of good order — such as Fascism seemed to represent in Italy — but on the maintenance of whatever continuities history has made available. Since European civilisation has been infused in all of its symbolism and patterns of feeling by Christianity, any denial of Christianity is a destruction of our connection with the past, a disruption of the continuity of association. The dissociation of sensibility could not be allowed to be complete if any modern English art was to be effective, and the bridge to the past is rebuilt by Eliot through the medium of the Church of England. The devaluation of Donne is again the prerequisite of this shift, a devaluation not in favour of Marvell, but in favour of Lancelot Andrewes. No longer can Eliot approve the anarchic energy with which Donne's mind was 'merely seizing the object in order to express itself',[89] objects are not all of equal value in what they give expression to, and the mind that can express the greatest value is the one which can most submit itself to a hierarchy of objects and emotions:

Donne is a 'personality' in a sense in which Andrewes is not: his sermons, one feels, are a 'means of expression'. He is constantly finding an object which shall be adequate to his feelings; Andrewes is wholly absorbed in the object and therefore responds with the adequate emotion.[90]

Through Andrewes the tradition speaks, a tradition not merely of the English world but of the whole of Europe, for Andrewes is a part of the Catholic church which joins the modern world to the ancient, and at the same time part of a national church which joins the new post-Renaissance world of Europe to its medieval heritage. Despite the fact that the Church of England was a product of the Reformation and had divorced itself from Rome, it had maintained the bridge of culture unbroken, combining the interests of nation and state, locality and European tradition, so that,

> in Hooker and Andrewes . . . we find also that breadth of culture, an ease with humanism and Renaissance learning, which helped to put them on terms of equality with their Continental antagonists and elevate their Church above the position of a local heretical sect. They were fathers of a national Church and they were Europeans . . . the voice of Andrewes is the voice of a man who has a formed visible Church behind him, who speaks with the old authority and the new culture.[91]

The dialectic of 'old authority' and 'new culture' matches the dialectic of modernism itself, and the combiners of European tradition with the needs of a new national spirit are, like Eliot, holding together past and future, keeping the bridges intact. That is why in Andrewes' sermons Eliot found a language that yielded analytically the effects that poetry ought to achieve suggestively:

> Andrewes may seem pedantic and verbal. It is only when we have saturated ourselves in his prose, followed the movement of his thought, that we find his examination of words terminating in the ecstasy of assent. Andrewes takes a word and derives the world from it; squeezing and squeezing the world till it yields a full juice of meaning which we should never have supposed any word to possess.[92]

Associationist poetry always tries to force us to 'derive the world from it', and as Eliot's test of Andrewes' success is that his prose is full of 'flashing phrases which never desert the memory',[93] so associationist art depends upon a mind which is no desert, but rich in the increment of the past.

Eliot's conception of society could never be as revolutionary as Pound's, because the continuity of past and present had to be preserved through time — it could not be recreated as a re-established relation with the natural world. But its implications for contemporary society were not dissimilar, for despite the fact that he was not committed to the soil as such, he was committed to the continuity that could only be achieved in a stable community, and stability depended on ensuring that

> the land of the country should be used and dwelt on by a stable community engaged in its cultivation . . . No one would pretend that life on the land is a very good one for a man with a family whose wage is only a few shillings more than the dole; but agricultural life is capable of being the best life for the majority of any people. And it is hardly too much to say that only in a primarily agricultural society, in which people have local attachments to their small domains and small communities, and remain, generation after generation, in the same place, is genuine patriotism possible . . .[94]

And this was not just Eliot's opinion in the crisis of 1931, when it was written, but was to be repeated after the Second War in *Notes towards the Definition of Culture*, in which Eliot argued for a society in which there will be 'groups of families persisting, from generation to generation, each in the same way of life'.[95] 'Generation after generation' must remain in the same way of life in order to ensure the kinds of memory 'rich in generations of experience' required by the poet — who, of course, is freed by talent from submitting to the same pattern of life. The 'reverence for past and future'[96] which poets and aristocrats share must be ensured among the lower orders by a pattern of society which is, essentially, that described by Yeats in 1907 in 'Poetry and Tradition':

> Aristocracies have made beautiful manners, because their place in tho world puts them above the fear of life, and the countrymen have made beautiful stories and beliefs, because they have nothing to lose and so do not fear, and the artists have made all the rest, because Providence has filled them with recklessness. All these look back to a long tradition . . .[97]

That the bridge of memory be unbroken the society of those who look back to a long tradition, whether out of choice or, as with the countryman, out of necessity, must be maintained.

9 THE POLITICS OF POETRY

The underlying dynamics of the associationist theory of poetry manifest themselves in Yeats, Pound and Eliot in the parallel patterns running through the development of their work. An art based, initially, on exploiting the associational effects to be gained from within the realm of art gives way to a despair at the collapse of memory; and the recovery of memory through the application of political remedies to the amnesiac society follows upon or is a prelude to a more personal recovery of memory as an ontological reality of the universe in which we live. The recovery of a universal memory is not necessarily, however, a buttress against political insistence, because the realisation of memory as a fundamental truth of the world may only intensify the poet's commitment to enforcing the values of memory upon the structure of his society. For all three, on the other hand, the poetry is at maximum pressure when despair at the maintenance of memory is greatest: when the poetry has to become the reservoir of the totality of memory it ought to be able to assume in the world around it, it reaches the fullest expression of its own inherent principles. It is as though the poetry needs to have its political and historical objectives destroyed as facts before it can express them fully: it needs to have them return as memories before they can be integrated into art. But that does not nullify the political commitments: the same drive to shape a society in accord with the principles of memory will find other outlets when one set of possibilities has been exhausted: Yeats's regret at the destruction of the Anglo-Irish aristocracy was not to remain a merely elegiac passion but was to fuel his support for the Blueshirts; Pound found his way back, in the 1950s, to many of the same positions he seemed to have renounced in *The Pisan Cantos*; Eliot found in sociology justifications for patterns of society that had been supported only by dogma when the 'new conservatism' of the 1950s replaced the ideas of the *Action Française* he had drawn on in the 1930s. The impulse to implement the values of the poetry is constant, even if the political form of Fascism was only the momentary shape by which such implementation seemed possible.

This does not mean that the relationship with Fascism is the result of a historical accident, the accidental conjunction of two entirely different processes which, because occurring together, might be mistakenly identified. Such would be the view of those critics who would see in Yeats and Eliot, in particular, men whose politics were essentially conservative, but never Fascistic. In part this is a recoil from the emotive meanings the term 'Fascism' acquired after 1945, but it is a warping of the poet's views to make their politics mere nostalgia for a past age, let alone approval for contemporary conservatisms. Yeats and Pound would have agreed with Eliot when he wrote of conservatism in 1926, that it 'believed explicitly in progress, and believed implicitly that progress consists in things remaining much as they are'.[1] Yeats, Eliot and Pound wanted things to be very different from what they were, and wanted change that was not a mere progression from past into future, but the complete remaking of the future on values drawn from an entirely different historical pattern than that of their own society. The virtues of T.E. Hulme's position, as described by Eliot, are ones all of them would have seen as central both to their politics and their literature: Hulme, Eliot suggested, was 'the forerunner of a new attitude of mind, which should be the twentieth century mind, if the twentieth century is to have a mind of its own. Hulme is classical, reactionary and revolutionary: he is the antipodes of the eclectic, tolerant and democratic mind of the last century.'[2] It is the fact that they are reactionary *and* revolutionary that makes the poets kin with Fascism and distances them from any straightforward conservatism. What they wished upon their societies was not a preservation of the inherent values of its existing structure but something that would be the 'antipodes' of the democratic, industrial and plural societies of which they were the citizens. Eliot expressed their common disgust with contemporary politics when he wrote in 1929 that, 'Everyone who cares for civilization must dread and deplore that waste of time, money, energy and illusion which is called a General Election.'[3] He added that 'no country pays so heavily for this undesirable luxury as Britain.'[4] Throughout his career Eliot insisted that people were not fit for the burdens of democracy, and his obsession in the 1930s was with the destruction of democracy by the extension of the franchise: every extra voter was a reduction of the electorate's power over its parliamentary representatives.[5] Equally, the effort to educate people for democracy was, for Eliot, a betrayal of the true needs of the culture. When he expresses his desire, in the conclusion of *The Use of Poetry and the Use of Criticism*, for 'as large and miscellaneous an audience as possible', but preferably for one 'which could neither read nor write',[6] he is, essentially, proposing as an appropriate society the model of Yeats's Ireland of aristocrats and peasants. Responsible government, for Yeats, depends upon maintaining power in the hands of the Few 'who through possession of hereditary wealth, or great personal gifts, have come to identify their lives with the life of the State', as opposed to the 'lives and ambitions of the Many' which are entirely 'private'.[7] At the same time the Few must rule over a 'people' rather than a discrete mass, and a 'people, a community [is] bound together by imaginative possessions, by stories and poems which have grown out of its own life, and by a past of great passions which can still waken the heart to imaginative action'.[8] The people is created by its memory of art, and art requires a people so that it can fulfil its own nature:

> Does not the greatest poetry always require a people to listen to it? England or any other country which takes its tune from the great cities and gets its taste from the schools and not from old custom may have a mob, but it cannot have a people ... The poet must always prefer the community where the perfected minds express the people, to a community that is vainly trying to copy the perfected minds.[9]

What Fascism offered was the means, the political means, to recreating a people with a memory: 'TO ORGANISE in our barbarism, in our utter and rabbity inconsequence, an hierarchy and order ... [10] For Pound, Fascism offered an escape from the barbarism of a people become a mob, allowing the poet access again to 'the one everlasting repository, the MIND of the people'.[11]

Political authoritarianism was one means of re-establishing a proper community, but it was, as Pound insisted, 'a matter of decades':[11] it offered a solution to the poet's problem but not one that would be effective until there had been time for minds to acquire again the values of 'old custom'. But there was another way in which the poet could intervene directly in order to transform the mob into a people, and that was by providing them with a public art which would enjoin upon them shared experience and common memories — an art in the theatre:

> Victor Hugo has said that in the theatre the mob becomes a people, and, though this could be perfectly true only in ancient time when the theatre was part of the ceremonial of religion, I have some hope that ... we may help to bring a little ideal thought into the common thought of our times. The writers, on whom we principally depend, have laboured to be citizens ... of that ancient and eternal Ireland which has lived in old times ...[12]

The theatrical performance is the medium through which the writer in touch with the values of the past can create a common bond of memory again amongst his audience. In the context of an urban society lacking 'old custom', Eliot, too, saw the theatre as a means of transforming mob into people:

> The ideal medium for poetry, to my mind, and the most direct means of social 'usefulness' for poetry, is the theatre. In a play of Shakespeare you get several levels of significance. For the simplest auditors there is the plot, for the more thoughtful the characters and conflict of character, for the more musically sensitive the rhythm, and for auditors of greater sensitiveness and understanding a meaning which reveals itself gradually.[13]

The unity which the theatre establishes is thus, for Eliot, one which would also maintain the social hierarchy as levels of responsiveness. Indeed, Eliot describes a play he himself had designed, in which the speech of one character 'should be on the plane of the most sensitive and intelligent members of the audience', so that there 'was to be an understanding between this protagonist and a small number of the audience, while the rest of the audience would share the responses of the other characters in the play'.[14] Such a discussion is not merely a matter of the formal attributes of a play: it is a projection of a pattern of society in which an 'aristocracy' of sensitiveness and intelligence are the essential ingredient for the successful creation and transmission of the work of literature. Eliot is, in fact, echoing Yeats's discussion, in *The Cutting of an Agate*, of the divisions within the Elizabethan theatre, formal divisions between 'the humourous realism' and the 'great speeches' which mirror social divisions between 'the common citizen standing on the rushes of the floor' and the aristocratic patrons: the great tragic dramas and the great speeches are 'written by poets who remembered their patrons in the covered galleries'.[15] The poets remember that their patrons have a memory: the theatre directed at the aristocracy of culture but integrating all levels of the society is the means, for both Yeats and Eliot, to re-establishing a unified and yet hierarchical society in a world in which the peasantry can no longer be a focus for 'old custom' and common beliefs. The audience in such a theatre is a model for the whole pattern by which modern society could be renovated.

Recovery along these lines depends, however, on the maintenance of an aristocracy;[16] even if the peasantry has been destroyed, the aristocracy still connects with the past, and decay of the upper classes therefore attracts some of the poets' severest strictures on their society. In arrogant inversion of the relationships of rich and poor, Yeats, in 1919, complained that,

> All exploitation of the life of the wealthy, for the eye and the ear of the poor and the half-poor, in plays, in popular novels, in musical comedy, in fashion papers, at the cinema, in *Daily Mirror* photographs, is a travesty of the life of the rich; and if it were not would all but justify some Red Terror; and it impoverishes and vulgarises the imagination, seeming to hold up for envy and to commend a life where all is display and hurry, passion without emotion, emotion without intellect, and where there is nothing stern and solitary.[17]

The exploitation of the rich to satisfy the (imaginative) hungers of the poor is a reduction of their riches to mere wealth, an impoverishment of the true riches which both ought to have by depriving them of their proper role within the overall emotional and intellectual economy of the state. The same problem was the one that seemed central to Eliot in his discussion of class in *Notes towards the Definition of Culture*:

> This disintegration of classes had already led to an exaggerated estimate of the social importance of the right school and the right college at the right university, as giving a status which formerly pertained to birth. In a more articulated society — which is *not* a society in which the social classes are isolated from each other: that is itself a kind of decay — the social distinction of the right school or college would not be so coveted, for social position would be marked in other ways.[18]

Envy is only possible where one might have had the attributes of a member of a higher class in society: a society based on birth and heredity is one in which envy is impossible since one could not have acquired a different genealogy. The effect of industrial society has been to destroy the upper class to which all high art is attached: 'You cannot make an aristocrat out of a company chairman, though you can make him a peer; and in a thoroughly industrial society the only artist left will be the international film producer.'[19] The artist needs aristocrat and people: or, at least, the poet does, whose art, according to Yeats, does 'its work by suggestion, not by direct statement' and is 'always reminding and half-reminding those who understand it of dearly loved things'.[20] Only an aristocracy, accumulating riches through generations, and a peasantry, living in the same place generation after generation, can provide the appropriate kind of memory for the poet: that social configuration informs Yeats's and Eliot's political discussions throughout their careers and is the pattern their revolution is intended to re-establish.

Pound, believing more in the independence of the frontiersman than the traditions of peasant or aristocrat, might seem to stand aside from Yeats and Eliot on this. He has little sympathy for aristocracy:

> It seems fairly proved that privilege does NOT breed a sense of responsibility. Individuals, let us say exceptional individuals in privileged classes, maintain the sense of responsibility, but the general ruck, namely 95 per cent of all privileged classes, seem to believe that the main use of privileges is to be exempt from responsibility, from responsibilities of every possible kind.[21]

And he believes that more or less any political system would do as long as it had a sound understanding of economics: 'The point is that the orders of an omniscient despot and of an intelligent democracy would be very much alike in so far as they affected the main body of the country's economics.'[22] The important quality is one that can be had by an elite, a democracy, or an individual but which, given the economic corruption by which Pound thinks we are surrounded, tends only to focus in our time on the individual, and that quality is energy, 'will'; the great leader, Jefferson or Mussolini has it:

> There is also the opportunism of the artist, who has a definite aim, and creates out of the materials present. The greater the artist the more permanent his creation. And this is a matter of WILL.[23]

And yet what that will is directed towards has much in common with Yeats's or Eliot's prescription. Pound sees in Jefferson and Mussolini men who 'both hate machinery or at any rate the idea of cooping up men and making 'em into UNITS, unit production, denting in the individual man',[24] and they are therefore both concerned with the values of the land, 'a sense of the "root and branch" '.[25] Pound does not see memory as instantiated in any particular social class, but it is memory nonetheless that his 'volitional' politics are directed towards. In 'A Visiting Card', originally written in Italian and published in 1942, he defined three components as the essentials of a 'culture':

(1) a direction of the will;

(2) certain ethical bases, or a general agreement on the relative importance of the various moral, intellectual and material values;

(3) details understood by specialists and members of the same profession.[26]

It is a conception of culture which would seem to have much in common with the culture made up entirely of elites from which Eliot, in *Notes towards the Definition of Culture*, wished to preserve us by maintaining the central role of an aristocracy that would act as a linch pin for the continuity of the society's general, as opposed to specialist, values. For Pound that function will be provided only by the vaguely agreed 'certain ethical bases'; such shared values are, however, subsidiary to 'a direction of the will'. It is the will that gives meaning and direction to life, the will, as Pound found it in Mussolini and in Lenin, not to power, but to order.[27] What that order will be, however, is revealed in the immediately following paragraphs of the same essay:

> To replace the marble goddess on her pedestal at Terracina is worth more than any metaphysical argument.
> And the mosaics in Santa Maria in Trastevere recall a wisdom lost by scholasticism, an understanding denied to Aquinas.[28]

The will is towards the re-establishment of an ancient memory which will provide the ethical base from which action can proceed. Will is primary, but it is a will to the recovery of the past as well as the creation of the future.

Pound's 'will' is a politics for the preservation of memory just as much as Yeats's or Eliot's, but their insistence on the powers of memory did not mean that they neglected the will. In fact the realm of Hodos Chameliontis in which Yeats had found himself trapped was a memory which could have no impact on life because it connected with no will-power. What Yeats needed to meet in the depths of the mind, at the end of the chain of association, was that 'other will' that comes through Image or Mask, that gives impulse and direction to action.[29] And through action, Yeats thought, we find a more profound meaning, a more fundamental Image, that will harmonise all the aspects of our life. As with Pound, the active passions are not a denial but a fulfilment of the needs of memory:

We are becoming interested in expression in its first phase of energy, when all the arts play like children about the one chimney, and turbulent innocence can yet amuse those brisk and active men who have paid us little attention of recent years. Shall we be rid of pride of intellect, of sedentary meditation, of emotion that leaves us when the book is closed or the picture seen no more; and live among thoughts that can go with us by steamboat and railway as once upon horseback, or camel-back, rediscovering, by our reintegration of the mind, our more profound Pre-Raphaelitism, the old, abounding, nonchalant reverie.[30]

A reverie still, but one that can be fitted to the active as well as to the meditative passions, that can incorporate the will. The reason for this modification of Yeats's original conception of poetic purpose is the result of his recognition that the values of poetry cannot be maintained if they are always in flight from the present moment into the past. From the past there has to return the values which will shape the future; there has to be not only the quantitative accumulation of memories, but also the uncovering of some ultimate Image, some one fundamental symbol, by which our actions can be governed and the future created. Memory makes the future and the future, therefore, is always a recall of some forgotten potentiality of the mind, an eternal return. Action and reverie are merely different completions of the same underlying principle, different chains of association within the workings of the universal memory.

Eliot would never have committed himself to the values of heroic action as Yeats did, but in a very similar way he too came to assert the value of the will. It appears most clearly, perhaps, in the following passage, part of his long-running debate with Middleton Murry and an attack, too, on a conception of memory with which the associationist conception might be confused:

No sane person supposes that one age is exactly like another, or that it can wholly explain another, or even wholly explain in what ways it is different from another. But the Bergsonian time doctrine, which Mr. Murry accepts implicitly, goes much further than this; it reaches the point of fatalism which is wholly destructive. It is a pure naturalism. What is true for one age is not true for another, and there is no external standard. If Mr. Murry would say plain and pat that St. Thomas is wrong, that Aristotle is wrong, that their 'systems' are altogether wrong, I should not mind. But he simply says that St. Thomas has gone. The cheese is mouldy today, he seems to say, but what a magnificent cheese it was until yesterday. This sort of false ecstasy of admiration for something you do not believe in is the perquisite of the time philosophies like those of Bergson and Mr. Murry. The *Summa* is admirable for me only in so far as I can find some crumbs of truth in it ... But in Mr. Murry's fluid world everything may be admired, because nothing is permanent. There is no place in it for the human will.[31]

It is to the direction of the 'will' that Eliot's Christianity, however self-doubtingly, is committed – and to its curbing, of course. But as in the case of Pound, though challenging each other on the specific nature of truth, the will is to the reconstitution of past truth as eternally present, as permanently in need of re-enactment in the present. Eliot attacks the Bergsonian conception of memory because he sees it as reducing the power of memory by turning it into a pure automatism. For the associationists, no matter how true it might be that everything had its place in the memory, memory was not an automatic inheritance; the whole of the historical past did not gather itself around us like some enormous rolling snowball, as it does in Bergson's conception. Memory was dependent, for Yeats, Eliot and Pound, on sustained cultural effort: it was precisely the fact that it could be and was in the process of being lost that gave urgency to their politics of poetry. In Bergson's conception whatever might be useful to the future would automatically be there, available, when we needed it, but for the poets it would only be there if a whole social framework that kept us in touch with the past were sustained to give foundation, and to offer completion, to what the poet himself could provide. No doubt, in the light of intellectual history, there is enough common ground between Bergsonian ideas of time and memory and those of associationism to make them more alike than distinguishable; but at the time the divide was sharp, and Yeats, Eliot and Pound all saw themselves on Wyndham Lewis's side and opposed to the 'time philosophy', though they would see each other in the opposite camp. That this was possible was because each was trying, from different perspectives, to maintain the values both of memory and of will; the will to order that would produce a society in which memory was maintained. As Eliot, paraphrasing Machiavelli, wrote in 1927: 'Liberty is good; but more important is order; and the maintenance of order justifies every means.'[32] For Eliot the essential feature in maintaining order was the religion that maintained continuity with the past, and thus the politics of Machiavelli

and the bridge to the past of the Anglican Church come to be identified
with each other:

> [Machiaveilli] says still more positively, in words which Archbishop
> Laud would have approved:
>   'The rulers of all States, whether Kingdoms or Commonwealths,
> who would preserve their government firm and entire, ought above
> all things to take care that Religion is held in the highest venera-
> tion, and its cermonies at all times uncorrupted and inviolable; for
> there is no surer prognostication of impending ruin in any State,
> than to see Divine worship neglected or despised.'[33]

Such a view of the demands of order as a support for preserving spiritual
values, and the preservation of spiritual values for the support of order,
was also Pound's, though with an explicit commitment to Fascism:

> The fascist revolution was FOR the preservation of certain liberties
> and FOR the maintenance of a certain level of culture, certain
> standards of living, it was NOT a refusal to come down to a level
> of riches or poverty, but a refusal to surrender certain immaterial
> prerogatives, a refusal to surrender a great slice of the cultural
> heritage.[34]

The immaterial creates order, order defends the immaterial values of
the cultural heritage. Fascism is, for Pound, a reactionary revolution,
a revolution of preservation, and, like the associationist poem, its
dynamic towards the future is a recovery of the past; it maintains
what our democratic social world has forgotten, but does so by a
revolution which, though committed to continual renewal, is also
committed to continual preservation. The formal attributes of an
art of memory are homologous with the political purposes of Mussolini's Fascism.

To assert such an analogical relation takes us to the heart of the
problem of the politics of poetry. In the first place it is clear that no
man or work of art ever equals a particular abstract ideology: we are
even more insistently tempted to divorce the artist from any such
identification because the ideology of the artist (a pervasive one in our
culture) demands that he be utterly unique, that he fulfil the individuality all of us aspire to but cannot achieve. Pound, who in some of his
statements identifies himself with an ideology, can also assert in his
essay 'The State':

As to our 'joining revolutions' etc. It is unlikely. The artist is concerned with producing something that will be enjoyable even after a successful revolution . . . The artist, the maker is always too far ahead of any revolution . . . and no party programme ever contains enough of his programme to give him the least satisfaction.[35]

This was written in 1927, before Pound's admiration for Mussolini came to its fruition, but it is a defence we are likely to feel suitable for any writer. In the second place, the results of Fascism were so horrific that we have a tendency to wish to exculpate from any implication in it all who were not so monstrous as to have willed its conclusions; or, alternatively, to wish to use the term only for those whose beliefs we want to categorise as monstrous. This is why it seems particularly unacceptable to apply the term 'Fascist' or 'Fascistic' to anyone who has not effectively participated in a Fascist political organisation: if we intend the word to have a specific meaning we cannot apply it to general political orientation — it is too damning; if we use the word to cover general political orientation it becomes virtually meaningless because it has been reduced to a mere term of abuse, one that has no identifiable ideological content. As Noel Stock said in his study of Pound, *Poet in Exile*, Fascism 'is a topic upon which one is expected to utter a simple "yes" or "no" whether one knows anything about it or not, which puts it outside the bounds of rational discussion'.[36] But Stock, among others, has therefore taken it to be the case that any parts of the poet's political and social views which reveal rational consideration of serious issues that might concern the vast majority of thinking people cannot be part of a Fascist politics,[37] in other words that a Fascist stance in politics includes only the monstrous, that no one with 'decent' feelings could, in 1928 or 1930 or even 1933, have been a Fascist. It is an assumption which makes the politics of the poetry and the nature of Fascism equally beyond our understanding — something which, conveniently in Pound's case, can be put down to mental aberration, or which, as in the case of Eliot, can be dismissed because he was more concerned with Christian belief than with politics. Roger Kojecky, for instance, notes that Eliot in 1961

again referred to the benefit he had derived from the literary essays of Maurras, whose clear distinction between classicism and romanticism had been useful. And in a talk on 'The Literature of Politics' in the mid-1950s, he regretted what had happened to Maurras, as well as some of the views he had expressed. He suggested that Maurras would have achieved more by confining himself to litera- ture, and to the theory rather than the practice of politics.[38]

But if Maurras would have achieved more, would it have been more in the same line as his collaboration with Nazism, but retained purely within the bounds of theory? Kojecky allows Eliot's division between the theoretical and the practical to stand unchallenged, as does his dis- avowal that there was anything 'Fascistic' about the *Action Française*[39] — that may be so, but can we accept it merely on Eliot's own assertion?

The real problem lies in the problem of defining Fascism itself. We have tended to refuse to attempt this in order to preserve in ourselves the emotional recoil upon which our disgust for it is based, an emo- tional recoil which may prevent us recognising elements in our thought which we share with Fascism. On the other hand, it may seem that discussion of Fascism accords it intellectual respectability, thus en- couraging tendencies whose recurrence seems, at the date of writing, all too possible. The conflagration caused in Italy by the publication in 1974 of Renzo de Felice's work on Mussolini[40] was partly based on this feeling: to treat Fascist ideology with intellectual seriousness is to encourage its re-entry into the political arena. And yet if we do not treat it seriously how are we to understand why the history of Europe in the first half of our century took the shape it did? How are we to know whether the ideas that animated Fascism still form an integral part of our political assumptions? The problem of understanding Fascism is not helped by the way in which the 'classic' interpretations of the phenomenon developed.[41] These divided largely along the lines of whether one saw intellectual, political or social factors as the primary determinants of historical events. The earliest views of Fascism, those that were emerging from within Germany in particular, tended to stress that Fascism was an intellectual or moral disease, one which was endemic to Western thought but particularly virulent in Germany. The sources of this disease were sometimes claimed to lie in Enlighten- ment rationalism, with its emphasis on the value of individual fulfil- ment, or on Romantic irrationalism, with its emphasis on freeing the self from traditional constraints: in either case what was produced was a mass belief in the right to self-assertion, both individual and national, of those most in touch with the irrational powers of the universe or most elevated by rational superiority.[42] Fascism was, in this context, a new religion of political and social opportunities, promising to pro- vide in this life what had previously, within a Christian context, been withheld till the hereafter. Those, however, who regarded the political as the major determinant of historical change, tended, in the years after the Second World War, to see the causes of Fascism as specific to Germany and Italy, and as a function of their retarded national integration and their belated entry into the competition for overseas empires. The rise of Fascism in this context is seen as the unique product of specific political and social situations whose roots lie in the fact that Italy and Germany did not develop on parallel lines to Britain and France, though coming within the sphere of influence of 'developed' economies whose achievements they would try to emulate.[43] The third, and perhaps most pervasive interpretation, is that of Marxism, which sees in Fascism the final effort of the bourgeoisie to keep economic power when its political power is being challenged by the revolutionary working class movement. Fascism is a counter-revolution, defending the class state by overthrowing the liberal political establishment behind which economic exploitation of the working class had been concealed in order to preserve the power position of the ruling classes within the society. The Fascist seizure of power was assimilated in this view to Marx's analysis of Bonapartism: the state executive was not the expression of a specific class, but was tolerated by the economically dominant classes in order to sustain their privileges.[44] On a more detailed level, this same view often appears as the linking of Fascism to the economic pressure experienced by the lower middle classes who, in the economic crises following the war, feared the loss of their differentiation from the proletariat.[45]

There are problems with all three of these views: the first does not account for the failure of Fascism in the other European nations, such as Britain, where it did not take hold, and tends to see everything in European thought prior to Fascism as, in some sense, entailing it, as though no other outcome was possible and as though the values by which we criticise Fascism were not also the products of the same intellectual history. The second view prevents us connecting German and Italian Fascism with the Fascisms of other countries, and prevents us taking it seriously as an ideology: for one of the things that has become clear from recent work on Fascism is that it does have an ideology and is not merely a piece of political opportunism possible only in the context of the specific political and historical circumstances that obtained in Italy and Germany after the First World War. The third view — that of Fascism as a counterrevolution to prevent workers taking control of the state — is the most problematic of all, because the metaphor of 'left' versus 'right' has become such an insistent part of our sense of political relationships. Yet the view of Fascism as a 'right-wing' phenomenon was not so self-evident in the 1920s as it appears now; and it was not at all clear what kind of 'right-wing' movement it was, whether it was a product of dying capitalism or the backlash of the rural against the urban. Indeed, much of our common currency of thought about Fascism is the result of the effort by left-wing writers to explain why there should be a mass movement which could succeed in taking power where the Communists had failed. As Eugen Weber has commented, we still see Communism as the revolutionary movement, and 'the only one entitled to the label', and Fascism as therefore necessarily its opponent from the other end of the spectrum:

> But: they opposed each other. This cannot be denied. It need not be. Fascist revolutions were in effect directed against Communists — not exclusively, but also. In this sense, which has been treated as decisive and which is almost accidental, Fascisms were counter-revolutionary: revolutions against a rival revolution. They did not seek ... to carry one revolution beyond a given stage; but to carry another revolution in a different direction, to define its aims (often similar to the other's) in terms of other principles, to define its foes (often similar too) in terms of different values. The coincidences so many have noted were denounced by the Communists and their friends as camouflage; they were stressed by the Communists' enemies to smear the Communists. No one thought to remark that it is possible to react to similar problems in different ways — even on the immoderate plane.[46]

In effect, it was the Communists who placed Fascism on the political spectrum at the opposite point from themselves in order to ensure that they could not be seen as a rival revolutionary party, and also, as Plumyène and Lasierra show in their study of French Fascisms, in order to bring Socialists and Communists into a new unity in the face of a common enemy.[47]

The conception of Fascism which these three views promulgated was, of course, apparently validated by historical circumstance: the conception of an intellectual disease accounted for concentration camps, the alliance of Italy and Germany confirmed the theory of Fascism's specific historical configuration in relation to the development of those two nations, and the victory of the Allies, combining capitalist democracies and Communists, confirmed the opposition of

Fascism to both of these. The historical end of Fascism must not, however, deceive us as to its historical origins, and the picture that emerges from recent research breaks up the pattern which the classical interpretations have placed on the Fascisms of the 1920s and early 1930s. The men who made up the vanguard of Fascism — and to which Fascism very often appealed in those countries which did not develop a powerful Fascist party — were the front line veterans of the war. Return to peace time conditions in which they would no longer be accorded the status which, for many of them, the war had made possible; return to a peace in which their suffering gave them no special claims upon the community; but perhaps, fundamentally, the return to a class-divided society after the coherence and camaraderie of the army: all those provoked the desire for a politics which would bring into the ordinary social world of peacetime the values and the prestige of the military. Those who had fought were the new aristocracy, an aristocracy that was going unrecognised by the civilians who had not fought and the leaders who had ignored or used their suffering but no longer paid heed to their demands. As Juan Linz has written:

> The rigid status structures of pre-World War I society in which the aristocracy still occupied a distinct position particularly among the professional officers, in which educational differences defined social position, could be contrasted with the reality of social equality in front of the enemy, the opportunities for promotion for valour to non-commissioned and even officer status, that represented a new experience of solidarity. The return to civilian life with its lower-class hostility and upper-class snobbism and a basically unchanged status structure of society shocked many veterans.[48]

In addition, the ethos of the veterans had taken on the tone of a generational conflict with the 'old men' of the pre-war world, and for the young who had just missed the opportunity to fight, who had learned to identify themselves with the heroism of the soldiers they were expected to become if the war did not end, and who found themselves in a world where there was the enormous gap between themselves and their elders owing to the slaughter of those four years, Fascism offered the opportunity to fulfil the values that peace had made irrelevant.[49]

The nucleus which such emotions provided for Fascism could not have been so effective had not there been an ideology already to hand for their use — or, at least, a crisis of ideology which they could exploit. We return here to the issue of history and the collapse, in the face of

the experience of the war, of the ideologies of history which had provided the motor force of Western thought in the nineteenth century.
It was not just liberalism which suffered the destruction of its expectations of history in the attrition of the Western front: Marxism suffered
too, and if anything more severely, for the working classes of Europe
failed to put their class commitment and their class solidarity before
their nationalistic emotions. Conflicts which had been developing within Marxist and Socialist thought were suddenly brought to a crisis by
the war, and the crisis was focused on the role of the nation, a role to
which Marxism had given very little theoretical attention, assuming
it to be a function of the bourgeois phase of history which would necessarily be transcended by the internationalist commitments of the
working-class movement. Zeev Sternhell places this as the core of a
transformation which was to create Fascism out of Socialism:

> The collapse of the Socialist International on the eve of the war
> and the inability of the working classes to prevent the clash, the
> haste and near unanimity with which they ranged themselves,
> physically and morally, behind the established order, and at one
> blow shattered the solidarity of the proletariat, were tangible proof
> that the concepts of class carried less weight, as a factor of solidarity,
> than the concept of nation. Confronted by the fervour which the
> idea of the nation aroused, the idea of class was shown up in all
> its artificiality: the nation was the reality, which the International
> could never aspire to be. In the course of the war the socialists
> were a legion who reached the same conclusion, particularly if they
> belonged among the syndicalists and revolutionaries of the far
> left.[50]

The war brought to a head the tensions which had been developing
within Marxism as it came under the influence of the social theories
of Mosca and Pareto, asserting the central role in any society of ruling
elites, and the conceptions of mass behaviour of Le Bon, with its insistence that the masses were moved only by their irrational reaction
to emotive images and symbols.

In the light of the failure of the working-class movement to mobilise
itself to prevent the war, it seemed that such analyses of society and
of mass motivation were only too accurate. The Socialists who had
assumed that, at the moment of crisis, the masses would energise themselves for conflict, were forced into seeing themselves as leaders to
people who would not gather revolutionary momentum except under

the direction of some kind of 'collective hallucination' such as Le Bon had asserted to be the psychological reality of crowds, and ideas of class and of economic justice could not be made to appeal to such a mentality. In fact, Le Bon's analysis of the mind of the crowd is a public equivalent to the associationist conception of the private experience of the reader of poety:

> crowds are not to be influenced by reasoning, and can only comprehend a rough-and-ready association of ideas. The orators who know how to make an impression on them always appeal in consequence to their sentiments and never to their reason. The laws of reason have no action on crowds. To bring home conviction to crowds it is necessary first of all thoroughly to comprehend the sentiments by which they are animated, to pretend to share these sentiments, then to endeavour to modify them by calling up, by means of rudimentary associations, certain eminently suggestive notions . . .[51]

Le Bon's advice to the orator — 'first of all to thoroughly comprehend the sentiments by which they are animated, to pretend to share these sentiments' — is identical with the advice of Hallam to the reader of associationist poetry: 'clearly to apprehend the leading sentiment in the poet's mind, by their confirmity to which the host of associations is arranged'. The political leader must be a kind of artist — or the equivalent of Eliot's perfect critic — who can gather the associations of the crowd, and, by making them cohere, give them a new direction. His business is the aesthetic business of creating and sustaining illusions:

> it is always the marvellous and legendary side of events that more specially strike crowds. When a civilisation is analysed it is seen that, in reality, it is the marvellous and the legendary that are its true supports. Appearances have always played a much more important part than reality in history, where the unreal is always of greater moment than the real . . . Nothing has a greater effect on the imagination of crowds of every category than theatrical representations. The entire audience experiences at the same time the same emotions, and if these emotions are not at once transformed into acts, it is because the most unconscious spectator cannot ignore that he is the victim of illusions . . . Sometimes, however, the sentiments suggested by the images are so strong that they tend, like habitual suggestions, to transform themselves into acts.[52]

It is through the aesthetic and its associative impact that the masses are to be made coherent and given their direction. History was not, under such conceptions, to be made by deterministic forces unfolding themselves to their necessary conclusions, nor by the forces of reason and justice, but by the will to power of those who could activate the myths by which societies were governed. It was a transformation of Marxism which was to be common both to the Bolsheviks and the Fascists,[53] but it was Fascism which most thoroughly 'modernised' Marxist ideology to bring it into line with what it took to be the truths of the human psyche and of the social organism, truths which were equally at work in the transformation of poetry represented by modernism.

It was in the work of Sorel, and especially in the *Reflections on Violence*, that these elements had already been brought into a theoretical amalgam before the outbreak of the war. As James Gregor points out,

> by 1900 Sorel was arguing that the behaviour of men was significantly influenced by psychological factors, and that any account of revolution must necessarily consider the ideals producing purposive and self-sustaining behaviour. What was missing, Sorel maintained, in the Marxism that had been inherited from Marx and Engels was a competent psychological theory, one that might persuasively relate collective behaviour to the social and economic realities of any determinate period.[54]

But from being a rewriting of Marx's theory of what shaped history, Sorel's conceptions shifted to seeing in Marx's work not a scientific theory at all, but an effective myth competing with other myths to prompt men to historic action.[55] As myth, no matter what its rationalist claims, Marx's theories, like all others, are fundamentally an aesthetic appeal to the irrational, and it is the myth which can most effectively tap the irrational sources of human motivation which will dominate future history. Like all such theories, of course, Sorel's was already imbued with its own myth, one motivated by hatred of bourgeois society's lack of mythic values, its timid complacence: 'The highest good is the heroic action performed with a sense of impersonal consecration to the ends of a restricted group bound together in fervent solidarity and impelled by passionate confidence in its ultimate triumph in some cataclysmic encounter.'[56] In France particularly, where Socialist parties had come to be seen, after the Dreyfus affair, as supporters of the Republic and therefore of the political *status quo*, Sorel's theories became the rallying point for all who were opposed to their society: through Sorel political groups and moral attitudes of very different colours found themselves in harmony:

> Sorel and his associates contrived the synthesis of all the ideas and contemporary trends of thought which had in common the advocacy of revolt against a bourgeois society and all its moral and political values, revolt against the doctrine of natural rights, and revolt against liberalism and democracy. Revolutionary syndicalists and nationalists, as well as anti-democrats and anti-liberals of every colour, had now found common ground; and the shift from revolutionary syndicalism to nationalism, or vice versa, had never in theory been beyond the bounds of possibility, and by the time the first war loomed on the horizon it had taken on the appearance of inevitability.[57]

In Sorel's theories those who opposed their society because of its economic injustices and those who opposed their society because of its middle-class philistinism and lack of aristocratic *élan* could join forces in reactionary revolution. Among those who accepted his analysis was Charles Maurras.

One more element had to be added to Sorel's transformation of Marxism before it could become a fully-fledged political ideology, and that was the translation of Marx's conception of the proletariat from the class to the nation. It was in Italy that this shift occurred: from the 1890s it had been argued by many Italian intellectuals that the problems of Italy were different from those of industrial nations, and that class warfare could only jeopardise still further Italy's economic development. The problem in Italy was not, in effect, the problem to which Marx had given his attention: the problem in Italy was not the unequal distribution of wealth, but the need to create wealth. It was not the need to take from the bourgeoisie the wealth they had created by exploiting the proletariat, but the need to prevent the exploitation of Italy by the already industrialised nations of Europe; the need, in other words, to perform in Italy that transformation of the productive base which was, historically, the purpose of the bourgeoisie, but a purpose which the Italian bourgeoisie might be incapable of carrying out because of Italy's underdeveloped condition in relation to the other major nations of Europe. Class conflict of the Marxist variety could, Mussolini and the syndicalists argued, only further weaken the Italian nation and so harm the economic situation of the masses. Only national unity, fitness for the Darwinian struggle of nations for the riches of the world, could be the path forward for a nation which was proletarian not in being largely working class, but in being exploited by those nations in which large industry and therefore a working class had already been developed:

> If great industry was the necessary antecedent to socialism, socialism was hardly a prospect for most of the world in 1920, and certainly not for Italy in the foreseeable future. The syndicalists and Mussolini argued that the vast majority of the nations of the world faced bourgeois tasks — national independence, integration, and the generation of great industry. If the bourgeoisie proved inadequate to their historical mission, revolution must intercede. It would be a revolution led by men fired by a mythic vision and mobilizing masses to their purpose, masses innocent of the consciousness that would otherwise have to wait for the advent of large scale industry.[58]

Nationalism and Socialism; nationalism for the establishment of the conditions in which Socialism would be possible, but a Socialism which knew that the masses would always have to be led by myths, such was the fusion that created the first Fascism.

The ideology of Fascism which I have been abstracting from the works of Gregor, Laqueur, Sternhell, Mosse and de Felice can be summed up in three basic propositions: first, that men in society operate as groups and not as individuals; secondly, that groups are motivated by irrational forms of consciousness, by myths, and that these are organised and controlled by elites within the society; and thirdly, that the most effective myths are those associated with the nation, which, because of this and its role in organising economic life, becomes the essential carrier of historical development. Such an ideology makes of Fascism not an eccentric and accidental element in our historical development, but a central pattern whose elements — though calling themselves something different — have appeared repeatedly in situations where revolutionary parties have sought to create the conditions for a proletarian society in a country where no industry existed to form a proletarian class. Under such conditions the revolution has to be its own justification; there is no conceivable end to which it is working other than maintaining the dynamic of its own revolutionary development: 'The Fascist spirit shuns everything that arbitrarily mortgages the mysterious future.

We do not believe in dogmatic programmes.'[59] So Mussolini wrote in 1921: Fascism is voluntaristic because it is based in the will to make a revolution rather than the knowledge that it is bound to happen; the form the future will take is therefore also open, 'mysterious'. It is this which at once makes Fascism so amenable to transference from one country to another and makes it, at the same time, so difficult to reduce to a definite identity: since it is based on a nationalist set of myths and a national trajectory of development each type of Fascism will have a different character. Indeed, the destructiveness of Fascism in its most virulent forms stems from the temptation — obvious in the development of Mosley — to reduce the myths to the most crass prejudices of the community in order to activate social feelings on which the party can draw. The Fascism which was developed by Mussolini from the class theories of Pareto, the psychology of Sorel, and the nationalism of Corradini had none of the anti-Semitism we have come to take as typical of Fascist thought:[60] the anti-Semitism was the irrational element, the myth, upon which in Germany Fascism could feed and which, in the wake of its military superiority, it could enforce on its allies. It is impossible to ignore the anti-Semitism which was such an integral part of Nazism, for it is the sign of what an acceptance of irrationalism will unleash, but it would be wrong to identify that with Fascism itself: anti-Semitism, as Walter Laqueur has shown, was so pervasive in European society that even the opponents of Fascism could not bring themselves to try to defend the Jews from the full effects of Hitler's plans.[61] The essence of the Fascist stance is a fusion of past and future: towards an unstated future the myths of the past will mobilise the nation; out of action and conflict a new morality and a new society will be born that will be based, even as it refuses to fix itself, on the values of the national past.

It was because of this psychology of action that Fascism used — or rather abused — the realm of the aesthetic more than other political organisations. The power of myth had to be made manifest, had to have an effective form that could bridge the gulf between thought and action; the Futurists, for whom the aesthetic was a way of living rather than a thing to be created, provided Mussolini's Fascism with its style. It provided the theatre of the streets upon which the myth of dynamic movement towards the future could be played out, while also, in its aristocratic elitism, recalling the heroic values of a past, recalling men to the patriotism that had justified heroism: 'We want to glorify war — the only cure for the world — and militarism, patriotism, the destructive gesture of the anarchists, the beautiful ideas which kill.'[62] It was

Futurism which gave its style to the 'aristocracy of the trenches' who wanted a future in keeping with the values they had learned in war. Some commentators have seen a contradiction in Fascism's apparent commitment to a conservative set of myths and an activist ideology, to the technological management of industrialisation and the return to irrational sources of motivation. Adrian Lyttelton, for instance, argues that,

> There was a fundamental contradiction between such a rational and conservative notion as the restoration of the authority of the State, and the irrationalist activism which had inspired the Fascist movement. Ideas of constitutional reform, or any kind of effective organization, were regarded by this mentality as antipathetic or at least irrelevant. Camillo Pallizi ... expressed this attitude with eloquence: 'Fascism fought for a principle of authority ... Authority: but not that of a written law or a constitutional system.' And again: 'The genuine Fascism had a repugnance for being crystallized into a State ... The Fascist State is, more than a State, a dynamo.'[63]

Lyttelton also argues, and he is not alone in this, that Fascism changed character after taking power: that in order to maintain the authority of the State, Mussolini and Hitler both had to purge their party of those old Fascists who would have insisted on the dynamic irrationalism of their actions rather than their subjection to the will of the established authority. The issue is a complex one which I do not intend to follow further: the point which is of interest to me is that in the 1920s at least, Fascism seemed to have found a way of combining modernity, the commitment to movement, development, change, with conservation, retention of the values of home, family, nation, all of the past. Under Fascism mankind could accept the impulsion towards the future without the alienation from the past that it would seem to necessitate: Fascism was a journey into the future in order to recover the values that bourgeois society had destroyed, to re-establish the greatness that the world had once owned. Fascism was therefore balanced between the symbol of the pilot – image of modernity, of transcendence, of the heroic individual who can use machines to the glorification of the human – and the peasant – symbol of continuity, of the enduring value of the land and its folk, gatekeeper of all the values of the national past. Pound, who was close enough to have the feel of the ideology in the texture of life – or at least of the propaganda – was responsive to both these sides of the Fascist equation. He wrote in

Jefferson and/or Mussolini: 'The Fascist revolution is infinitely more *interesting* than the Russian Revolution because it is not a revolution according to a preconceived type.'[64] Indeed, Pound's justification for relating the two leaders with whom his book deals is not that they in any way share an ideology, but a frame of mind 'when faced with the unending problem of CHANGE'.[65] At the same time the aspect which he does find in common between them is their relation to the land and its cultivation:

> Both he [Mussolini] and T.J. had sympathy with the beasts. They still plough with oxen in Italy and they say that the sentimental foreigner with his eye for the picturesque and the classic scholar who likes to be reminded of Virgil etc. are not at the root of it. The *bue* IS indisputably *simpatico*. I don't believe even Marinetti can help liking the sight of a pair of grey oxen scrunching along under olive trees, or lugging a plough up an almost vertical hillside. There are plenty of fields in Italy where a tractor would be little use and larger farm machinery no economy.
>
> However, the Duce is capable of, as T.J. was capable, of putting a prejudice or a sentiment in his pocket. He has looked over a few model factories, he is all for machinery when it means machines in the open air in suitable places . . .[66]

The mixture – confusion perhaps – of retention of the past with renovation towards a very different future is founded in the dialectic between past and future that is of the essence of Fascism. The dynamic of the machine is harnessed to the emotive image of the oxen in an assertion of economic and psychological health, at once open to change and retaining all that is valuable of the past.

If we are to understand Fascism we have to recognise that it could present itself as the truly modern ideology, founded on the most advanced conceptions of society and of the psyche: it was not utopian, but pragmatic, bringing into the open the elements which had always operated within societies but which had been kept covert or concealed. In asserting the value of elites it at the same time offered every man a place within the elite that was the whole nation in its struggle to fulfil itself. It fundamentally replaced bourgeois man in the most important way – as its ideology saw it – that he could be replaced, in people's myth of themselves. For those already predisposed, in the 1920s, against the 'levelling' effects of Communism, or for those who had seen the war as a refutation of Marxist theories of class, Fascism did not offer a 'reactionary' philosophy: it offered a different conception of a revolutionary philosophy, a revolution not to reinstantiate the classless society that had been at the beginning of history and would also be its end, but a revolution to join history into a single unity that would preserve past tradition while maintaining a dynamic trajectory towards the future. It acknowledged what was inescapable, the arrival of mass society, but it envisaged what the masses seemed in other politics to abolish, common purpose and individual nobility. Fascist society, organised to meet the true nature of humanity, could ensure the success of national struggle in a world whose fundamental economic units were nations and empires, and by ensuring the success of the nation it ensured the preservation of those values which other political ideologies demanding change or conservation would either cast into redundancy or allow to be eaten away.

Fascism drew — and draws — its support, therefore, from two different impulses which might seem on the surface to be opposed, but ones which under the conditions of the modern world seem to be ineluctably drawn together, though it is only under the supreme authority of the State that they can be held together. On the one hand is the impulse to dynamic transformation and to modernisation of society, a change which can, however, only be achieved by using the symbols of the traditional community which can mobilise the mass of the population; on the other hand is the traditionalist, the agrarian impulse, which sees that only by controlling the energies of mass society can its values be maintained. Supporters of Fascism no doubt tend towards one or other pole, but there is an element of both impulses in all Fascist pronouncements: it has to be both national and socialist.[67] And that doubleness is also to be found in the fact that Fascism is fundamentally an urban movement, and yet draws its values from rural and traditional sources: Fascism, as so many commentators have pointed out, offers a sense of homeland to those who live in the cosmopolitan world of the modern city: it does not overthrow the city and its mode of life, but it roots its lifestyle back into its hinterland, back into the soil. The fact that Yeats, Eliot and Pound were all exiles seeking a rootedness for a language which was neither quite their own nor quite that of the country they belonged to may well have intensified their desire for a politics that could combine the international, cosmopolitan world of the modern machine with the traditional agrarian virtues, the agriculture in which a culture and a language are rooted. One could list the features which the poets share with Fascist ideology and there would remain always the claim that these features are marginal to the poets' thinking or that they are not central to Fascism:[68] what connects the poetry to the politics is that they both strive to be modern in exactly parallel ways. Both attempt to bring change and innovation, a radical and dynamic movement towards the future, under the control of the desire to retain the traditional values of the past that contributed to national greatness and a healthy community; both saw the linchpin through which past and future could be connected as the irrational motivation of men through images, an irrational motivation that put the poet at the very crux of historical process. And at the centre of this shared nexus of ideas is the associationist aesthetic which performs in itself precisely the same relation between past and future that Fascism adopts: it moves forward into the openness of the reader's associations, into the future, only to reach deeper back into the past, and recalls the past only to set loose the uncontrollable flow of images into the future. Like Fascism, the associationist aesthetic inevitably demanded an authoritarian hierarchy to control the dynamic of the powerful irrationalities it unleashed, an authoritarian hierarchy so that the dynamic could be allowed to continue.

No poetics can, of course, be identical with a politics once it is in action: the former remains always relatively unconditioned in the realm of thought; the latter turns from ideology into action. But while Fascism was still an ideology, with all its historical consequences as yet unrevealed, Yeats, Pound and Eliot all found in it, though to different degrees, a politics whose pattern matched the developing needs of their art of memory. Fascism would ensure the preservation of the culture on which their poetry depended without destroying the dynamic of historical process, without merely conserving as dead remnants a residue of the past that happened to have survived into the present. In his diary of 1930 Yeats wrote:

> Spengler is right when he says all who preserve tradition will find their opportunity. Tradition is kindred. The abrogation of equality of rights and duties is because duties should depend on rights, rights on duties. If I till and dig my land I should have rights because of that duty done, and if I have much land, that, according to all ancient races, should bring me still more rights. But if I have much or little land and neglect it I should have few rights. This is the theory of Fascism and so far as land is concerned it has the history of the earth to guide it and that is permanent history.[69]

The combination of a desire for preservation and, at the same time, for the dynamic of history ('will find their opportunity'), of history both as a universal and permanent system but, at the same time, as founded upon native tradition, upon kindred, makes Yeats's identification of his views with Fascism no accident. And the transfer of terminology from the literary to the social and political, a transfer which we have seen already in the poets' works, is made possible, of course, because Fascism places the aesthetic at the very core of its conception of motivation. The transfer is revealed in another passage in the same diary entry in which the new society of the future is seen as an echo of the literary mode Yeats himself has developed:

> Our civilisation which began in A.D. 1000 approaches the meridian and once there must see the counterbirth. What social form will that birth take? It is multitudinous, the seat of the congeries of autonomous beings each seeing all within its own unity.[70]

The one and the multitude: the dialectic between them defines Yeats's politics as well as his aesthetics. The poet's image with its multitudinous effects is mirrored in a multitudinous world focused upon a single unity; and if the image does not itself produce the transformation of men's minds that the poet seeks, then history may do it by forcing upon people circumstances in which traditional values will again be relevant:

> If human violence is not embodied in our institutions the young will not give them their affection, nor the young and old their loyalty. A government is legitimate because some instinct has compelled us to give it the right to take life in defence of its laws and its shores.
> Desire some just war, that big house and hovel, college and public house, civil-servant — his Gaelic certificate in his pocket — and international bridge-playing woman, may know they belong to one nation.[71]

Belonging to one nation they will share the same images, their multitudinousness resolved into unity, their unity spreading out into multitude.

Yeats's politics are fundamentally agrarian and it is the destruction of rural by urban society that he hates:

> I came on a great house in the middle of the night,
> Its open lighted doorway and its windows all alight,

And all my friends were there and made me welcome too;
But I woke in an old ruin that the winds howled through;
And when I pay attention I must out and walk
Among the dogs and horses that understand my talk.

('The Curse of Cromwell'; CP, p. 351)

But those agrarian values can find their dynamic equivalent in the urban mass whose revolution is carried out in obedience to the image of the nation and its glories:

Come gather round me, players all:
Come praise Nineteen-Sixteen,
Those from the pit and gallery
Or from the painted scene
That fought in the Post Office
Or round the City Hall,
Praise every man that came again,
Praise every man that fell.
From mountain to mountain ride the fierce horsemen.

. . .

Some had no thought of victory
But had gone out to die
That Ireland's mind be greater,
Her heart mount up on high;
And yet who knows what's yet to come?
For Patrick Pearse has said
That in every generation
Must Ireland's blood be shed.
From mountain to mountain ride the fierce horsemen.

('Three Songs to One Burden'; CP, p. 373)

There is no division now between the aesthetic and the heroic: in recall the events of 1916 become drama, an image to be maintained with the others that connect us with all our monumental history — 'From mountain to mountain ride the fierce horsemen' — a history essentially at one with the land and the landscape. It is precisely the preparedness for a dynamic engagement in history undertaken under the direction of the images of the national past and for the reconstitution of the ideals of the national past that takes Yeats into alliance with O'Duffy's Blueshirts. That history did not provide him with the opportunity to fulfil those politics, as it did for Brasillach or Drieu La Rochelle or Maurras or Pound, is his good fortune, but no reason for denying the connection. The modern in poetry, after the First World War, and the modern in politics are based on the same transformations in our view of the human being and his society: both Fascism and modernism were founded on the same effort to build a bridge between the European past and the European future across the gulf of the collapse of European history in the war.

The case of Eliot is without doubt the most problematic, and is so in part because of the fundamental evasiveness of Eliot's writings. Just as the objective correlative is explained only in terms of a negative instance, so his politics are defined in terms of refusals of positions rather than their assertion. In one sense, of course, Eliot refuses to be political at all, because all that pertains to the world of action is necessarily failed in the perspective of the eternal, but he also refuses to be political because he claims only to be interested in political ideas, not in politics, and even then to be interested from a point of view of jaundiced scepticism. Thus, in his essay on 'The Literature of Fascism' he early on announces that he is 'interested in political ideas, but not in politics',[72] and concludes that 'both Russian Communism and Italian Fascism seem to me to have died as political ideas in becoming political facts.'[73] And at the heart of his attitude is a sense of the utter futility of political commitments:

> The human craving to believe in *something* is pathetic, when not tragic; and always, at the same time, comic. I still believe, however, that religious beliefs (including, of course, Atheism), are on a different plane. Some so-called religious beliefs are really political beliefs in disguise; but many political beliefs are substitutes for religious beliefs.[74]

The phrasing — 'human craving to believe in something is pathetic . . . I still believe' reveals Eliot's sense of the irony of his own position, because it is based not only on a distinction of planes of belief (a distinction Eliot's own qualifications make problematic), but also on the belief that all action is insignificant, that action is necessarily a revelation of inconsequentiality. Thus, in an earlier essay in the *Criterion*, he had put forward the following distinction:

> I am also an admirer of Machiavelli; Machiavelli also seems to me an honest thinker, and no politician; and I should say on the basis of

Machiavelli's works alone, that a man who could write so honestly was a simple fellow with no skill in 'practical politics' – a belief which is borne out by what we know of Machiavelli's career. This is (without prejudice) one difference between Machiavelli and Maurras on the one hand and Mussolini on the other; the two former, who have not 'succeeded' are men of thought; that last, who has 'succeeded', is a man of action, a man of histrionic ability.[75]

Success is necessarily failure, a revelation of mere histrionic ability; failure is necessarily success, a revelation of honesty in a corrupt world; success, indeed, is a revelation that what was on offer is polluted by being already in harmony with the degraded potentialities of common humanity. Eliot's reason for distancing himself from Fascism and Communism is, as he summed it up in a review article of 1929, that,

> They have both been already partially absorbed by the popular mind, so that in the intellectual sense, there is nothing 'shocking' about them; and as they seem to be so easily absorbed by the popular mind, one suspects that they must have a good deal in common with what was in the popular mind already. They are both, in other words, perfectly conventional ideas . . . [76]

A mind so determined to separate itself from anything tainted by the acceptance of the populace is of necessity driven to a political theory which can either never be fulfilled or which, when fulfilled, must be deemed to have denied its own validity. Eliot views himself as the true revolutionary because his ideas have no popular support: talk to the common man

> about the divine right of kings, or the advantages of an hereditary oligarchy, he will either retort with open derision and hearty giggles, or with the patient gentleness with which he treats a harmless maniac. These ideas are, as ideas, and whether true or false, revolutionary.[77]

Fascism, for Eliot, has denied itself the role of truly revolutionary reactionary idea by becoming political fact: it is to the royalism of the *Action Française* that Eliot remains loyal, because, having failed as a political movement, it retains in ideal purity the thought of the reactionary revolution.

Eliot was not a supporter of any post-Mussolini Fascist movement:

he supports the ideas which created Fascism but despairs of action sufficiently to see its instantiation as a denial of its ideas. At the same time we must recognise that Mussolini's Fascism was, for Mussolini himself, of purely Italian significance. Pound, in insisting that he had never advocated Fascism for any other country than Italy, was being accurate to Mussolini's sense of his movement, for, as a nationalism, it could only develop within the possibilities of the national past — within the myths that that past made available. When Eliot satirised the aims of the British Fascist journal the *British Lion*, which had asserted its support for the monarchy, by suggesting that 'the *British Lion* might very well uphold these things without dressing itself up in an Italian collar',[78] he was only repeating what Mussolini had said when he insisted that Fascism was not for export. The elements of Fascism which could be exported were only those connected with its sense of dynamism: the 'agrarian' and 'traditionalist' myths which provided the psychological impetus to dynamism were necessarily unique to specific cultures. There is also a fundamental difference between the 'Fascism' of an already industrialised country and the Fascist ideology that had been developed in order to aid the development of the under-developed, between, as many commentators would claim, Italian and German versions of Fascism.[79] But though there may be intellectual justification for Eliot's complaints about 'sentimental Anglo-Fascism',[80] the consistent thread that runs throughout his essay on 'The Literature of Fascism' is his petulance at support for Fascism by a Roman Catholic hierarchy which had condemned Maurras: 'I should not like to see it [the Roman Church] accept in Rome what it has denied in Paris; and I should like to have it explained to me why Fascism can perhaps be swallowed, when the *Action Française* is spewed out.'[81] Because of national conditions Eliot continues to believe that the future of Britain will be determined by French rather than Italian models of reactionary revolution, whatever the Vatican might say about Maurras:

the aim of Fascism appears to be centralization. The theory of the *Action Française* carries decentralization to the farthest possible point, and in this respect represents a reaction against the Napoleonic system, with which Fascism has some analogies. It is to be admitted, of course, that Italy has centuries of chaotic decentralization to overcome, and that perhaps the Italian needs for a generation or so a powerful dose of central authority; and that the difference between France and Italy in this respect is diametrical. My point is, however, that the situation with respect to England is nearer to the situation of France than it is to that of Italy.[82]

Thus Eliot's refusal of Fascism is based not on opposition to its general ideology but on the ways in which that ideology can be applied to specific national situations. When he writes that he has 'a preference for Fascism in practice', rather than Communism, and that he 'will not admit that this preference is itself wholly irrational' because the 'Fascist form of unreason is less remote from my own than is that of the Communists',[83] he is not merely playing with words: the *Action Française* represented a social philosophy based on the same linking of the irrational with the dynamic that had given rise to Fascism.

In France, since the Second World War, there has been a strong line of argument that has tried to draw a definite distinction between the extreme conservatism of the French right and the Fascist movements in France. But as Robert Soucy has shown, 'the two philosophies shared many common denominators which were often far more important in determining their political behaviour than the elements which separated them',[84] and the distinction between the two breaks down particularly in the case of the *Action Française*, for Maurras 'acknowledged that when a monarchist state came to power again it might have to institute a temporary dictatorship'[85] and the means of bringing about such a new state included the activities of the *Camelots du Roi*, the shock troops of a political upheaval that would start in the streets. Zeev Sternhell points to the ways in which Maurras' philosophy was integral to developing Fascist ideology in the period immediately before the war:

In 1911-12, Sorel — the revolutionary syndicalist — put out a review called *L'Independence*, which was nationalist and anti-Semitic, at about the same time as two other publications were launched that rank among the more interesting and significant harbingers of Fascism: *Les Cahiers du Cercle Proudhon* in France, and *La Lupa* in Italy. The Cercle Proudhon was founded by Charles Maurras, with George Sorel as its moving spirit. It embraced both syndicalists and nationalists belonging to Action Française. A month later the first edition of *Les Cahiers* . . . was published, and among its promoters two names stand out that are symbolic of the nature of the enterprise: George Valois, who belonged with the left wing of Action Française, who was the author of *La Monarchie et la Classe Ouvrière*, and who went on to found the Faisceau in 1925; and

Edouard Berth, a disciple of Sorel's who in the 1920s shifted from the radical right to the extreme left. Nationalists and syndicalists alike were in agreement that 'democracy was the greatest mistake of the last century,' that ... 'if we wish to conserve and increase the moral, intellectual and material capital of civilization, it is absolutely imperative to destroy the institutions of democracy.'[86]

We may draw the lines at various points on the complex political spectrum of right and left that this fusion of nationalism and socialism produced: there can be no doubt, however, that the *Action Française* was a part of the transformation of nationalism and socialism that led in Italy to Fascism, and that, being the earlier movement, the *Action Française* had tended to lose its most dynamic supporters after Mussolini's Fascism seemed to point the way to a more effective means of implementing the same underlying principles.[87] But if, for the more agrarian wing of this political upsurge, the dynamism of Mussolini was unacceptable in itself, because implying an insufficient attention to tradition, it was also unnecessary in countries which had the option of re-establishing the strength of the monarchy as the focus of an ordered and authoritarian social system. Thus Eliot insisted that 'the *Action Française* does not contemplate a powerful dictator and a nominal king — but a powerful king and an able minister.'[88] The basis of kingly power, however, would lie in the same psychological forces that Fascism sought to tap in the irrational motivation of men (Eliot felt that Mosley's programme on which British Fascism was to be based lacked an 'enthusiasm', the element of 'unreason' integral to any political philosophy[89]) and in England such irrational motivation would be intensified by the monarchical leader being head, too, of a national Church. The monarch in England would be the true inheritor of the mantle claimed by the Italians:

The old Roman Empire is a European idea; the new Roman Empire is an Italian idea, and the two must be kept distinct ... The general idea is found in the continuity of the impulse of Rome to the present day. It suggests Authority and Tradition certainly, but Authority and Tradition (especially the latter) do not necessarily suggest Signor Mussolini. It is an idea which comprehends Hooker and Laud as much (or to some of us more than) it implies St. Ignatius or Cardinal Newman.[90]

It was not to Mussolini that Eliot turned for help from Italy for his views, but to Machiavelli: 'It is quite possible that an established National Church, such as the Church of England, might have seemed to Machiavelli the best establishment for a Christian commonwealth; but that a religious establishment of some kind is necessary to a nation he is quite sure.'[91] What Mussolini's Fascists try to achieve through a single party totalitarian state can be achieved, in England or France, by reconstituting the institutions which assert the divine right of kings, for, as Machiavelli had noted,

> the introduction of Religion at Rome by Numa was one of the causes that chiefly contributed to its grandeur and felicity: for Religion produced good order, and good order is generally attended with good fortune and success in any undertaking. And, as a strict observance of Divine worship and religious duties always tends to the aggrandizement of a State, so a neglect or contempt of them may be reckoned amongst the first causes of its ruin.[92]

Maurras' problems with the Vatican had arisen from his apparent use of Christianity as part of a political programme without believing in it: for Eliot belief in Christianity becomes an added inducement to the support of Maurras' politics.

The Toryism which Eliot adopted in the 1930s, was neither directly related to the traditions of English conservatism nor to the British Conservative party of his own day: it was an English version of Maurras, but one in which religion was not merely an instrument of political policy, focusing, like the political structure, upon the person of the monarch, but an essential act of faith without which no political philosophy could hope to gain the kind of support that would allow it to survive. Nationalism by itself was inadequate; only the nationalism inscribed in an established religious institution would be adequate to the challenge of Communism:

> The Bolsheviks at any rate believe in something which has what is equivalent for them to a supernatural sanction; and it is only with a genuine supernatural sanction that we can oppose it. The theory of nationalism, as advanced in Italy, is not good enough; it becomes both artificial and ridiculous ... The only hope is in a Toryism which, though not necessarily distinct for parliamentary purposes, should refuse to identify itself with that Conservatism which has been overrun first by deserters from Whiggism and later by business men. And for such a Toryism not only a doctrine of the relation of

the temporal and spiritual matters of Church and State is essential, but even a religious foundation for the whole of its political philosophy. Nothing less can engage enough respect to be a worthy adversary of Communism.[93]

The respect for Communist beliefs implied in the final statement of this passage did not extend to the people Communism claimed to represent or whose interests it sought to advance. Eliot's respect was for a parallel elite of believers, suffering the same fate as his own:

> They have joined that bitter fraternity which lives on a higher level of doubt; no longer the doubting which is just play with ideas . . . but that which is a daily battle. The only end of the battle, if we live to the end, is holiness; the only escape is stupidity, and stupidity, for the majority of people, is no doubt the best solution of the difficulty of thinking; it is far better to be stupid in a faith, than to be stupid and believe nothing.[94]

The conception of society which this implies is one in which contending elites strive for the adherence of the irrational multitude. There is no validation of the elites' views in terms of the multitude, because their need is for something to believe in. Eliot treats Communism primarily in terms of its quality as a focus of belief, not in terms of its social aims, and he sympathises with it in so far as it is, at least, a belief:

> I would even say that, as it is the faith of the day, there are only a small number of people living who have achieved the right not to be communists. My only objection to it is the same as my objection to the cult of the Golden Calf. It is better to worship the Golden Calf than to worship nothing; but that, after all, is not, in the circumstances, an adequate excuse. My objection is that is happens to be mistaken.[95]

But elsewhere Eliot does have a different test for Communist society: 'the kind of art it produces. Art in its highest development, both in Europe and in Asia, can hardly exist without a sense of individuality, a sense of tragedy, for which Communism does not seem to leave room.'[96] Individuality, a value regularly invoked by Eliot, is no more here, than it was in his early critical essays, something that can be achieved in isolation from an ordered social structure and an ordered development of past into present. He quotes, in 1934, some of the young writers of the *Action Française* to the effect that 'the law of French society does not consist in an utter devotion . . . of the individual to the State, but in the restoration of a right equilibrium and of right relations between the State and the individual' while, at the same time, 'protecting the rights, the duties, the forces, and the amenities of the family'.[97] What kind of law is being invoked? It is a natural law of the society's inherent development, and the social system within which such natural developments can take place is made clear in *The Idea of a Christian Society*:

> You cannot expect continuity and coherence in politics, you cannot expect reliable behaviour on fixed principles persisting through changed situations, unless there is an underlying political philosophy: not of a party, but of the nation. You cannot expect continuity and coherence in literature and the arts, unless you have a certain uniformity of culture, expressed in education by a settled, though not rigid agreement as to what everyone should know to some degree, and a positive distinction — however undemocratic it may sound — between the educated and the uneducated.[98]

It is not by the imposition of a social system from above, it is not by the crude means of a Fascist organisation invoking potent irrational images, that past and future will be linked and the powers of memory retained; in countries such as France and England, where vestiges of a traditional society still remain within a powerful and developed imperial economy, the pattern of an ordered, hierarchical, authoritarian society can be managed by ensuring that the mass of the people stay loyal to those symbols which have unified the society in the past, and that can be achieved through the educational system — 'A nation's system of education is much more important than its system of government'[99] — so that those intended to play the role of the 'unconscious' in relation to the consciousness of high culture, those intended to represent the continuity of family rather than the achievements of individuality, will do so, and the stupid will not be tempted to betray the virtues of their stupidity through education.

Yeats, always more dramatic than Eliot, was writing of the same kind of society in the same years — 1938-9 — but on the assumption that it was already upon us:

> I assume some tragic crisis shall so alter Europe and all opinion

that the Irish Government will teach the great majority of its school-children nothing but ploughing, harrowing, sowing . . . coat-cleaning, trouser-patching, and playing upon the squiffer, all things that serve human dignity, unless it decide that these things are better taught at home, in which case it can leave the poor children at home.[100]

The art of memory leads always to the same social organisation, the same stress on avoiding the education of the masses that they might be the carriers of the wisdom for which they are fitted and from which the poet can draw sustenance. With his acceptance of Christianity, Eliot stepped back from the dynamic aspects of Fascist programmes, but like them he saw, as Roger Kojecky puts it, that 'a society with an over-arching ideology was positive', while 'a liberal or secular society which denies the ideological perspective was negative, and could only exist as a transitional phase'.[101] The 'tragic crisis' that Yeats foresaw was one which Eliot hoped would also force upon people the recognition that they must positively assert the residual ideology of the existing nation, the ideology not of the actual institutions that had developed within the nation's history, but those that were implicit in its History — the institutions of Church and State. Eliot's politics remain always within Maurras' conception of a people living on the land and led by a hereditary class which also draws to it the elite of other groups: between them they can perform society's essential function, preservation of the continuity of history through sustained memory of the generations that have gone before them. Eliot could not have accepted the Fascism of Mosley not only because of his refusal to make temporal commitments, but also because Mosley's Fascism was essentially of the dynamic variety: it was a Fascism of the trench veterans committed to ceaseless action rather than a conscious defence of past values. Mosley's Fascism did not harness the desire for 'rooted-ness' and never got beyond the ambience of those whom both Mussolini and Hitler found they had to drop once they achieved power. Eliot's politics remains within the agrarianism of Fascism's ideological roots before the war, rather than its dynamism after the war. What Fascist ideology insisted had to be made to happen, Eliot left to that passive accumulation of history which it was the business of politics to make possible, but which could not be manufactured. Making it possible, however, brought Eliot to the point that he describes in *The Use of Poetry and the Use of Criticism*, the point at which, 'when a man takes politics and social affairs seriously the difference between revolution and reaction may be the breadth of a hair'.[102] In the early years of the

1930s an enabling politics for the true values of historical continuity was so lacking that the times seemed to demand the imposition of new values if History was not to be altogether lost: 'the asceticism must first, certainly, be practised by the few, and it must be definite enough to be explained to, and ultimately imposed upon the many; imposed in the name of something in which they must be made to believe.'[103]

Fascism's aggressive modernity is a function of the fact that it does not actually belong to the modern world, but to the modernising world. It is an ideology which encourages modernisation within the terms of the security of the national past. Sociologically, it is no doubt significant that Yeats, Pound and Eliot were all from areas which had, in their youth, undergone rapid social change, and that their values were formed on the frontier between a 'traditional' agricultural society and a modern urban one. Eliot, for instance, found himself deeply in tune with the Southern Agrarians, whose

> complaint is not merely that the South was ruined and subjected by the Civil War, but that it is now well on the way to being modernized; that coal, oil, iron and factories have altered the relation of man to the world, and that the Good and Happy life is becoming less possible. The old Southern society, with all its defects, vices and limitations, was still in its way a spiritual entity, and now the organisation is wholly materialistic.[104]

But Eliot said this as someone himself committed to urban values: the desolation of modernity that Eliot saw in the South and in his own New England, the destruction of healthy individualism that Pound saw as the development from a pioneer confrontation with the natural world to an industrial barbarism, the uprooting of a society of aristocrat and peasant and its replacement by capitalist agriculture that made Yeats despair of Ireland, were attitudes adopted within a commitment to the cosmopolitan culture of the city. All three had imbibed, and nowhere more so than in their own area of specialisation – poetry, the ethos of aggressive change of a modernised society. Their art and their politics try to hold together these two poles: it is a dynamic development which attempts to restrain its own dynamism within the continuing values of a 'spiritual entity' that joins the present to the past. The aesthetics of associationism provided the context in which that dialectic could find expression, because in image and in language it allowed them, even as they committed themselves to the modern world, to invoke the memory of the past. And the value of associationist theories to poetry in general was that, in transferring the source of aesthetic experience from the beautiful in the world, as described by the poet, to the psychological stimulation of memories in the reader, it made possible a poetry of the ugly, the banal, the quotidian. The modern urban world which had no hold upon the poetic mind as traditionally conceived could find its place in a poetry whose images were not valued in themselves, but in what stimulus they offered to the reader's recall. The modern world could be faced in the confidence that its use was not a displacement of the past nor of past forms of beauty from poetry.

Equally, the structures which associationist poetry encouraged mirrored, in their fragmentation, their disruptive juxtapositions and violent conclusions, common responses to the psychological impact of modern urban life. Even if its purpose was not mimesis, associationist art could be read as a transcription of the flickering incoherence of the mind in the face of the rapidity of change, the collisions of different levels of experience, the lack of continuity that was the daily experience of anyone on a city street. More importantly, however, behind the mimetic façade, and asserting its parallel existence within the society, there remained a covert unity: the real experience of art or society was the experience of the elite in touch with a totality the world had lost. 'I want,' wrote Yeats, 'to create for myself an unpopular theatre and an audience like a secret society where admission is by favour and never to many.'[105] The poetry reflects a fragmented world, but does so in the knowledge that it will not fully 'exist but for those who do in some measure share its traditional knowledge, a knowledge learned in leisure and in contemplation'[106] that will deny the world with which they are forced to live. On the one hand the unity of the work implies the unity of history working its secret purposes, a spiritual impulse which will overthrow the old world and revitalise it, as Fascism would claim to do; on the other it implies the secret unity of the intellectual, maintaining inviolable his wholeness of consciousness by his participation in a knowledge which saves him from the modern world and to which the masses will never gain access:

> nothing matters but the quality
> of the affection —
> in the end — that has carved the trace in the mind
> dove sta memoria.

(Canto 76; p. 457)

But are all affections worthy of remembrance, all memories worthy of affection; memory our only matter in the end?

Endless memory is the central postulate of associationist theories of poetry and has remained central, as a result, to much of our contemporary poetic theory. Its impulse, in opposing the brutalising uniformity of the multinational and bureaucratic, in refusing to submit to a single dimensional international culture, is humanistic, but when memory itself is reified, when it ceases to have any connection with common processes of recollection and their ordinary scale among the mass of humanity, it becomes the justification for repressive political doctrines which deny people significant humanity in proportion to their failure to maintain or gain entry to the memory validated by poetry. The attempt to match poetry to the assumptions of the associationist aesthetic produced, in the work of Yeats, Eliot and Pound, profound innovations – the climactic image, the allusive method, the incomplete poem – innovations which succeeded in encompassing both the experience of loss and the sense of dynamic opportunity for which the First World War, in its decisive rupture of European history, was the catalyst and a mass technological society the fundamental cause. It was a poetic able to utilise the 'unpoetic' ingredients of the modern world because the poetry was in the process of recollection; and it was a poetry, too, in whose essential incompletion both the exhilarating and the terrifying possibilities of a world of relentless change were caught. But the defence of memory which the poetry demanded was to lead directly to a politics which, like the poems themselves, would move dynamically forward only to recover the order of the past, and to recover that order not only in mind or gesture, but as an active encouragement of political systems in which memory was to be power, in which the future was to be shaped by a past revealed, retained and eternally recreated through poetry, in which politics and poetry were to to be equal associates in the arts of memory, the memories of art.

ABBREVIATIONS AND EDITIONS OF TEXTS CITED

Yeats

Au.   *Autobiographies* (Macmillan, London, 1955)
CP   *The Collected Poems of W.B. Yeats* (Macmillan, London, 1950)
E   *Essays* (Macmillan, London, 1924)
E&I   *Essays and Introductions* (Macmillan, London, 1961)
Ex.   *Explorations* (Macmillan, London, 1962)
M   *Mythologies* (Macmillan, London, 1962)
Mem.   *Memoirs: Autobiography – first draft – and Journal* (Macmillan, London, 1972)
UP, 1   *Uncollected Prose*, vol. 1 (Macmillan, London, 1970)
UP, 2   *Uncollected Prose*, vol. 2 (Macmillan, London, 1975)
Var.   *The Variorum Edition of the Poems of W.B. Yeats* (New York, Macmillan, 1973)
V   *A Vision* (Macmillan, London, 1962)

Eliot

ASG   *After Strange Gods: a Primer in Modern Heresy* (Faber, London, 1934)
CP   *Collected Poems 1909-1962* (Faber, London, 1963)
FLA   *For Lancelot Andrewes: Essays on Style and Order* (Faber, London, 1970)
IC   *The Idea of a Christian Society* (Faber, London, 1939)
K&E   *Knowledge and Experience in the Philosophy of F.H. Bradley* (Faber, London, 1964)
NDC   *Notes towards the Definition of Culture* (Faber, London, 1960)
OPAP   *On Poetry and Poets* (Faber, London, 1957)
SE   *Selected Essays* (Faber, London, 1951)
UPUC   *The Use of Poetry and the Use of Criticism* (Faber, London, 1964)
SW   *The Sacred Wood* (London, Methuen, 1960)

Pound

ABC	*ABC of Reading* (Routledge, London, 1934)
	The Cantos of Ezra Pound (Faber, London, 1975)
CSP	*Collected Shorter Poems* (Faber, London, 1968)
G-B	*Gaudier-Brzeska: A Memoir* (John Lane, London, 1916)
GK	*Guide to Kulchur* (Peter Owen, London, 1938)
J/M	*Jefferson and/or Mussolini* (Stanley Knott, London, 1935)
LE	*Literary Essays of Ezra Pound* (Faber, London, 1960)
SP	*Selected Prose 1909-1965* (Faber, London, 1973)
SR	*Spirit of Romance* (Peter Owen, London, 1952)

NOTES

Chapter 1: Introduction

1. *The Letters of W.B. Yeats* (Rupert Hart-Davis, London, 1954), p. 812.
2. Ibid., p. 811.
3. Pound, *The Cantos*, p. 202.
4. Pound, *J/M*, p. 12.
5. Eliot, *ASG*, p. 12.
6. Ibid., p. 20.
7. Yeats, *UP*, 1, p. 410; 'Greek Folk Poesy', 1896.
8. Ibid.
9. Yeats, *CP*, p. 267.
10. Yeats, *Mem.*, p. 156.
11. Yeats, *E&I*, p. 259; 'Poetry and Tradition', 1907.
12. Yeats, *Ex.*, p. 423; 'Tomorrow's Revolution', 1939.
13. Ibid., p. 425.
14. Yeats, *CP*, p. 400.
15. The text of one of Pound's broadcasts is given in an appendix to William M. Chace, *The Political Identities of Ezra Pound and T.S. Eliot* (Stanford University Press, Stanford, 1973), pp. 224ff. The citation is on pp. 231-2.
16. Pound, Canto 52, p. 257.
17. The most useful accounts of Pound's economics are probably those of Noel Stock, *Poet in Exile: Ezra Pound* (Manchester University Press, Manchester, 1964), Chs. XI and XII; Hugh Kenner, *The Pound Era* (Faber, London, 1972), pp. 301ff; and Earle Davis, *Vision Fugitive: Ezra Pound and Economics* (University Press Kansas, Kansas, 1968).
18. Pound, *G-B*, p. 106.
19. Pound, *SP*, p. 250.
20. See, for instance, Chace, *The Political Identities of Ezra Pound and T.S. Eliot*, p. 85.
21. See, for example, the Introduction to Roger Kojecky, *T.S. Eliot's Social Criticism* (Faber, London, 1971); Kojecky allows Eliot the benefit of liberal interpretation, e.g. 'The notorious passage in *After Strange Gods* [p. 19] is capable of the interpretation that a community of *orthodox* Jews would be socially "desirable" ' (p. 12).
22. *Times Literary Supplement*, 23 August 1957.
23. *Criterion*, VIII, 31, (December 1928) p. 288.
24. Ibid., pp. 288-9.
25. Ibid., p. 287.
26. *Criterion*, VIII, xxxiii, (July 1929), p. 690.
27. Eliot, *NDC*, p. 48.
28. Ibid., p. 45.
29. Ibid., p. 107.
30. Conor Cruise O'Brien, 'Passion and Cunning: an essay on the politics of W.B. Yeats' in A.N. Jeffares and K.G.W. Cross, *In Excited Reverie* (Macmillan, London, 1965), p. 207. See also the reply to O'Brien by Patrick Cosgrave, 'Yeats, Fascism and Conor O'Brien', *London Magazine*, 7. 4 (July 1967). On Eliot see Allen Austin, *T.S. Eliot: The Literary and Social Criticism* (Indiana University Press, Bloomington, 1971) and on Pound, C.D. Heyman, *Ezra Pound: The Last*

Rower: A Political Profile (Faber, London, 1976).

31. John Harrison, *The Reactionaries* (Gollancz, London, 1966), p. 15.

32. Ibid., p. 16.

33. Ibid., p. 59.

34. Stephen Spender, 'Writers and Politics', *Partisan Review*, 34 (1967), pp. 372-3.

35. Roland Barthes, 'From Work to Text' in J.V. Harari (ed.), *Textual Strategies: Perspectives in Post-Structuralist Criticism* (Methuen, London, 1979), p. 76.

36. W.H. Auden, 'The Public v. the late Mr. William Butler Yeats', *Partisan Review*, 6, 3 (Spring 1939); reprinted in W.H. Pritchard, *W.B. Yeats: A Critical Anthology* (Penguin, Harmondsworth, 1972), p. 142. Auden's poem 'In Memory of W.B. Yeats' is also given in its original form in Pritchard's anthology.

37. Ibid.

38. Eric Homberger, 'Ezra Pound and the Ostriches', *Cambridge Review*, 89, 2156 (November 1967); reprinted in J.P. Sullivan (ed.), *Ezra Pound: A Critical Anthology* (Penguin, Harmondsworth, 1970), p. 352.

39. See particularly Freud's essay of 1908, 'The Relation of the Poet to daydreaming', *Collected Papers of Sigmund Freud*, IV (London 1924), pp. 173-83.

40. Eliot, Review of *The Philosophy of Nietzsche* by A. Wolf, *International Journal of Ethics* (Chicago), XXVI (April 1916), p. 426.

41. Freidrich Nietzsche, *Human, All Too Human*, trans. Helen Zimmern, *The Complete Works of Nietzsche*, ed. Oscar Levy (T.H. Foulis, Edinburgh, 1909), p. 27.

42. *Criterion*, II, 8 (July 1924), a review of 'The Growth of Greek Civilisation' by W.J. Perry, p. 490.

43. Ibid.

44. Frank Kermode, *The Sense of an Ending* (Oxford University Press, London, 1968), p. 40.

45. Ibid., p. 39.

46. Ibid., p. 112.

47. Ibid., pp. 39-40.

48. Yeats, *E&I*, p. 74.

49. Pound, *GK*, p. 299.

50. Yeats, *Ex.*, p. 369; 'The Philosophy of Shelley's Poetry', 1900.

51. George Dekker, *Sailing After Knowledge: The Cantos of Ezra Pound* (Routledge and Kegan Paul, London, 1963), p. 62.

52. See Boris de Rachelwitz, 'Pagan and Magic Elements in Ezra Pound's Works' in Eva Hesse (ed.), *New Approaches to Ezra Pound* (Faber, London, 1969), pp. 186ff.

53. Pound, *SR*, p. 92.

54. Yeats, *Au.*, p. 167.

55. Eliot, 'Reflections on Contemporary Poetry', *The Egoist*, IV, 9 (October 1917), p. 133.

56. *Criterion*, IV, 3 (June 1926), p. 420.

57. Yeats. *Mem.*, p. 188.

58. Ibid., p. 179.

59. Pound, *CSP*, p. 205.

60. Pound, *SP*, p. 293.

61. *Criterion*, VI, 5 (November 1927), p. 386.

62. William Hazlitt, 'Coriolanus', *The Complete Works of William Hazlitt*, ed. P.P. Howe (J.M. Dent, London, 1930) 4, pp. 214-15.

63. That these problems are not dead has been revealed by recent writings about poetry and politics. See, for instance, *Stand*, 20, 2 (Winter 1979) and

subsequent issues.

64. Kermode, *Sense of an Ending*, p. 108.

Chapter 2: The Associationist Tradition

1. Edmund Wilson, *Axel's Castle* (Scribner's, New York, 1931); Cleanth Brooks, *Modern Poetry and the Tradition* (Poetry London, London, 1948).

2. Eliot, *SE*, p. 287.

3. Robert Langbaum, *The .Poetry of Experience* (Chatto and Windus, London, 1957); Frank Kermode, *Romantic Image* (Routledge, London, 1961).

4. Kermode, *Romantic Image*, p. 2.

5. The most prominent of the critics who have refused to go along with the 'romanticising' of modernism are Monroe K. Spears, *Dionysus and the City: Modernism in Twentieth Century Poetry* (Oxford University Press, New York, 1970) and J. Hillis Miller, *Poets of Reality: Six Twentieth Century Writers* (Harvard University Press, Cambridge, Mass., 1966).

6. Northrop Frye, *A Study of English Romanticism* (Random House, New York, 1968); Harold Bloom, *The Ringers in the Tower: Studies in Romantic Tradition* (University of Chicago Press, Chicago, 1971); George Bornstein, *Yeats and Shelley* (University of Chicago Press, Chicago, 1970).

7. Denis Donoghue, *Yeats* (Fontana, London, 1971), p. 121.

8. Bloom, *Ringers in the Tower*, p. 190.

9. Eliot, *UPUC*, pp. 147-8.

10. Ibid., p. 88.

11. Kermode, *Romantic Image*, pp. 92-3. Probably the most influential exponent of this conception of romantic development is M.H. Abrams, *The Mirror and the Lamp: Romantic Theory and the Critical Tradition* (Oxford University Press, New York, 1953).

12. Eliot, *SE*, p. 285; 'The Metaphysical Poets', 1921.

13. Ibid., p. 282.

14. Yeats, *M*, p. 344.

15. Richard Ellmann, *The Identity of Yeats* (Faber, London, 1958), pp. 65-6.

16. Sigmund Freud, *New Introductory Lectures on Psychoanalysis*, trans. James Strachey (Penguin, Harmondsworth, 1973), pp. 39-40.

17. Ibid., p. 41.

18. Anna Balakian, *The Symbolist Movement: A Critical Approach* (Random House, New York, 1967), p. 164.

19. George Bornstein, *Transformations of Romanticism in Yeats, Eliot and Stevens* (University of Chicago Press, London, 1976), p. 136, sees in much of Eliot's poetry 'mental conflict between imagination and association', but does so on the assumption that imagination is good, association bad.

20. The best account of the centrality of associationist thinking to modern theories of language is probably Bernard Harrison, *Meaning and Structure: An Essay on the Philosophy of Language* (Harper and Row, New York, 1972). Harrison gives the following example, p. 11, from the work of W.V.O. Quine, *Word and Object* (MIT Press, Cambridge, Mass., 1960) as typical of what he calls the 'empiricist theory of language': 'the power of a non-verbal stimulus to elicit a given sentence commonly depends on earlier associations of sentences with sentences . . . Thus someone mixes the contents of two test tubes, observes a given tint, and says, "There was copper in it". Here the sentence is elicited by a non-verbal stimulus, but the stimulus depends for its efficacy upon an earlier network of associations of words with words, viz. one's learning of chemical theory.'

21. See, for instance, Noam Chomsky, *Problems and Knowledge and Freedom* (Fontana/Collins, London, 1972), p. 44.

22. Roland Barthes, 'Literature as Rhetoric', in Elizabeth and Tom Burns (eds.), *Sociology and Literature of Drama* (Penguin, Harmondsworth, 1973), p. 195. Originally in *Littérature et Société: Problèmes Méthodologiques en Sociologie de la Littérature* (Institute de Sociologie, Bruxelles, 1967), p. 31.

23. Yvor Winters is the only critic, though an unsympathetic one, to have taken the associationist principle as a central and continuing influence on modern poetry; see *The Function of Criticism* (Routledge, London, 1962), p. 47, and *Forms of Discovery: Critical and Historical Essays on the Short Poem in English* (Allen Swallow, Denver, 1967).

24. David Hartley, *Observations on Man* (J. Johnson, London, 1791), vol. I, p. 65.

25. Yeats, *CP*, p. 240.

26. John Locke, *An Essay Concerning Human Understanding*, ed. Peter H. Nidditch (Clarendon Press, Oxford, 1975), Bk 2, Ch. xxxiii, sect. 5, p. 395.

27. Ibid., p. 396.

28. David Hume, *A Treatise on Human Nature*, ed. L.A. Selby-Bigge (Clarendon Press, Oxford, 1967), p. 92.

29. Hartley's popularity was not achieved until the 1780s, when Joseph Priestley was their chief propagandist through his *Lectures on Oratory & Rhetoric* (1777). See the discussion of the development of associationist theory in Walter J. Hipple, *The Beautiful, The Sublime and the Picturesque* (Southern Illinois University Press, Carbondale, 1957), Ch. 11, and particularly p. 169: 'There is no trace of a physiological basis for association; Alison's system is wholly ideal. Indeed, it bears a far greater resemblance to the system of Hume than to the system of Hartley . . . Alison thought that his analysis of material beauties into mental coincided with the doctrine of the "PLATONIC SCHOOL".' Hipple goes on to point out that, 'In the second edition Alison reformulated his doctrine to conform to the "Platonist" position. The various "relations" are shown to be merely indirect expressions of mental qualities, and the ultimate conclusion is restated accordingly: "that the beauty and sublimity which is felt in the various appearances of matter, are finally to be ascribed to their expression of mind." '

30. See Martin Kallich, *The Association of Ideas and Critical Theory in Eighteenth Century England: A History of a Psychological Method in English Criticism* (Mouton, the Hague, 1970), pp. 222ff.

31. The importance of Alison's work has been noted particularly by Hipple, and by Ernest Lee Tuveson, *The Imagination as a Means of Grace: Locke and the Aesthetics of Romanticism* (University of California Press, Berkeley, 1960), who links Alison and Yeats, see pp. 194ff.

32. Archibald Alison, *Essays on the Nature and Principles of Taste* (Bell and Bradfute, Edinburgh, 1793); pp. 4-5; references are to the 1811 edition, hereafter cited as *Essays*.

33. Ibid., p. 5-6.

34. Ibid., p. 10.

35. Yeats, *M*, p. 344.

36. Alison, *Essays*, p. 12.

37. Yeats, *E&I*, pp. 89-90.

38. See Arthur Beatty, *William Wordsworth: his Doctrines of Art in their Historical Relations* (University of Wisconsin, Madison, 1927).

39. Alision, *Essays*, p. 90.

40. Yeats, *E&I*, pp. 156-7.

41. Ibid., pp. 157-8.

42. Alison, *Essays*, p. 42.

43. Yeats, *E&I*, pp. 215-16; 'Emotion of Multitude', 1903.

44. Edward Engelberg, *The Vast Design: Patterns in W.B. Yeats's Aesthetic* (University of Toronto Press, Toronto, 1965), pp. 124-5.

45. Ibid.

46. Yeats, *E&I*, p. 195; 'The Moods', 1895.

47. Alison, *Essays*, p. 397.

48. Yeats, *E&I*, p. 87; 'The Philosophy of Shelley's Poetry', 1900.

49. Bornstein, *Transformations of Romanticism*, p. 37, suggests that Yeats adopts Shelley's definition of 'revery': 'To receive these images mind entered the state Yeats named *revery*, for which he quoted Shelley's definition', but Yeats in fact quotes this passage (*E&I*, pp. 79-80) in order to distinguish the mystical state of reverie from the aesthetic, with which it is related but not identical.

50. Alison, *Essays*, p. 42.

51. Yeats, *E&I*, p. 159; 'The Symbolism of Poetry', 1900.

52. Ibid., pp. 240-1; 'The Tragic Theatre', 1910.

53. Yeats, *Ex.*, p. 141; 'Samhain', 1904.

54. Alison, *Essays*, p. 13.

55. Ibid., p. 62.

56. Yeats, *E&I*, p. 292; 'Discoveries', 1906.

57. Ibid., p. 7.

58. Alison, *Essays*, p. 45.

59. Yeats, *E&I*, pp. 161-2; 'The Symbolism of Poetry', 1900.

60. William Wordsworth, 'Preface to *Lyrical Ballads*', writes that his intention was 'to choose incidents and situations of common life, and to relate them, throughout, as far as possible, in a selection of language really used by men, and, at the same time to throw over them a certain colouring of the imagination, whereby ordinary things should be presented to the mind in an unusual aspect; and further, and above all, to make these incidents and situations interesting by tracing in them truly though not ostentatiously, the primary laws of our nature: chiefly as far as regards the manner in which we associate ideas in a state of excitement.' The rustic nature of his tales provides a more basic account of the 'primary laws of our nature' because his characters are not 'under the influence of social vanity'. *Collected Prose Works*, ed. Alexander Grossart (Edward Moxon, London, 1876), II, p. 81.

61. See Alison, *Essays*, p. 15.

62. Ibid., p. 16.

63. Ibid., p. 23.

64. Yeats, *UP*, 2, p. 140; 'The Irish Literary Theatre', 1899.

65. Yeats, *Mem.*, p. 248.

66. Yeats, *UP*, 1, p. 104; 'The Poetry of Sir Samuel Ferguson – II', 1886.

67. Alison, *Essays*, p. 47.

68. Yeats, *W.B. Yeats: Letters to Katharine Tynan*, ed. Roger McHugh (Clonmore and Reynolds, Dublin, 1953), p. 55 and p. 86.

69. Yeats, *E&I*, p. 349; 'Art and Ideas', 1913.

70. Yeats, *Ex.*, pp. 28-9; 'Gods and Fighting Men', 1904.

71. See, for instance, Martin Kallich, who, though ending by arguing that 'eighteeenth-century critics have formulated a theory of criticism more complex that we had been given to believe, and in the best applications a theory to which writers today may ascribe with few apologies' (p. 275), none the less sees the fundamental value of associationist theory in the fact that 'with the new social, political and moral adaptation of Hartley's theory by Godwin & Bentham, and their disciples, it helped form the intellectual milieu in which the psychological and critical conception of Wordsworth and Coleridge first took shape' (p. 266).

72. See, for instance, John Margolis, *T.S. Eliot's Intellectual Development*

1922-1939 (University of Chicago Press, Chicago/London 1972).

73. Francis Jeffrey, 'Alison on Taste', *Edinburgh Review*, XXXV (May 1811); for the importance of this essay, see Thomas Crawford, *The 'Edinburgh Review' and the Romantic Poets* (University Press, Auckland, 1955), pp. 5ff.

74. Dugald Stewart, *Philosophical Essays* (William Creech and Archibald Constable, Edinburgh, 1810); Thomas Brown, *Lectures on the Philosophy of the Human Mind* (W. and C. Tait, Edinburgh 1820); James Mill, *Analysis of the Phenomena of the Human Mind* (Baldwin and Craddock, London, 1829).

75. He had taken it out twice from Edinburgh University library in the 1790s; see Bain, *James Mill: A Biography* (Longmans Green, London, 1882) p. 18.

76. John Stuart Mill, *Dissertations and Discussions*, I (John W. Parker, London, 1859), p. 82.

77. Wordsworth, *Collected Prose Works*, II, p. 81.

78. James Mill, *Analysis of the Phenomena of the Human Mind*, ed. J.S. Mill (Longmans Green, Reader & Dyer, London, 1869), p. 90.

79. John Stuart Mill, *Logic, Collected Works*, VIII (Routledge and Kegan Paul, London, 1974), p. 853.

80. John Stuart Mill, 'Thoughts on Poetry and its Varieties', *Dissertations and Discussions*, I, (John W. Parker, London, 1859), p. 82.

81. See George P. Landow, *The Aesthetic & Critical Theories of John Ruskin* (Princeton University Press, Princeton, 1971), pp. 100ff.

82. John Stuart Mill, *Dissertations and Discussions*, III (John W. Parker, London, 1875), p. 135.

83. John Stuart Mill, *The Later Letters, 1849-1873, Collected Works*, XV, p. 645.

84. Isobel Armstrong, *Victorian Scrutinies: Reviews of Poetry 1830-1870* (Athlone Press, London, 1972), p. 14.

85. See Olivier Brunet, *Philosophie et Esthétique chez David Hume* (Paris, 1965).

86. Armstrong, *Victorian Scrutinies*, p. 19.

87. Hallam's essay first appeared in *The Englishman's Magazine*, i (August 1831); it is reprinted in Armstrong, *Victorian Scrutinies*, pp. 84-102, to which my references refer; p. 89.

88. Yeats, *UP*, I, p. 277.

89. Yeats, *Ex.*, p. 490; the phrase follows a discussion of Hallam and the Aesthetic School as an influence on the young Yeats.

90. Arthur Symons, *The Symbolist Movement in Literature* (Heinemann, London, 1899), p. xix.

91. Ibid., pp. 133-4.

92. James Webb, *The Flight from Reason* (Macdonald, London, 1971), pp. 100-1.

93. A.G. Lehmann, *The Symbolist Aesthetic in France, 1885-1895* (Basil Blackwell, Oxford, 1968), p. 46.

94. Remy de Gourmont, *Le Problème du Style* (Mercure de France, Paris, 1902), p. 69.

95. Ibid., p. 81.

96. Ibid., p. 39.

97. Eliot, *SW*, p. 3.

98. Ibid., p. 7.

99. Ibid., p. 15.

100. Ibid.

101. Pound, *LE*, p. 3. This was the first of three propositions which Pound claimed had been drawn up 'by "H.D.", Richard Aldington and myself' in 1912;

F.S. Flint probably had more than a little to do with them, however; see Peter Jones (ed.), *Imagist Poetry* (Penguin, Harmondsworth, 1972), pp. 18ff. for an account of the power struggle between Pound and Flint for theoretical leadership of the group.

102. Pound, *SP*, p. 33; 'I Gather the Limbs of Osiris' (1911-12).

103. Pound, 'Vorticism', *The Fortnightly Review* (September 1914), pp. 461-2; quoted in Jones, *Imagist Poetry*, p. 21.

104. Yeats, *E&I*, p. 161.

105. Pound, *LE*, p. 4; 'A Retrospect', from 1912/13.

106. Ibid.

107. Yeats, *E&I* p. 161.

108. Pound, *LE*, p. 5.

109. See Jones, *Imagist Poetry* for a discussion of the Imagists' use of the term, and see, for example, 'The Symbolism of Poetry', *E&I*, p. 160, for an instance of Yeats's use of it: 'Besides emotional symbols, symbols that evoke emotions alone . . .'

110. Pound, *G-B*, p. 106.

111. Ibid., p. 97.

112. Ibid., p. 99.

113. Ibid., p. 106.

114. Wallace Martin, 'The Sources of the Imagist Aesthetic', *Publications of the Modern Language Association of America*, 85, 2 (March 1970), p. 198. Martin argues that it is not to de Gourmont that Pound and Hulme are indebted, but to the French psychologist Ribot. However, Ribot was one of the group with whom de Gourmont was connected and which published its work in the *Revue Philosophique*; see Garnet Rees, *Remy de Gourmont: essai de biographie intellectuelle* (Boivin, Paris, 1940), pp. 157ff. Whichever source we decide on as the primary, the line of continuity from empiricist psychology to the image remains clear.

115. Eliot, *SE*, p. 283; 'The Metaphysical Poets', 1921.

116. Eliot, 'Isolated Superiority', *The Dial*, 84 (January 1928), p. 6.

117. Eliot, *SE*, p. 315; 'John Dryden', 1921.

118. Eliot, 'Reflections on Contemporary Poetry', *The Egoist*, iv, 8 (September 1918), p. 118.

119. Eliot, *SE*, p. 145.

120. Ibid.

121. Eliot, *OPAP*, pp. 32-3; 'The Music of Poetry', 1942.

122. Yeats, *E&I*, p. 6; 'What is "Popular Poetry"?', 1901.

Chapter 3: Openings

1. Yeats, *E&I*, pp. 117-18; 'Blake's Illustrations to Dante', 1897.

2. Kermode, *Romantic Image*, p. 102.

3. See, for instance, T.E. Hulme's essay 'Romanticism and Classicism', *Speculations* (Kegan Paul, London, 1924), p. 111, in which he argues for the primacy of fancy over imagination. Commentators have tended to take this as a *jeu d'esprit* rather than a real qualification about how we think of the workings of the imagination.

4. Eliot, *UPUC*, pp. 77-8; 'Wordsworth and Coleridge' (1933).

5. Thomas Carlyle, *Sartor Resartus, Works* (Chapman and Hall, London, 1896), I, p. 175.

6. Yeats, *E&I*, p. 6.

7. Ibid., p. 245; 'The Tragic Theatre', 1910.

8. Umberto Eco, 'The Poetics of the Open Work', *20th Century Studies*,

12 (1974), p. 6; the essay can now be found in Eco, *The Role of the Reader: Explorations in the Semiotics of Texts* (Indiana University Press, Bloomington, 1979), pp. 48-9.

   9. Eco, *The Role of the Reader*, p. 55.

   10. St-Jean Perse, *Anabasis*, trans. T.S. Eliot (Faber, London, 1959), pp. 9-10.

   11. D.H. Lawrence, *The Rainbow* (Heinemann, London, 1955), pp. 361-2.

Chapter 4: Yeats: the Art of Memory

   1. Yeats, *E&I*, p. 495; 'Modern Poetry', 1936.

   2. Ibid., p. 227; 'Certain Noble Plays of Japan', 1916.

   3. Ibid., p. 516; 'A General Introduction for my Work', 1937.

   4. Yeats, *Mem.*, p. 180.

   5. Yeats, *E&I*, pp. 255-6; 'Poetry and Tradition', 1907.

   6. Ibid., p. 206; 'Ireland and the Arts', 1901.

   7. Ibid.

   8. Yeats, *UP*, 1, p. 101; 'The Poetry of Sir Samuel Ferguson', originally published 1886.

   9. Ibid., p. 104.

   10. Ibid.

   11. Yeats, *E&I*, pp. 8-9; 'What is "Popular Poetry"?', 1901.

   12. Ibid., pp. 250-1; 'Poetry and Tradition', 1907.

   13. Ibid., p. 243; 'The Tragic Theatre', 1910.

   14. Ibid., p. 245.

   15. Yeats, *UP*, 2, p. 188; 'The Literary Movement in Ireland', 1889.

   16. Yeats, *UP*, 1, p. 164; 'Bardic Ireland', 1889.

   17. Yeats, *E&I*, p. 352; 'Art and Ideas', 1913.

   18. Yeats, *UP*, 2, p. 193; 'The Literary Movement in Ireland', 1889.

   19. Ibid.

   20. P.B. Shelley, 'Alastor', ll. 406-8. Compare some other passages from 'Alastor' which utilise the same motif:

> His eyes beheld
> Their own wan light through the reflected lines
> Of his thin hair, distinct in the dark depth
> Of that still fountain: as the human heart
> Gazing in dreams over the gloomy grave
> Sees its own treacherous likeness there.
>
> (ll. 469ff.)

>   leaping rivulet, and evening gloom
> Now deepening the dark shades, for speech assuming,
> Held commune with him, as if he and it
> Were all that was; only – when his regard
> Was raised by intense pensiveness – two eyes,
> Two starry eyes, hung in the gloom of thought,
> And seemed with their serence and azure smiles
> To beckon him.
>
> (ll. 486ff.)

   21. See Thomas Parkinson, *W.B. Yeats Self-Critic: A Study of his Early Verse* (University of California Press, Berkeley and Los Angeles, 1951), pp. 123ff.

   22. See Donald R. Pearce, 'Flames Begotten of Flame', *Sewanee Review*, LXXIV (1966), p. 649. Pearce examines effectively the various sources of the

poem and argues that Horace, Keats and Yeats have written out of their predecessor's work. The associationist theory would justify our including all of such a recall as part of the experience of the poem, but would also justify many more possible connections. See Jon Stallworthy, *Between the Lines: Yeats's Poetry in the Making* (Oxford University Press, London, 1963), p. 100 for a discussion of the bird's possible sources and connections.

23. Stallworthy, *Between the Lines*, p. 99: the original form of the lines was:

And set in golden leaves to sing
Of present past and future and to come
For the instruction of Byzantium.

24. Harold Bloom, *Yeats*, (Oxford University Press, London, 1970), p. 346.
25. Engelberg, *The Vast Design*, p. 107.
26. Yeats, *E&I*, p. 162; 'The Symbolism of Poetry', 1900.
27. Yeats, *Ex.*, p. 145; 'Blake's Illustrations to Dante', 1897.
28. Yeats, *E&I*, p. 109; 'At Stratford-on-Avon', 1901.
29. Yeats, *Mem.*, p. 184.
30. Yeats, *E&I*, p. 294; 'Discoveries' 1906.
31. Ibid., pp. 49-50; 'Magic', 1901.
32. Samuel Taylor Coleridge, *Biographia Literaria* (Scolar Press, Menston, Yorkshire, 1971; reprint of 1817 ed), 1, p. 296.
33. Yeats, *E&I*, pp. 77-8; 'The Philosophy of Shelley's Poetry', 1900.
34. Ibid., p. 74.
35. Ibid., p. 50; 'Magic', 1901.
36. Yeats, *Var.*, pp. 131-2.
37. Kermode, *Romantic Image*, p. 97.
38. Graham Martin, 'The Wild Swans at Coole' in Denis Donoghue and J.R. Mulryne (eds.), *An Honoured Guest: New Essays on W.B. Yeats* (Edward Arnold, London, 1965), p. 55; D.J. Gordon and Ian Fletcher, *I, the Poet William Yeats* (Descriptive Guide to the University of Reading, Yeats's Photographic Exhibition, 1957), p. 33.
39. Kermode, *Romantic Image*, p. 38.
40. Dudley Young, *Out of Ireland: Poetry of W.B. Yeats* (Carcanet, Cheadle, 1975), p. 52.
41. Bloom, *Yeats*, pp. 193ff.
42. Marjorie Perloff, 'The Consolation Theme in Yeats's "In Memory of Major Robert Gregory" ', *Modern Language Quarterly*, 27 (1966), p. 307.
43. Yeats, *Au.*, p. 318.
44. Daniel Harris, *Coole Park and Ballylee* (Johns Hopkins University Press, Baltimore and London, 1977), p. 135.
45. Yeats, *E&I*, pp. 212-13; 'The Galway Plains', 1903.
46. Perloff, *MLQ*, 27, p. 315.
47. Yeats, *Au.*, p. 194.
48. Ibid., p. 216.
49. Ibid., p. 272.
50. Yeats, *Var.*, p. 846; the note is to the revised edition of *Poems* (1895), published in 1899.
51. Bloom, *Yeats*, p. 133.
52. See, for instance, Northrop Frye's essay, 'Yeats and the Language of Symbolism', *Toronto Quarterly*, xvii (1947-8), p. 1: 'In reading any poem we have to know at least two languages: the language the poet is writing and the language of poetry itself. The former exists in the words the poet uses, the latter in the images and ideas which the words express. And just as the words of the

language are a set of verbal conventions, so the imagery of poetry is a set of symbolic conventions. This set of symbolic conventions differs from a symbolic system, such as a religion or metaphysic, in being concerned, not with content, but with a mode of apprehension.' Though reflexive upon the psyche of the reader, Frye's symbolism is still a language system with its conventional and publicly-established meanings.

53. Yeats, *UP*, 2, p. 134; 'A Symbolic Artist and the Coming of Symbolic Art', 1898.

54. Yeats, *CP*, p. 280.

55. Yeats, *UP*, 2, p. 136.

56. Ibid., p. 134.

57. Yeats, *E&I*, pp. 289-90; 'Discoveries', 1906.

Chapter 5: Eliot, Pound and the Memory of Art

1. Eliot, 'A Foreign Mind', *The Athenaeum*, 4653 (4 July 1919), p. 553.

2. Ibid.

3. Ibid.

4. Yeats, *E&I*, p. 286; 'Discoveries', 1906.

5. Eliot, *The Egoist*, IV (July 1917), p. 90.

6. Yeats, *E&I*, p. 286.

7. Hugh Kenner, *The Invisible Poet: T.S. Eliot* (Methuen, London, 1965), p. 5.

8. Eliot, *SE*, pp. 325-6; 'Swinburne as Poet', 1920.

9. Stephen Spender, *Eliot* (Fontana/Collins, Glasgow, 1975), p. 39.

10. Eliot, *SE*, p. 419; 'Baudelaire', 1930.

11. Grover Smith, *T.S. Eliot's Poetry and Plays: a study in sources and meaning* (University of Chicago Press, Chicago, 1956), p. 24.

12. Ibid.

13. Eliot, *UPUC*, p. 78.

14. Ibid., p. 148.

15. See Lewis Freed, *T.S. Eliot: The Critic as Philosopher* (Purdue University Press, West Lafayette, Indiana, 1979), pp. 142ff. for a detailed examination of the development of this aspect of Bradley's terminology in Eliot's early work.

16. For the background to English Idealism, see A.J. Milne, *The Social Philosophy of English Idealism* (George Allen and Unwin, London, 1962) and Melvin Richter, *The Politics of Conscience: T.H. Green and his Age* (Weidenfeld and Nicholson, London, 1964). The best account of Bradley is probably Richard Wollheim, *Bradley* (Pelican, Harmondsworth, 1959) and he has examined Eliot's indebtedness in 'Eliot and F.H. Bradley: an account', in Graham Martin (ed.), *Eliot in Perspective* (Macmillan, London, 1970), p. 169. See also, Anne C. Bolgan, *What the Thunder Really Said: A Retrospective Essay on the Making of 'The Waste Land'* (McGill-Queen's University Press, Montreal, 1973).

17. Bradley, Eliot notes, is parodying the explanation by Bain of how, on associationist principles, 'an infant comes to recognise a lump of sugar: 'A young child, or one of the lower animals, is given on Monday a round piece of sugar, eats it and finds it sweet. On Tuesday it sees a square piece of sugar, and proceeds to eat it ... Tuesday's sensation and Monday's image are not only separate facts, which, because alike, are therefore *not* the same; but they differ perceptibly both in quality and environment. What is to lead the mind to take one for the other?

'Sudden at this crisis, and in pity at distress, there leaves the heaven with rapid wing the goddess Primitive Credulity. Breathing in the ear of the bewildered infant she whispers, The thing which has happened once will happen once more. Sugar was sweet, and sugar will be sweet. And Primitive Credulity is accepted forthwith as the mistress of our life . . .' (*SE*, p. 446)

18. Eliot, *SE*, p. 448; 'Francis Herbert Bradley', 1927.

19. See Sir William Hamilton, *Lectures on Metaphysics and Logic*, ed. Mansel and Veitch (Edinburgh, 1859), II, p. 237, for the source of this concept in Mill's major opponent in Victorian philosophy.

20. Eliot, *SE*, p. 19.

21. F.H. Bradley, *Collected Essays* (At the Clarendon Press, Oxford, 1935), I, p. 212, from the essay 'Association and Thought', first published *Mind*, o.s. xii, 47 (July 1887), p. 354.

22. See C.K. Stead, *The New Poetic: Yeats to Eliot* (Penguin, Harmondsworth, 1967).

23. Eliot, *K&E*, p. 22.

24. Ibid., p. 90.

25. Eliot, 'Kipling Redivivus', *The Athenaeum*, 4645 (9 May 1919), p. 298.

26. Eliot, *SE*, p. 159; 'Ben Jonson', 1919.

27. Ibid., p. 148.

28. Ibid.

29. Ibid., p. 158.

30. Ibid., p. 148.

31. Eliot, *The Athenaeum*, 4657 (1 August 1919), p. 680; 'Was there a Scottish Literature?'

32. Eliot, *SE*, p. 14.

33. Eliot's use of Conrad is discussed in more detail in Chapter 8.

34. The phrase occurs in Marlow's description of the savages on the river bank: 'They howled and leaped, and spun and made horrid faces; but what thrilled you was just the thought of their humanity – like yours – the thought of your remote kinship with this wild and passionate uproar. Ugly. Yes, it was ugly enough; but if you were man enough you would have to admit to yourself that there was in you just the faintest trace of a response to the terrible frankness of that noise, a dim suspicion of there being a meaning in it which you – you so remote from the night of first ages – could comprehend. And why not? The mind of man is capable of anything – because everything is in it, all the past as well as all the future.' (*Heart of Darkness*, *Works of Joseph Conrad*, vol. 5, *Youth* (Heinemann, London, 1921).

35. Eliot, *Athenaeum*, 4668 (17 October 1919), p. 1036; 'War Paint and Feathers'.

36. Ibid.

37. Eliot, *SE*, pp. 155-6.

38. *Criterion*, III, 3 (April 1925), p. 341.

39. Eliot, *SE*, p. 362; 'John Bramhall', 1927.

40. Eliot, *OPAP*, p. 33.

41. Eliot, *SE*, p. 17.

42. Ibid., p. 29; 'The Function of Criticism', 1923.

43. Ibid., p. 14.

44. Eliot, *The Dial*, 83 (September 1927), p. 260.

45. Ibid.

46. *Blast*, 1 (June 1914), p. 7.

47. Pound, *LE*, p. 92; 'The Tradition', 1913.

48. Ibid., p. 76; 'Date Line', 1934.

49. Pound, *G-B*, p. 106.

50. Pound, *LE*, p. 92.

51. Pound, *GK*, p. 44.

52. See de Rachelwitz, 'Pagan and Magic Elements in Ezra Pound's Works', in Hesse, *New Approaches to Ezra Pound*.

53. Donald Davie, *Ezra Pound: Poet as Sculptor* (Routledge and Kegan Paul, London, 1965).

54. Herbert Schneidau, 'Pound and Yeats: The Question of Symbolism', *English Literary History*, XXXII (1965), p. 220. The quote from Pound is from *Poetry*, 1 (January 1913), p. 125.

55. Pound, *LE*, p. 380; 'Date Line', 1934.

56. Davie, *Poet as Sculptor*, p. 176.

57. Pound, *G-B*, p. 84.

58. Pound, *ABC*, pp. 20-1.

59. Ibid., p. 47.

60. Pound, *SP*, p. 291; 'A Visiting Card': 'In this last category [logopoeia] Eliot surpasses me; in the second category [melopoeia] I surpass him. Part of his logopoeia is incompatible with my main purpose.'

61. Herbert Schneidau, *Ezra Pound: The Image and the Real* (Louisiana State University Press, Baton Rouge, 1969), p. 123.

62. Ibid.

63. Pound, *GK*, p. 204.

64. Schneidau, *Ezra Pound: The Image and the Real*, p. 70.

65. Pound, *GK*, p. 80.

66. Yvor Winters, *The Function of Criticism* (Routledge and Kegan Paul, London, 1959), p. 47.

67. Davie, *Ezra Pound: Poet as Sculptor*, p. 218.

68. Daniel Pearlman, *The Barb of Time: on the Unity of Ezra Pound's Cantos* (Oxford University Press, London, 1969), p. 46.

69. Pound, *GK*, p. 286.

70. Ibid., p. 57.

71. Ibid., p. 195.

72. Ibid., p. 33.

73. Hugh Kenner, 'Blood for the Ghosts', in Hesse, *New Approaches to Ezra Pound*, p. 331.

74. Pound, *GK*, p. 126.

75. Pound, *LE*, p. 91.

76. Pound, *SP*, pp. 58-9; 'Terra Italica', 1931.

77. Pound, *GK*, p. 126.

78. John J. Espey, *Ezra Pound's Mauberley* (University of California Press, Berkeley and Los Angeles, 1955), p. 98.

79. Quoted by Forrest Read, 'The Pattern of the Pisan Cantos', *Sewanee Review*, LXV (1957), p. 400. Carne-Ross's essay appeared in the *Boston University Journal* (Winter 1972).

80. Yeats, *E&I*, pp. 215-16.

81. Pound, 'Wyndham Lewis at the Goupil', *The New Age*, XXIV, 16 (20 February 1919), p. 264; the passage is cited by Ronald Bush, *The Genesis of Ezra Pound's Cantos* (Princeton University Press, Princeton, 1976), p. 46.

82. Pound, *The Egoist*, I, 12 (15 June 1914), p. 233.

83. Bush, *Genesis of Ezra Pound's Cantos*, p. 46.

84. Yeats, *V*, p. 4, gives these as Pound's own account of his intentions.

85. Eliot, *Athenaeum*, 4668 (17 October 1919), p. 1036.

Chapter 6: Closures

1. Eliot, *SE*, p. 14.

2. Quoted H. Stuart Hughes, *Spengler* (Charles Scribner's, New York, 1952), p. 12.

3. Arthur Schopenhauer, *The World as Will and Idea*, trans. Haldane and Kemp (Routledge and Kegan Paul, London, 1883), I, p. 326. See Patrick Gardener, *Schopenhauer* (Penguin, Harmondsworth, 1967) for a succinct account of Schopenhauer's views.

4. Quoted by Hayden White, *Metahistory: The Historical Imagination in Nineteenth Century Europe* (Johns Hopkins Press, Baltimore and London, 1973), p. 259.

5. Friedrich Nietzsche, *Complete Works*, ed. Oscar Levy (T.N. Foulis, Edinburgh, 1909-13), vol. 2, *Thoughts out of Season*, the first part of which is *The Use and Abuse of History*, p. 9.

6. Ibid., p. 31.

7. Ibid., p. 39.

8. Ibid., p. 52.

9. Ibid., pp. 53-4.

10. White, *Metahistory*, p. 372.

11. Nietzsche, *Use and Abuse of History*, p. 23.

12. Ibid., p. 9.

13. For the influence of Nietzsche on Yeats in particular, but also on Pound, see Patrick Bridgwater, *Nietzsche in Anglosaxony* (Leicester University Press, Leicester, 1972), Chs. 6 and 10.

14. Eliot, *SE*, p. 14.

15. Nietzsche, *Use and Abuse of History*, p. 10.

16. Bridgewater, *Nietzsche in Anglosaxony*, p. 147, points out that Nietzshce's greatest sales in Britain came at the point, in 1914, when he had passed from an intellectual influence to being the 'execrable Neech', source of German militarism.

17. Nietzsche, *Use and Abuse of History*, p. 57.

18. Pound, *GK*, p. 60.

19. Pound, *SP*, p. 236; 'John Buchan's *Cromwell*', 1935.

20. Pound, *GK*, p. 30.

21. Ibid., p. 194.

22. Yeats, *Ex*., p. 236; 'Samhain 1908'.

23. Eliot, *Criterion*, VIII, 13 (July 1929), p. 686.

24. See Bradley's essay, 'The Presuppositions of Critical History' in *Collected Essays*, 1, p. 1.

25. Eliot, *SE*, p. 14.

26. Eliot, *Times Literary Supplement* (11 November 1926), p. 787.

Chapter 7: Yeats: the Loss and Recovery of Memory

1. Yeats, *Au*., pp. 194-5.

2. Ibid., p. 195.

3. Yeats, *E&I*, p. 259; 'Poetry and Tradition', 1907.

4. Ibid., p. 344; 'John Shawe-Taylor', 1911.

5. Ibid., p. 260; 'Poetry and Tradition'.

6. Ibid., p. 250.

7. Yeats, *UP*, 2, p. 188; 'The Literary Movement in Ireland', 1899.

8. Yeats, *E&I*, p. 251.

9. Ibid., p. 203; 'Ireland and the Arts', 1901.

10. Ibid., p. 205.

11. Ibid., p. 203.

12. Yeats, *UP*, 2, p. 141; 'The Irish Literary Theatre', January 1899.
13. Ibid.
14. Yeats, *E&I*, p. 227; 'Certain Noble Plays of Japan', 1916.
15. Ibid., p. 364; 'Edmund Spenser', 1902.
16. Ibid., p. 372.
17. Ibid., p. 347; 'Art and Ideas', 1913.
18. Ibid., p. 350.
19. Ibid., p. 345.
20. Ibid., p. 352.
21. Ibid., p. 227; 'Certain Noble Plays of Japan', 1916.
22. Ibid., p. 229.
23. Ibid., p. 286; 'Discoveries', 1906.
24. Ibid., pp. 275-6.
25. Yeats, *Mem.*, p. 169.
26. Ibid., p. 168.
27. Ibid.
28. Yeats, *E&I*, p. 151; 'Symbolism in Painting', 1898.
29. Yeats, *Mem.*, p. 151.
30. Ibid., pp. 178-9.
31. Ibid., p. 140.
32. Ibid., p. 178.
33. Ibid., p. 215.
34. Yeats, *E&I*, p. 276; 'Discoveries', 1906.
35. Yeats, *Mem.*, p. 207.
36. Ibid., p. 209.
37. Ibid., p. 210.
38. Ibid., p. 198.
39. See George Mills Harper, *Yeats's Golden Dawn* (Macmillan, London, 1974), for a full account of the crises which tore apart the Golden Dawn between 1900 and 1903.
40. Yeats, *E&I*, p. 253; 'Poetry and Tradition', 1907.
41. Ibid., p. 313.
42. Yeats, *Au.*, p. 234.
43. Yeats, *E&I*, p. 43; 'Magic', 1901.
44. Yeats, *Au.*, p. 263.
45. See Graham Martin, 'The White Swans at Coole' in Donoghue and Mulryne (eds.), *An Honoured Guest*, pp. 5ff. for an analysis of the writing and compiling of the volume.
46. The details are given by Richard Ellmann, *Yeats: The Man and the Masks* (Faber, London, 1965), p. 199; the visitation is recorded by Yeats in his journal, *Mem.*, p. 264.
47. Yeats, *Ex.*, p. 56.
48. Ibid., p. 36.
49. Yeats, *E*, pp. 522-3.
50. Ibid., p. 527.
51. Ibid., p. 518.
52. Ibid., p. 517.
53. Ibid., p. 519.
54. Yeats, *Ex.*, p. 35.
55. Yeats, *E*, p. 526.
56. Yeats, *V*, p. 29.
57. Yeats, *E&I*, p. 245; 'The Tragic Theatre', 1901.
58. Dudley Young, *W.B. Yeats: Out of Ireland*, pp. 65-6.
59. Thomas Whitaker, *Swan and Shadow: Yeats's Dialogue with History*

(University of North Carolina Press, Chapel Hill, 1964), p. 223.

   60. D.J. Gordon and Ian Fletcher, *I, the Poet William Yeats* (Descriptive Guide to the University of Reading, Yeats's Photographic Exhibition, 1957), p. 26; quoted by Giorgio Melchiori, *The Whole Mystery of Art: Pattern into Poetry in the Work of W.B. Yeats* (Routledge and Kegan Paul, London, 1960), p. 201.

   61. Bloom, *Yeats*, p. 391; the quotation is from Yvor Winters, *The Poetry of W.B. Yeats* (Alan Swallow, Denver, 1960), p. 12.

   62. Yeats, *Ex.*, p. 328; 'Pages from a Diary in 1930', 20 September.

   63. Ibid., p. 344; 'Introduction to *The Words Upon the Window-Pane*', 1931.

   64. Ibid., p. 351.

   65. Gustave Le Bon, *The Crowd: A Study in the Popular Mind* (T. Fisher Unwin, London, 1897), p. 54.

   66. Yeats, *Ex.*, pp. 357-8.

   67. Yeats, *CP*, p. 213; 'A Prayer for my Daughter'.

   68. Yeats, *Ex.*, p. 354.

   69. Yeats, *Var.*, p. 828.

   70. O'Brien, 'Passion and Cunning', in Jeffares and Cross (ed.), *In Excited Reverie*, p. 274.

   71. Ibid., p. 246; O'Brien writes that 'O'Higgins's biographer, Mr. Terence de Vere White, while noting that it became the fashion to call him "the Irish Mussolini", maintains that he was in fact "an intense believer in democracy" . . . the important point is that it was as an "Irish Mussolini" that Yeats rightly or wrongly saw him.'

Chapter 8: Eliot, Pound: Memory's Broken Bridge

   1. Yeats, *E&I*, p. 365.

   2. Ibid., p. 365.

   3. Eliot, *SE*, p. 293.

   4. Ibid., p. 294.

   5. Ibid., p. 303.

   6. Eliot, *NDC*, p. 111.

   7. *Criterion*, VII, 3 (March 1928), p. 194.

   8. See Remy de Gourmont, *La Culture des Idees* (Mercure de France, Paris, 1900) and *Le Chemin de Velours* (Mercure de France, Paris, 1902); For a detailed discussion of Eliot's indebtedness to de Gourmont, see T.R. Rees, 'Eliot, Remy de Gourmont and dissociation of sensibility', in W.F. McNeir (ed.), *Studies in Comparative Literature* (Louisiana State University Press, Baton Rouge, 1962).

   9. See, for instance, part one of *ABC of Economics*, subtitled 'Dissociations: Or preliminary clearance of the ground', *SP*, p. 203.

   10. Eliot, *SW*, p. 37.

   11. Eliot, *SE*, p. 88.

   12. Eliot, *The Dial*, 71 (August 1921), pp. 216-17.

   13. Eliot, *SE*, p. 286.

   14. Ibid., p. 287.

   15. Ibid.

   16. Ibid., p. 293.

   17. Ibid., p. 292.

   18. Ibid., p. 303.

   19. Ibid., p. 295.

   20. Ibid., p. 296.

21. Ibid., p. 292.
22. *Criterion*, V, 2 (May 1927), p. 253; 'Popular Theologians'.
23. Eliot, *OPAP*, p. 57; 'What is a Classic?'.
24. Ibid., p. 55 and 61.
25. Eliot, *Athenaeum*, 4643 (25 April 1919), p. 237; 'American Literature'.
26. Eliot, *OPAP*, p. 57.
27. Eliot, *SE*, p. 155; 'Ben Jonson', 1919.
28. Ibid., p. 300; 'Andrew Marvell', 1921.
29. Ibid., p. 27; 'The Function of Criticism', 1923.
30. Eliot, *NDC*, p. 106.
31. Eliot, *SE*, p. 458; 'Marie Lloyd', 1928.
32. Ibid., pp. 459-60.
33. *Criterion*, V, 2 (June 1927), pp. 285-6.
34. *Criterion*, V, 1 (January 1927), p. 122.
35. Eliot, *The Egoist*, V, 5 (May 1918), p. 70; 'Observations', which appeared under Eliot's 'nomme de guerre', T.S. Apteryx.
36. Pierre Gaxotte, 'Fustel de Coulanges', trans. T.S. Eliot, *Criterion*, VIII, 31 (December 1928), p. 269.
37. Eliot, *The Egoist*, V, 5 (May 1918), p. 70; 'Observations'.
38. For a discussion of Eliot's attitude to Blake and its relation to his critical stance at the time of its writing see Ernest J. Lovell, Jr, 'The Heretic in the Sacred Wood; or the Naked Man, the Tired Man and the Romantic Aristocrat: William Blake, T.S. Eliot and George Wyndham' in *Romantic and Victorian: Studies in Memory of William, H. Marschall*, ed. Paul Elledge and Richard L. Hoffman (Harleigh Dickinson, New Jersey, 1971).
39. Eliot, *SE*, p. 317 and 321; 'William Blake', 1920.
40. Eliot, *Athenaeum*, 4657 (1 August 1919), p. 680; 'Was there a Scottish Literature'.
41. *Criterion*, VI, 4 (June 1927), p. 680.
42. Eliot, *SW*, p. 26.
43. *Criterion*, VI, 2 (August 1927), p. 98.
44. Ibid.: 'It is a hopeful sign that a small number of intelligent persons are aware of the necessity to harmonize the interests, and therefore to harmonize first the ideas, of the civilized countries of Western Europe.'
45. Eliot, *NDC*, p. 45: 'The real revolution in that country was not what is called the Revolution in the history books, but is a consequence of the Civil War; after which arose a plutocratic elite; after which the expansion and material development of the country was accelerated; after which was swollen that stream of mixed immigration, bringing (or rather multiplying) the danger of development into a *caste* system.'
46. *The Waste Land*, l. 404.
47. Eliot, *SW*, p. 15.
48. Eliot, *The Family Reunion* (Faber, London, 1963), p. 57.
49. Yeats, *Au.*, p. 270.
50. Yeats, *E*, p. 55.
51. See Tom Paulin, *Thomas Hardy: The Poetry of Perception* (Macmillan, London, 1975), pp. 24ff., which argues the case for Hardy's conception of association, perhaps accounting for the ghosts which haunt his poetry.
52. Bush, *Genesis of Ezra Pound's Cantos*, p. 54.
53. Ibid., p. 62.
54. Yeats, *UP*, 2, p. 206; ' "Maive" and Certain Irish Beliefs', 1900.
55. Eliot, *SE*, p. 321; 'William Blake', 1920.
56. Pound, *SP*, p. 71; 'Statues of Gods', 1939.
57. Bush, *Genesis of Ezra Pound's Cantos*, p. 54.

58. Ibid., pp. 55-6.
59. Ibid., p. 59.
60. Ibid., p. 55.
61. Yeats, *V*, p. 29.
62. Forrest Read, 'The Pattern of the Pisan Cantos', *Sewanee Review*, LXV (Summer 1957), p. 400.
63. I.A. Richards, *Principles of Literary Criticism* (Routledge and Kegan Paul, London, 1967), p. 231.
64. *The Waste Land: a Facsimile*, p. 113. The conception of the poem has having its unity in a 'protagonist' stems largely from Cleanth Brooks, *Modern Poetry and the Tradition* (Poetry London, London, 1948), and has been given one of its most interesting formulations by Robert Langbaum, New Modes of Characterization in *The Waste Land*' in A. Walton Litz (ed.), *Eliot in his Time: Essays on the Occasion of the Fiftieth Anniversary of the Waste Land* (Princeton University Press, Princeton, 1973).
65. Joseph Frank, 'Spatial Form in Modern Literature' in *The Widening Gyre: Crisis and Mastery in Modern Literature* (Rutgers University Press, New Jersey, 1965).
66. Yeats, *E&I*, p. 352; 'Art and Ideas', 1913.
67. Yeats, *E&I*, p. 6; 'What is "Popular Poetry"?', 1901.
68. Friedrich Nietzsche, *Complete Works*, ed. Levy, *The Birth of Tragedy*, trans. Haussman, p. 174.
69. Ibid.
70. Nietzsche, *Complete Works*, ed. Levy; *Human, All Too Human*, trans. Zimmern, pp. 6-7.
71. Bridgwater, *Nietzsche in Anglosaxony*, p. 142.
72. Nietzsche, *The Birth of Tragedy*, p. 162.
73. *The Waste Land: a Facsimile*, p. 3.
74. Nietzsche, *The Birth of Tragedy*, pp. 158-9.
75. Ibid., pp. 168-9.
76. F.N. Lees, *Notes and Queries* (October 1964), pp. 386-7, first drew attention to the connection between Eliot's objective correlative and Nietzsche's concept, as well as to the possible link through the Wagner quotation in *The Waste Land*; Bridgwater, pp. 139ff. adds a little to this but, finding little evidence of Eliot's having given much time to Nietzsche, traces the influence no further.
77. Nietzsche, *The Birth of Tragedy*, p. 156.
78. Ibid., pp. 156-7.
79. Ibid., p. 157.
80. Ibid., pp. 186-7.
81. Bryant Knox, 'Allen Upward and Ezra Pound', *Paideuma*, 3, 1 (Spring 1974), p. 77. The quotation is from Upward's *The New Word* (1910).
82. Pound, *Social Credit: An Impact* (Stanley Nott, London, 1935), p. 4.
83. Ibid., p. 9.
84. Ibid., p. 7.
85. Ibid., p. 9.
86. Pound *J/M*, p. 33.
87. Ibid., p. 36.
88. Eliot, *FLA*, p. 102.
89. Eliot, 'Reflections on Contemporary Poetry', *Egoist*, IV, 8 (September 1917), p. 118.
90. Eliot, *FLA*, pp. 24-5.
91. Ibid., pp. 14-15.
92. Ibid., pp. 19-20.
93. Ibid., p. 22.

94. *Criterion*, II, 42 (October 1931), p. 72.
95. Eliot, *NDC*, p. 48.
96. Ibid., p. 44.
97. Yeats, *E&I*, p. 251; 'Poetry and Tradition', 1907.

Chapter 9: The Politics of Poetry

1. Eliot, *Nation and Atheaeum*, XL, 11 (18 December 1926), p. 426; 'Whitman And Tennyson.
2. Eliot, *Criterion*, II, 7 (April 1924), p. 231.
3. *Criterion*, VIII, 32 (April 1929), p. 377.
4. Ibid.
5. E.g. 'The men of letters seem to agree, and a great many obscure people will agree with them, that to have one fifty-thousandth part in choosing a representative (of whom one may know next to nothing) who himself will have only a small part in indicating the nomination of a Prime Minister, who will himself be obliged to choose his cabinet for various reasons, is a very poor kind of "self-government" . . .' Ibid. p. 380.
6. Eliot, *UPUC*, p. 152; 'Conclusion', 1932.
7. Yeats, *Ex.*, p. 351; 'The Words Upon the Window-Pane', 1931.
8. Yeats, *E&I*, p.213; 'The Galway Plains', 1903.
9. Ibid.
10. Pound, *SP*, p. 135; 'National Culture', 1938.
11. Ibid.
12. Yeats, *UP*, 2, p. 141; 'The Irish Literary Theatre', 1899.
13. Eliot, *UPUC*, p. 153.
14. Ibid.
15. Yeats, *E&I*, p. 227; 'Certain Noble Plays of Japan', 1916.
16. Eliot's *Notes towards the Definition of Culture* is explicitly 'a plea on behalf of a form of society in which an aristocracy should have a peculiar and essential function' (p. 48).
17. Yeats, *Ex.*, pp. 244-5; 'A People's Theatre', 1919.
18. Eliot, *NDC*, p. 103.
19. Eliot, *Criterion*, X, 40 (April 1930), p. 484.
20. Yeats, *Ex.*, p. 255.
21. Pound, *SP*, p. 217; 'ABC of Economics', 1933.
22. Ibid., p. 218.
23. Pound, *J/M*, pp. 15-16.
24. Ibid., p. 63.
25. Ibid., p. 64.
26. Pound, *SP*, p. 290; 'A Visiting Card', 1942.
27. Pound, *J/M*, p. 99: 'Power is necessary to some acts, but neither Lenin nor Mussolini show themselves primarily as men thirsting for power. The great man is filled with a very different passion, the will to *order*.'
28. Pound, *SP*, p. 290.
29. Yeats, *Au.*, p. 274.
30. Yeats, *E&I*, p. 355; 'Art and Ideas', 1913.
31. Eliot, *Criterion*, VI, 4 (October 1927), p. 346; 'Mr. Middleton Murry's Synthesis'.
32. Eliot, *FLA*, p. 46.
33. Ibid., pp. 44-5.
34. Pound, *J/M*, p. 127.
35. Pound, *SP*, pp. 184-5; 1927.

36. Stock, *Poet in Exile*, p. 127.

37. See, for instance, his defence of Pound, *Poet in Exile*, pp. 128-9: 'He gave thought to the problem of war, peace and disarmament . . . He was also interested in the part played in world affairs by the manufacturers of armaments . . . he was interested in the American negro . . . If Pound was interested in Mussolini, he was also interested, though to a lesser extent, in Stalin and Congressman George Holden Tinkham . . .'

38. Roger Kojecky, *T.S. Eliot's Social Criticism* (Faber, London, 1971), p. 69.

39. Ibid., p. 68.

40. See Michael A. Ledeen, 'Renzo de Felice and the Controversy over Italian Fascism' in George L. Mosse (ed.), *International Fascism: New Thoughts and New Approaches* (Sage, London and Beverly Hills, 1979).

41. See Francis L. Carsten, 'Interpretations of Fascism' in Walter Laqueur (ed.), *Fascism: A Reader's Guide* (Wildwood House, London, 1976), p. 415, as well as Renzo de Felice, *Interpretations of Fascism*, trans. Brenda Huff Everett (Harvard University Press, Cambridge, 1977).

42. de Felice, *Interpretations of Fascism*, pp. 14ff. See also George L. Mosse, *The Crisis of German Ideology: Intellectual Origins of the Third Reich* (Grosset and Dunlap, New York, 1964).

43. See de Felice, *Interpretations of Fascism*, pp. 24ff. See also Paul M. Hayes, *Fascism* (George Allen and Unwin, London, 1973), pp. 123ff.

44. See de Felice, pp. 30ff. See also George Watson, *Politics and Literature in Modern Britain* (Macmillan, London, 1977), Ch. 5, for a discussion of the development of the distinction between 'left' and 'right' in British politics in the 1930s.

45. See Juan J. Linz, 'Some Notes Toward a Comparative Study of Fascism in Sociological Historical Perspective', in Laqueur (ed.), *Fascism: A Reader's Guide*, p. 3, for a detailed analysis of Fascist support.

46. Eugen Weber, 'Revolution? Counterrevolution? What Revolution?' in Laqueur (ed.), *Fascism: A Reader's Guide*, p. 450.

47. J. Plumyène and R. Lasierra, *Les Fascismes Français* (Editions du Seuil, Paris, 1963), pp. 19ff.

48. Juan J. Linz, 'Comparative Study of Fascism' in Laqueur (ed.), *Fascism: A Reader's Guide*, p. 38.

49. The 'Marxism' of the generation of the 1920s was also a product of such emotions: see, for instance, Christopher Isherwood, *Lions and Shadows* (Methuen, London, 1953), pp. 78-9.

50. Zeev Sternhell, 'Fascist Ideology' in Laqueur (ed.), *Fascism: A Reader's Guide*, p. 335.

51. Gustave Le Bon, *The Crowd*, pp. 108-9.

52. Ibid., pp. 54-5.

53. See particularly A. James Gregor, *The Fascist Persuasion in Radical Politics* (Princeton University Press, New Jersey, 1974) for a wide-ranging argument along these lines; Domenico Settembrini, 'Mussolini and the Legacy of Revolutionary Socialism' in Mosse (ed.), *International Fascism*, also has comparisons to make between Lenin's and Mussolini's development: see particularly, pp. 14ff.

54. A. James Gregor, *Young Mussolini and the Intellectual Origins of Fascism* (University of California Press, Berkeley, 1979), p. 24.

55. Ibid., p. 27: 'In his work, according to Sorel's interpretation, Marx had consciously or unconsciously employed not science by "social poetry".'

56. George Sorel, *Reflections on Violence*, p. 18.

57. Sternhell, 'Fascist Ideology' in Laqueur (ed.), *Fascism: A Reader's Guide*, p. 332.

58. Gregor, *Young Mussolini*, p. 247.
59. Quoted by Settembrini in *International Fascism*, p. 114.
60. Ibid., pp. 115ff.
61. See Walter Laqueur, *The Terrible Secret* (Weidenfeld, London, 1980).
62. Quoted by Sternhell, 'Fascist Ideology' in Laqueur (ed.), *Fascism: A Reader's Guide*, p. 334.
63. Adrian Lyttelton, 'Fascism in Italy: The Second Wave' in Mosse (ed.), *International Fascism*, p. 47.
64. Pound, *J/M*, p. 24.
65. Ibid., p. 11.
66. Ibid., pp. 63-4.
67. The 'socialism' need not imply, however, the 'socialism' of bureaucratic public ownership: see Robert Soucy's analysis of the politics of Drieu La Rochelle in Mosse (ed.), *International Fascism*, pp. 261ff. Soucy points out that French Fascism was much more elitist, much less oriented towards the masses than German Nazism, and, like Eliot, Drieu had little sympathy for dictators: 'He concluded that while the masses, being "a little female", were prone to abandon themselves to these "living gods" (dictators), a truly virile elite would always resist this kind of subservience' p. 262). See, too, the article entitled 'Laudian Marxism', by Joseph Needham, in *Criterion*, XII, 46 (October 1932), which quotes some Lancelot Andrewes, and asks, 'Does not this catalogue of divine actions curiously resemble the programme of the socialist state?' The socialist element in Fascism is rather an insistence on economic planning than on a planned economy.
68. See, for instance, Tom Gibbons, 'Modernism and Reactionary Politics', *Journal of Modern Literature*, 3, 5 (1974), p. 1140: Gibbons clearly shows the relationship between modernist thought and social Darwinism, but this neither establishes nor refutes the claim that the modernists are reactionary, since the idea is common also to many left-wing, non-fascist writers. It is, however, an integral element in the world-View of Fascism, even if it is not a defining one.
69. Yeats, *Ex.*, p. 312.
70. Ibid., p. 311.
71. Ibid., p. 441; 'Ireland After the Revolution', 1939.
72. Eliot, *Criterion*, VIII, 31 (December 1928), p. 281; 'The Literature of Fascism'.
73. Ibid., p. 290.
74. Ibid., p. 282.
75. *Criterion*, VII, 4 (June 1928), p. 374.
76. *Criterion*, VIII, 33 (July 1929), pp. 682-3.
77. Ibid., p. 683.
78. *Criterion*, VII, 2 (February 1928), p. 98.
79. See George Mosse, 'Towards a General Theory of Fascism' in Mosse (ed.), *International Fascism*, pp. 1ff.
80. Eliot, *Criterion*, VII, 2 (February 1928), p. 186; 'The Action Française, Mr. Maurras, and Mr. Ward'.
81. *Criterion*, VIII, 31 (December 1928), p. 286.
82. Ibid., p. 289.
83. *Criterion*, VIII, 33 (July 1929), p. 690; 'Mr. Barnes and Mr. Rowse'.
84. Robert Soucy, 'The Nature of Fascism in France' in Mosse (ed.), *International Fascism*, p. 249.
85. Ibid., p. 250.
86. Sternhell, 'Fascist Ideology' in Laqueur (ed.), *Fascism: A Reader's Guide*, p. 333.
87. Soucy, 'Nature of Fascism in France' in Mosse (ed.), *International*

Fascism, pp. 244ff. charts the departure from the *Action Française* of Valois, Brasillach and others as they found in it a more aggressive stance towards the achievement of their views: as a result, however, French Fascism retains much of the 'mélange of authority and indiscipline, tradition and insubordination' (p. 249) which had characterised the *Action Française*.

88. *Criterion*, VIII, 31 (December 1928), p. 289.

89. *Criterion*, X, 40 (April 1930); Eliot also felt that 'the fundamental objection' to Mosley's programme was that it was 'not fundamental enough. The changes are propounded in the same old cautious and sensible, and at the same time, catchy, phrasing, as any other political manifesto.'

90. *Criterion*, IV, 2 (April 1926), p. 221.

91. Eliot, *FLA*, p. 45.

92. Ibid., p. 44.

93. *Criterion*, XI, 42 (October 1931), p. 71.

94. *Criterion*, XII, 48 (April 1933), p. 472.

95. Ibid., p. 473.

96. *Criterion*, XI, 44 (April 1932), p. 471.

97. *Criterion*, XIII, 53 (July 1934), p. 630.

98. Eliot, *ICS*, p. 40.

99. Ibid., p. 41.

100. Yeats, *Ex.*, p. 438.

101. Kojecky, *T.S. Eliot's Social Criticism*, p. 137.

102. Eliot, *Criterion*, X, 39 (January 1931), p. 313.

103. Eliot, *UPUC*, p. 73.

104. Eliot, *Criterion*, X, 40 (April 1931), p. 484.

105. Yeats, *Ex.*, p. 254; 'A People's Theatre', 1919.

106. Ibid., p. 251.

SELECT BIBLIOGRAPHY

The material on Yeats, Eliot and Pound is, of course, vast, and readers can find some guidance on Yeats in K.G. Cross and R.T. Dunlop, *Bibliography of Yeats Criticism* (Macmillan, London, 1971) and in John E. Stoll, *The Great Deluge: A Yeats Bibliography*; on Eliot in Mildred Martin, *A Half-Century of Eliot Criticism* (Kaye and Ward, London, 1972); and on Pound in the pages of *Paideuma: A Journal Devoted to Ezra Pound Scholarship* (Orono, Maine), from 1972 onwards. I have provided here a selection of the material relating to three different areas of interest, on poetry and politics, on associationism and related aesthetic matters, and on Fascism.

Poetry and Politics

Alvarez, A., 'Eliot and Yeats: Orthodoxy and Tradition', *Twentieth Century*, CLXII (1957), pp. 149-63 and 224-34

Austin, Allen, *T.S. Eliot: The Literary and Social Criticism* (Indiana University Press, Bloomington, 1971)

Block, Haskell M., 'Some Concepts of the Literary Elite at the Turn of the Century', *Mosaic*, 5, 2 (1972), pp. 57-64

Bowra, C.M., *Poetry and Politics 1900-1960* (Cambridge University Press, London, 1966)

Bradbury, Malcolm, *The Social Context of Modern English Literature* (Basil Blackwell, Oxford, 1971)

Brooks, Van Wyck, *New England: Indian Summer* (Dent, London, 1940)

Chace, William M., *The Political Identities of Ezra Pound and T.S. Eliot* (Stanford University Press, Stanford, 1973)

Davis, Earle, *Vision Fugitive: Ezra Pound and Economics* (University Press Kansas, Kansas, 1968)

Donoghue, Denis, *The Ordinary Universe: Soundings in Modern Literature* (Faber, London, 1968)

Eagleton, T., *Exiles and Emigrés: Studies in Modern Literature* (Chatto and Windus, London, 1970)

Fishman, Solomon, *The Disinherited of Art* (University of California Press, Berkeley, 1953)

Frank, Joseph, *The Widening Gyre: Crisis and Mastery in Modern Literature* (Rutgers University Press, New Brunswick, 1963)

Gibbons, Tom, 'Modernism and Reactionary Politics', *Journal of Modern Literature* 3, 5 (1974), pp. 1140-57

Gross, Harvey, *The Contrived Corridor: History and Fatality in Modern Literature* (Michigan University Press, Ann Arbor, 1971)

Hamburger, Michael, *The Truth of Poetry: Tensions in Modern Poetry from Baudelaire to the 1960s* (Weidenfeld and Nicolson, London, 1969)

Harrison, John, *The Reactionaries* (Gollancz, London, 1966)

Heyman, C.D., *Ezra Pound: The Last Rower: A Political Profile* (Faber, London, 1976)

Heller, Erich, *The Artist's Journey into the Interior* (Secker and Warburg, London, 1966)

Howe, Irving, *The Decline of the New* (Gollancz, London, 1971)

Kenner, Hugh, *The Pound Era* (Faber, London, 1972)

Kermode, Frank, *The Sense of an Ending* (Oxford University Press, 1968)

Kojecky, Roger, *T.S. Eliot's Social Criticism* (Faber, London, 1971)

Lucy, Sean, *T.S. Eliot and the Idea of Tradition* (Cohen and West, London, 1960)

Lukacs, Georg, *The Meaning of Contemporary Realism* (Merlin Press, London, 1962)

Margolis, John D., *T.S. Eliot's Intellectual Development* (University of Chicago Press, Chicago, 1972)

Morris, J.A., *Writer and Politics in Modern Britain, 1880-1950* (Holmes and Meier, New York, 1977)

O'Brien, Conor Cruise, *The Suspecting Glance* (Faber, London, 1972)

Poggioli, Renato, *The Theory of the Avant-Garde* (Harvard University Press, Cambridge, Mass., 1968)

Raban, Jonathon, *The Society of the Poem* (Harrap, London, 1971)

Rosenberg, Harold, *The Tradition of the New* (Paladin, London, 1970)

Spears, Monroe K., *Dionysus and the City: Modernism in Twentieth Century Poetry* (Oxford University Press, New York, 1970)

Spender, Stephen, *The Destructive Element* (Hamish Hamilton, London, 1953)

— *Eliot* (Fontana/Collins, Glasgow, 1975)

Stock, Noel, *Poet in Exile: Ezra Pound* (Manchester University Press, Manchester 1964)

Torchiana, D.T., *W.B. Yeats and Georgian Ireland* (Oxford University Press, London, 1968)

Watson, George, *Politics and Literature in Modern Britain* (Macmillan, London, 1977)

Watson, G.J., *Irish Identity and the Literary Revival: Synge, Yeats, Joyce, and O'Casey* (Croom Helm, London, 1979)

Whitaker, Thomas R., *Swan and Shadow: Yeats's Dialogue with History* (University of North Carolina Press, Chapel Hill, 1964)

Zwerdling, Alex, *Yeats and the Heroic Ideal* (Peter Owen, London, 1966)

Associationism

Abrams, M.H., *The Mirror and the Lamp: Romantic Theory and the Critical Tradition* (W.W. Norton, New York, 1953)

Armstrong, Isobel, *Victorian Scrutinies: Reviews of Poetry 1830-1870* (Athlone Press, London, 1972)

Bate, Walter Jackson, *From Classic to Romantic* (Harvard University Press, Cambridge, Mass., 1949)

Beatty, Arthur, *William Wordsworth: His Doctrines of Art in their Historical Relations* (University of Wisconsin, Madison, 1927)

Bornstein, George, *Transformations of Romanticism in Yeats, Eliot and Stevens* (University of Chicago Press, Chicago and London, 1976)

Bruns, Gerald L., *Modern Poetry and the Idea of Language* (Yale University Press, New Haven and London, 1974)

Coffman, Stanley, J., *Imagism: A Chapter for the History of Modern Poetry* (University of Oklahoma Press, Norman, 1972)

Eco, Umberto, *The Role of the Reader: Explorations in the Semiotics of Texts* (Indiana University Press, Bloomington, 1979)

Engelberg, Edward, *The Vast Design: Patterns in W.B. Yeats's Aesthetic* (University of Toronto Press, Toronto, 1965)

Hough, Graham, *Image and Experience: Studies in a Literary Revolution* (Duckworth, London, 1960)

Hughes, Glenn, *Imagism and the Imagists: a Study in Modern Poetry* (Bowes and Bowes, London, 1960)

Kallich, Martin, *The Association of Ideas and Critical Theory in Eighteenth Century England* (Mouton, the Hague, 1970)

Levine, Bernard, *The Dissolving Image: The Spiritual-Aesthetic Development of W.B. Yeats* (Wayne State University Press, Detroit, 1970)

Martin, Graham Dunstan, *Language, Truth and Poetry* (Edinburgh University Press, Edinburgh, 1975)

Massey, Irving, *The Uncreating Word: romanticism and the object*

(Indiana University Press, Bloomington, 1970)

Rosenthal, M.L., 'The Waste Land as an open strucutre', *Mosaic*, 6, 1 (1972), pp. 181-9

Schneidau, Herbert, *Ezra Pound: The Image and the Real* (Louisiana State University Press, Baton Rouge, 1969)

Stead, C.K., *The New Poetic: Yeats to Eliot* (Penguin, Harmondsworth, 1967)

Toveson, E.L., *The Imagination as a Means of Grace* (University of California Press, Berkeley, 1960)

Fascism

De Felice, Renzo, *Fascism: An Informal Introduction to Its Theory and Practice* (Transaction Books, New Brunswick, 1976)

— *Interpretations of Fascism*, trans. Brenda Huff Everett (Harvard University Press, Cambridge and London, 1977)

Glaser, Hermann, *The Cultural Roots of National Socialism*, trans. Ernest E. Menze (Croom Helm, London, 1978)

Gregor, A. James, *The Fascist Persuasion in Radical Politics* (Princeton University Press, New Jersey, 1974)

— *The Ideology of Fascism: The Rationale of Totalitarianism* (Collier Macmillan, London, 1969)

— *The Young Mussolini and the Intellectual Origins of Fascism* (University of California Press, Berkeley, 1979)

Hamilton, Alastair, *The Appeal of Fascism: A Study of Intellectuals and Fascism*. (Anthony Blond, London, 1971)

Hayes, Paul, *Fascism* (George Allen and Unwin, London, 1973)

Laqueur, Walter (ed.), *Fascism: A Reader's Guide: Analyses, Interpretations Bibliography* (Wildwood House, London, 1976)

Mosse, George L., *The Crisis of German Ideology: Intellectual Origins of the Third Reich* (Grosset and Dunlap, New York, 1964)

— (ed.), *International Fascism: New Thoughts and New Approaches* (Sage, London and Beverly Hills, 1979)

Nolte, Ernest, *Three Faces of Fascism: Action Française, Italian Fascism, National Socialism* (Weidenfeld and Nicolson, London, 1965)

Plumyène, J. and R. Lasierra, *Les Fascismes Français 1923-1963* (Seuil, Paris, 1963)

Soucy, Robert, *Fascism in France: the Case of Maurice Barrés* (University of California Press, Berkeley, 1972)

Sternhell, Zeev, *La Droite Revolutionnaire 1885-1914: les origines françaises du fascisme* (Seuil, Paris, 1978)

Turner, Henry A., *Reappraisals of Fascism* (New Viewpoints, New York, 1975)

Weber, Eugen, *Action Française* (University of Stanford Press, Stanford, 1962)

— *Varieties of Fascism: Doctrines of Revolution in the Twentieth Century* (Van Nostrand / Anvil, Princeton, 1964)

Weiss, John, *Conservatism in Europe 1770-1945: Traditionalism, Reaction and Counter-Revolution* (Thames and Hudson, London, 1977)

Woolf, S.J., *European Fascism* (Weidenfeld and Nicolson, London, 1968)

INDEX

Abbey Theatre 21, 165
Abrams, M.H. 29n11
Action Française 7, 212, 251, 279, 280, 282-5
Africanus, Leo 179
Aldington, Richard 57n101
Alison, Archibald 36-9, 41-6, 48-9, 50, 51, 52, 54, 59
Andrewes, Lancelot 132, 248-9
anti-Semitism, 2, 271
Armstrong, Isobel 51
associationism 26-64, 67, 75-6, 87, 94-5, 125-32, 134-40, 163-6, 168-9, 172, 177-8, 179-82, 185-6, 191, 193-5, 209, 226, 245-6, 247-8, 287-9
    and ghost 220-6
    and Great Memory 105-6, 109-10, 123, 182-3
    and symbol 88-90, 106-7, 259
    dissociation 205-8
    free association 31, 121, 137
    redintegration 125-6
Auden, W.H. 13
Austin, Allen 9n30

Bain, Alexander 50-1, 125
Balakian, Anna 33
Barthes, Roland 12
Beatty, Arthur 39n38
Bergson, Henri 58, 258-9
Berkeley, George 22, 180
Blake, William 65, 212, 223
Bloom, Harold, 26, 27, 28, 105, 191
Blunden, Edmund 132
Bolgan, Anne C. 125n16
Bon, Gustave Le 196, 266-7
Bornstein, George 26
Bradley, F.H. 124-9, 153
Brasillach, Robert 278, 282n87
Bridgwater, Patrick 239
Brooks, Cleanth 26
Brown, Thomas 48
Browning, Robert 19, 221, 224
Brunet, Olivier 51n85
Buchan, John 152
Burckhardt, Jacob 148, 154
Burke, Edmund 197

Bush, Ronald 144

Carlyle, Thomas 51, 166, 207
Carne-Ross, D.S. 143
Carsten, Francis L. 262n41
Catullus 207
Cavalcanti, Guido 140
Chace, William M. 9
Chaucer, Geoffrey 162, 204, 233
Chomsky, Noam 33
Coleridge, Samuel Taylor 28, 30, 36, 51, 65, 66, 77, 89, 120, 125
Conrad, Joseph 128, 130, 135, 209, 240
Corradini, Enrico 271
Cosgrave, Patrick 9n30
Coulanges, Fustel de 212
Cuchulain 100, 107-8, 195, 202

Daniel, Arnaut 140
Darwin, Charles 29
David, Thomas 156
Davie, Donald 134, 137-8, 139, 143
Davis, Earle 6n17
Dekker, George 19n51
Donne, John 14, 30, 61, 206, 207, 248
Donoghue, Denis 26-8
Douglas, Clifford Hugh 6, 247
Dreyfus Affair 7, 268
Drieu La Rochelle, Pierre 274n67, 278
Dryden, John 60

Eco, Umberto 67, 68
Edinburgh Review 51
Eliot, T.S. 3, 6, 8, 14, 29, 51, 54-6, 66, 67, 69, 71, 112-32, 140, 144, 151-3, 204-22, 225, 231-46, 248-50, 251-62 *passim*, 274-5, 278-87
    and *Action Française* 7, 212, 262, 280, 281, 284
    and associationism 29-30, 55-6, 60-2, 63-4, 69-71, 114, 124-6, 209, 214, 259
    and Bradley 124-9, 130
    and Coleridge 66
    and dissociation 205-7, 218

319

and Fascism 7-8, 278-86
and de Gourmont 54-5, 205-6
and history 129-31, 153-4, 207-8,
    236
and Maurras 8-9, 280, 281, 283,
    286
and memory 66, 121-4, 131-2,
    214, 215, 217-18, 226-7,
    234-5
and Nietzsche 151-2, 236-45
and objective correlative 62-3,
    112-13, 138, 242
and Yeats 112-14, 119-20, 204-5,
    219-20, 227, 233-4, 252-3,
    254-5
works: *After Strange Gods*, 3, 7;
    'Burbank with a Baedeker:
    Bleistein with a Cigar' 212-14;
    Criterion 7, 20, 212, 278;
    The Family Reunion 213;
    Four Quartets 225-7;
    'Gerontion' 218-21; *The Idea of
    a Christian Society* 285; *Knowl-
    edge and Experience in the
    Philosophy of F.H. Bradley* 128;
    'The Literature of Fascism'
    7-8, 278; 'The Love Song of J.
    Alfred Prufrock' 114-20, 121,
    214, 219; 'Marina' 124; 'The
    Music of Poetry' 63; *Notes
    towards the Definition of
    Culture* 8, 255, 257; 'The
    Perfect Critic' 55, 61, 112,
    126; 'Rhapsody on a Windy
    Night' 120-3, 124; *The Sacred
    Wood* 3, 55; 'Seneca in Eliza-
    bethan Translation' 205;
    'Sweeney Agonistes' 215, 233;
    'Sweeney Among the Night-
    ingales' 216-18, 219, 233;
    'Sweeney Erect' 215, 233;
    'Tradition and the Individual
    Talent' 130, 146, 154, 219;
    *The Use of Poetry and the Use
    of Criticism* 29, 123, 252; 'The
    Waste Land' 3, 33, 69-71, 146,
    218, 225, 229, 230-46; 'What
    is a Classic?' 208
Ellmann, Richard 31
emotion of multitude 39-41, 143,
    189-90, 193, 234
Engelberg, Edward 40, 87
Espey, John J. 143

Fascism 2-9, 197-203, 251-89

and Eliot 7, 261-2, 278-85
and Pound 8, 248, 260-1, 272-3
and Yeats 197, 199-203, 275-8
ideology 265-71
interpretations of 262-5
Felice, Renzo de 262, 270
Fenellosa, Ernest 136, 140
Fletcher, Ian 95, 190
Ford, Ford Madox 135
Frank, Joseph 232
Freud, Sigmund 14, 32-3
Frye, Northrop 26, 105

Gardener, Patrick 147n3
Gaudier-Brzeska 58
Gibbons, Tom 275n68
Gonne, Maud 95, 105, 167, 168, 197
Gordon, D.J. 95, 190
Gourmont, Remy de 54-5, 205, 206
Grattan, Henry 156
Gregor, A. James 268, 270
Gregory, Augusta 4, 48, 100, 102, 107,
    188
Gregory, Robert 96-104, 197
Gyles, Althea 106

Hallam, Arthur 51-3, 90, 267
Harper, George Mills 167n39
Harrison, Bernard 33n20
Harrison, J.R. 9, 10
Hartley, David 29, 30, 34, 36, 49, 51
Hawthorne, Nathaniel 208
Hayes, Paul M. 263n43
Hazlitt, William 23, 245
Hegel, G.W.F. 147, 148
Herbert, George 30, 132
Heyman, C.D. 9n30
Hipple, Walter J. 36
Hitler, Adolf 271, 272
Hooker, Richard 132, 154, 249, 282
Hughes, H. Stuart 147n2
Hulme, T.E. 57-8, 252
Hume, David 22, 35, 51

Imagism 57-60
Isherwood, Christopher 265n49

Jefferson, Thomas 3, 256, 273
Jeffrey, Francis 48n73
John, Augustus 21
Johnson, Lionel 101, 102
Johnson, Samuel 205
Jonson, Ben 43, 128-9
Joyce, James 22, 112, 232

Kallich, Martin 36n30
Kenner, Hugh 6n17, 114, 139, 143
Kermode, Frank 15-19, 24, 26, 29, 56, 92, 96
Khan, Gustave 54
Knox, Bryan 246
Kojecky, Roger 7n21, 9, 261-2, 286

Laforgue, Jules 120
Lane, Hugh 171
Langbaum, Robert 26, 232n64
Laqueur, Walter 270, 271
Lasierra, R. 264
Lawrence, D.H. 70
Ledeen, Michael A. 262n40
Lees, F.N. 242n76
Lehmann, A.G. 54
Lenin, V.I. 257, 268n53
Lewis, Wyndham 143-4, 259
Linz, Juan 265
Litz, A. Walton 232n64
Lloyd, Marie 210
Locke, John 29, 34-6
Lyttelton, Adrian 272

MacBride, Major John 167
MacDonagh, Thomas 164-5
Machiavelli, Nicolo 259-60, 278-9, 283
Malatesta, Sigismondo 153
Mallarmé, Stéphane 14, 53, 68, 188
Margolis, John 48n72
Martin, Graham 95, 125n16, 178n45
Martin, Wallace 59
Marvell, Andrew 205-7, 208-9, 248
Marx, Karl 147, 148, 197, 268, 269
Maurras, Charles 7, 8, 261-2, 269, 278, 281, 283, 286
Mill, James 48
Mill, John Stuart 49-51, 56, 125
Miller, J. Hillis 26n5
Milne, A.J. 125n16
Milton, John 223
More, Henry 180
Morris, William 4, 209
Mosley, Oswald 271, 282, 286
Mosse, George L. 262n42, 270
Murry, Middleton 209, 258-9
Mussolini, Benito 2, 196, 256, 257, 260, 261, 262, 268n53, 269, 271-3, 280, 282

Nietzsche, Friedrich 15, 148-51, 154, 237-44

O'Brien, Conor Cruise 9, 199
O'Connell, Daniel 155
O'Duffy, Eoin 2, 277
O'Higgins, Kevin 202
O'Leary, John 155, 156, 173

Pareto, Vilfredo 266, 271
Parkinson, Thomas 83n21
Parnell, Charles Stewart 73, 155, 171-2, 199
Pater, Walter 51, 188
Pearce, Donald R. 85n22
Pearlman, Daniel 138
Perloff, Marjorie 96, 97
Perse, St-Jean 69
Plumyène, Jean 264
Poe, Edgar Allen 208
Pollexfen, Alfred 99
Pollexfen, George 99, 102, 184
Pound, Ezra Loomis 2, 5, 8, 14, 18, 25, 54, 57-9, 66, 71, 87, 114, 132-45, 151-3, 205, 221, 222-4, 225, 227-31, 246-8, 251-61 *passim*, 272-3, 274, 275, 278, 288
    and associationism 57-60, 134-8, 143
    and emotion of multitude 143-5
    and Fascism 5-6, 8, 248, 260-1, 277
    and history 152-3, 221-2
    and Imagism 57-60, 135
    and memory 66, 139-40, 145, 222, 224, 228-30, 247, 257
    and Mussolini 2-3, 138-9, 248, 256-7, 261, 273
    and tradition 140-2
    and Yeats 133-5, 139-40, 143
    works: *ABC of Reading* 136; *Cantos* 32, 137-40, 144, 146, 224-5, 229-31, 246; 'A Girl' 246; *Guide to Kulchur* 18, 137, 152; 'Hugh Selwyn Mauberley' 21, 142; 'In a Station of the Metro' 59; *Jefferson and/or Mussolini* 2, 273; *Pisan Cantos* 14, 228-30, 251; *Social Credit: An Impact* 247; *The Spirit of Romance* 19; 'The State' 260; 'Surgit Fama' 141; 'Terra Italica' 140; 'A Visiting Card' 256
Priestley, Joseph 36n29

Quine, W.V.O. 33n20

Read, Forrest 229

Rees, Garnet 60n114
Rees, T.R. 205n8
Richards, I.A. 231n63
Richter, Melvin 125n16
Ruskin, John 50, 51

Schneidau, Herbert 134
Schopenhauer, Arthur 147, 154
Shakespear, Olivia 2
Shakespeare, William 22, 23, 88, 89,
    129, 131, 190, 212, 222-3, 254
Shawe-Taylor, John 155
Shelley, Percy Bysshe 20, 39, 52, 79,
    88, 89, 105
Smith, Grover 121
Sorel, Georges 196, 197, 268-9, 271,
    281
Soucy, Robert 274n67, 281
Spears, Monroe K. 26n5
Spencer, Herbert 50
Spender, Stephen 10, 11, 12, 16, 115,
    120
Spengler, Oswald 147, 275
Spenser, Edmund 70, 159-60, 181
Stallworthy, Jon 86n23
Sternhell, Zeev 266, 270, 281
Stewart, Dugald 48
Stock, Noel 261
Swedenborg, Emanuel 179, 181
Swift, Jonathan 196, 197
Swinburne, Algernon Charles 19, 60,
    114
Symons, Arthur 53-4, 55-6, 112, 188
Synge, John Millington 101, 102, 112,
    175

Tennyson, Alfred 19, 51
Tuveson, Ernest Lee 36n31
Tynan, Katharine 47

Upward, Allen 134, 246

Valéry, Paul 215
Valois, Georges 281, 282n87
Van Buren, Martin 3, 152
Vaughan, Henry 132

Wagner, Richard 239
Watson, George 263n44
Webb, James 54
Weber, Eugen 264
Wells, H.G. 207-8
Whibley, Charles 205
Whitaker, Thomas 188

White, Hayden 149
Whitman, Walt 208
Wilde, Oscar 11
Wilson, Edmund 26
Winters, Yvor 138, 191
Wollheim, Richard 125n16
Woolf, Virginia 22, 146, 205
Wordsworth, William 39, 45, 51, 65
Wyndham, George 214

Yeats, J.B. 113
Yeats, W.B. 2, 5, 9, 13, 24-5, 30,
    31, 37-48, 52-3, 54, 57, 64, 65, 67,
    71, 72-111, 112-14, 120, 126,
    133, 135, 139, 140, 151, 155-203,
    204, 209, 210, 219, 220, 225,
    227, 228, 250-9, 275-8, 285
  and Archibald Alison 38-9, 41-8
  and associationsim 30, 37-48, 67,
    75-6, 121, 165-6, 168-9, 172,
    177, 179-81, 184-5, 188-208
    passim, 258
  and Eliot 56, 64, 112-14, 119-20,
    204-5, 219-20, 227, 233-4,
    252-3, 254-5
  and Fascism 2, 10, 13, 251-2, 275-7
  and memory 65-6, 72-6, 88-90,
    104-5, 109, 110-11, 155, 169-
    203 *passim*, 258
  and nationalism 155, 157-8, 177
  and Pound 57, 133-5, 139-40, 143
  and realism 158-9, 163-4
  and symbolism 87-9, 106-7
  works: 'Art and Ideas' 161, 233;
    'At Galway Races' 168; Auto-
    biographies 177; 'Blood and the
    Moon' 4; 'Broken Dreams' 171;
    'Byzantium' 190-6; 'The Cold
    Heaven' 169-71, 184; 'Coole
    Park and Ballylee 1931' 197;
    'Cuchulain's Fight with the Sea'
    107; 'The Curse of Cromwell'
    277; *The Cutting of an Agate*
    112, 254; *Discoveries* 43, 113;
    'Easter 1916' 173-8; 'Edmund
    Spenser' 204; 'Fallen Majesty'
    169; 'Fergus and the Druid'
    81-2, 83; 'The Fisherman' 167;
    'The Folly of Being Comforted'
    95; 'A General Introduction for
    my Work' 72; 'He Remembers
    Forgotten Beauty' 108-9;
    In the Seven Woods 178; 'The
    Indian to his Love' 82, 84, 85;

'In Memory of Major Robert Gregory' 95-104; 'An Irish Airman Foresees his Death' 98, 99; 'The Lamentation of the Old Pensioner' 90-2; 'Leda and the Swan' 199-202; 'Lines Written in Dejection' 168; 'The Lover asks Forgiveness because of his Many Moods' 93-4; 'The Madness of King Goll' 78-81, 90, 119; 'Magic' 181; 'Meditations in Time of Civil War' 146, 198; 'The Moods' 193; 'The Mountain Tomb' 178; 'Nineteen Hundred and Nineteen' 32, 185-9, 196; 'Old Memory' 94-5; *Per Amica Silentia Lunae* 30; 'The Philosophy of Shelley's Poetry' 18, 38; 'Poetry and Tradition' 74, 169, 250; 'Reprisals' 98; *Responsibilities* 178; 'The Rose' 228; 'Sailing to Byzantium' 83-7, 191; 'The Second Coming' 110-11; 'September 1913' 172-3, 212; 'The Statues' 100; 'A Symbolic Artist' 106; 'The Symbolism of Poetry' 41, 44; 'Three Marching Songs' 198-9; 'Three Songs to One Burden' 277; 'Three Songs to the Same Tune' 198-9; 'To a Friend Whose Work has Come to Nothing' 169; 'To a Shade' 171; 'To some I have Talked with by the Fire' 193; 'The Tower' 66, 86, 146, 229; *The Trembling of the Veil* 97; 'The Two Trees' 92; 'Under Ben Bulben' 202; 'Under Saturn' 183; 'Upon a House Shaken by the Land Agitation' 160; *A Vision* 32, 184, 190; 'What is Popular Poetry?' 43, 64; *The Wild Swans at Coole* 178; *The Winding Stair* 14; *The Words upon the Window-Pane* 19

Young, Dudley 96, 186